MULTI-LEVEL GOVERNANCE

CONCEPTUAL CHALLENGES AND CASE STUDIES FROM AUSTRALIA

MULTI-LEVEL GOVERNANCE

CONCEPTUAL CHALLENGES AND CASE STUDIES FROM AUSTRALIA

EDITED BY KATHERINE A. DANIELL
AND ADRIAN KAY

Australian
National
University

PRESS

ANU PRESS

the Australia and New Zealand
School of Government

Published by ANU Press
The Australian National University
Acton ACT 2601, Australia
Email: anupress@anu.edu.au
This title is also available online at press.anu.edu.au

National Library of Australia Cataloguing-in-Publication entry

Title: Multi-level governance : conceptual challenges and case
            studies from Australia / edited by
            Katherine A. Daniell, Adrian Kay.

ISBN: 9781760461591 (paperback) 9781760461607 (ebook)

Series: Australia and New Zealand School of Governance (ANZSOG)

Subjects: Federal government--Australia--Case studies.
            Decentralization in government--Australia.
            Australia--Administrative and political divisions.

Other Creators/Contributors:
            Daniell, Katherine A., editor.
            Kay, Adrian, editor.

Cover design and layout by ANU Press. Cover photograph by Redd Angelo on Unsplash.

Contents

List of Figures and Tables vii

List of Acronyms. ix

Foreword xiii
Helen Sullivan

Part 1: Conceptual Challenges

1. Multi-level Governance: An Introduction 3
    Katherine A. Daniell and Adrian Kay

2. Multi-level Governance and the Study of Australian Federalism. . .33
    Adrian Kay

3. Rethinking Federalism: Network Governance, Multi-level
    Governance and Australian Politics. 57
    Paul Fawcett and David Marsh

4. Accountability in Multi-level Governance: The Example
    of Australian Federalism 81
    Richard Mulgan

5. Multi-level Governmentality. 101
    Paul Dugdale

6. Multi-level Governance as Political Theory 121
    Russell Kerr

Part 2: Education and Social Policy

7. Negotiating the Early Childhood Education Revolution:
    An Exercise in Multi-level Governance .161
    Trish Mercer and Wendy Jarvie

8. The Deployment of an Epistemic Model of Multi-level
    Governance: A Study of Differences in Hearing. 187
    Anthony Hogan

9. Multi-level Governance in Aboriginal Community
    Development: Structures, Processes and Skills for
    Working across Boundaries 211
    Wendy Jarvie and Jenny Stewart

Part 3: Spatial and Planning Policy

10. Multi-level Housing Policy in Australia .233
    Patrick Troy

11. Multi-level Governance in Integrated Land Use and Natural
    Resource Planning on the Urban Fringe: A Case Study of
    Processes and Structures for Governing across Boundaries. . .255
    Iris Iwanicki, Kathryn Bellette and Stephen Smith

12. Regional Solutions for Multi-level Governance Challenges
    in Australian Coastal and Climate Change Planning 281
    Barbara Norman and Nicole Gurran

13. Multi-level Governance in the Lake Eyre Basin:
    Meeting in the Middle? 305
    Kate Andrews

Part 4: Environmental and Agricultural Policy

14. Natural Resource Management as a Form of Multi-level
    Governance: The Impact of Reform in Queensland and
    Tasmania 327
    Allan Dale, Sarah Ryan and Kathleen Broderick

15. Multi-level Integrated Water Governance: Examples from
    New South Wales and Colorado. 361
    Andrew Ross

16. Private Actors in Multi-level Governance: GLOBALG.A.P.
    Standard-setting for Agricultural and Food Products 385
    Anne McNaughton and Stewart Lockie

17. Breaking Down the 'One-Size-Fits-All' Approach to Rural
    and Regional Policy: Enhancing Policy Initiatives through
    Multi-level Governance 403
    Katherine A. Daniell, Anthony Hogan and Jen Cleary

18. What Remains Unwritten? Developing a Critical Evaluation
    of Multi-level Governance and its Futures in Australian Public
    Policy and Politics 429
    Katherine A. Daniell and Trish Mercer

List of Contributors. 451

List of Figures and Tables

Figure 7.1: The Early Childhood Development (ECD) Subgroup work program, 2008 172

Table 7.1: COAG Early Childhood Development Subgroup 2008: What worked – at a glance. 179

Figure 9.1: Bureaucratic complexity: Murdi Paaki governance structures 2006 217

Figure 11.1: Willunga Basin – a geographic area, the majority of which was in the District Council of Willunga prior to 1997, and subsequently Onkaparinga Council, which amalgamated the councils of Happy Valley, Noarlunga and Willunga 258

Figure 11.2: The Onkaparinga Catchment Water Management Board Area – showing council boundaries 262

Figure 11.3: The relationship between the *Development Act, Water Resources Act* and state and local government roles 265

Figure 11.4: Multi-level governance reform – the development plan amendment 271

Table 12.1: Governance of regional coastal collaborations 299

Figure 13.1: NRM MLG structures and roles in 2011 313

Table 13.1: Comparison of the Lake Eyre Basin Intergovernmental Agreement and community initiative. 315

Table 15.1: Water entitlements and management instruments in New South Wales and Colorado 367

Table 15.2: Water governance in New South Wales and Colorado . . 370

Figure 18.1: MLG cultural typology (based on Grid-Group
       Cultural Theory) 441

List of Acronyms

ACAA	Australian Coastal Advocacy Alliance
ADF	Australian Defence Force
AEDI	Australian Early Development Index
ALP	Australian Labor Party
ANZSOG	Australia and New Zealand School of Government
ATSIC	Aboriginal and Torres Strait Island Commission
ATSIS	Aboriginal and Torres Strait Islander Services
BHA	Better Hearing Australia
COAG	Council of Australian Governments
CSHA	Commonwealth–state Housing Agreements
CURF	Canberra Urban and Regional Futures
DAA	Department of Aboriginal Affairs (NSW)
DC	District Council
DEEWR	Department of Education, Employment and Workplace Relations
DEST	Department of Science, Education and Training
DET	Department of Education and Training (NSW)
DEWR	Department of Employment and Workplace Relations
DIMIA	Department of Immigration and Indigenous Affairs
DOHA	Department of Health and Ageing
EC	exceptional circumstances
ECD	early childhood development
ECE	early childhood education
ECEC	early childhood education and care

EPA	Environment Protection Authority
EU	European Union
EUREP	Euro-Retailer Produce Working Group
EYLF	early years learning framework
FaCS	Family and Community Services
FaCSIA	Families, Community Services and Indigenous Affairs
GAP	Good Agricultural Practice
GFC	global financial crisis
HIP	Home Insulation Program
IFA	Integrated Farm Assurance
IGA	intergovernmental agreement
IPA	Indigenous Protected Area
LEB	Lake Eyre Basin
LEBCG	Lake Eyre Basin Coordinating Group
MDB	Murray–Darling Basin
MDBA	Murray–Darling Basin Authority
MLG	multi-level governance
NAL	National Acoustic Laboratory
NBN	National Broadband Network
NDIS	National Disability Insurance Scheme
NRM	natural resource management
NSTF	National Sea Change Taskforce
NSW	New South Wales
NWI	national water initiative
OECD	Organisation for Economic Co-operation and Development
OECECC	Office of Early Childhood Education and Child Care
OHS	Office of Hearing Services
OMC	open method of coordination
PAR	Plan Amendment Report
PAWG	Productivity Agenda Working Group
QSCC	quality standards in child care

RDA	Regional Development Australia
RDC	research and development corporation
RRRC	Reef and Rainforest Research Corporation
SCCG	Sydney Coastal Councils Group
SECA	South East Coastal Adaptation
SHHH	Self Help for Hearing
SoE	state of the environment
SPP	specific purpose payment
WTO	World Trade Organization

Foreword

Helen Sullivan

How do we explain Australia's governance to itself, let alone to others? Why is it that the constitutional settlement between the Commonwealth and states and territories remains intact even though it is regularly breached and fails to acknowledge the key institution of local government? How can Australia's system of governance be sustained in the face of structural funding inequities, such as vertical fiscal imbalance? And what are we to make of a coordinating instrument – Council of Australian Governments (COAG) – that is more impressive the further away from it you are?

Not everyone will agree with the above critique, but even the most ardent defender of Australia's institutions and their power to adapt and survive must acknowledge that Australia's system of governance is operating sub-optimally. There are trade-offs in any system, even the most unitary, between democracy and efficiency. But Australia's present condition appears to be making the best of neither. Citizens are frustrated with the performance of politics and politicians and are less inclined than they were to consider Australia's democratic framework as able to solve the nation's most pressing problems. Likewise, the business of administering governance is regularly critiqued as policy innovations fail to overcome powerful lobby groups, programs suffer poor implementation because of insufficient expertise or overreaching governments, and reforms do not provide hoped-for returns.

There may be some comfort in the fact that governments all over the world are experiencing a loss of public confidence and trust in their ability to govern effectively. While this creates opportunities for mutual learning, it also suggests that governments have limited time in which to restore confidence. While this is not an easy task in any country, the Australian context adds some particular difficulty. A combination of historical, geographical, demographic, political, economic and cultural factors make Australia's present and future governance internally complicated – the failure to reach a satisfactory governance settlement that affords appropriate recognition to Aboriginal and Torres Strait Islander peoples is the clearest example of this, and externally difficult – such as accounting for the growing power of neighbours with different governing histories, traditions and practices.

Such circumstances lend themselves to different approaches and radically new ways of thinking. This volume takes up the challenge by exploring the possibilities offered by re-imagining Australia through the lens of multi-level governance (MLG).

As is typical of many useful social science concepts, MLG can be defined or interpreted in a variety of ways. This elasticity is both confounding and liberating because it opens up the possibility that governing Australia can be understood in multiple ways, which overlap and are contingent upon the conditions of different policy and political pasts as well as actors' agency in specific time and space.

The volume offers a unique insight into the various understandings of MLG and how these interact with or confront different Australian contexts and norms. It also provides an encyclopaedic interrogation of the application of MLG ideas to different policy issues and questions.

Throughout the volume, it is possible to discern at least four different meta-level perspectives on MLG. For some, it is an outcome: a normative end state that promises a more effective and sustainable (if not simple) system of governance. Here the job is to design the institutions and tools to secure this future state. Elsewhere, MLG is used as a container to hold a range of linked, but distinct, conceptual and empirical developments including collaboration, networks and polycentrism. In this case, the task is to figure out what works in a particular context and to find ways of enabling the different processes to function together. Another version sees MLG as a description of the rather fragmented and dysfunctional institutions, policy tools and levers and processes that have emerged over time. The task here is to make the parts work better together. Finally there is MLG as an analytical lens, a way of looking at the Australian condition to explore its workings from a variety of perspectives and positions.

Each of these meta-level perspectives is illuminating and the chapters in which they are considered allow the reader to think about them in different policy, community and political settings.

There is always more to say on a topic like this and this volume provides policymakers, scholars and practitioners with the foundations and tools for informed future conversations.

Part 1: Conceptual Challenges

1

Multi-level Governance: An Introduction

Katherine A. Daniell and Adrian Kay

Background

In an increasingly globalised and rapidly changing world, decision-making processes associated with the development, implementation and monitoring of public policies are becoming increasingly complex. Individual governments or government departments now rarely have all the power, resources and governance structures that are required to adequately respond to public policy challenges under their responsibility and effectively govern their constituencies. This means that they are required to work with, or seek the aid of, others from the public, private, non-government organisation or community spheres, and often across a range of sectors, to achieve their objectives. Understanding and managing the issues associated with governing across a range of boundaries are thus paramount to achieving positive public policy outcomes in today's environment.

In Australia, public debates about the constitutional status of the Australian federation, and how to create effectively functioning mechanisms for the distribution of power and resources between levels of government, do not always capture the complexity of the country's multi-level governance (MLG) systems. There are, therefore, both practitioners and academics working in the public policy, political science and associated fields that are looking for conceptualisations of governance systems and processes that can bridge the boundaries of academic disciplines and governance practice in different policy domains. An expanded version of the concept of MLG, stemming in large part from the study and practice of governance in the European Union (EU) (e.g. Hooghe and Marks 2003; Bache and Flinders 2004; Enderlein et al. 2010), is increasingly attracting the attention of policymakers and academics around the world, including in Australia. This rapidly increasing usage may be due to its capacity to act as a mobilising 'metaphor', where the term is sufficiently ambiguous that room is left for individuals to attach their own meaning and criteria for success to it, hence maintaining their support for its use (Porter 1995; Mosse 2004). Examples of the use of the term 'multi-level governance' in the Australian context include Stilwell and Troy (2000), who use it to describe the issues associated with the coordination of urban development policies and plans across three tiers of government and with other sectoral policies; Painter (2001), who takes the standard EU definitions and uses MLG as a frame to examine collaborative federal institutions; and Fenna (2006), who, in his analyses of the uses of federalism, refers to MLG as a general term for systems of divided jurisdiction over a territory, of which federalism is just one type. More recently, the term 'multi-level governance' has also been appropriated in the feminist literature to provide an alternative, more flexible version of governance where power is shared between different tiers of government and with non-state actors, including international bodies, non-government organisations, community groups and private corporations (Haussman et al. 2010). It is also increasingly found in the environmental and natural resource management literature, along with the terms 'adaptive governance', 'polycentric governance' and 'collaborative governance', to emphasise the transfers of power and responsibility to a variety of stakeholders and scales of governance that do not fit typical government administrative boundaries (Marshall 2008; Lockwood et al. 2009; Pahl-Wostl et al. 2010; Daniell et al. 2011).

In all these contexts, the concept of MLG tends to refer to systems of governance where there is a dispersion of authority upwards, downwards and sideways between levels of government – local, regional, national and supra-national – as well as across spheres and sectors, including states, markets and civil society. However, beyond a broad consensus that effective governance increasingly requires coordination and continuous negotiation across multiple levels and sectors, there is little convergence on best practice models of how to design and effectively operate MLG systems for different contexts and policy issues.

This book stems from the premise that, without ideal models, a pragmatic, problem-driven approach to investigating MLG is required that can support improvement in public policy practice in Australia and further afield. The contents have been developed as a result of a 'Multi-level Governance Symposium' held at The Australian National University in 2010 and subsequent workshops in 2011 that brought together policy experts and practitioners from government and universities to consider distinctive features of existing and proposed MLG models for a range of key Australian policy challenges.

In this book, we first provide a number of chapters on different conceptual challenges of MLG, followed by case study chapters that range across social and environmental policy domains. The preliminary chapters on conceptual challenges present current theoretical challenges and issues related to the MLG concept, written in most part by political scientists and public policy academics. Each of the case studies then represent different periods or 'snapshots' of governance workings and negotiations at or through different points in time for particular policy issues or systems. They have typically been written by practitioner-academics from a range of public policy–related disciplines, who have been involved in the development of, and negotiations within, these MLG systems. Due to the two distinct sections of this book, we have chosen to provide the connections between these perspectives and, thereby, reveal what these two distinct viewpoints can add to our understanding of MLG and other governance systems and policymaking practices in general. This introduction thus provides a more general introduction into the concept of MLG and the types of themes and questions that the book addresses through its chapters. The final chapter of the book (*Daniell and Mercer, Chapter 18*)[1] synthesises these themes and presents a critical view of what the book can help us to understand about MLG and its practice in the Australian context, what forms it takes under different political regimes and how and why preferences for particular types of systems appear to come about, as well as how these governance systems can be researched in the future.

---

1   References to chapters in this book are provided in italics.

Due to the lack of consensus on the use of the MLG concept, this introduction provides a definition for the dominant way in which we interpret the term that has shaped the analysis of the case studies. The key elements of each of the book's chapters, the key questions investigated and the aspects highlighted throughout are then discussed.

Defining MLG and its conceptual components: Systems of continuous negotiation for governing across boundaries

Unless otherwise defined by the authors of individual chapters, we take the European view of MLG processes, which can be defined as systems of 'continuous negotiation among nested governments at several territorial tiers' (Marks 1993: 392), where authority is not only dispersed vertically between levels of administration but also horizontally across different sectors of interest and spheres of influence, including non-government actors, markets and civil society (Bache and Flinders 2004). Following our earlier discussion on the complexity of public policy challenges, the need and appearance of these kinds of negotiation systems can be premised on the fact that 'governance must operate at multiple scales in order to capture variations in the territorial reach of policy externalities' (Marks and Hooghe 2004: 16; see also Daniell and Barreteau 2014 on issues of scale and externalities). These negotiation systems represent a form of flexible and adaptive governance where both formal and informal structures can be developed to engage stakeholders from a range of appropriate levels and spheres of influence for the negotiated development of mutually acceptable, collectively analysed and implementable policies. MLG, taking this definition, is not an umbrella concept that can be used in place of 'federalism', 'intergovernmental relations' or 'polycentric governance', even though many instances of governance analysed through these frames may resemble MLG's negotiated processes. Negotiations do not have to lead to consensus; they may operate in many modes, including accommodating, competitive or collaborative modes (Thomas and Kilmann 1974). This leaves the door open to consider to what extent each instance of governance or policy-specific governance systems in Australia's federalist system exhibits typical MLG characteristics, as well as how this alternative concept can add to existing Australian public policy scholarship.

In terms of typical forms of MLG systems, European scholars note two ideal types of continuous negotiation systems (Marks and Hooghe 2004). As Bache and Flinders (2004: 5) describe, the first type (Type I) commonly portrays characteristics and structures considered important in federalist thought, including stability of authority and clear lines of accountability due to only a 'limited number of non-overlapping jurisdictional boundaries at a limited number of levels'; the second type (Type II), portrays characteristics typical of some described in the adaptive governance literature where negotiation systems are constituted of 'a complex fluid patchwork of innumerable overlapping jurisdictions', which tend to be flexible and adaptable to meeting new policy demands. In light of these two types, it can be considered that MLG approaches to policy development and implementation can 'provide a more flexible mode of optimising the policymaking process by allowing multi-directional shifts both vertically and horizontally in decision-making authority and power' (Stein and Turkewitsch 2008: 26). Fostering such shifts can allow the investigation and development of 'appropriate' multi-level mechanisms for policy design and delivery, which are suited to manage specific policy issues and contexts, although to what extent such flexibility is desirable and can promote adequate accountability mechanisms can be seen to be strongly contested by some political and public service leaders, or at least be a significant challenge to existing accountability frameworks (e.g. APSC 2012; see also Bovens et al. 2014). Open negotiation systems can also foster arenas of policy experimentation and learning that can lead to greater innovation, increased problem-solving capacity and broadly beneficial and acceptable policies (Scharpf 1994; Swanson et al. 2010), even though risk-averse governments can see this kind of governance system as a threat to stability and maintaining control over the direction of policy development and implementation.

Thus, despite the conceptual power that policy analysis based on MLG systems can potentially bring, putting effectively functioning systems in place can pose a number of challenges. One of the first issues involves the maintenance of two values upon which many of our traditional governance systems were based: clear lines of accountability and representative democracy. Peters and Pierre (2004: 85) summarise this challenge as the potential 'Faustian bargain' of MLG, where there is potential that the 'core values of democratic government are traded for accommodation, consensus and purported efficiency in governance'. Often when negotiated multi-level systems develop organically or informally, their transparency to external observers and the knowledge of who can be held to account for decisions that stem from the negotiations can be considered as less than desirable.

To effectively implement MLG systems that seek to overcome these issues, there are two further challenges that require attention. The first is understanding and developing systems that can fit and function within our legal systems. The second relates to understanding the importance of 'meta-governance' of MLG systems (see Jessop (2004) and Glasbergen (2011) or Daniell et al. (2010) and Daniell (2012) for a view on the similar concept of 'co-engineering') and how the development of organisational rules, guidelines and supportive mechanisms or incentives can be developed to aid and encourage the development of legal, accountable and transparent MLG systems for policy development and delivery.

What can be found in this book?

Considering these definitions and already highlighted tensions and challenges found in different types of governance systems for developing and implementing effective public policy, this book seeks to contribute to both the theoretical and practical debates surrounding MLG. It also seeks to contribute to investigating the pertinence of using MLG as a theoretical and practical concept specifically within the context of Australian public policy.

As we have previously outlined, this book is structured in two parts. The first concentrates on *conceptual challenges* related to MLG in the Australian context. Specifically, in Chapter 2, *Kay* investigates MLG and how it compares to the study of Australian federalism; in Chapter 3, *Fawcett and Marsh* look at the linkages between network governance, MLG and Australian politics; in Chapter 4, *Mulgan* analyses the important issue of accountability in MLG systems through the example of Australian federalism; in Chapter 5, *Dugdale* looks at the mentality of governing in MLG systems or what he terms 'multi-level governmentality'; and, in Chapter 6, *Kerr* investigates MLG as political theory, analysing the concept's potential for reconsidering the relationship between sovereignty and cross-boundary governance.

The second part comprises three sections of case studies, which focus on the domains of *education and social policy, spatial and planning policy* and *environmental and agricultural policy.* Each case study makes an appraisal of the potential usefulness of the MLG concept in analysing and understanding different Australian public policy challenges and reforms. More or less directly, each case study addresses the questions of and provides information on:

1. the background or history of the policy or governance challenge
2. what levels/actors/sectors were involved – and hence, which boundaries were being governed across
3. what (and who) were driving the negotiations
4. timelines and resources involved over the case study period
5. the resulting policy actions or outcomes
6. to what extent the policy succeeded or addressed the governance challenge, and why
7. key points of interest
8. emerging questions.

The case studies range in temporal scope from historical pictures of how MLG systems have been enacted and reformed through time for certain policy domains (*Troy; Hogan*) to more distinct phases of negotiation for specific policy or governance reforms that have taken place under different governments over the past couple of decades (*Mercer and Jarvie; Iwanicki et al.; Jarvie and Stewart*) and individual MLG systems that have been driven by the private sector (*McNaughton and Lockie*). Others use a comparative approach across governance programs or institutional arrangements (*Andrews*), regional case studies (*Norman and Gurran; Dale et al.*), policy sub-sectors (*Daniell et al.*) or countries (*Ross*) to draw conclusions about different instances of MLG systems and to provide suggestions for improving these systems in the future.

In the first case study section on *education and social policy,* in Chapter 7, *Mercer and Jarvie* analyse the extent to which the negotiations around the Rudd Labor Government's 'Early Childhood Education Revolution' and work through the Council of Australian Governments (COAG) could be considered an exercise in MLG. Chapter 8 by *Hogan* looks at the governance of differences in hearing and how an epistemic model of MLG has historically been able to assume primacy over others in this policy domain in Australia. Chapter 9, by *Jarvie and Stewart*, investigates the

Howard Government's Murdi Paaki Aboriginal community development COAG policy trial in New South Wales and the structures, processes and skills required in this case for effectively working across boundaries.

The second case study section concentrates on different components of *spatial and planning policy* in Australia. In Chapter 10, *Troy* analyses the history of MLG in Australia's housing policy and the impacts of different periods of reform. In Chapter 11, *Iwanicki, Bellette and Smith* examine the MLG involved in integrating land-use development and natural resource planning in the Willunga region, South Australia, on the southern peri-urban fringe of Adelaide in the early 2000s. Chapter 12, by *Norman and Gurran*, then looks at a range of contemporary regional solutions for addressing MLG challenges in Australian coastal and climate change planning. Chapter 13, by *Andrews*, analyses MLG in the Lake Eyre Basin and provides a comparison of the effectiveness of different types of structures for providing regional governance.

The final case study section focuses on issues of *environmental and agricultural policy*. In Chapter 14, *Dale, Ryan and Broderick* investigate natural resource management (NRM) in Australia as a form of MLG, looking specifically at the impacts of NRM policy reforms in Queensland and Tasmania and areas for enhancing future Australian NRM reforms. In Chapter 15, *Ross* provides a comparison of multi-level water governance examples from Australia and the United States, focusing on the Namoi region of New South Wales and the South Platte region of Colorado. Chapter 16, by *McNaughton and Lockie*, then specifically analyses the important roles that private actors can play in MLG, using the case of the international GLOBALG.A.P. standard-setting arrangements for agricultural and food products. In Chapter 17, *Daniell, Hogan and Cleary* investigate the need to break down the common 'one-size-fits-all' policy development and implementation approaches to rural and regional policy, and provide some specific priorities for how future policy initiatives could be enhanced through MLG.

The book concludes in Chapter 18 with a synthesis by *Daniell and Mercer* of the book's main contributions and a critical evaluation of the MLG concept's use and future in the Australian policy context.

Use and contributions of MLG conceptualisations and theory to knowledge and practice

Through existing literature and the contributions in this book, we note that there are three principal types of uses to which conceptualisations and theory of MLG can be put. First, MLG can be used analytically, in order to better understand decision-making and policy processes. Second, it can be used empirically, as in the case of many MLG studies in the EU. Finally, it can be used normatively, in order to offer potential improvements to governance arrangements.

As we alluded to at the beginning of this introduction, the great appeal of MLG to scholars of European integration, and in the study of Australian public policy, is its ability to capture and simplify novel multi-scalar configurations of policymaking for analysis in which both formal powers and informal capacity to act are dispersed and redistributed. This can involve the creation of new institutions for new policy spaces within and across existing political–administrative jurisdictions, which may not always be counted as conventionally 'public' (see, for example, *McNaughton and Lockie*). Instead, MLG encourages us to think about the potential for hybridity in novel governance arrangements. For those who accept that the complexity of contemporary Australian policymaking is no longer captured adequately and usefully by a Commonwealth versus state dichotomy, MLG may provide a welcome means of casting light on an analytical terrain that contains the potential to improve policymaking.

At the core of MLG system theory are shifting interdependencies in policymaking, such that no level or scale of policymaking is able to effectively enforce its ambitions or requirements onto other levels in an ongoing and permanent manner. Instead, compliance is an outcome of negotiation and the ability of different actors at different levels to exert influence within those negotiations and to hold others within them to account for their actions over a specific period of time. This may, for example, require the development of complex policy coalitions that are able to steer these negotiations and subsequent reforms (Daniell et al. 2014; *Hogan*). All of the empirical case study chapters in this book explore and attempt to gauge the influence of certain actors, or groups of actors, and trace this through to the observed outcomes in their cases of MLG policymaking. The volume shows that the concept of MLG contributes to an understanding of these influences as diverse – for example, processes driven and organised by different levels of government, private sector actors, community groups and researchers or other experts/professionals – and complementary or in conflict, but certainly not unidirectional in Australian policymaking.

The challenge for those seeking to deploy the concept in Australia is twofold: first, to consider the extent to which MLG contributes to an improved understanding of policymaking above and beyond governance conceptualisations already in more common use but also, second, to consider to what extent it helps the organisation of evidence and inquiry about how to improve policymaking processes and capacity in Australia.

At a conceptual level, MLG encourages us to think about governance arrangements for policy dilemmas that are no longer contained within the boundaries of a zero-sum 'blame game' between state and federal governments. It thus links to the studies in federalism that show how alternative conceptualisations of the roles and relative powers of these two levels of government, and how they influence each other or work together, can create very different policy development and implementation outcomes (Smullen 2014; *Kay*). Specifically, an ideal form of MLG holds the promise of policy learning as repeated interactions in novel arrangements, including beyond governments, to help transform interests, build trust and allow evidence to be used and respected in a less partisan manner. In doing so, this may contribute to a policy practice that is able to surmount the well-established roadblocks in Australian policy reform. In a less than ideal form, however, it could lead to undermining representative democracy and traditional mechanisms of accountability, and lead to new forms of stakeholder power-grabbing and a reduction in fairness of policy outcomes across the country due to individualised, rather than standardised and centralised, governance processes. In either case, we consider that better understanding the alternative values that are present in governance systems can be clearly addressed through the critical application of the MLG concept.

It is thus not surprising that the empirical evidence from the EU about MLG's contribution to policy capacity is also debated and contested. Stephenson (2013) summarises different generations of scholarship over 20 years of use of the MLG concept. Much of the celebration of MLG is in EU regional and cohesion policy, and the extent to which new spatial scales of policy thinking and novel sub-national arrangements of implementation have been observed, as well as around the open method of coordination (OMC), which has enabled non-hierarchical policy development and coordination beyond constitutionally entrenched limits to policy integration. This OMC policy dynamic (see also *Kay*) and the perspective of moving beyond the nation state that it implies helps to analyse of the plurality of policy reform processes and cast doubt on any claims that there is one jurisdiction that has all the answers. To what extent it functions effectively in practice and leads to these desirable outcomes in each instance – instead of policy gridlock, as some spectators of the recent European crises (both economic and linked to migrating refugees) may attest – is, however, certainly a topical area of popular and academic debate (e.g. Song 2011; Barcevičius and Weishaupt 2014).

As a contribution to this debate on MLG specifically in the Australian context, this book provides some insights into the potential for functional, task-specific MLG policy arrangements in Australia (i.e. there is a strong focus on Type II MLG from the aforementioned definitions), which, while relatively enduring, do not get locked in, creating sticky legacies for future policymakers to overcome. As *Fawcett and Marsh* point out, MLG and most studies associated with it also draw our attention to three important themes: moving beyond formal institutions, taking a multi-scalar focus and developing a more networked approach (see also Torfing et al. 2012). *Andrews* likewise points to Peters and Pierre's (2004) characteristics of MLG, which include a wide and diverse set of actors, being non-hierarchical (i.e. not controlled from above), not being constrained by formal agreements or rules (which means informal bargaining can be as important as formal power) and largely ignoring structure (instead focusing on process and outcomes). This implies a need to focus more on the politics of scale and the interests of different actors involved in processes of negotiation that lead to rescaling and new governance systems and institutions (especially informal) that are fit for the negotiated purpose and prevailing political interests (see also Mukhtarov and Daniell 2017 and discussion in *Daniell and Mercer*).

Whilst better policy outcomes – specifically those that 'fit' with local and differentiated needs among stakeholders – may be the driver of moving towards MLG, there is the normative question of accountability. Do novel, flexible and adaptable arrangements in response to changing policy challenges create an accountability deficit – in particular, by marginalising representative institutions of democracy in Australia? *Mulgan* considers this question and the extent to which accountability may be ensured.

The democratic deficit dilemma of certain MLG-type arrangements exists within Australian policymaking. However, as the concept expands its ambit to include international and global arenas (see, for example, *McNaughton and Lockie*), or to look at the potential for policy transfer, translation and learning across jurisdictions and cultures (e.g. Evans and Davies 1999; Daniell 2014; Mukhtarov and Daniell 2017; *Ross*), there is likely to be an ongoing theoretical and practical question to investigate in future MLG studies on the interplay of global governance institutions and extant domestic policymaking processes in Australia. On top of issues of accountability, this could also include novel investigations of sovereignty, as suggested by *Kerr*. The studies of advantages of Type I, Type II and hybrids of these ideal types in different policy areas is just one way of approaching some of these challenges (see, for example, the analyses of *Mercer and Jarvie* and *Ross*).

The last section of this introduction digs further into a number of these questions, highlighting some preliminary responses about the utility of MLG conceptualisations and understandings of practice in Australia, drawing on the contributions to this volume.

MLG for Australia and abroad: Emerging themes and questions

The richness of the MLG concept and its relatively recent introduction into Australian public policy results in an abundance of research themes and questions to explore. Here we outline the seven themes and insights addressed in this volume, with example insights from chapters related to them. This discussion is expanded in a more critical manner in *Daniell and Mercer* at the end of the book, specifically looking at examples of additional governance systems and how these might allow us to further theorise on the usefulness of the concept for future research and public policy practice.

Processes and structures for 'governing across boundaries'

The first research theme of importance addressed in this book relates to how MLG is about the processes and structures for 'governing across boundaries' – specifically, around investigating *what types of processes and structures are most effectively used for governing across boundaries and whether these differ for different types of boundaries?* An MLG viewpoint has also allowed consideration of not only how governing across boundaries occurs, but also for whom this is carried out and, subsequently, *who is involved* (Hooghe and Marks 2003; *Kerr*).

Each of the case study chapters provide a number of examples of more or less successful processes and structures. They also discuss who is involved in governing across a range of boundaries, typically different arenas of negotiation – such as COAG-driven working groups (e.g. *Mercer and Jarvie; Jarvie and Stewart*) or regional networks and structures (e.g. *Iwanicki et al.; Andrews; Dale et al.; Norman and Gurran; Daniell et al.*) – a number of which will be discussed in the next research theme, and so are not detailed here. The boundaries that are governed across predominantly include levels of administration or spatial territories, but also include sectors and knowledge types (e.g. traditional indigenous/community knowledge, administrative knowledge, commercial knowledge, academic research). Research on cross-boundary (or multi-scalar) working and governance has been blossoming in recent years from both theoretical and practical points of view (e.g. Cash et al. 2006; Daniell and Barreteau 2014), but merging this with research on policymaking and politics is less common and could provide a fruitful avenue for Australian MLG research, as will be discussed in *Daniell and Mercer*.

From the chapters, we can see that MLG cross-boundary working can be formalised to a certain extent through legislation (e.g. *Iwanicki et al.; Troy; Dale et al.; Ross*) or more informally developed using new or existing organisations and relationships (e.g. *Mercer and Jarvie; Jarvie and Stewart; Andrews*). However, most governance systems are hybrids of both – like they are between Type I/Type II MLG – especially when it comes to the construction of the negotiation arenas and who is personally involved in them.

Looking to the future, our chapters and other authors also note other structures of importance for governing across borders that deserve further investigation in the Australian context, including those related to performance monitoring and compliance (where legal or equivalent frameworks exist). Investigating such issues in the EU, for example, linked to OMC (e.g. De la Porte et al. 2001; Arrowsmith et al. 2004; *Kay*), has yielded useful research to inform policymaking across, and negotiations between, member states in a range of policy areas. Similar potential exists for cross-boundary working between Australian states especially, as *Mulgan* notes, if common objectives can be agreed on. These negotiations can be complex (*Mulgan*), however, due to the variety of objectives and areas of interest requiring data for management purposes that may not match between levels of government and other stakeholders (*Dugdale*), which complicates the development of data collection and coordination systems.

In such a setting, the importance of private actors and markets, as well as the need to maintain some checks and balances on them (*Dugdale*), should not be overlooked. This means governments at different levels must, to some extent, engage in MLG systems and performance monitoring. Differences in existing data systems (e.g. across states or industry sectors) can also be a challenge to reporting on negotiated common objectives, but serious efforts in Australia on some policy areas have been occurring in recent years following work by the COAG Reform Council (e.g. the development of the 'MySchool' website[2] and national education testing). Some governments, however, continue to lack interest in acting upon performance indicators (McClintock 2012), at least in federal–state/territory agreements. Yet, this lack of willingness can alter when other stakeholders from outside government are involved and push for change (*Mulgan*), or when more innovative collectives of state and non-state actors run the processes for data management and systems interoperability (see *Dugdale*). Thus, there are a growing numbers of areas, such as in social and environmental policy, where having an overview of environmental conditions or social indicators across the country is helping to inform the development of MLG systems to cope with the diversity of situations and priorities identified, as well as empowering communities and other public and private actors in the governance system to act and invest in order to seek system improvements (see, for example, *Mercer and Jarvie* and *Dale et al.*). In areas such as natural resource management policy, some progress is being made towards nationally agreed targets (*Dale et al.*), but changes to funding arrangements, such as competitive grants from government for short-term projects, can decrease the ability to maintain local interest and ties long-term community/business funding to their identified priorities, and reduces collaboration and engagement more generally across levels and sectors.

---

2   www.myschool.edu.au [Accessed: 29/12/2014].

Some performance systems are developed for information only, whereas others may monitor adherence to standards or legislation, thus requiring complementary compliance systems to be developed. In many traditional MLG systems in Australia, policy and intergovernmental agreements are developed at higher administrative levels (e.g. federal, state), then implemented at lower levels (e.g. state, local), and it is at these lower levels that compliance mechanisms also have to be developed. Other actors, such as courts, may play a role in compliance, though this may be more developed in other countries such as the United States (e.g. *Ross*). When resources are not allocated or available for compliance monitoring and rectification, however, it can lead to policy failure, such as the appearance of slum housing in Australia (*Troy*).

Mechanisms of authority sharing: Successes and failures

The second theme this book investigates relates closely to the idea of policy learning, hence questioning *what can be learnt from successes and failures of MLG systems, especially around the mechanisms of authority sharing and their ultimate impacts?* It is specifically through case study analyses that authors address this question, although there is room for additional research to contribute to this theme through theoretical investigations around the nature of authority (e.g. Barnett and Finnemore 2004), accountability (e.g. *Mulgan*), risk-sharing and uncertainty management (e.g. Matthews 2009) and what this means for working in 'multi-accountable' groups (e.g. Daniell 2012).

For example, as initial offerings to this theme from our case study chapters, we can see that the Commonwealth–state working groups on early childhood education (ECE) reform (*Mercer and Jarvie*) were successful in developing innovative working relationships, but some issues of authority to make decisions were encountered, seemingly due to the arrangement of federal and state public service officials working under a Commonwealth minister, where state ministers were not involved. This led to the requirement for significant communication from the work-group members back to numerous departments to reassess positions in the negotiations. Since high levels of trust were built, however, decisions from negotiations were still taken quickly while ensuring the required flexibility of the process. A similar approach across Australia between federal government and the states to agree on regional NRM plans and resource allocation in the early 2000s also saw success and encountered challenges (*Dale et al.*).

Other successful strategies seen in the indigenous policy trial in *Jarvie and Stewart* included flexible budgeting and a range of inter-organisational mechanisms to drive the governance system and implementation of its decisions; intergovernmental and government–community networks with non-hierarchical structures that could involve rotating chairs and joint objective-setting/decision-making; and trust-building through ongoing and regular engagement and listening to others (see also *Mercer and Jarvie* on trust-building). On the other side, challenges that could lead to failure included instability in authorising environments (federal government or communities), including changing philosophical positions and structures in ways that do not help maintain relationships important for advancing the project, and the requirement of significant resources for collaborative approaches that may or may not finally provide value for money in terms of results, both politically and practically (*Jarvie and Stewart*).

Some of these challenges are linked to 'pure politics' in terms of competing rationalities and scales of thinking that are prioritised by different governments (e.g. (laissez faire) market approach, coercive/ strongly regulation-driven government, bottom-up community pressure/ driving a reactive government approach). One successful MLG initiative for agricultural standard setting, GLOBALG.A.P., led to business, rather than government, driving the standard-setting in response to community discontent/fear and the need to secure markets and consumer confidence (*McNaughton and Lockie*). Other authors identified that staff turnover and lack of expertise in multiple areas can also be a barrier to successful implementation of 'integrated' policies (*Iwanicki et al.*) and that regulation alone may provide a base standard for management but may not lead to further improvement of practices (*Dale et al.*) without other drivers (social or competitive/economic). It was also evident that different MLG systems can lead to similar outcomes (not necessarily optimal), as demonstrated in the United States/Australian integrated groundwater/surface water management issue in *Ross*, and thus most can likely be further improved through ongoing policy learning, adaptations and negotiations.

Questions of MLG system visibility

The third theme investigated through the book relates to the issue of whether negotiations in MLG systems are in the political spotlight or occur under the radar, and to what extent this influences outcomes. For example, *are 'under the radar' or informal activities more conducive to a collaborative approach to governing*? Both theoretical and practical contributions to this theme are presented.

For example, accountability – or at least holding actors to account in MLG systems – can occur through outlets like the media and social networking. There could obviously be issues about 'under the radar' governing from such an accountability perspective, but it may also allow more effective progress and results, rather than processes and issues, to be assessed. This is less likely to hamper progress in the particular direction chosen by the collective. Such governance systems with multiple stakeholders can also be more open and transparent than traditional monolithic hierarchical structures (*Mulgan*). They can also facilitate the negotiation of individual grievances and then quickly move forward, thus providing 'bottom-up' instead of 'top-down' accountability (*Mulgan*).

Moreover, conceptualising accountability as being constructed in an ongoing fashion, including between partners in the MLG network, rather than being a forced condition of work, opens an important line of inquiry for Australian research. Internationally, this book provides the interesting case of private actors in governance (*McNaughton and Lockie*) where formal accountability or 'standard adherence' mechanisms and sanctions can be set up as both informal and/or legally binding if state actors make reference to such standards.

Similar processes of accountability development can also occur in MLG systems with high proportions of community actors, as in the Lake Eyre Basin community initiative (*Andrews*) where high trust and organising principles can be developed, but actions may end up being constrained by other initiatives in the operating environment. As *Andrews* notes: 'MLG should now represent models that create new forms of accountability and empowered relationships between people and their institutions.' In a complementary fashion, MLG can be seen and investigated as a process of authorising and legitimating particular actors (*Kerr*).

Preliminary insights from the contributions in this volume also lead us to postulate that much work that occurs 'under the radar' in MLG systems remains there because it is successful and generally welcome and is thus often not considered newsworthy or of academic interest (*Mulgan*). This book contributes to illuminating some of these kinds of negotiating systems (see, for example, *Jarvie and Stewart; Mercer and Jarvie; Iwanicki et al.; Andrews*). The findings from these Australian cases coincide with Bache and Flinders's (2004: 199) EU analysis that 'MLG is likely to be more evident in "low politics" issues, where the stakes are less significant and the politics are less fraught', as noted by *Mercer and Jarvie. Jarvie and Stewart*, however, also note that working under the political radar can prove detrimental to the maintenance of good relationships with the bureaucratic and political hierarchy. There also remains the issue of who receives the political pay-off and if it can be made visible, as Commonwealth or state governments are typically less likely to act if there is no political gain (see, for example, *Troy* on these challenges, including budget allocations in the housing policy domain).

Organisation of negotiation arenas

The fourth theme investigated through the book relates to the organisation of negotiation arenas for integrated policies – specifically, *who is involved in this organisation and what enabling conditions are required?* This can also relate to issues of meta-governance at both the macro (e.g. structural) and micro (e.g. individual actor) level.

From our chapters, we can see that some issue areas like climate change and agricultural trade and standards have global reach and immediacy, and so find that a greater range of state and non-state actors are involved in negotiations (and their organisation) at a range of levels, as it is rare that Type I governance solutions will work (see Betsill and Bulkeley 2006; *Fawcett and Marsh; Norman and Gurran; Daniell et al.; McNaughton and Lockie*). Social policy areas typically require the involvement of community groups and frontline service providers (*Jarvie and Stewart; Hogan*), although the extent to which they may be engaged from the beginning of policy development varies (see *Mercer and Jarvie* on the COAG-dominated approach to ECE reform, and *Daniell and Mercer* for further discussion on this point), as can the eventual level of support for or resistance to the resulting policy. This leads to the importance of designing negotiation arenas to include community engagement (*Dugdale*). Specifically, trust (and openness) can enable the development of 'win–win' outcomes, as there is generally a need for high trust to permit the effective functioning of MLG policy systems, especially in the implementation phase (*Dugdale*).

While it can be of particular use to have actors involved in the negotiation arena who have an interest in final outcomes, those organising the arenas may have a less prominent personal stake but a strong interest in ensuring negotiation effectiveness. How this is done and what procedural objectives are considered to be of importance can be linked to different mentalities of governing or 'governmentalities' (Foucault 2007) and hence different preferred governance or MLG negotiation systems (*Dugdale*). In our cases, we have evidence of negotiation arenas that are self-organised by communities, for communities, with support from government and specific facilitators or organisers (*Andrews*). There was one case where community and government champions were important in negotiations to align actions at different levels and across groups involved in the MLG system (*Jarvie and Stewart*).

Other MLG processes have researchers playing an important role in driving innovation and/or the organisation of MLG systems (Daniell et al. 2014), yet, in order to gain maximum benefit over larger geographical areas, such as regions, more coordinated research bodies or brokers at these levels may be required to ensure adequate knowledge and consideration of innovation and investment across these areas (see *Dale et al.* and *Daniell et al.* for examples), rather than individual researchers driving innovation in one area around their own interests. Ideally, these regional research programs should be strongly linked to 'end-user' or community needs, with these stakeholders helping to set the research priorities and helping to follow the research through (e.g. in a participatory research set-up – see Barreteau et al. (2010) – with direct links then made to the use of this research and knowledge to help inform the decision-making processes and innovation in the MLG system). This has been the case in some of the regional bodies and negotiation arenas presented in *Norman and Gurran*, such as the Canberra Urban and Regional Futures (CURF) initiative. Perceived failures across levels and scales to organise such negotiations in multiple or specific governance systems may, however, lead to a major shift in governance approach, such as a strong reversion to hierarchical and centralised control mechanisms and exclusion of non-government condoned entities (see also *Daniell and Mercer*), as discussed in the next section.

Drivers of coordination and tension in MLG systems

The fifth theme of this book relates to the internal dynamics of MLG systems – specifically, *what are the drivers of coordination and tension in MLG systems?* Theoretical issues in this area include issues of legitimacy of, and trust between, participants of MLG systems (see *Kay*) and the ongoing tensions between Type I and Type II systems due to their advantages and disadvantages (see *Fawcett and Marsh*; Brown and Bellamy 2010; *Ross, Daniell and Mercer*).

For example, a potential lack of transparency in Type I negotiation processes (e.g. *Mercer and Jarvie*) is likely, as public servants are often bound by stricter codes of conduct over the release of information than other non-state actors. This can often lead to lesser involvement of community stakeholders and greater potential for conflict between governments and communities (*Ross*). Type II systems have the potential for more innovation but can also lack coherence and consistency across MLG systems, or have issues due to the lack of higher-level oversight (*Ross*).

A significant driver of tension within MLG systems, as alluded to in previous discussion, can be the different ideological origins of policies within and across administrations and stakeholder groups (*Troy*; *Hogan*); for example, a reliance on markets versus the need for state-funded welfare support, or a technological solution aimed to 'fix a problem' compared to a societal or person-focused intervention to appreciate and support difference. As Hogan notes, there can be a battle of ideas, politics and influence in negotiations and other governing processes that results in the subjugation of certain people, where ideas that do not benefit a minority come to dominate policy (*Hogan*).

Another similar tension can be the different experiences of policymakers versus implementers, who are often at lower administrative levels or external to administrations (*Troy*). In this case, a lack of mutual understanding can affect negotiations. The other associated challenge and cause of tension is that unilateral actions taken at one level or by one group of actors can undermine the value or position of a collective agreement if the results have strong impacts on the policy area under question, rendering inoperable the range of options initially considered (see *Troy* for an example of the Commonwealth push for home ownership that undermined the states' room to manoeuvre on housing policy).

Other tensions and areas where coordination is typically necessary to work through issues are between territory- or jurisdiction-specific needs compared to general needs and priorities of a larger area jurisdiction (e.g. a water basin area versus a larger regional area). Tensions here, for example, have been observed between NRM developed by the federal government, regional systems of governance and 'organically' evolved community basin initiatives between regions, with agreed specific priorities (*Andrews*). The existence of regional and inter-regional systems indicates the national 'one-size-fits-all' structures do not function equally well for all territories (*Daniell et al.*).

Tensions can come from other issues, such as the relative weight of representational democracy versus participatory or deliberative democracy in MLG systems. This can lead to additional questions of research interest, such as *what are the advantages and disadvantages of voluntary (community) participation versus statutory frameworks for participation/partnership working in MLG systems?* On top of accountability and representation issues with different forms of participation in decision-making, it is clear that in many policy domains public participation is key to ensuring policy support, understanding and successful implementation. As *Iwanicki et al.* outline, public involvement and education are key for driving local reforms like catchment management, since the processes are little known and investments in engagement need to be made to bring the community along with the work. This can be trickier to do in larger geographical areas, however, as there can be a relative loss of community control under statutory or legislated frameworks and less flexibility to include issues of interest for the community (see *Andrews* for a comparative analysis on some advantages and disadvantages of different systems). Yet, over Australia's public policy history, there have been examples of sophisticated public engagement campaigns linked to complex negotiations (see, for example, Combet and Davis (2014) on industrial relations policy) that warrant further investigation as MLG case studies.

MLG system change: Entry points and the importance of individuals

The sixth theme treated through the chapters of this book focuses on the dynamics of change in MLG systems – specifically, looking at *what are the entry points into different MLG systems to bring about change and empower individuals?* Both theoretically and practically, this involves questioning the role of the identity of individuals involved in MLG systems who are seeking to drive change, including those individuals (and/or organisations) involved in boundary spanning, facilitation or brokering.

In terms of the mechanisms used for driving change in our case studies, *Mercer and Jarvie* note that the chairing of complex groups by 'outsiders' (e.g. a consultant) in the state/Commonwealth reform group, as well as an initial cash injection from the Commonwealth to the states, helped to demonstrate good faith and helped to build trust in the governance/ reform process. Other authors similarly note the importance of bringing in facilitators to work through different issues within and between groups for planning or the importance of brokering work to 'join up the dots' (e.g. *Jarvie and Stewart*; see also Sabatier and Jenkins-Smith 1999; Daniell et al. 2014). For example, individuals with expertise across multiple policy domains can act as knowledge brokers or boundary spanners to help bring actors and relevant information together (e.g. across catchment management and land planning, as in *Iwanicki et al.*).

Individuals with in-depth historical and local knowledge of past work/ policies can also be invaluable change agents to support policy learning and to help avoid repeating policies that had previously failed; they have insights that can help to select policies that are more likely to be locally viable for implementation. These individuals may be people in positions such as 'project officers', working under stakeholder steering committees, who do the hard work of engaging people in the process and providing this bridging service (e.g. *Andrews*). There is, however, also a need to support widespread change in developing the skills of all actors involved in the MLG system in engaging across boundaries. This can, for example, be built through the process of negotiating and partnership working, as discussed in the case of *Jarvie and Stewart*, although they also highlight the importance of ongoing support of a champion and leadership – collaborative rather than directive – so that others in the system are not alienated.

Not all MLG systems are collaborative and, thus, some individuals – such as ministers, engineers or other intermediaries (e.g. *Ross*) – have key decision-making powers or capacities to formulate plans that shape the rest of the MLG system and negotiations, thus acting as key agents for system change.

Regional-level groups (e.g. catchment boards) can also help drive coordination in MLG systems both vertically and horizontally, including acting as facilitators between state and local levels (e.g. *Iwanicki et al.*; *Norman and Gurran*; see also *Andrews* and *Dale et al.*). Yet, this is also one of the messiest and most contested areas of policy development, as regions or regional governance may also find themselves subject to changing policy environments in the formal levels of government (see, for example, *Daniell et al.*). Personal relationships and networks with people in other levels of governance/spheres can help to get things working, as trust exists already (*Iwanicki et al.*). Individuals can also hold multiple roles, especially in Type II systems, having a position at, say, a local and regional level, while being the local representative on a national body. Many of the seemingly more successful and connected regional groups form organically as part of Type II systems with voluntary membership (e.g. local governments, universities or community groups). This allows groups with specific targeted interests, such as climate change adaptation or coastal planning, to build a coalition large enough to seek change, but small enough to maintain close connections to local issues, priorities and knowledge (*Norman and Gurran*). Such groups also tend to promote more experimentation in governance systems, as will be discussed next.

Experimentation and innovation: Driving MLG forward

The final theme explicitly addressed in this volume relates to innovation and how this can drive public policy forward. In particular, there are questions to investigate, such as *what is the experimental or innovative potential of certain types of MLG systems?* And *what can be learnt from the successes of innovation in certain areas and the potential failures for these innovations to be taken up and extended across broader MLG systems?* These questions again relate to policy learning in a different, more systematic way, where potential policy solutions can be experimented with and evaluated, or left to emerge and be learnt from.

From the contributions of our authors, it can be considered that the fluidity of goal-setting in MLG systems may lead to an intensification of policy innovation, creativity and entrepreneurialism of actors (*Dugdale*). It can also be seen that innovation may be easier in arenas where there is not a long history of adversarial politics/strong positions and media interest in the debate. Hence, in ECE policy, in comparison to schools policy, it was easier to openly investigate new and more innovative solutions to issues (*Mercer and Jarvie*). Authors also noted that small innovative programs can make a difference to the people involved, but expanding them against a dominant policy landscape (including values and resourcing) means that their ultimate spread, expansion or fate may not be assured (see examples in *Andrews* and *Hogan*, as well as in Daniell et al. 2014). Where there is no strong opposition group, however, MLG innovations may have greater take-up and spread, as occurred with the private European agricultural standards system 'EurepGAP'. This system first expanded to have global reach in GLOBALG.A.P. and is now reintegrating and supporting national and local 'gap' systems in both developed and developing countries, showing the MLG system's capacity for both responsiveness and innovation (*McNaughton and Lockie*), as well as the power of non-state actors within them.

It was also seen that with changing authorising environments, innovations at more local levels can be short-lived (e.g. integration of catchment management and land planning in *Iwanicki et al.*), although strong voluntary coalitions of groups with similar issues and objectives may help to maintain alliances and continue to drive innovation through difficult political times (e.g. *Norman and Gurran*; *Andrews*). In terms of MLG system types, it is generally considered that there is greater (or at least easier) innovation potential from Type II or nested (polycentric) systems, due to their adaptation and flexibility potential. This is shown in the examples of a regional board driving change up and down the nested system in *Iwanicki et al.*, and a regional community initiative supporting the development of an intergovernmental agreement in *Andrews*.

Recent research, however, also shows that more centralised Type I systems may have solid potential for innovation, including by developing a culture of policy experimentation and trials across the system that can be learnt from before final policies are developed and rolled out. This has, for example, been the case in China (e.g. Daniell et al. 2014), where the Chinese national government has the willingness and resources to take an experimental approach. In some policy areas, such an approach has also been used in Australia (see, for example, *Jarvie and Stewart* on Indigenous policy trials and *Daniell et al.* on the drought policy trial). However, there remains the challenge of having a long enough term of government and strategy to actually learn from such trials, complete further testing and policy development and have the resources for eventual broad scale rollout.

Australian public policy and MLG systems thus have some unique challenges, some linked to cultures of relative government risk-aversion and short-term thinking (Daniell 2014) and others linked to rapidly shifting political frameworks and national leaders in recent years, as will be expanded upon in *Daniell and Mercer* at the end of this book. Yet, by considering different meta-governance systems that can create the enabling conditions for greater risk-taking, entrepreneurialism and learning from both successes and failures (see also Matthews 2009, 2013), more effective MLG systems of Types I and II and hybrid varieties may be created and reformed over time to enhance and drive Australian public policy forward more effectively.

Acknowledgements

The initial MLG forum and workshops, around which the content of this volume was designed, was funded by a research grant from the ANU College of Asia and the Pacific. Katherine Daniell would like to thank her colleagues at the Centre for Policy Innovation (Research School of Social Sciences), HC Coombs Policy Forum, ANU Centre for European Studies and ANZSOG Institute for Governance (in the Muarry–Darling Basin Futures Sustainable Communities project) for their ongoing support of this project from 2010–14. We would also like to thank John Wanna and the staff at ANU Press for their support in the development and realisation of this volume, Trish Mercer for her willingness to review the case study chapters, and Anne Daniell and Justine Molony for their copyediting of the volume. The editors and authors take full responsibility for any remaining errors or omissions in the book.

References

APSC (2012). *Tackling Wicked Problems: A Public Policy Perspective.* Australian Public Service Commission, www.apsc.gov.au/publications-and-media/archive/publications-archive/tackling-wicked-problems [Accessed: 01/06/16].

Arrowsmith, J., Sisson, K. & Marginson, P. (2004). What Can 'Benchmarking' Offer the Open Method of Co-ordination? *Journal of European Public Policy*, 11(2): 311–28. doi. org/10.1080/1350176042000194458

Bache, I. & Flinders, M. (eds) (2004). *Multi-level Governance*. Oxford University Press. doi.org/10.1093/0199259259.001.0001

Barcevičius, E. & Weishaupt, T. (2014). *Assessing the Open Method of Coordination: Institutional Design and National Influence of EU Social Policy Coordination*. Palgrave Macmillan, Basingstoke. doi.org/ 10.1057/9781137022622

Barnett, M. & Finnemore, M. (2004). *Rules for the World: International Organizations in Global Politics*. Cornell University Press, New York.

Barreteau, O., Bots, P.W.G. & Daniell, K.A. (2010). A Framework for Clarifying 'Participation' in Participatory Research to Prevent its Rejection for the Wrong Reasons. *Ecology and Society*, 15(2): 1. doi.org/10.5751/ES-03186-150201

Betsill, M.M. & Bulkeley, H. (2006). Cities and the Multilevel Governance of Global Climate Change. *Global Governance*, 12(2): 141–59.

Bovens, M., Goodin, R.E. & Schillemans, T. (eds) (2014). *The Oxford Handbook of Public Accountability*. Oxford University Press. doi.org/ 10.1093/oxfordhb/9780199641253.001.0001

Brown, A.J. & Bellamy, J.A. (2010). In the Shadow of Federalism: Dilemmas of institutional design in Australian rural and remote regional governance. *The Australasian Journal of Regional Studies*, 16(2): 151–81.

Cash, D.W., Adger, W., Berkes, F., Garden, P., Lebel, L., Olsson, P., Pritchard, L. & Young, O. (2006). Scale and Cross-Scale Dynamics: Governance and information in a multilevel world. *Ecology and Society*, 11(2): 8. doi.org/10.5751/ES-01759-110208

Combet, G. & Davis, M. (2014). *The Fights of my Life*. Melbourne University Press.

Daniell, K.A. (2012). *Co-engineering and Participatory Water Management: Organisational Challenges for Water Governance.* UNESCO International Hydrology Series, Cambridge University Press. doi.org/10.1017/CBO9780511998072

———. (2014). *The Role of National Culture in Shaping Public Policy: A Review of the Literature.* HC Coombs Forum Discussion Paper, June 2014, The Australian National University, Canberra, tinyurl.com/national-culture-public-policy [Accessed: 29/12/2014].

Daniell, K.A. & Barreteau, O. (2014). Water Governance Across Competing Scales: Coupling land and water management. *Journal of Hydrology*, 519(Part C): 2367–80. doi.org/10.1016/j.jhydrol.2014.10.055

Daniell, K.A., Coombes, P.J. & White, I. (2014). Politics of Innovation in Multi-level Water Governance Systems. *Journal of Hydrology*, 519(Part C): 2415–35. doi.org/10.1016/j.jhydrol.2014.08.058

Daniell, K.A., Manez Costa, M.A., Ferrand, N., Kingsborough, A.B., Coad, P. & Ribarova, I.S. (2011). Aiding Multi-level Decision-making Processes for Climate Change Mitigation and Adaptation. *Regional Environmental Change*, 11(2): 243–58. doi.org/10.1007/s10113-010-0162-0

Daniell, K.A., White, I., Ferrand, N., Riborova, I.S., Coad, P., Rougier, J.-E., Hare, M., Jones, N., Popova, A., Perez, P. & Burn, S. (2010). Co-engineering Participatory Water Management Processes: Theory and insights from Australian and Bulgarian interventions. *Ecology and Society*, 15(4): 11. doi.org/10.5751/ES-03567-150411

De la Porte, C., Pochet, P. & Room, B.G. (2001). Social Benchmarking, Policy Making and New Governance in the EU. *Journal of European Social Policy*, 11(4): 291–307. doi.org/10.1177/095892870101100401

Enderlein, H., Wälti, S. & Zürn, M. (eds) (2010). *Handbook on Multi-level Governance.* Edward Elgar, Cheltenham.

Evans, M. & Davies, J. (1999). Understanding Policy Transfer: A multi-level, multi-disciplinary perspective. *Public Administration*, 77(2): 361–85. doi.org/10.1111/1467-9299.00158

Fenna, A. (2006). *What Use is Federalism Anyway?* Australasian Political Studies Association Conference, University of Newcastle, www-cms. newcastle.edu.au/Resources/Schools/Newcastle%20Business%20 School/APSA/PanelFederalism/Fenna-Alan.pdf [Accessed: 12/12/2014].

Foucault, M. (2007). *Security, Territory and Population. Lectures at the College De France 1977–78.* Palgrave MacMillan, New York.

Glasbergen, P. (2011). Mechanisms of Private Meta-governance: An analysis of global private governance for sustainable development. *International Journal of Strategic Business Alliances*, 2(3): 189–206. doi.org/10.1504/IJSBA.2011.040886

Haussman, M., Sawer, M. & Vickers, J. (2010). *Federalism, Feminism and Multilevel Governance.* Ashgate, Surrey.

Hooghe, L. & Marks, G. (2003). *Unraveling the Central State, But How? Types of Multi-level Governance.* Political Science Series. Institute for Advanced Studies, Vienna.

Jessop, B. (2004). Multi-level Governance and Multi-level Metagovernance. In: Bache, I. & Flinders, M. (eds). *Multi-level Governance.* Oxford University Press, pp. 49–74. doi.org/10.1093/0199259259.003.0004

Lockwood, M., Davidson, J., Curtis, A., Stratford, E. & Griffith, R. (2009). Multi-level Environmental Governance: Lessons from Australian natural resource management. *Australian Geographer*, 40, 169–86. doi.org/10.1080/00049180902964926

Marks, G. (1993). Structural Policy and Multilevel Governance in the EC. In: Cafruny, A. & Rosenthal, G. (eds) *The State of the European Community Vol. 2: The Maastricht Debates and Beyond.* Longman, Harlow, pp. 391–410.

Marks, G. & Hooghe, L. (2004). Contrasting Visions of Multi-level Governance. In: Bache, I. & Flinders, M. (eds). *Multi-level Governance.* Oxford University Press, pp. 15–30. doi.org/ 10.1093/0199259259.003.0002

Marshall, G. (2008). Nesting, Subsidiarity, and Community-based Environmental Governance beyond the Local Scale. *International Journal of the Commons*, 2: 75–97. doi.org/10.18352/ijc.50

Matthews, M. (2009). Fostering Creativity and Innovation in Cooperative Federalism – The Uncertainty and Risk Dimensions. In: Wanna, J. (ed.) *Critical Reflections on Australian Public Policy*. ANU E Press, Canberra, pp. 59–70, epress.anu.edu.au/anzsog/critical/pdf/ch06.pdf [Accessed: 29/12/14].

——. (2013). *Managing Innovation and Risk in a Public Sector Context*. TMF Risk Management Conference: NSW Government 'Manage Risk – Drive Performance', 7 November, Australian Technology Park, Sydney.

McClintock, P. (2012). Harnessing Federalism – The Missing Key to Successful Reform. Sir Roland Wilson Lecture. Crawford School of Public Policy, Canberra, crawford.anu.edu.au/news/200/harnessing-federalism-missing-key-successful-reform [Accessed: 12/12/14].

Mosse, D. (2004). Is Good Policy Unimplementable? Reflections on the Ethnography of Aid Policy and Practice. *Development and Change*, 35: 639–71. doi.org/10.1111/j.0012-155X.2004.00374.x

Mukhtarov, F. & Daniell, K.A. (2017). Diffusion, Adaptation and Translation of Water Policy Models. In: Conca, K. & Weinthal, E. (eds) *The Oxford Handbook of Water Politics and Policy*. Oxford University Press.

Pahl-Wostl, C., Holtz, G., Kastens, B.& Knieper, C. (2010). Analyzing Complex Water Governance Regimes: The management and transition framework. *Environmental Science and Policy*, 13: 571–81. doi.org/10.1016/j.envsci.2010.08.006

Painter, M. (2001). Multi-level Governance and the Emergence of Collaborative Federal Institutions in Australia. *Policy and Politics*, 29: 137–50. doi.org/10.1332/0305573012501260

Peters, B.G. & Pierre, J. (2004). Multi-level Governance and Democracy: A 'Faustian bargain'? In: Bache, I. & Flinders, M. (eds), *Multi-level Governance*. Oxford University Press, pp. 75–89. doi.org/10.1093/0199259259.003.0005

Porter, D.J. (1995). Scenes from Childhood: The homesickness of development discourse. In: Crush, J. (ed.) *Power of Development*. Routledge, London, pp. 61–84.

Sabatier, P.A. & Jenkins-Smith, H. (1999). The Advocacy Coalition Framework: An assessment. In: Sabatier, P.A. (ed.) *Theories of the Policy Process*. Westview Press, Boulder, CO, pp. 117–66.

Scharpf, F.W. (1994). Games Real Actors could Play – Positive and Negative Coordination in Embedded Negotiations. *Journal of Theoretical Politics*, 6: 27–53. doi.org/10.1177/0951692894006001002

Smullen, A. (2014). Conceptualising Australia's Tradition of Pragmatic Federalism. *Australian Journal of Political Science*, 49(4): 677–93. doi.org/10.1080/10361146.2014.964660

Song, W. (2011). Open Method of Coordination and the Gloomy Future of Social Europe. *Asia Europe Journal*, 9(1): 13–27. doi.org/10.1007/s10308-011-0300-4

Stein, M. & Turkewitsch, L. (2008). *The Concept of Multi-level Governance in Studies of Federalism*. International Political Science Association (IPSA) International Conference *International Political Science: New Theoretical and Regional Perspectives*, Concordia University, Montréal, Canada.

Stephenson, P. (2013). Twenty Years of Multi-level Governance: Where does it come from? What is it? Where is it going? *Journal of European Public Policy*, 20(6): 817–37. doi.org/10.1080/13501763.2013.781818

Stilwell, F. & Troy, P. (2000). Multilevel Governance and Urban Development in Australia. *Urban Studies*, 37: 909–30. doi.org/10.1080/00420980050011154

Swanson, D., Barg, S., Tyler, S., Venema, H., Tomar, S., Bhadwal, S., Nair, S., Roy, D. & Drexage, J. (2010). Seven Tools for Creating Adaptive Policies. *Technological Forecasting and Social Change*, 77: 924–39. doi.org/10.1016/j.techfore.2010.04.005

Thomas, K.W. & Kilmann, R.H. (1974). *Thomas-Kilmann Conflict Mode Instrument*. Consulting Psychologists Press, Inc., Palo Alto, CA.

Torfing, J., Peters, B.G., Pierre, J. & Sørenson, E. (2012). *Interactive Governance Advancing the Paradigm*. Oxford University Press. doi.org/10.1093/acprof:oso/9780199596751.001.0001

2

Multi-level Governance and the Study of Australian Federalism[1]

Adrian Kay

Introduction

The concept of multi-level governance (MLG) has yet to gain wide currency in either public or academic discussion of policymaking in Australia (important exceptions are Painter 2001; and Gleeson 2003). Although, as an academic term, MLG is now 20 years old, much of the practice and process in multi-level systems that it labels are far older. Emerging originally in the study of the European Union (EU), MLG is particularly linked to the EU regional policy framework where new policy and administrative territorial spaces have been created, often overlapping existing national and sub-national boundaries. This is part of the 'Europe of the Regions' project, in turn linked to discussions of the 'new regionalism' in which contemporary geo-economic processes have putatively restructured the spatial scales of effective economic policymaking away from the national level to simultaneously the global and the regional/local levels (e.g. Gleeson 2003). The distinctive governance features of EU regional policy are that the European Commission deals directly with the novel territorial jurisdictions rather than through member-state

1   This chapter is a republication (with permission and with minor adjustments) of the paper: A. Kay (2015). Separating Sovereignty and Sharing Problems: Australian federalism and the European Union. *Australian Journal of Public Administration*, 74(4): 406–18.

governments as intermediaries and these interactions generally operate without a hierarchy, are relatively informal in character and, in the most effective cases, are based on a shared commitment to problem-solving.

The MLG concept is not faddish. It remains immediate and relevant to understanding contemporary processes of European integration, well beyond its origins in regional policy. For example, the transformation of economic governance in the EU between 2010 and 2015 following the sovereign debt crisis; the rescue packages for Ireland, Portugal and Greece; and the European Financial Stability Facility, the Euro Plus Pact, and the Fiscal Compact Treaty[2] all amount to an expansion of EU-level powers at the expense of national fiscal autonomy – powers that were previously jealously guarded. The issuing of EU-backed bonds and the establishment of a rescue fund apparently contravenes the 'hard' constitutional rules of the EU budget. In fiscal federalism terms, while the member-states remain at the centre of analysis, they have delegated finance powers – limited in scope but large in potential size – upwards to the larger, EU level in response to a policy challenge that is only surmountable at the Eurozone spatial scale. Whilst collectively the changes have had a significant impact on European economic governance, not all of the measures formally belong to the EU.

The MLG concept has merit in gaining leverage in the case of sovereign debt crises because it places experimentation and innovation in policy coordination across different spatial levels at its analytical core. It is possible to abstract from governance changes observed in the EU context to cast light on experiments in creating cross-jurisdictional policy capacity in Australia, across and between different governance jurisdictions to match the territorial scale that is functional for effective policy response. In such terms, this chapter argues that the MLG concept can contribute to the analytical value of the concept of 'pragmatic' federalism in Australia that is advanced by Hollander and Patapan (2007), in which there is a dynamic within federalism that allows it to adjust to changes in the territorial scales of policy problems.

As an indication of its value as a label for a core aspect of EU policymaking, the MLG concept has crossed the academic–practice boundary. Several institutions of the EU, in various prominent documents, have talked

---

2   Colloquially known as the Fiscal Compact Treaty, its full title is: Treaty on Stability, Coordination and Governance in the Economic and Monetary Union.

about methods or modes of 'doing' MLG (e.g. European Commission 2001; Committee of the Regions 2009). Even though the practice of MLG in Australia long predates its conceptualisation in the EU, there is advantage in applying the term in Australia. Notably, it facilitates a self-conscious reflection on both examples of experimentation and innovation in multi-level interactions within the settled constitutional boundaries of the federation, as well as cases where the policy agenda is more sclerotic and reform efforts hamstrung by a divided polity. Such reflexivity can help provide a novel thematic within venerable studies of Australian federalism and contribute to the analysis of changes in Australian fiscal federalism in response to the beginning and end of what former Treasury secretary Ken Henry has called the 'greatest external shock' in the history of the Australian economy – the mining resources boom and bust (Kelly 2010).

This chapter advances the argument that the MLG term can contribute to understanding the capacity for, and barriers to, dynamism and innovation in the Australian federation. This does not rely on an empirical comparison of the EU and Australia, but rather the advantages of placing the quality of the interactions between different jurisdictions at different spatial scales at the centre of analysis. Here the MLG concept serves both to complement and extend long-established seams of work on the constitutional allocation of competences between levels or analyses of the distribution of fiscal authority over revenue/expenditure. In particular, the chapter accepts the widely diagnosed centralising dynamic in Australian federalism as an enduring feature, but argues that a focus on the characteristics of harmonisation and coordination can sometimes obscure from view the potential for experimentation, variety and difference in multi-level policymaking in Australia.

The Reform of Federation white paper being developed in 2015 has the organising thematic that 'every level of government will be sovereign in its own sphere' (Abbott 2014). This is linked to well-rehearsed concerns about vertical fiscal imbalance that are being tackled in the tax white paper process running simultaneously. From an MLG perspective, the appeal to sovereignty is curious. There is nothing in the pragmatic history of Australian federalism to suggest constitutional answers to the shifting geographies of policy problems; indeed, the absence of seminal, big bang constitutional reforms is noteworthy. Sovereignty is a problematic concept in political theory and, although it is not for this paper to review the history of political thought on the question, we can state initially that sovereignty, in the sense of clearer constitutional roles and responsibilities, does not imply capability. To be sovereign is not the same as being functional in a public administration and policy sense, as the history of Australian federalism attests.

The EU has dealt with the problems of sovereign borders and the nature of policy problems that span many of these; indeed, it is, on many influential accounts, the motor of European integration. Similarly, it appropriated the concept of subsidiarity in parallel with the Council of Australian Governments (COAG) at the end of 1991. This chapter uses the concept of MLG to strike a sceptical note on both the desirability and feasibility of a big bang, once-in-a-generation reform of the federation. The capacity for shared, cross-jurisdictional policy coordination is not a neat function of constitutional design; far from it, the story of economic integration across territorial space shows the need for plasticity, innovation and adaptation as key aspects.

The following steps are taken in the chapter. The first defines the main elements of MLG and sets out what it may add to the existing understanding of Australian federalism and its reform. The next section considers the general characteristics of MLG observed in contemporary Australian federalism. The final section presents the open method of coordination (OMC) form of MLG as helping understand Australian fiscal federalism since the December 2008 Intergovernmental Agreement (IGA) on Federal Financial Relations, the structural changes in the economy brought about by the mining boom and subsequent bust, as well as the limitations of the current Reform of the Federation white paper.

MLG: What is it?[3]

The term multi-level governance was coined in Marks (1993: 392) to refer to 'a system of continuous negotiation among nested governments at several territorial tiers'. This has acted as a serviceable baseline definition to underpin subsequent refinements of the term that stress the non-hierarchical, informal and deliberative aspects of the negotiations under scrutiny (e.g. Hooghe and Marks 2001; Sabel and Zeitlin 2007). There

---

3   This chapter uses the MLG term analytically as an aid in understanding decision-making across different jurisdictional levels. However, Stein and Turkewitsch (2010) argue that there are (at least) two other distinct senses in which the MLG term is employed: (i) an empirical description of a specific governance form, particularly the EU; and (ii) normatively, to evaluate improvements in intergovernmental decision-making.

is some variation in the MLG literature about the extent to which non-government actors need to be included for a process to be categorised as MLG. For example, Peters and Pierre (2004) stress the governance aspect in MLG, arguing that this introduces a potentially wider cast of policy actors than in conventional accounts of intergovernmental relations.

In this analysis, MLG is a subset of governance, and thus the distribution of authority and policy capacity sideways must be taken into account across different sectors and spheres, including states, markets and civil society, and not just on the vertical plane upwards and downwards. Hooghe and Marks (2001) distinguish between Types I and II of MLG. Federalism is the exemplar of Type I MLG, where authority is dispersed to a limited number of general purpose jurisdictions, which are stable across time and do not overlap. Type II MLG, in contrast, is characterised by fluidity with the potential for a patchwork of numerous overlapping jurisdictions. These often have single tasks rather than multiple and general purposes, and include explicitly and formally non-government actors. In addition, they are potentially short-lived, with their continued existence depending directly on the nature of the governance challenge they are established to confront.

This typological separation of MLG helps to sidestep the Peters and Pierre (2004) issue by broadening the scope of the concept: *both* government and governance interactions can be usefully located on *both* vertical and horizontal dimensions. In such light, MLG is revealed as a composite construction: it brings key governance insights from studies of non-hierarchical, informal and continuous interactions between public organisations into federal studies and, at the same time, it identifies a particular governance problem in federal systems – multi-level policy coordination – within broader governance debates. The manifest scholarly challenge is to conceptualise and explain the relationships between the relatively enduring Type I features of Australian federalism and Type II issue-based, territorially novel and often ephemeral policy responses to particular governing challenges.

Of course, the trade-off for broadening the scope of MLG with the Hooghe and Marks (2001) typology is a reduction in its analytical precision. If any governmental or governance process located on a vertical and horizontal dimension counts as MLG, what does the term add to our understanding? The answer for the study of Australian federalism is that its distinctiveness lies in the emphasis on policymaking and policy coordination across different territorial jurisdictions outside a formal, institutionally prescribed vertical order. The problematic nature of the vertical ordering of different levels or spatial scales of policy analysis distinguishes the MLG concept within that of governance more generally. The MLG concept serves to organise analysis of situations in which that vertical ordering is not neatly constitutional, because formal powers are concurrent or overlapping or simply ambiguous, but where there is a powerful vertical interdependence in the control of governing resources and policy instruments.

One persistent theme in the study of European integration is that EU multi-level policy coordination has been successful, even in the absence of a constitutionally prescribed, vertical order, because EU policymaking is, to a significant degree, deliberative and technocratic. The EU's enormous comitology structure of expert committees (whose membership is drawn from the EU institutions, member-states and sometimes outside organisations) has had the putative consequence of socialising different national and sub-national interests into a shared enterprise through regular and frequent discussion and sustained argument. This socialisation mechanism can lead to a problem-solving mode of policy coordination among policy actors representing different levels in which starting policy preferences are adjusted and adapted through reasoned debate. Although this mechanism has not been universally observed, evidence of its effect may be read in many fields from monetary union to environmental policy, where the EU has been able to move beyond simple intergovernmental bargaining in which progress is limited by the lowest and fixed common denominator policy preference.

MLG processes in the EU tend to be informal: the rules that govern them are tacit and uncodified rather than explicit; unofficial rather than official; and emergent and self-enforcing rather than purposely designed with a third-party enforcer. The central point in Types I and II of MLG is that order and policy coordination between levels cannot be read off or anticipated in formal legal instruments or constitutional provisions. Instead, MLG is a negotiated order. For some, this informality is the great advantage of MLG because it allows extra-legal workarounds to circumvent some of the blockages apparent in the EU's formal institutional design.

What does the concept of MLG add to the study of federalism?

As an analytical term, there is the obvious challenge for MLG: to specify what it adds to the long-standing study of federalism in Australia. Two initial contributions can be identified. The first is to give the Australian constitutional grid a degree of policy dynamism in terms of trans-boundary agenda setting, the flow of different ideas, and the development of shared arrangements for feedback on policy performance. Notably, the concept allows the insight that these flows do not follow straight, constitutionally prescribed lines of transmission. For example, Brumby and Galligan (2015: 83) outline the benefits of 'healthy competition' between states and instances of policy mobility. Further, the New Zealand Government is a formal member of many coordination structures for intergovernmental relations – for example, the COAG Health Council – as is the president of the Australian Local Government Association. By giving a name to these kinds of processes, MLG serves to highlight potential sources of, and barriers to, institutional innovation in the Australian polity. In turn, this sets out a potential agenda for a seam of future research on Australian federalism. For example, the existing literature provides little on the relationship between intergovernmental processes and the socialisation of public servants from different jurisdictions towards a shared problem-solving perspective in Australia.

Second, MLG can be used to identify a variegated tendency within Australian federalism in the open economy era, in which analysis of policymaking that stresses distinctive sector-specific context and path-dependency, on the one hand, can be balanced adequately with common underlying tendencies towards centralisation on the other. Fenna (2009) reviews the seminal works on Australian federalism and, drawing on Sawer (1969) and Mathews (1977, 1982) in particular, sets out the distinct historical stages of coordinate, cooperative and integrated federalism through which Australia has passed. This periodisation is uncontentious (e.g. Hollander and Patapan (2007) draw similar epochal divides) and the general trajectory offered is familiar as a description of Australia's changing political economy: as national economic integration has deepened, so the Commonwealth has assumed increasing power, particularly in respect of control over taxation, to arrive at a situation where, as Sawer put it in the late 1960s, cooperative federalism is simply a euphemism for centralisation. In a widely expressed view, the upholding of the use of the corporations power s 51 (xx) in the *WorkChoices* case[4] indicates few legal limits on the Commonwealth's formal ability to reshape federalism.

Recent writing on Australian federalism, however, whilst not doubting the validity of this underlying narrative, has begun to offer more nuanced accounts of federalism after 1983 (see, for example, Carroll and Head 2010; Hollander and Patapan 2007; Brown 2007; Parkin and Anderson 2007; Keating and Wanna 2000). In these works, the process of centralisation is not unidirectional nor uniform across all policy sectors; Hollander and Patapan (2007) observe a 'pragmatic' federalism in Australia in which the federation has been continually reshaped by political dynamics to meet the policy demands of the day in the absence of an overarching political theory of federalism to inform party ideology and judicial policymaking. Within the political system, party allegiance no longer provides a reliable guide to federalism beliefs and the High Court has tended to see its role in terms of the particular disputes between parties rather than divining an overarching theoretical legal structure in Australian federalism. In such circumstances, pragmatist federalism bends and adapts according to the spatial scale of the policy challenges presented by particular circumstances in the political economy.

In response, Fenna (2012) argues that whatever the superficial attractions of the notion of a pragmatic federalism, it lacks a theoretical underpinning and therefore explanatory power. At best, the term offers a label for the mechanisms of intergovernmental adjustment but the challenge, for Fenna, is to articulate underlying general tendencies to centralisation in Australian federalism as well as account for observed sectoral variations in how pragmatic adjustments have played out in practice. The analysis in this chapter does not require a position on this criticism, instead it is sufficient to note that, if it holds at all, it pertains more broadly; there is an absence of a general theory of the dynamics of Australian federalism.

In this chapter, the pragmatic term is useful. It helps describe the characteristics of the development of COAG over 20 years or so into a permanent and standing body for the systematic organisation of intergovernmental relations (Carroll and Head 2010). Although the core executive of the Commonwealth Government exercises substantial

---

4   New South Wales v Commonwealth [2006] HCA 52; 81 ALJR 34; 231 ALR 1 (14 November 2006).

influence and control in COAG, consistent with centralisation, for others its arrival and potential future development serves as a counterpoint to immanent centralising tendencies and offers renewed multi-level collaborative potential in the Australian federation (Kildea and Lynch 2010; Painter 2001; contributions in Brumby and Galligan 2015; CEDA 2014).

The core of the pragmatist insight is that the federalist structure remains intact as the locus of policymaking moves in a centralising or decentralising direction as appropriate to the territorial scale of the governance challenge at hand. But, if that capacity for adaptation to the political economic exigencies of its day is large, does federalism matter in a policymaking sense? The pragmatist reply is that theirs is not a structuralist account in which the exigencies of the international economy explain formal changes in the Australian federal system; instead, the process of adaptation requires an active process of governing across multiple levels and jurisdictions with attendant uncertainties and contingencies. The distinguishing feature of Australia as a federation is the constitutionally entrenched position of the states in policy areas where they enjoy formal powers concurrent with the Commonwealth, as compared to policy coordination in non-federal multi-level systems where lower levels can be more easily reorganised. The states are a potential veto player in the process of federalism adaptation because they enjoy, at least formally, the option of acting unilaterally.

The Commonwealth Government is ineluctably involved in non-hierarchical policy coordination. Even if it enjoys the advantage of highly asymmetrical bargaining power, it still relies on the willingness of state governments to enter and engage in a process of negotiation. It can obviously set financial incentives to achieve this, but each government maintains a formal, constitutional right to refrain from coordination, and the involvement of COAG in coordination processes does not make them 'hierarchical'. MLG acts as a label for the policy problem-solving dilemma peculiar to federal systems where formal competences are divided and governing resources distributed between jurisdictions, however unevenly, such that coordination cannot be centrally (or hierarchically) imposed on any of the participating governments.

In the abstract, different non-hierarchical modes of coordination to solve collective policy problems can be stated, ranging from mere policy emulation between and among different levels of government, to ad hoc coordination, to informal political agreements, to formally binding rules.

To advance the contribution of the concept of MLG to understanding pragmatic federalism, two dimensions for organising non-hierarchical coordination in concurrent areas are salient in the MLG literature. The first dimension is the extent to which different governments are acclimatised to an interdependent policy environment; the second is the degree of institutionalisation of multi-level coordination.

At one end of the first dimension is the absence of coordination between levels, where each jurisdiction thinks and acts unilaterally. Further along the scale is a situation of mutual adjustment where, in the absence of any formal or informal agreement, each level takes the veto power of others into consideration in its policymaking but still acts unilaterally. Bargaining is further along still and refers to cases where actors from the different levels acclimatise to interdependence by being willing and able to enter a process of interaction and to adjust their interests in such a way that coordination becomes possible. The problem-solving mode sits at the opposite end of the scale to no coordination, standing analytically for a common-goal orientation in decision-making across levels, in which the individual interests that each level brings to the interaction are sublimated to a shared sense of the problem and solution.

The second dimension refers to variation in the institutionalisation of mechanisms for governing interaction across levels. Formal rules that compel negotiations across levels are prone to deadlock or may suffer Scharpf's (1988) famous 'joint decision trap', where the set of possible negotiating outcomes is limited to the lowest common denominator of starting-policy preferences. Where interaction across levels is not compulsory, however, there is the possibility of negotiation around principles and outcome-based standards for policy coordination. The OMC, discussed below, pioneered in the EU, is the exemplar of this possibility. Patterns of interaction based on broad principles for shared approaches to policy coordination may iteratively build trust and facilitate a problem-solving mode of governance.

Carroll and Head (2010) trace a history of COAG as a prominent indicator of the problem-solving capacity in the Australian federation on the first dimension. In a 'golden age' of reform (Head 2007), the structures of Australian federalism that might retard progress were successfully overcome through the gradual development of networks, institutions and processes for cooperation across levels. This is an important MLG tendency within federalism in Australia; within which has notably been the construction of an organisational capacity for political leaders to lead and direct the evolving intergovernmental system (Painter 2001). In terms of the second dimension above, the norm in COAG is consensus with the option reserved by all states and territories not to sign up to an agreement. Painter (1998) points out that there has been majority voting in ministerial councils from the late 1980s onwards.

At the two special premiers' conferences in November 1991 that established COAG, subsidiarity was stressed as a foundational and guiding principle (Australian Government 2015). This is the principle that functions should be performed by the lowest level of government able to do so effectively. Intriguingly, for understanding the role of EU MLG dynamics in Australian federalism, this principle in the foundation of COAG was embedded at the heart of the EU only a few weeks later in 1991 in the governance of intergovernmental relations under the famous Maastricht Treaty (formally the Treaty on European Union). Like the EU, Australia had found, and continues to find, constitutional change hard; subsidiarity was a concept recovered from the history of the Catholic Church as a way of thinking about how these Type I structures can be compensated for or, at least, adapted and reinterpreted for Type II sets of dynamics.

Before 1990, intergovernmental relations were largely decentralised, with policy issues addressed in a compartmentalised series of councils and committees. Carroll and Head (2010) describe the slightly ad hoc and unsystematic nature of this system and argue that it was not fit for the purpose of major microeconomic reforms that came in the late 1980s and into the 1990s. They conclude that the continuing development of COAG has enhanced the effective management of intergovernmental relations and, in an example of problem-solving in MLG, increased Australia's policy capacity for strategic, general interest reform.

Whilst acknowledging COAG's achievements in policy reform, it remains ad hoc in many important respects and, in the absence of a firm legal or constitutional footing, COAG's operation and its agenda remains at the discretion of the prime minister of the day (Brumby and Galligan 2015; Kildea and Lynch 2010). For example, there has been significant variation in the number of times that COAG has been held, from less than once a year in the early years of John Howard's government to four times a year under former prime minister Kevin Rudd. An important related consequence of prime ministerial discretion is that COAG has a tendency to centralise policy control at the expense of diversity, thus losing the advantages of diversity and learning between states (Anderson 2008; Brumby 2009; Brumby and Galligan 2015). Similarly, running through the Senate Committee Report's (2011: 53) agenda for reform of the Australian federation is a stress on 'joint ownership' in negotiations among the Commonwealth and state and territory governments, particularly with the latter having greater input in setting the agenda of COAG. Perhaps the most striking example of COAG's institutional frailty and lack of an independent, enduring status is the introduction in 2008 and subsequent abolition in 2014 of the COAG Reform Council.

Problem-solving in Australian conditions: Pragmatic diversity in changing economic geographies

For Australian federalism to be pragmatic, there must be potential for processes that push back against centripetal tendencies immanent in the system in circumstances where the nature of the policy challenge demands decentralisation and diversity. For example, if effective policy coordination requires an agenda with significant input from beyond the centre, and a toleration of cross-jurisdictional diversity, under the pragmatist account we would expect to observe decentralising adaptations in Australia. The development of COAG over 20 years may have worked in the field of microeconomic reform at the national, economy-wide scale, however, there are contemporary policy challenges whose scalar components are not so straightforward and where it is not obvious that COAG's previous success in producing general interest economic reforms at the national level can be replicated without some changes in the MLG template.

Several seams of ongoing political economy study, such as that on 'variegated' capitalism (Peck and Theodore 2007), the new economic geography (Krugman 1998; Porter 1998) and 'spatial' Keynesianism (Brenner 2004; Eisenschitz and Gough 1996) all suggest that there is no single or temporally fixed jurisdictional scale that defines the most effective institutional basis for successfully coordinating policy in core areas of economic development such as labour markets, vocational training and skill development and entrepreneurship (Brenner et al. 2010; Peck and Theodore 2010; Gleeson 2003).

The multi-level policy dilemma of the territorially uneven consequences of the Australian resources boom and bust is clear: a less uniform policy landscape and more adaptable fiscal federalism are required. The structural change resulted from the combination of rapidly improving terms of trade reversing a secular decline that has then unravelled as international commodity prices softened and Australia's terms of trade declined and investment in the mining sector fell. The multi-speed economy and attendant structural economic change presents a requirement for rethinking the scales of Australian public policymaking. Whilst this may be most readily apparent in fiscal federalism terms as the resources boom leads to significant changes in the states' net fiscal positions, there is an underlying catalyst: as the imperative of international competitiveness has become firmly embedded as a governing template, so public policy itself and the process by which it is made has become a factor in economic competitiveness (e.g. Campbell 2004).

This extends well beyond established debates about tax competition and internationally mobile capital to the main foundations of productivity: the quality of the microeconomic business environment. In a highly influential work, Porter (1998) argues that public policy has a prominent role here in areas such as training, infrastructure provision, procurement practice, locating airports and providing higher education services. Firms can derive competitive advantage from operating within an effective set of arrangements for multi-level policy coordination in these areas.

In Australia, the idea of public policy as a source of competitiveness has evolved distinctively. From its roots in the National Competition Policy and a focus on market regulation (Morgan 2003), the notion of policy competitiveness now envelops core human service delivery areas of government activity as well. In a related action, the Australian Government introduced a Commonwealth-wide Contestability Framework in the 2014–15 budget (Cormann 2015). Sectors that are conventionally seen in social policy terms, or at least involving some entitlement derived from social citizenship rights, are framed in the productivity agenda as an active ingredient of a competitive economy. In doing so, the appropriate territorial scale of policy action is refashioned as territorial equity and becomes less of a concern, replaced with the scales functional for economic policymaking and structural adjustment in a multiple speed economy characterised by a profound differential between resource and non-resource sector growth.

These scales tend to be smaller and more variegated than the universalism of social welfare provision. The result is that in many policy areas in Australia, in which formal powers are concurrent and have characteristics of both economic and social policies, as the recently published Harper Competition Policy Review sets out, the multi-level policy coordination challenge is to rethink policy spaces for effective intervention and their effective interrelationship in a federal system (Commonwealth of Australia 2015).

The open method of coordination

The story of EU constitution-making is not one of settled or seamless progress but, rather, is marked by delay, deep-seated disagreements about the nature of *la construction européenne*, and populist success in defeating constitutional referenda. In response, the EU has been forced to develop new and creative forms of governance to meet the problems of multi-level policymaking without a constitutional state to provide vertical order. In such terms, the EU is an 'experimentalist' form of governance (Zeitlin and Sabel 2009), and one of its distinctive innovations is the OMC. In this form of MLG, bespoke institutions for multi-level policy coordination are established for particular policy challenges and agreed in advance by participating governments as able to be revised rather than being fixed.

These institutions contain relatively broad, open-ended policy objectives, and include an agreement on how to chart progress towards those objectives on a common measure. Critically, in multi-level policy coordination terms, lower-level jurisdictions enjoy substantial discretion in how to design and implement policy directed towards achieving those objectives. Under the OMC, this discretion comes with an extensive and public reporting requirement on progress towards the common objectives. This allows transparent comparison between the different jurisdictions pursuing different means to achieve the same shared goal. In theory, the result of this system is an iterative process of learning and deliberative problem-solving in which both the rules and goals are regularly revised based on the experiences of implementing them.

The intention of the OMC is that this learning can lead to a convergence of both policy agendas and the general direction of travel in performance, but not of specific programs, policy instruments or settings. This tolerance of diversity is a political *sine qua non* of EU multi-level policymaking in many fields; for example, the OMC has been extensively used in areas of employment policy where deep-rooted differences in national institutions and policy legacies have served to substantially limit opportunities for European-level harmonisation. The ambition to reconcile common EU-level action with legitimate national and sub-national diversity has become heightened with the enlargement of the EU to 27 members over the last decade, each presenting singular economic histories, labour market institutions and social welfare systems.

In Australia, the OMC model of MLG is useful for the analysis of adjustments in pragmatic federalism. The increasing diversity and unevenness in the economic geography of Australia demands a recovery of the early policy justifications for the Australian federation (Moran 2011; Brumby and Galligan 2015): a laboratory for natural experiments in policy that enhance opportunities for cross-jurisdictional learning through comparison of different approaches to related problems. There are some cases of partial, OMC-type experiments available in the contemporary history of Australian federalism; for example, Parkin (1988) analysed interrelations between, and diversity within, Commonwealth–state housing agreements, where there were compromised but shared goals alongside substantial local discretion in implementation. However, it is the December 2008 IGA on new fiscal federal arrangements that marks the critical juncture in an OMC trend within Australian federalism.

This intergovernmental fiscal reform is significant in both its scale and its awkwardness for the centralisation narrative of Australian federalism. The 2008 IGA is designed to reduce Commonwealth Government prescriptions on service delivery by the states, and allow them increased flexibility in policymaking with the corollary of policy diversity. The cornerstone is a major reduction in the number of specific purpose payments (SPPs) to the states, from over 90 to five. These are supported by national agreements, which establish the broad policy objectives and an extensive performance and assessment framework, publicly reported and administered by the COAG Reform Council.

National agreements need to be distinguished from the national partnership agreements, included in the same IGA. The latter are time limited and involve fiscal incentives via payments to the states that are linked with specific reform activities or projects (O'Loughlin 2011). The national agreements are salient as the nascent OMC feature in Australian public policy; they set out the objectives, outcomes, outputs and performance indicators by sector, which have been agreed in advance between all jurisdictions. They do not include financial or other resource input controls on policy by the state and territory governments, and there is no provision for national SPPs to be withheld in the case of a jurisdiction not meeting a performance benchmark specified in a national agreement. The five SPPs give block grants by sector, and the states and territories have full budget discretion to allocate funds within that sector to achieve the agreed objectives for that sector. Importantly, the policy areas covered by the national agreements are at the core of the microfoundations of productivity: education, skills and workforce development, health care, affordable housing and disability services.

The 2008 IGA gave the now defunct COAG Reform Council significant responsibilities for performance assessment and reporting under national agreements. The COAG Reform Council provided annual reports to COAG on each of the agreements based on a comparative analysis of governing performance against the established benchmarks for progress in reform and improvements in service delivery. In November 2013, the COAG Reform Council published a five-year report card on the 2008 IGA on fiscal federal reform, which, in broad terms, shows measured progress on the ambitious goals set in 2008 to have been mixed (Brumby 2013). Of particular relevance to this chapter, the COAG Reform Council (2013) report also provides analysis of the actual process of COAG reform to supplement the existing large number of performance reports in the key areas of the 2008 agreement. Among other things, this process analysis highlights weaknesses in implementation, the need for better performance data and agreement on higher-quality indicators, as well as observing the well-known tendency of governments making or inheriting long-term commitments to move away from outcome measures and lose sight of program logic, reverting instead to input or activity measures.

It is premature to infer any firm lessons on changes to multi-level policy capacity in Australia from the OMC tendency in the 2008 IGA. This is because the OMC is designed as a learning process where standard policy evaluation logic only applies imperfectly; although Moran (2011) expresses some doubts about whether the performance management systems at the state level have eventuated to match national agreements entered into, sustained comparative and longitudinal analysis is required for more concrete conclusions. At this stage, and for the purposes of this chapter, the concept of the OMC is offered as a potential way of diagnosing a changing dynamic in Australian federalism. This conceptualisation of the 2008 IGA may help inform studies of its effects on policy orientation and thinking across, and between, levels in the Australian federation; the nature of the analytical work undertaken on benchmarking, peer review, monitoring and iterative redesign; and whether there is evidence of cross-jurisdictional policy learning.

In EU terms, the OMC has been established as a means of extending EU involvement in a range of policy domains where it has no formal or legal competence, but simultaneously protecting member-states' authority in those areas. In the Australian case of concurrent constitutional powers and strong interdependence in terms of policy capacity, the 2008 IGA reveals the potential of OMC to substitute in some cases for detailed COAG agreements on a uniform, national policy framework. Despite the fact that the OMC is not legally binding, the EU and many scholars regard the OMC as effective in achieving policy coordination in certain cases (e.g. Hodson and Maher 2001). There is burgeoning research in EU studies on the conditions for a 'soft' and non-binding governance method to be effective. In particular, attempts are underway to identify the mechanisms to explain why member-state governments might pursue policies aimed at OMC objectives even though they are not legally obliged to do so and are not threatened by sanctions other than 'naming and shaming' by the EU Commission (Sabel and Zeitlin 2007; Zeitlin and Sabel 2009).

There are sceptics on the effectiveness of the OMC compared to 'hard law' EU policy and suggestions that the OMC cannot influence national policymaking due to its non-bindingness and lack of sanctions (e.g. Chalmers and Lodge 2003). As discussed above, however, the MLG term has been freighted to label circumstances in which a hierarchical mode of policy-making is ineffective: where there is a substantial implementation gap between central edicts and control of policy on the ground. Softness is likely to be more successful than hardness in such circumstances, particularly if different states in Australia disagree strongly about the policy instruments and settings appropriate to their social and economic conditions or want to retain their authority over a particular policy area.

Trust-building in the Australian federation

MLG processes are, by definition, non-hierarchical and relatively informal; it is the capacity to influence and persuade rather than command and control that is central in bringing about problem-solving as the dominant mode of interaction. In particular, for the OMC to be effective, tolerance of diversity in approach and performance is essential. Trust is an essential ingredient in this; without it, differentials are liable to be exploited politically, producing strong centralising pressures for territorial uniformity. This reveals that MLG in the EU is founded to an extent on the socialisation of actors involved, and its relative success or failure in any domain is a function of the degree to which this socialisation can be captured in enduring institutions – formal and informal – over time. We might hypothesise that this is more easily found in the Australian context, with only nine governments involved, but we know little about this. This is the challenge to academic study of Australian federalism: to understand systematically the emergence of intergovernmental trust in particular policy sectors and draw robust lessons of how this facilitates a problem-solving orientation.

There are two basic ways to understand the role of trust in the interaction of representatives from multiple levels. The first is in assisting with problem-solving amongst self-interested, rational actors; the alternative is in developing commitments towards a shared view of the problem and/or obligations towards certain normative schemes. They are not mutually exclusive and, in practice, we may observe both roles coexisting.

Under the first approach, it is the system of negative and positive incentives to MLG actors that will determine how successfully the problem-solving mode of governance operates in achieving collective ends. The basic motivations behind compliance with MLG 'soft' demands are the benefits that actors may gain from the acceptance of these demands and/or the avoidance of the costs of non-adoption. Repeated interaction helps build high trust in the commitments of others to certain action and, following the insights from repeated, non-cooperative game theory, a non-hierarchical equilibrium may be achieved. Actual practice in Australia can, however, make such an analysis appear exclusively academic: the turnover and churn of political leaders and senior bureaucrats presents the question of how trust and a shared problem-solving commitment can endure and become institutionalised. This is again an area where we lack systematic data on what has worked in the past in Australia.

In the second analytical avenue, shifting the normative considerations of appropriateness of the divergent demands will influence the scope of possible policy coordination. This is where deliberation leads to policy change that coordination implies must be considered as correct and legitimate by relevant decision-makers at each level in order to be adopted and implemented. Socialisation contributes to high trust through regular personal and official contacts, and its possible effect in terms of a degree of normative convergence over time about 'what ought to be done' is enforced by norms of shame and loyalty/kinship. In this problem-solving mode, the reliance is not on high-powered incentives to policy action but rather the use of high trust to support norms that persuade, shame or otherwise encourage policy actors into accepting the required policy change.

Conclusion

MLG in the Australian context moves us away from simply viewing Commonwealth–state relations as a zero sum game of formal authority and fiscal power to considering the possibility of enhanced policy capacity through experimentation and innovation in multi-level interactions. It encourages a research focus on the relationship between Type I and Type II MLG in the Australian federation, notably the extent to which a shared problem-solving approach can be achieved in a particular policy sector. The OMC is a distinctive mode of MLG Type II, developed in the EU to exploit the potential for within-Treaty innovation, given the ongoing constitutional problems of European integration; problems that, far from perfectly analogous, bear a strong resemblance to debates about coordinate federalism in Australia. This chapter has presented the OMC not as a soft, second-best option to hard legislation or command-and-control authority but rather as a prominent Type II MLG; a non-binding mechanism for policy coordination appropriate to many contemporary governance challenges. The 2008 IGA exhibits certain OMC characteristics: in the national agreements, the policy design and implementation functions remain at state level and diversity is encouraged. When the consequences of structural change in the Australian economy are uncertain and widespread but presenting territorially diverse policy challenges, an OMC approach to multi-level policy coordination is liable to be more effective than a uniform standardised policy framework imposed from the centre.

References

Abbott, T. (2014). Speech to Sir Henry Parkes Commemorative Dinner, Tenterfield, 25 October 2014, ahha.asn.au/sites/default/files/docs/policy-issue/sir_henry_parkes_commemorative_dinner_speech_prime_minister.pdf [Accessed 29/06/2017].

Anderson, G.M. (2008). The Council of Australian Governments: A new institution of governance for Australia's conditional federalism. *University of New South Wales Law Journal* 31(2): 493–508.

Australian Government (2015). COAG and Federal Financial Relations, Reform of the Federation White Paper. Issue Paper 5. Department of the Prime Minister and Cabinet, Australian Government, Canberra.

Brenner, N. (2004). *New State Spaces: Urban Governance and the Rescaling of Statehood.* Oxford University Press, Oxford and New York. doi.org/10.1093/acprof:oso/9780199270057.001.0001

Brenner N., Peck J. & Theodore, N. (2010). Variegated Neoliberalization: Geographies, modalities, pathways. *Global Networks* 10(2): 1–41. doi.org/10.1111/j.1471-0374.2009.00277.x

Brown, A. (2007). Federalism, Regionalism And The Reshaping Of Australian Governance. In: Brown, A.J. & Bellamy, J. (eds) *Federalism and Regionalism in Australia: New Approaches, New Institutions?* ANU E Press, Canberra, pp. 11–33.

Brumby, J. (2009). Does Federalism Work? In: Wanna, J. (ed.) *Critical Reflections on Australian Public Policy.* ANU E Press, Canberra, epress. anu.edu.au/anzsog/critical/pdf/ch02.pdf [Accessed 18/07/2008].

——. (2013). Reform or Perish: 5 Years of National Reform. Speech to National Press Club, November 2013.

Brumby, J. & Galligan, B. (2015). The Federalism Debate. *Australian Journal of Public Administration*, 74(1): 82–92. doi.org/10.1111/1467-8500.12132

Campbell, J.L. (2004). *Institutional Change and Globalization.* Princeton University Press.

Carroll, P. & Head, B. (2010). Regulatory Reform and the Management of Intergovernmental Relations in Australia. *Australian Journal of Political Science*, 45(3): 407–24. doi.org/10.1080/10361146.2010.509310

CEDA (2014). *A Federation for the 21st Century*. Committee for the Economic Development of Australia, Melbourne.

Chalmers, D. & Lodge, M. (2003). *The Open Method Of Co-Ordination And The European Welfare State*. CARR Discussion Chapters, DP 11, LSE, London.

COAG Reform Council (2013). *Lessons For Federal Reform: COAG Reform Agenda 2008–2013*. Council of Australian Governments.

Committee of the Regions (2009). *White Chapter On Multi-level Governance*, CdR 89/2009. European Union, Brussels.

Commonwealth of Australia (2015). *Competition Policy Review*. Final Report. March 2015. Australian Government, Canberra.

Cormann, M. (2015). *Smaller, More Rational Government*. Minister of Finance Ministerial Paper, Commonwealth of Australia, Canberra.

Eisenschitz A. & Gough, J. (1996). The Contradictions Of Neo–Keynesian Local Economic Strategies. *Review of International Political Economy*, 3(3): 434–58. doi.org/10.1080/09692299608434364

European Commission (2001). *European Governance: A White Chapter*. COM (2001) 428, EU Commission, Brussels.

Fenna, A. (2009). Federalism. In: Rhodes, R.A.W. (ed.) *The Australian Study of Politics*. Palgrave Macmillan, Houndsmills.

———. (2012). Centralising Dynamics in Australian Federalism. *Australian Journal of Politics and History*, 58(4): 580–90. doi.org/10.1111/j.1467-8497.2012.01654.x

Gleeson, B. (2003). Learning About Regionalism from Europe: 'Economic normalisation' and beyond, *Australian Geographical Studies*, 41(3): 221–36. doi.org/10.1046/j.1467-8470.2003.00231.x

Head, B. (2007). Taking Subsidiarity Seriously: What role for the states? In: Brown, A.J. & Bellamy, J. (eds) *Federalism and Regionalism in Australia: New Approaches, New Institutions?* ANU E Press, Canberra, pp. 155–70.

Hodson, D. & Maher, I. (2001). The Open Method of Coordination as a New Mode of Governance: The case of soft economic policy coordination. *Journal of Common Market Studies*, 39(4): 719–46. doi.org/10.1111/1468-5965.00328

Hollander, R. & Patapan, H. (2007). Pragmatic Federalism: Australian federalism from Hawke to Howard. *Australian Journal of Public Administration*, 66(3): 280–97. doi.org/10.1111/j.1467-8500.2007.00542.x

Hooghe, L. & Marks, G. (2001). Types of Multi-level Governance. *European Integration Online Chapters* (EIoP) 5(11), eiop.or.at/eiop/pdf/2001-011.pdf [Accessed: 14/01/2014].

Keating, M. & Wanna, J. (2000). Remaking Federalism? In: Keating, M., Wanna, J. & Weller, P. (eds) *Institutions on the Edge?* Allen & Unwin, Sydney, pp. 126–55.

Kelly, P. (2010). Mission Is To Manage Politics Of Prosperity. *Australian*, 24 November 2010.

Kildea, P. & Lynch, A. (2010). *Entrenching 'Cooperative Federalism': Is it Time to Formalise COAG's Place in the Australian Federation?* Conference of the Australian Political Studies Association, University of Melbourne, Melbourne, 28 September 2010.

Krugman, P. (1998). What's New About The New Economic Geography? *Oxford Review of Economic Policy*, 14(2): 7–17. doi.org/10.1093/oxrep/14.2.7

Marks, G. (1993). Structural Policy and Multilevel Governance in the EC. In: Cafruny, A. & Rosenthal, G. (eds) *The State of the European Community: Volume 2*. Lynne Rienner, Boulder CO, pp. 391–410.

Mathews, R.L. (ed.) (1977). *State And Local Taxation*. Centre for Research on Federal Financial Relations, Australian National University Press, Canberra.

——. (1982). *Federalism in Retreat: The Abandonment of Tax Sharing and Fiscal Equalisation*. Australian National University Press, Canberra.

Moran, T. (2011). An Effective Federation in Delivering Australia's Next Wave of Reform. Address to the EIDOS Institute, 8 June 2011.

Morgan, B. (2003). The Economisation of Politics: Meta-regulation as a form of nonjudicial legality. *Social and Legal Studies*, 12(4): 489–523. doi.org/10.1177/0964663903012004004

O'Loughlin, M. (2011). Collaborative Reform: Lessons from the COAG Reform Council, 2008–2010. In: Lindquist, E., Vincent, S. & Wanna, J. (eds) *Delivering Policy Reform Anchoring Significant Reforms in Turbulent Times*, ANU E Press, Canberra, pp. 91–8.

Painter, M. (1998). *Collaborative Federalism*. Cambridge University Press, Melbourne. doi.org/10.1017/CBO9780511552236

——. (2001). Multi-level Governance and the Emergence of Collaborative Federal Institutions in Australia. *Policy & Politics*, 29(2): 137–50. doi.org/10.1332/0305573012501260

Parkin, A. (1988). Housing Policy. In: Galligan, B. (ed.) *Comparative State Policies*. Longman Cheshire, Melbourne, pp. 249–68.

Parkin, A. & Anderson, G. (2007). The Howard Government, Regulatory Federalism and the Transformation of Commonwealth–State Relations. *Australian Journal of Political Science*, 42(2): 295–314. doi.org/10.1080/10361140701320034

Peck J. & Theodore, N. (2007). Variegated Capitalism. *Progress in Human Geography*, 31(6): 731–72. doi.org/10.1177/0309132507083505

——. (2010). Labor Markets From The Bottom Up. In: McGrath-Champ, S., Herod, A. & Rainnie, A. (eds) *Handbook Of Employment and Society: Working Space*. Edward Elgar, Cheltenham, pp. 87–105. doi.org/10.4337/9781849806305.00014

Peters, G. & Pierre, J. (2004). Multi-level Governance and Democracy: A 'Faustian bargain'. In: Bache, I. & Flinders, M. (eds) *Multi-level Governance*. Oxford University Press, pp. 75–90. doi.org/10.1093/0199259259.003.0005

Porter, M.E. (1998). *The Competitive Advantage of Nations*. 2nd edn, Free Press, New York. doi.org/10.1007/978-1-349-14865-3

Sabel, C.F. & Zeitlin, J. (2007). *Learning from Difference: The New Architecture of Experimentalist Governance in the European Union*. European Governance Chapters (EUROGOV) No. C-07-02.

Sawer, G. (1969). *Modern Federalism*. Watts, London.

Scharpf, F.W. (1988). The Joint-Decision Trap. Lessons From German Federalism and European Integration. *Public Administration*, 66(2): 239–78. doi.org/10.1111/j.1467-9299.1988.tb00694.x

Senate Committee Report (2011). *Reform of the Australian Federation*. Commonwealth of Australia, Parliament House, Canberra.

Stein, M. & Turkewitsch, L. (2008). *The Concept of Multi-level Governance in Studies of Federalism*. International Political Science Association (IPSA) International Conference *International Political Science: New Theoretical and Regional Perspectives*, Concordia University, Montréal, Canada, pp. 184–202.

Zeitlin, J. & Sabel, C.F. (eds) (2009). *Experimentalist Governance in the European Union: Towards A New Architecture*. Oxford University Press, Oxford and New York.

3

Rethinking Federalism: Network Governance, Multi-level Governance and Australian Politics

Paul Fawcett and David Marsh

Introduction

There has been an explosion of interest in governance and multi-level governance (MLG) over the past 20 years. The literature on governance has drawn attention to the use of networked, collaborative and partnership-based approaches, whilst the concept of MLG has combined these concerns with a related set of questions about scale, including the dispersal of decision-making authority from the local to the global level. This combination of state transformation at both the vertical and horizontal levels has proven to be particularly successful at capturing the imagination of scholars both within and beyond the European Union (EU). At the same time, the literature on Australian federalism and intergovernmental relations has shown relatively little interest in directly engaging with the concept of MLG and associated debates.

Here, we argue that the MLG literature raises new and important research questions that currently remain relatively under-explored in the literature on Australian federalism. In our view, these questions merit further consideration because they have a potentially important impact on how we understand the changing nature of intergovernmental relations and the future of federalism more broadly conceived. It therefore seems appropriate to examine what insights can be drawn from this literature and the extent to which key concepts and ideas can be applied, with suitable adaptations, to reflect the particularities of the Australian context.

It is worth briefly noting at the outset that we are not arguing that one set of ideas or concepts must 'replace' another. Our main argument is that an MLG perspective can build on federalism's central focus on federal–state relations by drawing attention to the different scales and network of actors that play an increasingly active role in the policymaking process. As such, the literature on MLG provides one possible way of examining the trends associated with governance and their potential impact on federal systems.

This chapter is divided into three substantive sections. We begin by locating the concept of MLG in discussions about the changing nature of governance. Our argument is that MLG and federalism are not mutually exclusive; it is about federalism *and* MLG, rather than federalism *or* MLG. We then examine the literature on Australian federalism and compare it briefly with recent Canadian work, because much greater interest has been shown in applying the MLG concept there than in Australia. The third section extends this analysis by examining the extent to which the trends associated with MLG are evident in Australia. We draw on various empirical examples, which confirm that, whilst there may not be much direct discussion of MLG in Australia, there is a great deal of indirect discussion of its key features, challenges and concerns. In the conclusion, we briefly outline how some of these features, challenges and concerns could be explored within a federal context.

What is multi-level governance?

MLG is a concept that has gained popularity beyond its original application in EU studies (e.g. Stephenson 2013; Enderlein et al. 2010). It is now widely used to refer to vertical and horizontal changes within the state under the influence of such factors as globalisation, regionalisation and devolution, networks, privatisation and public–private partnerships respectively (Büchs 2009). These changes have generated particular interest within the EU due to its *sui generis* nature, but their impact is by no means limited to it.

This has prompted scholars to use the MLG concept in other fields such as global governance and federal studies. *Kay*, in Chapter 2, describes MLG as a 'composite construction' that 'brings key governance insights from studies of non-hierarchical, informal and continuous interactions between public organisations into federal studies' and 'identifies a particular governance problem in federal systems – multi-level policy coordination – within broader governance debates'. He further develops this baseline definition with reference to Hooghe and Marks's (2010) distinction between Types I and II of MLG.

Daniell and Kay have already outlined the key features of Type I and Type II MLG in their opening chapter, so we will not repeat these here. We only note that Hooghe and Marks (2010) argue that Type I and Type II MLG generate three forms of 'bias'. They argue that Type I MLG serves an intrinsic rather than extrinsic community (e.g. communities with a national, regional, local, religious or ethnic identity); prioritises voice through political deliberation in conventional liberal democratic institutions with high barriers to exit over jurisdictions that are organised around delivering a public good through a more voluntary membership; and privileges conflict articulation through structured political contestation and party competition on a left/right axis over consensus through specific purpose jurisdictions. As *Daniell and Kay* note in Chapter 1, these characteristics mean that some policy sectors maybe more susceptible to one form of MLG compared with another. It is also more likely that Type II arrangements will vary in their durability, fixity and geographical scope than Type I arrangements. This makes the distinction between Type I and Type II MLG particularly useful because it acts as a 'point of departure' for examining the extent to which each type coexists with the other in particular settings, how they coexist and why particular governance arrangements have evolved in the way that they have (e.g. Sutcliffe 2012). Most studies that have examined these questions have concurred with Hooghe and Marks's (2010: 23) conclusion that:

> Type II governance tends to be embedded in legal frameworks determined by Type I jurisdictions. The result is a large number of relatively self-contained, functionally differentiated Type II jurisdictions alongside a number of general-purpose, nested Type I jurisdictions.

This suggests that prevailing Type I arrangements will likely have an impact on Type II arrangements. By drawing attention to the role played by Type II arrangements, however, MLG also destabilises some of the more conventional analyses and concepts in the literature on federalism. In particular, it draws our attention to three themes that are common to most studies of MLG: a move beyond formal institutions, a multi-scalar focus and a more networked approach (Torfing et al. 2012).

Beyond formal institutions

One implication of the above discussion is that MLG pushes us to think beyond formal institutions, including the state, constitutional mandates, fiscal federalism and the formal agreements that exist between different levels of government. In particular, MLG blurs the distinctions found in more traditional approaches to intergovernmental relations, such as jurisdiction, subordination and control, by suggesting that these relationships are often less ordered than constitutional rules dictate. Institutions therefore have an important role in structuring a political system, but they may be less important than in the past, particularly in situations where the very nature of a public policy problem challenges long-held distinctions, such as those between the local, national and global, or the state and civil society. In such situations, agents may seek to bypass or work around existing institutional arrangements. This is clear in the growing role played by transnational and domestic private governance systems in areas such as forestry, coffee, food production, tourism and fisheries (e.g. Cashore 2002). More broadly, the growth of voluntary forms of self-regulation can also be taken as typical of this development (e.g. Provost 2012).

This suggests that studying patterns of interaction between agents within a political system (broadly defined) is as important as studying the distribution of power and resources within formal institutional arrangements. This more actor-centred perspective encourages an analysis of the interplay between multiple governmental tiers and the participation of sub-national units, organised interests and actors from the public and private sector in the policymaking process. It also encourages a view from the 'bottom up' in which a greater emphasis is placed on studying policymaking and its implementation 'on the ground' (e.g. Agranoff 2004; McGuire 2006).

A multi-scalar focus

It follows from the previous section that MLG approaches also have a more multi-scalar focus, placing greater emphasis on how different levels of government and governance interact with one another in a fluid relationship, rather than on the 'nested' hierarchy that has characterised the way in which intergovernmental relations have been classically analysed. In doing so, MLG approaches have drawn on arguments about the 'rescaling of the state', the 'politics of scale' and the 'political organisation of space' that have examined how power is deployed and experienced in different spatial arrangements beyond the nation state (for a review, see Brenner 2009).

A multi-scalar focus has also pushed those using an MLG approach to think about new levels of government and governance. This includes the interplay that exists between the domestic and international levels, as well as sub-national units, such as regional, local, city and community-based governance structures. In other words, there is a broader focus on the horizontal and vertical governmental and non-government policymaking structures operating at different levels and across different sectors. This is based on a recognition that resources, authority and agency flow between different institutional levels and networks. An examination of how and where actors at different levels and scales intersect with one another is, therefore, a crucial aspect of any MLG account.

A networked approach

The third implication from the previous discussion is that networks and networked interactions become an important focus of study. This follows from the more process-orientated and multi-scalar approach outlined above, in which networks provide agents with the opportunity to share knowledge, combine resources and generate political leadership through bargaining. This more horizontal orientation has been a particular focus within the literature on policy networks, which has developed a range of typologies to examine the different types of relationships that exist between state actors and private actors and their impact on the policymaking process (e.g. Marsh 1998; for recent applications, see Daugbjerg and Fawcett 2017; Fawcett and Daugbjerg 2012; Osborne 2010, Part V). This can include variation in the 'rules of the game', as well as the norms that underpin a network. A key distinction is often made in this literature between policy communities, which are tight, closed, highly integrated and highly institutionalised networks, and issue networks, which are weakly integrated, open and relatively dispersed. Policy communities often resist change, whereas issue networks often struggle to reach agreement due to the lack of consensus that exists between its members on basic policy objectives, policy principles and procedures.

The growth of networks may, however, also be used to highlight the broader disaggregation of the state. For example, many of the studies that have examined EU governance use networks to criticise existing concepts and applications for being too state-centric (e.g. Kohler-Koch and Rittberger 2006). Here, networks are used to refer to the multiplicity of linkages and interactions that exist between a large and wide number of actors from across all levels of government and society. For example, Sørenson and Torfing (2007: 3–4) have argued that:

> policy, defined as the attempt to achieve a desired outcome, is a result of governing processes that are no longer fully controlled by the government, but subject to negotiations between a wide range of public, semi-public and private actors, whose interactions give rise to relatively stable patterns of policy making that constitute a specific form of regulation, or mode of coordination.

Both of these uses of the network concept are present in the literature on MLG. Whilst these uses differ from one another in important respects, they nevertheless agree that networks present some common challenges in a more multi-scalar environment. This is particularly the case where networks privilege the priorities of their network over the priorities of any particular scale, do not align with pre-existing scalar boundaries and often act across multiple scales, due to their flexibility to respond to problems that cut across boundaries. This often results in a complex patchwork of networks that intersect at a variety of different scales with other networks that share similar, but not necessarily identical, concerns.

Multi-level governance and federalism

The preceding section identified some of the core characteristics of the literature on MLG. We now consider what sort of contribution it can make to the scholarship on federalism. Various metaphors and descriptive models have been used to capture different types of federalism. Federal systems have been described as cooperative, coordinative, polycentric, polyphonic, coercive, pragmatic and fuzzy. Some of these labels have more affinity with the concept of MLG than others, but what they share is the view that federalism is an ongoing project, as much as it is a formal arrangement for allocating authority and responsibilities (Clarke 2007). The more recent interest in MLG can be seen as a further extension of these concerns, although it is a development that has not been universally welcomed (e.g. Hueglin 2013).

In the next section, we briefly review the literature on federalism in Australia, emphasising that there is an overwhelming focus on the formal institutions of the state. We subsequently examine how the concept of MLG has been used beyond the EU. We focus on Canada, where more interest has been shown in how the MLG concept could be applied in a federal context. This is important as it suggests that a greater engagement with the Canadian literature on MLG may help to answer key questions, such as how and why the trends associated with MLG are having a more, or less, significant impact in Australia, compared with elsewhere.

Studying Australian federalism

Federalism has been a significant factor in Australian democracy for over a century, but it was not until mid-century that the academic study of Australian federalism began to gain ground (Fenna 2009). This can be partly explained by the early intellectual influence of British political studies, which understood government in terms of the Westminster Model. Australia's federal features were viewed with scepticism from this perspective due to the checks and balances that it imposed on the national level of government and its institutional and normative base in the American system of government (Parkin 2003). In these early days, Australia's federal inheritance was ignored, seen as an unwelcome distortion or regarded as fundamentally incompatible with the Westminster Model (Rhodes 2005). This has been reflected in the strongly normative tone that is evident in much of the literature on Australian federalism, including 'profound disagreement' over its legitimacy and relevance (Fenna 2009).

Institutional and comparative accounts of Australian federalism have focused on the changing relationship between different tiers of government – in essence, variation and changes within Type I MLG, but with an overwhelming focus on federal–state interactions. This has included studies that have examined the evolution of a relatively stable and consistent set of institutional arenas (e.g. executives, legislatures and courts), key actors (e.g. politicians and senior government officials) and processes (e.g. electoral forces) (Clarke 2007). A similar focus is also evident in the 'central topics' that have animated the interest of scholars working on Australian federalism, including *constitutional–juridical* change (e.g. the constitution and constitutional change or legal decisions taken by the High Court), *economic–fiscal* reform (e.g. the use of tied grants or the vertical fiscal imbalance between the Commonwealth and the states) or *governmental–political–administrative* relations (e.g. the role of the Senate or the reform of intergovernmental processes and institutions, such as the Council of Australian Governments, COAG) (Fenna 2009: 147). These studies have noted and assessed the impact of long-standing and contemporaneous developments on the character of Australian federalism, such as the relatively high degree of concurrency in key policy domains and the trend towards centralisation (Hollander and Patapan 2007; Galligan 2008; Fenna 2012). The changing relationship between different tiers of government has, however, been the starting point for much of this scholarship.

In other words, the literature on Australian federalism has been concerned with either normative issues, such as the compatibility between federalism and responsible government, or more institutional and legal issues. More recent scholarship has tended to focus on the institutional and legal aspects of Australian federalism, but that literature has been overwhelmingly state-centric in orientation. This has led to a particular focus on 'high politics' and executive federalism, but relatively little attention towards the issues raised by the literature on MLG. For example, there is no index entry on 'governance' in either of the two more recent volumes on Australian federalism (Appleby et al. 2012; Kildea et al. 2012). Yet, federalism in Australia appears to exhibit several of the key characteristics that have been identified by the literature on MLG.

One example can be seen in Galligan's (cited in Rhodes 2005: 142) description of federalism and intergovernmental relations as 'essentially untidy', a complex 'mixing and blending' of agencies with 'governments and parts of governments competing for a share in the action' in 'a communications network rather than a chain of command'. Concurrency contributes to this complexity, as roles and responsibilities in some policy areas are shared between the Commonwealth and states. Galligan (2008: 639) argues that: 'If there were ever a bottle with separate internal compartments for Commonwealth and state powers, the genie escaped long ago, and has so infused major policy domains that there is no putting it back.' Moreover, the need to address issues that traverse jurisdictional boundaries is becoming ever more urgent:

> Working out better arrangements and systems for intergovernmental management across jurisdictions within large policy areas is the biggest challenge facing modern Australian federalism, and is where our attention and effort should be focused. Happily, it is precisely these issues that are currently being tackled by COAG (Galligan 2008: 641).

This all contributes to an image of federalism as a 'policy matrix in which no government has a monopoly or complete authority' (Galligan, cited in Rhodes 2005: 142).

These conclusions are supported by other studies. For example, Fletcher (1991: 86–87) describes federal relations in Australia as a 'jurisdictional muddle … [a] complex picture of institutions … rather than a system of government organised into neat hierarchical functions'. Similarly, Stein and Turkewitsch (2010: 196) observe that there has been a more general shift in the literature on federalism away from descriptive models based in hierarchy towards models that have placed more emphasis on the shared or cooperative aspects of decision-making.

Studying federalism beyond Australia

It is within this context that there has been a noticeably greater openness to the concept of MLG in other jurisdictions. This has, however, worked both ways. On the one hand, EU scholars have been open to appropriating ideas, approaches and concepts in the literature on federalism. This has been noticeable in federal jurisdictions within the EU, such as Germany, as well as countries that have undergone devolution, such as the United Kingdom (e.g. Börzel and Hölsi 2003; Asare et al. 2009; Schmidt 1999; Benz and Zimmer 2010; Entwistle et al. 2012; Piattoni 2012). On the other hand, a number of studies have used MLG as a way of comparing the governance arrangements in the EU with pre-existing federal jurisdictions, particularly in the United States (e.g. Nicolaidis and Howse 2001; Menon and Schain 2007).

This transfer of ideas has also been evident in Canada where scholars have shown a particular willingness to experiment with the MLG concept. This interest is illustrated by the growing number of studies that have used the MLG concept to examine the governance arrangements in different policy areas, ranging from indigenous affairs and urban planning, to cross-border river disputes, immigration resettlement and climate change.[1]

Horak and Young's (2012) work on Canadian cities provides one example of this broader interest. Their argument is that federalism and the study of intergovernmental relations can no longer be confined to the interactions that take place between federal and provincial politicians and/or administrators. They argue that a suitably adapted version of MLG provides a more convincing fit with the changing nature of intergovernmental relations in Canada compared with the more restricted image provided by accounts grounded in executive federalism. Similarly, in reflecting on the particular public policy challenges that Canada now faces, Meekison et al. (2004: 23) have argued that:

> the sort of multi-centred collaboration that is now being contemplated, and that could involve federal, provincial, municipal, Aboriginal, and foreign governments, as well as transnational institutions, will be much more complex and increasingly political than earlier federal–provincial interactions.

They also note, however, that the challenges presented by emerging forms of MLG are 'only just beginning to be addressed' (Meekison et al. 2004: 24).

We certainly agree with Meekison et al. (2004) that we are only starting to address emerging forms of MLG, but even this brief review of the literature would appear to support the argument that there has been a greater engagement with the MLG concept in Canada, compared with Australia. We recognise that there are important differences between Australia and Canada that may help to explain some of this variation, but also note the tradition of comparison between them and the fact that they share some key institutional characteristics (see Rhodes et al. 2009). At the very least, this suggests that some further examination of the key trends associated with MLG could be useful.

---

1   See, for example, the recent Special Issue on Federalism and MLG in Canada, in *Canadian Public Administration*, Volume 56, Issue 2, June 2013.

Multi-level governance in Australia

We draw on various empirical examples in this section to further support our argument that an MLG perspective raises a number of insights that could make an important contribution to the literature on Australian federalism. We argue that, whilst there has been relatively little direct discussion about MLG in Australia, there has been a great deal of indirect discussion about MLG's key features, challenges and concerns. We illustrate our argument with examples from three areas: intergovernmental relations, sub-national governance and policymaking in environmental governance and natural resource management.

Intergovernmental relations

Intergovernmental relations in Australia continue to remain a relatively closed and secretive world in which the key actors are the Commonwealth prime minister, state premiers, portfolio ministers and their permanent officials (Painter 2001: 138). More recent scholarship has identified a trend towards a centralisation of power at the federal level, at the same time as it has been argued that federal–state relations have also become more collaborative (e.g. Hollander and Patapan 2007; O'Flynn and Wanna 2008; Jones 2010). As discussed earlier, this tension can be partly explained by the concurrency that exists in the Australian federation. For example, Hollander (2009: 141) argues that:

> While the Australian federation has been subject to strong centripetal forces in Australian federalism, the states, nevertheless, have continued to play a significant role in both policy making and implementation (Parkin 2003: 106–08), and the concurrency embedded in the Australian federation means that the system has continued to exhibit characteristics of Grodzin's 'marble cake' of shared activities.

Painter (2001: 139–40) further illustrates this tension by pointing to the two fundamental, and contradictory, sets of institutional forces and rationales at work in the relationship between officials and ministers at the Commonwealth and state level:

> The first set is centred on the domestic policy processes of the separate governments. It is deeply embedded in formal structures of accountability and control modelled on the Westminster system. The underlying principle of this set is command in hierarchy. In the second set, cross-jurisdictional intergovernmental networks and arenas of policy cooperation and conflict

shape relationships. They emerge in a context characterised by power sharing and interdependence, where cooperation rather than command is the underlying organising logic of effective policy making.

He notes that challenges often emerge as actors shift between these two different logics:

> Problem-solving strategies appropriate for the domestic setting are often countermanded by the rules of the game of the intergovernmental or multi-level context, and contradictions and tension may emerge that block the facilitation of joint action in the intergovernmental arena (Painter 2001: 140).

It is therefore understandable that centralisation may take place hand-in-hand with what Painter (2001: 149) has described as a 'long term trend towards the diffusion and institutionalisation of more collaborative forms of coordination in the Australian federation'. A similar trend has also been identified by Fels (2008: xii), who has argued that:

> Collaboration between governments could herald a new phase of federalism. If 'cooperative federalism' is about microeconomic reform and structural efficiencies, 'collaborative federalism' is about sharing intent, sharing goals and agreeing on delivery responsibilities. This new phase of federalism is likely to focus on social policies, national security and bio-security, the environment, infrastructure and communication. Above all, it is likely to dispense with the notion that 'government knows best', replacing it not just with intergovernmental agreements, but with community involvement in policy design and delivery. It could be more messy, but also more realistic and more results-based.

Fels's argument suggests that there may need to be more engagement with Type II forms of MLG, whereas most of the literature on intergovernmental relations has focused primarily on Type I MLG. As Fels suggests, such an endeavour would involve not only intergovernmental agreements, but also greater community involvement in policy design and delivery. Any attempts to move in this direction, however, will clearly take place against the backdrop of the competing logics described by Painter (2001).

Sub-national governance

There is a significant literature that has examined sub-national governance structures in Australia, such as local government, regional governance structures, cities, municipalities and local communities (e.g. Brown and Bellamy 2007; Jones 2008; Everingham et al. 2009; Acuto 2012); however, the literature on federalism and intergovernmental relations has tended to analyse these arrangements as either discrete entities or in the shadow of federal–state relations. At the same time, sub-national units have also been increasingly identified as an appropriate scale for tackling various policy issues. For example, the important role that regions play in certain policy areas supports Galligan's (2008: 618) argument that:

> regionalism is alive and well at the sub-State level for certain governance purposes and policy delivery regimes, and can be a preferred identifier for groupings of people concerned with or responding to certain issues.

Brown (2009, 2012) has gone somewhat further and argued that regions form an important part of the day-to-day political culture and practice of Australian citizens. This view is supported by Taylor's (2012: 507) study of the wheatbelt region of Western Australia in which he argues that 34 rural local governments were able to 'buffer state intervention and improve the effectiveness of their own cooperative planning and management activities for sustainable development' by adopting a defensive posture towards a state-led program of regionalisation for economic development and natural resource management.

These points are also illustrated by Brown and Bellamy's (2010) case study of the rural and remote region of central west Queensland in which at least 21 different regional bodies, programs, committees and community-based groups exist across a wide variety of policy areas from regional development, transport and integrated planning, to tourism, indigenous welfare and health and social services. Brown and Bellamy (2010) note the patchwork, informal and impermanent arrangements that exist in central west Queensland in which many services are delivered by project and network-based groups or public–private partnerships that involve a broader range of actors from the public, private and voluntary sectors. They argue that this has generated some challenges, including shortages in human capital, wider intergovernmental conflict, financial sustainability, misalignment between policy scales and responsibilities, legitimacy deficits and difficulties in securing sufficient policy capacity (Brown and Bellamy 2010: 180). They also noted the multiple, and sometimes blurred, spatial, functional and sectoral boundaries that can exist between different regional identifiers (Brown and Bellamy 2010: 172–75). Differences at this level existed not only between state and Commonwealth governments, but also between departments within any one given level of government.

They also note, however, that the partnership arrangements that exist in central west Queensland have also provided it with the flexibility and responsiveness to deal with various policy issues (Brown and Bellamy 2010: 190–91). So, whilst many of the participants in their study expressed concern that the system was 'supported only by weak regional institutional frameworks', they also noted the advantages that this brought. What this suggests is a struggle in central west Queensland between a desire to move further towards more institutionalised, Type I arrangements, combined with a concern that this would lead to a loss of flexibility and capacity to adapt to the more partnership- and project-based strategy found in Type II MLG arrangements. As Brown and Bellamy (2010: 191) note, the interviewees in their study:

> revealed little desire to sacrifice flexibility and informality, even when participants recognized the various signs of institutional weakness in the regional governance system, on the basis that this could limit their effective capacity to translate adaptive processes into outcomes.

Indeed, Brown and Bellamy's findings demonstrate how the participants in their study are balancing the various virtues and vices of Type I and Type II MLG that were discussed in the opening section of this chapter.

MLG and policymaking

MLG has also been used to examine the policymaking process, particularly in the literature on environmental governance and natural resource management (e.g. Morrison 2007; Lockwood et al. 2009; Daniell et al. 2011). In many instances, these difficulties can be located at the interface between Type I and Type II MLG. For example, Bellamy (2007: 104–05) argues that natural resource management in Australia increasingly involves:

> a complex system of multiple 'nested' or polycentric decision-making arrangements (versus being neatly hierarchical) being carried out concurrently across a range of political decision-making levels (e.g. national, state, region, local) and horizontally across a fragmented array of territorial and sectoral areas ... This system is continually evolving at all political and sectoral levels ... At each level of this complex multi-layered and polycentric system, there are different emergent properties and problems to be addressed.

Similarly, Bulkeley, in a series of single and co-authored contributions, has identified the emergence of a complex set of governance arrangements around climate change policy in Australia at the city/municipal level (e.g. Bulkeley 2005; Betsill and Bulkeley 2006; Bulkeley and Betsill 2013; see also Jones 2012, 2013). For example, Betsill and Bulkeley (2006: 151) argue that the inherently multi-level nature of the governance of climate change policy is leading to an active reconfiguration and renegotiation of the roles and responsibilities of state and non-state actors:

> While the nation-state may be responsible for legitimating and alleviating climate risks, this is a task that it cannot complete without addressing the source of risks (energy use) and without the involvement of the institutions and agents responsible for that use (industries and communities). In turn, non-state actors, which operate at different scales traditionally across discrete policy sectors, share responsibility with the state for defining problems and implementing solutions.

Bulkeley and Betsill (2013) argue that this renegotiation of roles and responsibilities is illustrated by the active role that several cities in Australia have played in various transnational municipal networks, such as the C40 network, the International Council for Local Environmental Initiatives' (ICLEI) Cities for Climate Protection (CCP) program and Climate Alliance. For example, they show how the city of Melbourne has developed a coordinated and strategic approach to climate change, despite the fragmented nature of local governance. Bulkeley and Betsill (2013) argue that Melbourne has been able to do this by providing strategic direction (e.g. the 2002 Victorian greenhouse strategy and the Zero Net Emissions by 2020 – Strategy Update), promoting Greenpower energy, supporting the ICLEI CCP program in regional and rural Australia and helping local councils to form partnerships known as regional greenhouse alliances.[2]

Bulkeley's overall argument is that these developments illustrate new spheres of authority that are not bound to a particular scale, but which are having a direct effect on the governance of climate change in various cities worldwide (e.g. Bulkeley 2005). She argues that these relatively new forms of Type II MLG in Australia also help illustrate at least three

---

2   Examples include Central Victoria Greenhouse Alliance, Eastern Alliance for Greenhouse Action, Gippsland Climate Change Network, Goulburn Broken Greenhouse Alliance, North East Greenhouse Alliance, the Northern Alliance for Greenhouse Action, the South East Councils Climate Change Alliance and Western Alliance for Greenhouse Action (see www.naga.org.au/alliances.html).

points. First, cities are playing an important role in addressing climate change in ways that nation-states have often failed to fully appreciate. Second, cities and local authorities can effectively bypass the nation-state, even when the actions that they take may contradict those that are being pursued by the national government. Third, cities and local governments have taken on functions that are typically associated with nation-states, such as the development of norms, rules for compliance and mechanisms for reporting and monitoring emissions. Betsill and Bulkeley (2006: 152) conclude that:

> This suggests that political power and authority lie not only with nation-states, but can accrue to transnational networks operating through a different form of territoriality.

Conclusion

This chapter has asked whether it is possible to draw ideas from a concept, such as MLG, beyond the particular context within which it was originally developed. We have argued that there appear to be some advantages in examining Australian federalism from an MLG perspective but it is obviously important that it is done with considerable caution.

The considerable differences that exist between the EU, as an emerging supra-national polity, and the federal system of government that exists in Australia, is one clear reason why it is necessary to proceed with caution. Most federal systems do not have a genuinely autonomous supra-national level of government like the EU; there are important differences in institutional architecture between the EU and Australia and the circumstances that gave rise to the federation in Australia are clearly different from those that gave rise to the EU. Bakvis (2013) underscores this point with reference to the Canadian context. He argues that, whilst non-hierarchical modes of coordination are used in Canada, hierarchy plays a more critical role in Canada than in the EU, due to its propensity for top-down control, the government's lack of willingness to engage civil society and a closed and elite-driven form of executive federalism:

> In the Canadian federation hierarchy plays a critical role, but not in direct relations between governments. Rather, as argued, hierarchy is found mainly within governments, with executive dominance the primary outcome, thereby affecting relations between governments: interactions

tend to be limited to those between governments (interstate federalism), mainly at a senior level and at the expense of inclusive networks and connections with civil society (Bakvis 2013: 215).

We have made a similar point when examining the nature of intergovernmental relations in Australia. So, factors such as those identified by Bakvis will clearly have an impact on the extent to which Type II MLG develops in Australia, given that these governance arrangements will be embedded within the legal frameworks and norms determined by Type I jurisdictions.

At the same time, we have also detailed several instances where Type I MLG is coexisting with Type II MLG in Australia. This raises important questions about how differences in institutional structure shape the extent to which Type II MLG emerges and how Type II MLG intersects and coexists with Type I MLG. The brief examples that we have provided suggest that this will vary across policy areas and between national contexts, but developing a better understanding of what drives this variation is clearly an important area for further research.

We have argued that greater engagement with the literature on MLG could act as a good starting point for this work. In particular, we have shown how taking an MLG perspective has opened up new lines of enquiry in other countries that share Australia's federal system of government. The different examples of Type II MLG that we have discussed suggest that similar trends are taking place in Australia. In our view, further research is now required in order to better understand how Type I MLG intersects and coexists with Type II MLG in Australia, including the effectiveness and legitimacy of such arrangements. The chapters in this volume are an important step in that direction.

References

Acuto, M. (2012). Ain't about Politics? The Wicked Power-Geometry of Sydney's Greening Governance. *International Journal of Urban and Regional Research*, 36(2): 381–99. doi.org/10.1111/j.1468-2427. 2011.01063.x

Agranoff, R. (2004). Researching Intergovernmental Relations. *Journal of Public Administration Research and Theory*, 14(4): 443–46. doi.org/10.1093/jopart/muh030

Appleby, G., Aroney, N. & John, T. (eds) (2012). *The Future of Australian Federalism*. Cambridge University Press, Melbourne.

Asare, B., Cairney, P. & Studlar, D.T. (2009). Federalism and Multilevel Governance in Tobacco Policy: The European Union, the United Kingdom, and devolved UK institutions. *Journal of Public Policy*, 29(1): 79–102. doi.org/10.1017/S0143814X09000993

Bakvis, H. (2013). 'In the shadows of hierarchy': Intergovernmental governance in Canada and the European Union. *Canadian Public Administration*, 56(2): 203–18. doi.org/10.1111/capa.12014

Bellamy, J. (2007). Adaptive Governance: The challenge for regional natural resource management. In: Brown, A.J. & Bellamy, J.A. (eds) *Federalism and Regionalism in Australia: New Approaches, New Institutions?* ANU E Press, Canberra, pp. 119–34.

Benz, A. & Zimmer, C. (2010). The EU's Competences: The 'vertical' perspective on the multilevel system. *Living Reviews in European Governance*, 5(1), www.europeangovernance-livingreviews.org/Articles/lreg-2010-1/download/lreg-2010-1Color.pdf [Accessed: 01/06/14].

Betsill, M. & Bulkeley, H. (2006). Cities and the Multilevel Governance of Global Climate Change. *Global Governance*, 12(2): 141–59.

Börzel, T.A. & Hösli, M. (2003). Brussels between Bern and Berlin. Comparative Federalism Meets the European Union. *Governance*, 16(2): 179–202. doi.org/10.1111/1468-0491.00213

Brenner, N. (2009). Open Questions on State Rescaling. *Cambridge Journal of Regions, Economy and Society*, 2(1): 123–39. doi.org/10.1093/cjres/rsp002

Brown, A.J. (2009). Thinking Big: Public opinion and options for reform of Australia's federal system. *Public Policy*, 4(1): 30–50.

———. (2012). Mapping Federal Political Culture and Support for Political Reform in the World's First 'Top-Down' Federation: the strange case of Australia. Paper Presented at the Triennial Meeting of the International Political Science Association, 8–11 July, Madrid, Spain.

Brown, A.J. & Bellamy, J.A. (eds) (2007). *Federalism and Regionalism in Australia: New Approaches, New Institutions?* ANU E Press, Canberra.

———. (2010). In the Shadow of Federalism: Dilemmas of institutional design in Australian rural and remote regional governance. *The Australasian Journal of Regional Studies*, 16(2): 151–81.

Büchs, M. (2009). Examining the Interaction Between Vertical and Horizontal Dimensions of State Transformation. *Cambridge Journal of Regions, Economy and Society*, 2(1): 35–49. doi.org/10.1093/cjres/rsn026

Bulkeley, H. (2005). Reconfiguring Environmental Governance: towards a politics of scales and networks. *Political Geography*, 24(8): 875–902. doi.org/10.1016/j.polgeo.2005.07.002

Bulkeley, H. & Betsill, M.M. (2013). Revisiting the Urban Politics of Climate Change. *Environmental Politics*, 22(1): 136–54. doi.org/10.1080/09644016.2013.755797

Cashore, B. (2002). Legitimacy and the Privatization of Environmental Governance: how non-state market-driven (NSMD) governance systems gain rule-making authority. *Governance*, 15(4): 503–29. doi.org/10.1111/1468–0491.00199

Clarke, S.E. (2007). 'Thinking Federally' from a Governance Perspective. In: Pagano, M.A. & Leonardi, R. (eds) *The Dynamics of Federalism in National and Supranational Political Systems*. Palgrave Macmillan Houndmills, pp. 55–85. doi.org/10.1057/9780230625433_4

Daniell, K.A., Máñez Costa, M.A., Ferrand, N., Kingsborough, A.B., Coad, P. & Ribarova, I.S. (2011). Aiding Multi-level Decision-making Processes for Climate Change Mitigation and Adaptation. *Regional Environmental Change*, 11(2): 243–58. doi.org/10.1007/s10113-010-0162-0

Daugbjerg, C. & Fawcett, P. (2017). Metagovernance, Network Structure, and Legitimacy: Developing a heuristic for comparative governance analysis. *Administration & Society*, 49(9): 1223–1245. doi.org/10.1177/0095399715581031

Enderlein, H., Wälti, S. & Zürn, M. (eds) (2010). *Handbook on Multi-level Governance*, Edward Elgar, Cheltenham.

Entwistle, T., Downe, J., Guarneros-Meza, V. & Martin, S. (2012). The Multi-level Governance of Wales: Layer cake or marble cake? *British Journal of Politics and International Relations*, 16(2): 310–25. doi.org/10.1111/j.1467-856X.2012.00541.x

Everingham, J., Cheshire, L. & Lawrence, G. (2009). Regional Renaissance? New forms of governance in nonmetropolitan Australia. *Environment and Planning C: Government and Policy*, 24(1): 139–55. doi.org/10.1068/c47m

Fawcett, P. & Daugbjerg, C. (2012). Explaining Governance Outcomes: Epistemology, network governance and policy network analysis. *Political Studies Review*, 10(2): 195–207. doi.org/10.1111/j.1478-9302.2012.00257.x

Fels, A. (2008). Foreword: Network governance and collaboration to improve outcomes. In: O'Flynn, J. & Wanna, J. (eds) *Collaborative Governance: A New Era of Public Policy in Australia?* ANU E Press, Canberra, pp. xi–xiii.

Fenna, A. (2009). Federalism. In: Rhodes, R.A.W. (ed.) *The Australian Study of Politics*. Palgrave, Houndmills, pp. 146–59. doi.org/10.1057/9780230296848_11

——. (2012). Centralising Dynamics in Australian Federalism. *Australian Journal of Politics and History*, 58(4): 580–90. doi.org/10.1111/j.1467-8497.2012.01654.x

Fletcher, C. (1991). Rediscovering Australian Federalism by Resurrecting Old Ideas. *Australian Journal of Political Science*, 26(1): 79–94. doi.org/10.1080/00323269108402137

Galligan, B. (2008). Processes for Reforming Australian Federalism. *UNSW Law Journal*, 31(2), 617–42.

Hollander, R. (2009). Rethinking Overlap and Duplication: Federalism and environmental assessment in Australia, *Publius*, 40(1): 136–70. doi.org/10.1093/publius/pjp028

Hollander, R. & Patapan, H. (2007). Pragmatic Federalism: Australian federalism from Hawke to Howard. *Australian Journal of Public Administration*, 66(3): 280–97. doi.org/10.1111/j.1467-8500.2007.00542.x

Hooghe, L. & Marks, G. (2010). Types of multi-level governance. In: Enderlein, H., Wälti, S. & Zürn, M. (eds) *Handbook on Multi-level Governance.* Edward Elgar, Cheltenham, pp. 17–31. doi.org/10.4337/9781849809047.00007

Horak, M. & Young, R. (eds) (2012). *Sites of Governance: Multilevel Governance and Policy Making in Canada's Big Cities.* McGill-Queen's University Press, Montreal and Kingston.

Hueglin, T.O. (2013). Comparing federalisms: variations or distinct models? In: Benz, A. & Broschek, J. (eds) *Federal Dynamics: Continuity, Change, & the Varieties of Federalism.* Oxford University Press, pp. 27–47. doi.org/10.1093/acprof:oso/9780199652990.003.0002

Jones, S. (2008). Can Australian Local Governments have a Role in Local Economic Development? Three cases of evidence. *Urban Policy and Research,* 26(1): 23–38. doi.org/10.1080/08111140701606785

———. (2010). The National Renewable Energy Target: An example of post-Machiavellian policy-making? *Australian Journal of Public Administration,* 69(2): 165–77. doi.org/10.1111/j.1467-8500.2010.00678.x

———. (2012). A Tale of Two Cities? Climate Change Policies in Vancouver and Melbourne – barometers of cooperative federalism? *International Journal of Urban and Regional Research,* 36(6), 1242–67. doi.org/10.1111/j.1468-2427.2011.01083.x

———. (2013). Climate Change Policies of City Governments in Federal Systems: An analysis of Vancouver, Melbourne and New York City. *Regional Studies,* 47(6): 974–92. doi.org/10.1080/00343404.2011.585150

Kildea, P., Lynch, A. & Williams, G. (eds) (2012). *Tomorrow's Federation: Reforming Australian Government.* The Federation Press, Sydney.

Kohler-Koch, B. & Rittberger, B. (2006). The 'Governance Turn' in EU Studies. *JCMS: Journal of Common Market Studies,* 44(s1): 27–49.

Lockwood, M., Davidson, J., Curtis, A., Stratford, E. & Griffith, R. (2009). Multi-level Environmental Governance: Lessons from Australian natural resource management. *Australian Geographer,* 40(2), 169–86. doi.org/10.1080/00049180902964926

Marsh, D. (ed.) (1998). *Comparing Policy Networks*, Open University Press, Buckingham.

McGuire, M. (2006). Intergovernmental Management: A view from the bottom. *Public Administration Review*, 66(5): 677–79. doi.org/10.1111/j.1540-6210.2006.00632.x

Meekison, P.J., Telford, H. & Lazar, H. (2004). The Institutions of Executive Federalism: Myths and realities. In: Meekison, P.J., Telford, H. & Lazar, H. (eds) *The State of the Federation 2002: Reconsidering the Institutions of Canadian Federalism*. McGill-Queen's University Press, Montreal and Kingston, pp. 3–34.

Menon, A. & Schain, M.A. (eds) (2007). *Comparative Federalism: The European Union and the United States in Comparative Perspective*. Oxford University Press.

Morrison, T.H. (2007). Multiscalar Governance and Regional Environmental Management in Australia. *Space and Polity*, 11(3): 227–41. doi.org/10.1080/13562570701811551

Nicolaidis, K. & Howse, R. (eds) (2001). *The Federal Vision. Legitimacy and Levels of Government in the United States and the European Union*, Oxford University Press.

O'Flynn, J. & Wanna, J. (eds) (2008). *Collaborative Governance: A New Era of Public Policy in Australia*. ANU E Press, Canberra.

Osborne, S.P. (ed.) (2010). *The New Public Governance?* Routledge, London.

Painter, M. (2001). Multi-level Governance and the Emergence of Collaborative Federal Institutions in Australia. *Policy & Politics*, 29(2): 137–50. doi.org/10.1332/0305573012501260

Parkin, A. (2003). The States, Federalism and Political Science: A fifty-year appraisal. *Australian Journal of Public Administration*, 62(2): 101–12. doi.org/10.1111/1467-8497.00329

Piattoni, S. (2012). Federalism and Its Competitors: Which template for contemporary Europe? *L'Europe en Formation*, 363(1): 9–20. doi.org/10.3917/eufor.363.0009

Provost, C. (2012). Governance and Voluntary Regulation. In: Levi-Faur, D. (ed.) *The Oxford Handbook of Governance*. Oxford University Press, pp. 554–68. doi.org/10.1093/oxfordhb/9780199560530.013.0039

Rhodes, R.A.W. (2005). Australia: The Westminster model as tradition. In: Patapan, H., Wanna, J. & Weller, P. (eds) *Westminster Legacies: Democracy and Responsible Government in Asia and the Pacific*. UNSW Press, Sydney, pp. 129–52.

Rhodes, R.A.W., Wanna, J. & Weller, P. (2009). *Comparing Westminster*. Oxford University Press. doi.org/10.1093/acprof:oso/9780199563494.001.0001

Schmidt, V.A. (1999). European Federalism and its Encroachment on National Institutions. *Publius*, 29: 19–44. doi.org/10.1093/oxfordjournals.pubjof.a030012

Sørenson, E. & Torfing, J. (2007). Introduction: Governance network research: towards a second generation. In: Sørenson, E. & Torfing, J. (eds) *Theories of Democratic Network Governance*. Palgrave, Houndmills, pp. 1–24. doi.org/10.1057/9780230625006_1

Stein, M.B. & Turkewitsch, L. (2010). Multi-level Governance in Canadian and American Intergovernmental Relations. In: Enderlein, H., Wälti, S. & Zürn, M. (eds) *Handbook on Multi-level Governance*. Edward Elgar, Cheltenham, pp. 184–200. doi.org/10.4337/9781849809047.00018

Stephenson, P. (2013). Twenty Years of Multi-level Governance: Where does it come from? What is it? Where is it going? *Journal of European Public Policy*, 20(6): 817–37. doi.org/10.1080/13501763.2013.781818

Sutcliffe, J.B. (2012). Multi-level Governance in a Canadian Setting: The reform of the Detroit River border crossing. *Regional and Federal Studies*, 22(2): 141–58. doi.org/10.1080/13597566.2012.668137

Taylor, B.M. (2012). Regionalism as Resistance: Governance and identity in Western Australia's wheatbelt. *Geoforum*, 43(3): 507–17. doi.org/10.1016/j.geoforum.2011.11.004

Torfing, J., Peters, B.G., Pierre, J. & Sørenson, E. (2012). *Interactive Governance Advancing the Paradigm*. Oxford University Press. doi.org/10.1093/acprof:oso/9780199596751.001.0001

4

Accountability in Multi-level Governance: The Example of Australian Federalism

Richard Mulgan

Introduction

This chapter examines accountability in Australian federalism as an instance of accountability in multi-level governance (MLG) and networked governance generally. The question of accountability in Australian federalism has long been seen as problematic, largely because of the overlapping responsibilities between the federal government and the governments of the states and territories. This overlap leads to continual bickering and the notorious 'blame game' between the two levels of government. The issue gained prominence under Kevin Rudd's Australian Labor Party (ALP) Government (2007–10), which revamped the Council of Australian Governments (COAG) structure in an attempt to clarify the respective responsibilities of each level of government and to remove the causes of the blame game. In spite of such efforts, however, recrimination between the two levels continues, helping to fuel growing public perceptions that federal and state and territory governments are not working well together (Griffith University 2014). Locating these problems within the wider context of accountability in multi-level and networked governance may help to explain the reasons for their intransigence, as well as throwing light on possible solutions.

Networked governance is a broad term referring to processes of governing undertaken by more than one organisation working together in partnership or collaboration (Rhodes 1997). It includes partnerships between different government organisations, as well as partnerships between government and private organisations. Federal divisions of authority, where two constitutionally independent levels of government – central and provincial – work together on common policies or problems, can therefore be counted as a species of networked governance. In this light, however, federalism as a species of networked governance fits only with those aspects of federalism that exhibit features of 'concurrent' federalism involving overlapping responsibilities (Galligan 1995; Painter 1998). It does not apply to those areas of government that fit the theory of 'coordinate' federalism, where each level of government operates separately within its own sphere of activity (though each separate jurisdiction may itself exhibit aspects of networked governance, for example, between its different government departments and agencies and between each government and non-government organisations).

Accountability, in turn, can be understood as the obligation to answer for the performance of duties, paired with the correlative right of someone else, typically the person for whom the duties are performed, to demand such an answer (Mulgan 2003: Chpt. 1; Bovens 2007; Bovens et al. 2014). It involves a number of elements or stages: reporting or informing (transparency); justifying and explaining (discussion); and the imposition of remedies, including compensation or sanctions (rectification). The accountability of democratic governments to their citizens typically involves a complex system of processes and institutions, including a range of different accountors (*who is accountable?*), different account-holders (*to whom are they accountable?*), different aspects of government operations (*for what are they accountable?*) and different mechanisms (*how are they accountable?*).

Accountability in networked governance

The question of accountability in networked governance turns on a comparison with the systems of accountability found in non-networked governance (i.e. in a unified governing system under a single controlling authority). From this perspective, the most important mechanisms of accountability in unitary systems of representative democracy operate through a chain of principal–agent relationships, linking the popular election of representative leaders with the control exercised by these leaders at the head of the hierarchically based organisations of executive bureaucracy. Within this chain, each agent is accountable to its respective principal, linking rank-and-file public officials to the voters.

The Westminster system of parliamentary government, operating at both the Commonwealth and state and territory levels, provides a classic example of such 'vertical' accountability within a single, unitary government structure. Under conventions of ministerial responsibility, ministers answer to parliament and the voters for the actions of their subordinates, fulfilling all three elements of accountability – providing information, discussing policy options and rationales, and imposing remedies in the light of public exposure and criticism. Members of the bureaucracy, in turn, help to implement this vertical accountability structure through internal accountability to their organisational superiors.

Vertical hierarchical accountability is not the only accountability mechanism operating in unified government systems. In addition, a number of 'horizontal' mechanisms supplement the overall accountability of the government by exercising the first two stages of accountability (informing and discussing) without being able to impose remedies. These include legislative committees and accountability agencies, such as auditors and ombudsmen, as well as more informal organisations such as the media and stakeholder groups. Although they lack the power of enforcement themselves, they often provoke the executive to take remedial action through the power of adverse publicity and potential reputational damage. In this sense, they operate 'in the shadow of hierarchy' (Schillemans 2008), relying on the background potential of controlling hierarchies to enforce their assessments. Unitary governments are also subject to judicial accountability, depending on the constitutional framework and the scope of administrative law, a form of accountability with both vertical and horizontal elements in which courts exercise the power of coercion but exist outside a structure of overall hierarchical control – this is dubbed 'diagonal' accountability (Bovens 2007).

Because networked governance, by definition, lacks a single central point of control, it is unable to provide vertical accountability in the same way as unified governing systems. There is no single person or body in charge and, therefore, no one who is obliged to answer to the public for the collective actions of the collaborating partners or to impose remedies when mistakes come to light. The absence of clear responsibility provides increased opportunities for blame avoidance and buck-passing (Mulgan 2003: 198–99). Moreover, when compared with unitary governments, multi-level governments such as federations do not offer the same range of horizontal accountability agencies to cover their joint activities because many such agencies – for instance, legislatures, auditors and ombudsmen – are constitutionally confined to investigating the actions of only one level of government. From this perspective, then, networked governance in general, and federal systems in particular, suffer from a serious 'accountability deficit' (e.g. Rhodes 2006; Michels and Meijer 2008; Mulgan 2014).

On the other hand, networked governance does not lack mechanisms of accountability. First, some forms of horizontal accountability certainly apply across jurisdictional boundaries (Michels and Meijer 2008; Papadopoulos 2007; Schillemans 2011). The news media, for example, can investigate and report on the outcomes of joint programs where responsibility is shared between different regimes. Individual citizens can share their own experiences of government networks through social media platforms.

Second, the pluralistic nature of many networks, in which different members pursue different, if overlapping, agendas, often allows for more open disclosure of information than is found in more closed, hierarchical structures (Mulgan 2003: 211–14). Networks, therefore, have the potential to be more transparent than monolithic hierarchies. Much depends on the nature of the network, on whether it is open and outward looking or closed and inwardly focused.

Third, at the local level, networks of committed professionals belonging to different organisations can offer individual citizens more direct accountability for government services than is provided through a standard hierarchical chain of command, provided they are given sufficient discretion to make their own decisions (Stoker 2006; Hupe and Hill 2007; Hendriks 2009). Because they are closely engaged with each other and with their communities, members of these networks can respond quickly and effectively to individual grievances without having to negotiate detailed and often inappropriate instructions from their separate bureaucratic superiors. This form of bottom-up accountability is well suited to networks in comparison with the more top-down, hierarchical accountability found in bureaucracies.

Fourth, networks can also subscribe to joint objectives, which is a common feature of successful collaborative partnerships based on shared values and mutual trust (Agranoff 2007). If members of the network also agree to public reporting of their performance in terms of meeting these objectives or to assessment by independent regulators, they also become more transparent and publicly accountable.

These different processes of horizontal accountability and transparency involve the first two stages of accountability (informing and discussing) but they can also lead to the final accountability stage of remedial action and rectification. For example, members of the network may be concerned to avoid adverse reputational consequences and may respond collectively to being named and shamed. The fact that responsibilities are divided and no one is clearly in charge can certainly offer more opportunities for shifting blame than in a unitary governmental system. But this does not mean that remedial consequences never follow from the exposure of faults in networked structures. In genuinely collaborative partnerships based on trust and shared values, as Agranoff (2012: Chpt. 8) points out, different partners with different limited rectification powers can each contribute to a collective solution.

Overall, then, networked governance may suffer from an accountability deficit because of the absence of a single point of authority, as well as the limited jurisdiction of some accountability agencies. In mitigation, networked arrangements have the potential to open government processes up to greater transparency and to stimulate voluntary rectification from network partners. Moreover, it should be remembered that unitary systems can also produce accountability deficits; for instance, through the tightness of their central control. In spite of their systems of vertical authority, rectification is not always straightforward in unitary governments where governments can often find means of avoiding consequences for mistakes; for example, through denial of responsibility and suppression of evidence (Mulgan 2014). The accountability ledger, therefore, is not wholly on the side of unified hierarchies, though the balance may be said to lie in their favour.

Notwithstanding any possible deficit in terms of accountability to the public, networked arrangements can also exhibit a number of characteristics that stem from their basis in shared values and partnerships and may compensate for deficiencies in terms of external accountability (Radin and Romzek 1996; Agranoff and McGuire 2001; Bogason and

Musso 2006). In the first place, partners in a network are often accountable to each other as they cooperate together in joint programs. For example, bureaucrats dealing with opposite numbers in cognate agencies regularly quiz each other on matters of common interest. This type of internal accountability need not be open to the public; in this case it does not count as a form of public accountability. It can help, however, to keep individual network members honest by requiring them to answer to people beyond their own organisation. Internal accountability built on mutual dialogue is particularly important in the not-for-profit private sector, which is generally less subject to external scrutiny than both the public sector and the commercial private sector, and relies more on the shared values and commitment of individual members (Goodin 2003).

More broadly, the extent to which members of a network are genuinely motivated to pursue generally accepted public values affects the extent to which they need to be subject to external supervision. In particular, not-for-profit charities engaged in providing public services can be trusted to act voluntarily in the public interest more than commercial contractors. Similarly, members of highly disciplined and regulated professions such as doctors and nurses, which are subject to their own professional regulatory bodies, need less additional scrutiny than mainline bureaucrats or commercial contractors. In networks involving such members, any accountability deficit associated with the networked nature of governance becomes less of an issue. If a network is based more on mutual trust and genuine commitment to the public interest it will be less subject to the opportunistic shirking and blame-avoidance, which the absence of vertical accountability encourages.

Some analysts sympathetic to the role of networks in governing have sought to defuse the impact of any supposed accountability deficit by redefining the concept of accountability itself, for instance, to include government responsiveness to the needs or preferences of citizens and communities without any obligation to answer publicly through the normal processes of accountability (Considine 2002). Accountability in governance has also been identified with public justifications made in terms of public reason and the public interest, thus, again, circumventing the need for political control (Weale 2011). Admittedly, accountability is a notoriously slippery concept (Mulgan 2000; Pollitt and Hupe 2011) and no definition can be categorically insisted on. Rather than extend the concept of accountability beyond its normal implication, however, it is preferable to admit that networks may be comparatively unaccountable but that other positive features of networks may counterbalance this deficiency.

Application of accountability in networked governance to federal–state relations in Australia

How, then, do these general conclusions about accountability in networked governance apply to federal–state relations in Australia? To begin with, the accountability deficit due to the absence of a single point of unified control in matters of overlapping responsibility is a familiar feature of Australian federalism. Its effects were well illustrated in the public criticism that surrounded two of the Rudd ALP Government's major spending programs designed to combat the global financial crisis (GFC) – the home insulation program and the school building program. In each case, the respective federal ministers were subject to fierce and continuing attack from the parliamentary opposition and sections of the media. Criticism centred on the federal government's role in authorising and supervising each program and led the government to implement substantial reviews and adjustments. Indeed, the minister in charge of the home insulation program, the minister for the environment, Peter Garrett, was replaced as minister in charge of the program and the program itself was abruptly wound down (Mulgan 2012).

State and territory governments, however, were also involved in each program. For example, in the home insulation program, the crucial function of occupational health and safety and safety inspection was a state and territory responsibility and, therefore, outside the direct control of the Commonwealth minister. The frenzy of media scrutiny prompted by the federal opposition's attack on the minister ignored this fact. Similarly, in the case of the school building program, most of the major failures were in government, rather than private, schools. Government schools are administered by state and territory bureaucracies who have their own agenda and are responsible to their own ministers with independent political priorities, which include extracting as much funding as possible from Commonwealth sources to use for their own purposes.

Because accountability was driven by a focus on federal politics, state and territory bureaucracies largely escaped being held to account for their delays and extravagance. In neither case did state nor territory ministers have any interest in the accountability of their departments for what were seen as primarily Commonwealth initiatives and failures. The Commonwealth Auditor-General, in his inquiries into the home insulation and school building programs, made pointed reference to the fact that he was unable to investigate or comment on the actions of state and territory governments and private contractors (ANAO 2010a; 2010b), even though they were heavily involved in the policy failures.

These examples confirm the absence of formal accountability mechanisms covering programs in which both levels of government are involved. They also underline the force of ministerial responsibility as a vertical accountability mechanism in Australia, which has both positive and negative effects for overall government accountability. The benefits flow from the pressures exerted on ministers and their departmental officials by opportunistic oppositions and sensation-hungry journalists. At the same time, concentration on the responsibilities and possible failings of federal ministers draws attention away from the contributions of state and territory governments and actively discourages public discussion of shared responsibilities. Ministers at both levels are encouraged to give highest priority to actions for which they and their governments can be seen to be directly responsible. By the same token, they have little incentive to claim a share in responsibility for joint programs, particularly when these programs come under public criticism.

If, like other instances of networked governance, Australian federalism experiences a clear deficit in terms of top-down vertical accountability, does it exhibit any of the other aspects of accountability found in networks? In the first place, joint policies involving both levels of government are certainly subject to horizontal accountability through public investigation in the media, which increases the transparency of such policies. Although some sections of the media, notably gallery journalists observing both levels of government, tend to concentrate on the actions of ministers and other politicians in one particular parliament, other sections of the media specialising in distinct policy areas, such as agriculture, industry or health, pursue particular policy outcomes across jurisdictional boundaries. Thus, media stories on irrigation in the Murray–Darling Basin cover the combined contributions of federal and state governments to the problem. Accounts of government responses to the impending closure of General

Motors' Holden factories in Victoria and South Australia referred to the intended input from both levels of government. Reporting of contentious issues often includes reference to the mutual recrimination between governments, providing continuing evidence of the notorious blame game and drawing attention to the lack of overall political responsibility. Such media exposure certainly increases transparency by giving publicity to joint government activities.

Second, Australian federalism provides a leading example of how the pluralistic nature of networked governance can open the processes of governing to wider scrutiny. The duplication of top-down vertical Westminster-style governments involved in joint programs may facilitate buck-passing and blame-shifting. But it also provides parallel sets of accountability institutions and processes, such as parliamentary inquiry and freedom of information legislation, that offer more points of contact between governments and the wider public, particularly for well-resourced and politically sophisticated interest groups and other stakeholders (Galligan 1995: Chpt. 1). Major interest groups, such as the Australian Medical Association or the National Farmers' Federation and its constituent organisations, have close relationships with both Commonwealth and state and territory bureaucracies and are able to gain access to a wide range of government information. In the discussions over proposed changes to the environmental assessment of development projects, involving both the Queensland and federal governments, environmental groups were able to put questions to both state and federal environment ministers and departments, thus widening public discussion of a contentious issue.

Third, Australian federalism, like other federal systems, may encourage bottom-up accountability by networks of committed professionals answering directly to local communities. Such networks are certainly found in service areas such as social and employment assistance, involving members of Commonwealth and state and territory governments, as well as local governments. Indigenous affairs, in particular, provides frequent examples of frontline administrators cooperating across institutional boundaries to serve local communities (O'Flynn et al. 2011; see also *Jarvie and Stewart*).

Such bottom-up accountability of professional networks is not confined to federations and can also be found in unitary systems (Hupe and Hill 2007). Federalism, through its constitutional division of powers and overlapping responsibilities, however, provides more opportunities for administrative discretion by frontline officials dealing with a greater range of different government agencies. It is not coincidental that theories of street-level administration and bottom-up accountability have been particularly influential in the United Sates, a federation with notably divided powers (e.g. Lipsky 1980; Agranoff 2007; 2012).

Fourth, Australian federalism has attempted to use performance reporting as a means of increasing accountability for joint Commonwealth–state and territory programs. First steps in this direction were taken by the annual reports on government services, which were introduced in the 1980s and coordinated by the Productivity Commission. But the COAG reforms that began in 2009 took the process much further. The new system has a number of foundations, beginning with the Intergovernmental Agreement on Federal Financial Relations (2008–09), the *Federal Financial Relations Act 2009* and an expanded role for the COAG Reform Council (established in 2006, since abolished in 2014) (O'Loughlin 2013).

Two main types of agreement have been associated with funding grants from the federal government. One type is national agreements, which deal with broad service sectors such as education, affordable housing, health care and Indigenous reform. Each national agreement sets out the agreed general objectives for the policy area as well as various outcomes, outputs and targets that contribute to these objectives. It then outlines the roles and responsibilities of the respective governments, including roles and responsibilities shared by both levels of government as well as those distinct to each level considered separately. Each agreement also stipulates mutually agreed performance indicators and benchmarks that can be used to assess governments' progress towards the agreed outcomes. The COAG Reform Council then reported publicly on the performance data received from each government, making comparisons and pointing out opportunities for improvement.

The national agreement system has certainly increased the level of public information about government performance in key areas of overlapping responsibilities. Both federal and state and territory governments are therefore more accountable in the sense of improving the public transparency of their achievements. On the other hand, like similar schemes in other federal systems, such as the United States (Radin 2006) and Canada (Anderson and Findlay 2010), the COAG reporting system did not meet all the hoped-for goals of its advocates.

One common problem is difficulty in collecting and collating comparable data. Though the COAG Reform Council exerted major efforts over the years into improving the quality and consistency of data, reported performance information still suffers from inconsistency because of the different priorities and incompatible administrative practices of different participating governments.

The adoption of performance reporting in networked governance assumes agreement between the partners on common objectives that can then be reported against as a measure of the network's joint success. In federations, however, such uniformity of purpose is not always forthcoming. The national agreements recognise this reality by allowing for some policy differences between individual states and territories and by tolerating a certain divergence in priorities. Such divergence, however, tends to undermine the attempt to use performance reporting as a mechanism of joint accountability. For this reason, the COAG Reform Council tended to adopt a unifying stance, placing its emphasis on common objectives and agreed measures.

In theory, COAG is a creature of all participating governments and stands in an equal relation to each one as it coordinates joint performance towards mutually agreed goals. In practice, however, COAG is driven by the Commonwealth Government and can easily be viewed by the states and territories as another instrument of Commonwealth control, more a centralising than a coordinating body. The Commonwealth is the main funder of services under the national agreements, while the states and territories are the main service providers and the main suppliers of performance data. Although the agreements talk the language of equality and consensus, the underlying reality is closer to that of purchaser and provider or principal and agent, a fundamentally unequal relationship that is associated more with vertical accountability.

A principal–agent approach is even more explicit in reporting for the other type of agreement under the 2008–09 intergovernmental arrangements, the national 'partnerships' (an Orwellian coinage, given that the partnerships are, in fact, less like genuine partnerships than the agreements). The partnerships have a similar structure of national policy objectives, defined outputs and performance benchmarks, but they differ from the agreements in that funds are located for specific activities or projects agreed to by each state or territory. In some cases the Commonwealth also offers reward payments on the basis of reported performance. In effect, the Commonwealth has used its funding power to forcibly impose a form of performance management on the states and territories in line with what is considered international best practice (Bouckaert and Halligan 2008).

In so far as the COAG reporting system is perceived as making separate states and territories individually more accountable for the performance of federally funded and defined services, it does not count as a form of genuine accountability for shared outcomes in networked governance. It is more akin to improving the accountability of states and territories to the Commonwealth as agents to principals, leaving the prime responsibility for the direction of policy with the Commonwealth. Alternatively, the states and territories are being treated as independent governments separately responsible for their own policies. For example, one of the benefits of the new reporting system claimed by COAG is that the system provides individual states and territories with measures of each other's performance, thus offering them benchmarks and encouraging a process of administrative learning. In either case, whether states and territories are seen as agents or independent governments, the background assumptions are coordinate rather than concurrent. Accountability is, therefore, allocated to one particular level, not shared between levels.

The lack of shared commitment to joint objectives may help to explain the general lack of interest in acting on the basis of performance information. As the former chairman of the COAG Reform Council, Paul McClintock, frequently complained (e.g. McClintock 2012), when the reports have been published they attract little public or political attention, which is a common feature of performance measurement reporting systems in general (Pollitt and Bouckaert 2011: 109). McClintock was particularly disappointed in the lack of political response to reports on progress towards national agreements. In contrast to successfully functioning networks, where partners willingly cooperate in imposing remedies and improvements, the general COAG experience has been that partner governments either ignore information of poor performance or else revert to the accustomed game of mutual recrimination. In this respect, the aim of eliminating, or even curtailing, the blame game, as championed by the COAG Reform Council, must be judged a failure.

On occasion, cooperative interaction across jurisdictional boundaries can support a form of performance reporting that is much closer to the networked governance model of accountability. For example, the National

Mental Health Commission was established by the Commonwealth Government in response to lobbying by mental health experts and consumer groups. It is made up of experts and consumer advocates in the field of mental health and collects and publishes information, both quantitative and qualitative, relevant to mental health provision in the different jurisdictions (Smullen 2016). Different mental health bureaucracies and institutions voluntarily contribute data and then make use of the joint information in decision-making. In this case, the members of the network are motivated by genuinely shared values and willingly embrace public accountability as a means of improving their individual and collective performance. The extent of voluntary cooperation, however, serves to highlight the contrast with other COAG-based agreements where the state and territory governments reluctantly acceded to performance regimes as the price of receiving Commonwealth funding.

Discussion

Overall, then, Australian federalism does exhibit some of the features of public accountability associated with networked governance. The extent of such accountability gains, however, does not appear to outweigh the undoubted deficits due to the lack of unified top-down control and external scrutiny. Such judgments, relying on patchy evidence and subjective impressions, are inevitably complex and contestable. But Australian federalism conforms to the general pattern that networked arrangements suffer from deficiencies in external accountability.

In this case, does Australian federalism display any of the countervailing features that are sometimes claimed to compensate for any deficit in external accountability in networked governance? For instance, does the networking between governments and government officials display a sufficiently high level of shared commitment to the public interest that would reduce the need to exercise external scrutiny? Can cooperating politicians and public servants in different jurisdictions be trusted to serve the public with as much dedication as, say, groups of social workers belonging to non-profit charities and government welfare agencies?

Again, the relationships between governments are too complex and disparate to allow any firm conclusions. In favour of a more optimistic view, we could point to the large body of uncontroversial, routine business regularly conducted between politicians and bureaucrats from different governments. A great deal of mutual cooperation occurs between members of the different governments, particularly among bureaucrats and professionals, either through the formal process of the ministerial councils and the officials' committees that support them, or informally through the regular interactions between opposite numbers in different bureaucracies. For the most part, cooperative relationships across jurisdictional boundaries operate informally and confidentially without being subject to public scrutiny. They may involve internal accountability between the respective partners as they question each other on relevant issues (Painter 1996) but they are typically not open to public view.

That much of this activity escapes public attention (and the interest of academics) is plausible *prima facie* evidence that it leads to outcomes that are generally welcome to the various sections of the public affected. These areas of genuine cooperation provide scope for the positive virtues of networks and partnerships, such as shared values and mutual trust. The fact that these aspects of federalism are largely unreported should not be allowed to minimise either their extent or their significance.

On the other hand, like other federations, Australian federalism provides ample opportunity for conflict between different levels of government. Relations between the respective governments of the Commonwealth and the states and territories are often marked more by self-interested competition and mutual suspicion than by trust and cooperation (Painter 1998: Chpt. 3). Open conflict with the Commonwealth is a perennial vote-winner for state and territory politicians, while their respective bureaucracies harbour entrenched antagonisms with their opposite numbers in the Commonwealth Government. Joint institutions, such as COAG leaders' meetings, are a site for political grandstanding and the self-interested pursuit of domestic advantage as much as for genuine interchange and cooperation.

This uncertainty over the respective extent of cooperation and conflict reflects the well-documented pragmatism that underlies Australian federalism (Hollander and Patapan 2007; Carroll and Head 2010). Intergovernmental relations are characterised by flexibility and the *ad hoc* use of institutions to suit current political imperatives without any strong commitment to constitutional federal principles. These imperatives, in turn, are set by the shifting agendas of federal governments, particularly prime ministers, as well as those of the state and territory governments.

It is to be expected, therefore, that patterns of interaction will adjust accordingly, displaying cooperation or conflict as the political dynamics demand.

Conclusions

In summary, federalism involves a clear deficit in terms of top-down accountability while offering certain accountability benefits through a higher number of points of access and potential for mutual scrutiny. Single-level government, conversely, can offer the advantages of top-down control and rectification, though at the cost of making government less transparent and less open to public questioning. Responses to these acknowledged differences in accountability structure vary according to the weight given to the different accountability mechanisms and also the value placed on decentred forms of governance and the institutional checks and balances they impose.

For some, the restrictions to top-down vertical accountability amount to a serious and insuperable accountability deficit in MLG and networks generally, when compared with single hierarchies (Rhodes 2006; Michels and Meijer 2008). Because these structures do not offer a single point of control, no one person or body is obliged to take ownership and responsibility of policy and programs and to impose remedies for failure. MLG provides opportunities for buck-passing and blame-shifting that can frustrate the public's demand for answers and solutions.

The demand for clear, hierarchical accountability has particular resonance in Westminster-style jurisdictions such as Australia, with their strong traditions of ministerial authority and responsibility. Criticisms of federalism centre on the alleged unaccountability of shared responsibility. By the same token, attempts to reform Australian federalism, whether by Commonwealth takeover of hospital services or by performance-based reward payments, are aimed at reducing the extent of shared responsibility by centralising control in Canberra. Calls to reduce vertical fiscal imbalance and restore more taxing power to states and territories are similarly driven by a preference for a single point of responsibility and accountability. Few voices are heard for the virtues of dispersed responsibility and cooperation.

The appeal of single-point vertical accountability, however, while strong in Westminster-style jurisdictions, carries less weight in other institutional systems that do not offer such an effective method of political accountability through elected leaders. In the United States, for example, the separation of powers and a more devolved bureaucratic structure mean that accountability through elected leaders is merely one of many external pressures facing government officials and is far from being the dominant relationship that it is for public servants in Westminster-style systems (Rhodes and Wanna 2009). Under such a system, more weight is likely to be given to the virtues of divided authority and multiple channels of accountability (Radin 2002). In Australia, too, liberal constitutionalists who value the checks and balances of federalism are more likely to emphasise the accountability gains that federalism offers (Galligan 1995). But theirs is a minority view. For the most part, Australians appear to prefer a structure that clearly allocates responsibility and accountability to a single level of government.

References

Agranoff, R. (2007). *Managing within Networks: Adding Value to Public Organisations*. Georgetown University Press, Washington.

——. (2012). *Collaborating to Manage*. Georgetown University Press, Washington.

Agranoff, R. & McGuire, M. (2001). Big Questions in Public Network Management Research. *Journal of Public Administration Research and Theory*, 11(3): 295–326. doi.org/10.1093/oxfordjournals.jpart. a003504

ANAO (Australian National Audit Office) (2010a). *Home Insulation Program*. Report 12, ANAO, Canberra, www.anao.gov.au/ Publications/Audit-Reports [Accessed: 12/12/14].

——. (2010b). *Building the Education Revolution*. Report 33, ANAO, Canberra, www.anao.gov.au/Publications/Audit-Reports [Accessed: 12/12/14].

Anderson, L. & Findlay, T. (2010). Does Public Reporting Measure Up? Federalism, Accountability and Child-care Policy in Canada. *Canadian Public Administration*, 53(3): 417–38. doi.org/10.1111/j.1754-7121.2010.00136.x

Bogason, P. & Musso, J. (2006). The Democratic Prospects of Network Governance. *American Review of Public Administration*, 36(1): 3–18. doi.org/10.1177/0275074005282581

Bouckaert, G. & Halligan, J. (2008). *Managing of Performance. International Comparisons*. Routledge/Taylor and Francis, London.

Bovens, M. (2007). Analysing and Assessing Accountability: A conceptual framework. *European Law Journal*, 13(4): 447–68. doi.org/10.1111/j.1468-0386.2007.00378.x

Bovens, M., Schillemans, T. & Goodin, R.E. (2014). Public Accountability. In: Bovens, M., Goodin, R.E. & Schillemans, T. (eds) *The Oxford Handbook of Public Accountability*. Oxford University Press. doi.org/10.1093/oxfordhb/9780199641253.013.0012

Carroll, P. & Head, B. (2010). Regulatory Reform and the Management of Intergovernmental Relations in Australia. *Australian Journal of Political Science*, 45(3): 407–24. doi.org/10.1080/10361146.2010.509310

Considine, M. (2002). The End of the Line? Accountable Governance in the Age of Networks, Partnerships, and Joined-Up Services. *Governance*, 15(1): 21–40. doi.org/10.1111/1468-0491.00178

Galligan, B. (1995). *A Federal Republic*. Cambridge University Press. doi.org/10.1017/CBO9781139084932

Goodin, R.E. (2003). Democratic Accountability: the distinctiveness of the third sector. *Archives Européennes de Sociologie*, 44(3): 359–96.

Griffith University (2014). *Australian Constitutional Values Survey 2014*. Centre for Governance and Public Policy, www.griffith.edu.au/__data/assets/pdf_file/0015/653100/Constitutional-Values-Survey-Oct-2014Results-2.pdf [Accessed: 19/10/17].

Hendriks, C.M. (2009). The Democratic Soup: mixed meanings of political representation in governance networks. *Governance*, 22(4): 689–715. doi.org/10.1111/j.1468-0491.2009.01459.x

Hollander, R. & Patapan, H. (2007). Pragmatic Federalism: Australian federalism from Hawke to Howard. *Australian Journal of Public Administration*, 66(3): 280–97. doi.org/10.1111/j.1467-8500.2007.00542.x

Hupe, P. & Hill, M. (2007). Street-Level Bureaucracy and Public Accountability. *Public Administration*, 85(2): 279–99. doi.org/10.1111/j.1467-9299.2007.00650.x

Lipsky, M. (1980). *Street-Level Bureaucracy: Dilemmas of the Individual in the Public Services*. Russell Sage Foundation, New York.

McClintock, P. (2012). Harnessing Federalism: The Missing Key to Successful Reform. Sir Roland Wilson Lecture. Crawford School of Public Policy, Canberra, crawford.anu.edu.au/news-events/news/200/harnessing-federalism-missing-key-successful-reform [Accessed: 12/12/14].

Michels, A. & Meijer, A. (2008). Safeguarding Public Accountability in Horizontal Government. *Public Management Review*, 10(2): 165–73. doi.org/10.1080/14719030801928490

Mulgan, R. (2000). 'Accountability': An Ever-Expanding Concept? *Public Administration*, 78(3): 555–73. doi.org/10.1111/1467-9299.00218

——. (2003). *Holding Power to Account*. Palgrave Macmillan, Basingstoke. doi.org/10.1057/9781403943835

——. (2012). Assessing Ministerial Responsibility in Australia. In: Dowding, K. & Lewis, C. (eds) *Ministerial Careers and Accountability in the Australian Commonwealth Government*. ANU E Press, Canberra, pp. 177–93.

——. (2014). Accountability Deficits. In: Bovens, M., Goodin, R.E. & Schillemans, T. (eds) *The Oxford Handbook of Public Accountability*. Oxford University Press.

O'Flynn, J., Buick, F., Blackman, D. & Halligan, J. (2011). You Win Some, You Lose Some: experiments with joined-up government. *International Journal of Public Administration*, 34(4): 244–54. doi.org/10.1080/01900692.2010.540703

O'Loughlin, M.A. (2013). Accountability and Reforms to Australia's Federal Financial Relations. *Australian Journal of Public Administration*, 72(3): 376–81. doi.org/10.1111/1467-8500.12035

Painter, M. (1996). Federal Theory and Executive Federalism. In: Halligan, J. (ed.) *Public Administration under Scrutiny.* Centre for Research in Public Sector Management, University of Canberra, pp. 77–96.

——. (1998). *Collaborative Federalism.* Cambridge University Press. doi.org/10.1017/CBO9780511552236

Papadopoulos, Y. (2007). Problems of Democratic Accountability in Network and Multilevel Governance. *European Law Journal*, 13(4): 469–86. doi.org/10.1111/j.1468-0386.2007.00379.x

Pollitt, C. & Bouckaert, G. (2011). *Public Sector Reform.* 3rd edn. Oxford University Press.

Pollitt, C. & Hupe, P. (2011). Talking about Government: The Role of Magic Concepts. *Public Management Review*, 13(5): 641–58. doi.org/10.1080/14719037.2010.532963

Radin, B. (2002). *The Accountable Juggler. The Art of Leadership in a Federal Agency.* CQ Press, Washington. doi.org/10.4135/9781483345215

——. (2006). *Challenging the Performance Movement: Accountability, Complexity and Democratic Values.* Georgetown University Press, Washington, DC.

Radin, B. & Romzek, B. (1996). Accountability Expectations in An Intergovernmental Arena: The National Rural Development Partnership. *Publius*, 26(2): 59–81. doi.org/10.1093/oxfordjournals. pubjof.a029855

Rhodes, R.A.W. (1997). *Understanding Governance: Public Networks, Governance, Reflexivity and Accountability.* Open University Press, Buckingham.

——. (2006). Policy Network Analysis. In: Moran, M., Rein, M. & Goodin, R.E. (eds) *The Oxford Handbook of Public Policy.* Oxford University Press, pp. 425–47.

Rhodes, R.A.W. & Wanna, J. (2009). Bringing the Politics Back In: public value in Westminster parliamentary government. *Public Administration*, 87(2): 161–83. doi.org/10.1111/j.1467-9299.2009.01763.x

Schillemans, T. (2008). Accountability in the Shadow of Hierarchy: the horizontal accountability of agencies. *Public Organization Review*, 8: 175–94. doi.org/10.1007/s11115-008-0053-8

——. (2011). Does Horizontal Accountability Work? Evaluating Potential Remedies for the Accountability Deficit of Agencies. *Administration and Society*, 43(4): 387–416. doi.org/10.1177/0095399711412931

Smullen, A. (2016). Not Centralisation but Decentralised Integration through Australia's National Mental Health Policy. *Australian Journal of Public Administration*, 75(3): 280–90. doi.org/10.1111/1467-8500.12153

Stoker, G. (2006). Public Value Management: A New Narrative for Networked Governance? *American Review of Public Administration*, 36: 41–57. doi.org/10.1177/0275074005282583

Weale, A. (2011). New Modes of Governance, Political Accountability and Public Reason. *Government and Opposition*, 46: 58–80. doi.org/10.1111/j.1477-7053.2010.01330.x

5

Multi-level Governmentality

Paul Dugdale

Introduction

The increased speed and reach of communication, together with the speed of personal travel and the number of people who can move around rapidly, have fundamentally changed the nature of territory and the government of populations within territories. The vast growth of governments' knowledge of each other's territory and society, and of each other's governing activities, has changed the nature of the interactions between them. For example, the possibilities for interaction between state and national governments in Australia have been radically transformed since federation.

This book focuses on the phenomenon whereby two or more governments with jurisdiction over the same population, at different levels (e.g. state and national government in a federation), actively cooperate in what has come to be called multi-level governance (MLG), where the various levels of governance are recognised as being more or less autonomous in their capacity for negotiating with stakeholders, making decisions and exercising power. The rise of MLG is salient for much of contemporary political theory; for example, theories of federalism, of international relations, of regionalism and of the empirical operation of democratic systems. This chapter considers MLG in relation to some current broader lines of political analysis to help understand the practical operation of

MLG arrangements and hopefully makes a contribution to understanding 'the character, causes, and consequences of multi-level governance' (Hooghe and Marks 2001: xii).

One of the consequences of MLG is that it expands the possibilities for governing and opens up new ways of governing, new things that can be governed and, consequently, new possibilities for imagining how and what to govern. The analysis of politics is not just concerned with who gets to govern; it is also concerned with how governing is done:

> the ways in which powers swarm through the territories of existence, flowing around circuits, through networks, devices, techniques ... power as it inheres in practices, calculations, strategies, tactics, technologies, relations, goals (Rose 2000: 142).

All enduring systems of governance see the development of a mentality of governing within their ambit. This mentality, or governmental rationality – what Michel Foucault has called governmentality – guides the imagination of actors, underlies the development of negotiating stances and is expressed in the shared understandings of what constitutes a problem to be addressed and what counts as a satisfactory solution to those problems. Foucault (2007) described the emergence of a governmentality in modern European states with an historical focus on the decades surrounding the French Revolution. This governmentality was, he argued, principally concerned with creating and operating administrative technologies that conjoined the security, territory and population problems they faced. These technologies of governmental power drew upon the techniques of pastoral care developed by the church, of financing and trade developed by the mercantilists, of violence by the military and of urban regulation developed by the bourgeoisie, and brought them together into the nascent assemblage of contemporary state government.

My task in this chapter is to take the basic concept of governmentality and apply it to the MLG arrangements that have emerged in Australia in the last few decades. The discussion here on multi-level governmentality begins with a consideration of the context of Australian federalism and the issues currently facing this when considered as a governmental assemblage. A specific governmental problem is the over-reliance on simple systems thinking in policy development and implementation, a hangover from the welfarist governmentality that emerged in the post-World War II period. However, in MLG, systematic approaches to implementation give way to continual negotiation as the dominant rationality and this has an effect on how federal governance is now conducted. This discussion is followed by a look at the pros and cons of the democratic deficit that has been identified as part of the character of MLG, and a discussion of the culture of MLG, particularly the development and impact of trust in the somewhat artificial and often corporatised arenas constructed for such governance. I conclude by sketching how Nicholas Rose's (1999) approach to understanding the neoliberal turn in governmental innovation over the last 20 years can be used to open up a fine-grained analysis of multi-level governmental arenas that recognises the way freedom from the unitary political rationality of single-level governmental systems allows these arenas to creatively generate new spheres of social action.

Multi-level government in the Australian federation

Hooghe and Marks (2001: xii) note, somewhat surprisingly, that in Europe, 'no policy area is more centralized at the national level in the year 2000 than in 1950, nor is there a single country in which regional governance has become weaker over the same period'. The latter also appears to be the case in Australia. Australia's federal constitution and the energetic regionalisation of administration by national and provincial governments over the last 30 years make for a wealth of interesting case study material on regional governance. Arguably, a self-aware and distinctive culture of MLG has been able to emerge in Australia. This is evident in the possibilities that are now being imagined in a wide variety of policy domains and can be seen in practice, as the case studies in this volume show. MLG, as a governmental technology that at its core moves functions and authority across jurisdictions (*Kay*), is now indispensable in fields where functions and authority overlap in Australia's federal system, such as health, education, corporate law and natural resource management.

MLG in Australia has expanded at the same time as there has been a shift from cooperative to integrated federalism (Fenna 2009; *Kay*). Cooperative federalism, namely intergovernmental cooperation through sharing out command-and-control functions in jointly designed programs of government, is still alive and well in the current Council of Australian Governments (COAG) arrangements. But it has been supplemented by more fluid and integrated schemes of networked governance, through which authorities with various heads of power continually negotiate their actions, ideally in a data-rich environment with multiple lines of public accountability. Corporate and trade practices regulation, regional resource management and health service quality improvement are all examples of this, and all have been developed through the multi-level arrangements of COAG.

Australia is prone to a burgeoning of government-sponsored corporate entities, either established by statute (federal or state), as wholly government-owned companies, or as not-for-profit companies established according to requirements published by governments with the mission of holding and executing government contracts. These quasi-autonomous non-government organisations may be explicitly formed to conduct MLG. Consider three examples from the health sector, the first two of which have roles in regional governance. In New South Wales, local health network governing councils have been established by state government statute in accordance with a COAG agreement, and are responsible for governing hospital network services that receive funding from both the state and federal governments. Even more innovative are the Primary Care Networks, private not-for-profit companies with self-sustaining boards that won government tenders – let as part of an intergovernmental agreement between the federal and state governments – to provide local governance of primary health care.

The third example relates to technical rather than regional governance. The National E-Health Transition Authority was established in 2005 as a company limited by shares, owned by all of Australia's health departments – 50 per cent Commonwealth and 50 per cent shared between the states – and whose board comprised most of the heads of those departments (bound under corporations law to act in the best interest of the company, not their respective governments) along with several independent directors. Its principal mission was to develop data and interoperability standards in information and communication technology for the health sector. It was superseded by a statutory Commonwealth agency in 2016.

All of these organisations are constituted by both state and national levels of government. They each include stakeholders from civil society and are charged with what effectively amounts to participating in continuous negotiations in the development of hospital services networks, primary health care coordination and e-health technology platforms respectively.

Part of the background for this recent burgeoning of MLG agencies was the adoption of the report reviewing the corporate governance of statutory authorities and office holders (Uhrig 2003). In particular, this has clarified that statutory authorities that receive the majority of their income from government are operated in accordance with the *Financial Management and Accountability Act 1997*, and those that earn most of their income from non-government sources are operated in accordance with the *Commonwealth Authorities and Companies Act 1997*. This regularised the governance and accountability of the field and, while it has led to many complaints by members of various authorities, it has produced certainty and consensus in the basic technical aspects of establishing such bodies.

Concurrently, the Australian Institute of Company Directors has embraced members of statutory authorities and non-government organisations in their fellowship, and has included consideration of their duties and conduct in the excellent guideline development and training work they engage in for their membership. While it may be going too far to say this is producing a convergence between private, non-government organisation and public sector governance, it has deepened the practical understanding of governance across these sectors and between the levels of government in Australia.

Beyond systems thinking

The development of a multi-level governmental rationality in Australia has taken place against a background of a broader evolution in the mentality of government since World War II. British sociologist Nicholas Rose and colleagues have described the evolution from a welfarist to a neoliberal mode of government amongst Western states (including Australia and New Zealand) in the second half of the 20th century. In World War II, government-directed command-and-control–based enterprises invaded every aspect of civilian activity. The following peace gave a major fillip to the power vested in the governments of wealthy nation states, manifested in a continued elaboration of state activity in a wide variety of social sectors. The state command–and–control technologies that developed during the world wars of the first half of the 20th century were applied to the postwar programs of social security and civic-infrastructure development.

The postwar form of government conducted by direct rule through state-run operations continued until the 1970s and has been described by Rose and colleagues as welfare statism (Miller and Rose 1990; see also Dean 1999). This resulted in a big government assemblage of state-owned and operated school systems, hospital systems, pension schemes, telecommunications systems, domestic and international transport systems, and energy production and distribution. Welfarist governmentality was deeply concerned with social engineering (Rose 1999) and its administration was largely done within the public sector and dominated by systems thinking.

Systems thinking is a pervasive metaphor in the mentality of program delivery. Having come through its broad development in engineering, biology and sociology from the 19th century, systems thinking is now strongly built into business administration, management accounting, political theory and sociology, among many other fields. It provides a ready shorthand for understanding the complex interplay between politicians, legislation, statutory agencies and the various stakeholders and contractors involved in regulation and welfare program delivery. One issue to be aware of in coming to understand MLG is the limit of traditional systems thinking. In the single level of government programs, systems thinking is plainly useful, even for interdepartmental programs. For intergovernmental programs – particularly those with multiple or contested objectives – the metaphor of the simple system can be more of a hindrance than a help. Some programs are, of course, almost ungovernable, but let us set that aside. The programs I have in mind are ones that are unengineerable. These can be governed, but not so as to deliver on an *a priori* or transcendental plan. Objectives need to evolve, relationships and alliances need to be crafted, and clientele need to be acquired, perhaps with an entrepreneurial spirit (e.g. see Ison et al. (2011) for a case study on water catchment management). This is public sector business development, with its attendant politics. Governance needs to engage politically in a way that is a far cry from a simplistic management by objectives approach often seen in policy implementation since the adoption of managerialism by the Australian Public Service in the 1980s (Dugdale 1993).

It could be argued that this kind of governance can be understood as the design of an interrelated set of self-steering systems (e.g. see Luhman 1985), of circuits in a complex social self-steering system (Parsons 1977), or as natural implementations of Ulrich's critical systems theory (Reynolds and Holwell 2010). While I would not disagree, such a conception is rarely held by the actors who are themselves involved. MLG is less about engineered systems and is more akin to institution building (e.g. see Goodin 1996). This has a different imagery from the ideas of social engineering that pervaded the collective imagination of welfare program designers in the post–World War II era (Rose 1999).

How does MLG figure in the shift from traditionally engineered systems thinking toward a practice of governance as negotiation? The distinctiveness of governance through multi-level mechanisms shows in agenda-setting, decision-making and implementation. Hooghe and Marks's (2001) analysis of MLG in Europe offers a specifically *political* analysis. They consider the politics, the manoeuvring, the location, operation and shifts of power, the alliances, the clash of interest and the formation of consensus for action in the evolving multi-level polity of late 20th/early 21st-century Europe. They describe the field of 'comitology' (Hooghe and Marks 2001: 24) – that is the field of knowledge concerning the design and operation of committees – an activity that is central to the creation of administrative power. The term was coined in relation to the work of the European Commission; however, we could consider that all senior bureaucrats in any jurisdiction are familiar with, and many consider they are somewhat expert in, the design and operation of the committee structures created by governments.

Committees may be created by statute or administrative fiat, they may have more or less vague terms of reference, and they often occur in complex concatenated chains of councils, committees and subcommittees with lateral and vertical lines of communication. Their membership may be more or less broad, and may span levels from ministers to managers, technocrats to consumers, lobbyists to business leaders. Hooghe and Marks note that in Europe:

> Comitology was designed to allow national governments to monitor the [European] Commission, but it has had the additional, and unintended, consequence of deepening subnational and group participation in the European political process (Hooghe and Marks 2001: 25).

This spans policy work from agenda-setting to decision-making and implementation. The committees form a:

> tree like structure … just about everywhere it institutionalises some form of direct contact between the Commission and subnational governments. Such links break open the mould of the state, so that multi-level governance encompasses actors beneath, as well as above, central states (Hooghe and Marks 2001: 25).

In Australia, supra-national governing bodies have, as yet, far less influence than in Europe. But at the infra-national level, Australian governments are taking an increasing interest in regional Australia – there has been a Commonwealth department with 'regional' in its title since 1993. Daniell et al. (2010) have shown how co-engineering processes in European and Australian water management involving multi-level policy and implementation forums use negotiation to turn a diversity of objectives into new opportunities and strategies. In another example noted above, local hospital network boards have been created at the regional level as part of the COAG national health reforms agreed to in 2011 to end the 'blame game' of states and the Commonwealth governments blaming each other for shortcomings in local health systems (Veronesi et al. 2014).

MLG, democratic ideals and trust

I will now look at the democratic character of MLG by considering its relations to the negative and positive connotations inherent in the idea of the democratic deficit. A case can be made both in favour and against MLG in relation to the ideals of democracy. It both suffers from and can work to overcome a democratic deficit, in which the institutions of government fail to satisfy democratic standards of accountability and legitimacy (Hindess 2002: 30). Like MLG, the term 'democratic deficit' was first used over 20 years ago in relation to the European Union (EU) as a result of the transfer of powers from the exercise of democratic member states to be exercised by the institutions of the EU, recognising that there was no EU-wide enfranchisement. It has since been applied to many different institutional arrangements, including intra-national federalist arrangements.

In general, a democratic deficit is seen as a negative thing, a problem to at least be recognised and preferably minimised. Against this pejorative use of the term, Hindess notes that classical analyses of the various forms of government identify democracy as prone to corruption (in its wide sense) by populism, and make the case for the institutional design in any notional democracy to reduce the influence of the populace on government:

> the conventional case in favour of democratic deficit reflects a more general concern to defend the proper work [of] government against corruption (Hindess 2002: 31).

This is at the heart of representative government, whereby there is democratic selection of representatives, who then govern in a system that ensures 'the total exclusion of the people, in their collective form' from the work of government (James Madison in 'The Federalist Papers' of 1788, quoted in Hindess 2002: 32). Since the time of 'The Federalist Papers', the term 'democratic government' has come to be understood as incorporating mechanisms of representation that buttress it against populist vices.

The creation of multi-level committees, agencies and companies for involvement in policy development and program implementation may be a positive strategy for good governance by responding to demands for more democracy outside the mechanisms based on voting for representatives. Let us examine this by considering approaches to citizen engagement in policymaking.

MLG can harness and channel the participation of the public in consultative and even deliberative activities within specific fields. Often, citizen engagement is a natural fit and the design of such participation can be more readily shaped to the contours of the governance task at hand than consultations organised by single levels of government (e.g. see Daniell et al. 2010). The latter face the pull of electoral pressures for any forthcoming electoral contest, or the push to secure the cooperation and gratitude of program beneficiaries, and the public consultations may be constrained because of these pressures. In MLG forums, however, the inclusion of participants from civil society – usually representing particular sectional interests rather than as individual citizens – can be seen by each government involved as a potential ally in the negotiations that are expected to come up.

The nature of the populace is itself constantly evolving. Stehr and Ericson (2000: 16) have noted:

> the growing volume of knowledge that is individually and collectively available not only is a constitutive factor of knowledge societies, but also plays a decisive role in the governance of present-day society.

It may be that the more knowledgeable the populace is, the less dangerous it is to good governance. Community engagement may increase the range of interests that need to be integrated and slow down decision-making in the formation of objectives and the arrangement of cooperative action. Increased participation can also, however, increase the legitimacy of the specific governmental activity that sponsors it. The increasing levels of education and access to knowledge of contemporary citizens are expanding the nuanced range of consultative possibilities available to the institutional participants in MLG, unconstrained by the narrow channels for influencing the makeup of democratic representation.

The rules of engagement – the concrete forms that the exercising of power takes – are different in MLG. In single-level government by representational democracy, the great contest of representational elections is confined to a brief period. The politics of representational democracy brings the representation of atomised personal interest to the fore in the hip-pocket politics of the electoral cycle. Notwithstanding the activities of a commentariat led by the media and opinion pollsters, elections are followed by years of cabinet government executed through performance-managed chains of authority in a hierarchical bureaucracy. The politics of interest group representation through lobbying and the media, and the search for consensual public support among the polity, bring sectional interests into the mix. MLG increases pressure for continual negotiation and fluidity of goal-setting that may intensify policy innovation and, with sufficient trust among the participants, can spur the creative development of win-win schemes for collaboration, or mutual advantage through compromise.

Fukuyama proposes that the level of trust in a culture determines its productivity:

> Past a certain point, the proliferation of rules to regulate wider and wider sets of social relationships becomes not the hallmark of rational efficiency but a sign of social dysfunction. There is usually an inverse relationship between rules and trust: the more people depend on rules to regulate their interactions, the less they trust each other, and vice versa (1995: 224).

Fukuyama contends that this is as true in relation to the nation-state as it is in the firm. Is it possible that MLG arenas, being outside the disciplines of single governmental administrations, are less rule-bound, and so potentially more productive?

Fukuyama, plausibly enough, argues that cooperation underpinned by trust drives productivity, and that governance, as the arrangement of cooperation, benefits from a culture of justified trust. Trust is a subjective measure of risk perception in social relationships. How do we build and justify trust in the business of governing? Fukuyama's answer draws a parallel between business and government:

The same propensity for spontaneous sociability that is key to building durable businesses is also indispensable for putting together effective political organizations (1995: 357).

But perhaps, in public policy terms, productive trust can be generated through the creation of accurate, relevant data on what we are interested in, coupled with transparent and intelligible decision-making. If these features are not present, trust can still be built on personal (and tribal) relationships and ideological alignment, but it is likely to be less productive and more fragile.

Multi-level neoliberalism

Foucault's analysis of liberal governmentality (Foucault 2007) has underpinned a flourish of political and social analysis over the last 20 years in Australia (Dean and Hindess 1998), the United Kingdom (Burchell et al. 1991) and elsewhere. Authors in the United Kingdom (such as Nicholas Rose, Peter Miller, Michael Power and Richard Osborne) and Australia (Barry Hindess and Mitchell Dean) have produced a powerful analysis of neoliberalism that considers how key social actors think about governing the conduct of the population for the purposes of social security, including its welfare, health and sustainability.

The welfarist mode of government of the post–World War II period became unstable in the 1970s as the population grew to be radically disenchanted with the increasingly narcissistic administrative apparatuses of state services (Offe 1984; Papadakis and Taylor-Gooby 1987), which was perhaps a manifestation of the phenomena of reduced trust following an intrusive proliferation of rules. The 1970s oil shocks – causing significant instability in oil prices and knock-on economic impacts – showed the potential instability of the economy and called into question the fiscal policies of big government upon which the welfarist mode of government relied. This opened the way for the neoliberal turn of the 1980s in the governments of Bob Hawke and Paul Keating in Australia, Ronald Reagan in the United States, Margaret Thatcher in the United Kingdom, and David Lange and Roger Douglas in New Zealand (popularly referred to as 'Reaganomics', 'Thatcherism' and 'Rogernomics'). This period saw the rhetoric, if not the actuality, of a drive to smaller government, combined with an expansion of the use of market-like mechanisms for the governance of public sector endeavour and the rise of government through commercial contracts. These governments called for deregulation and favoured light-touch regulatory systems designed along classical liberal lines that empowered more or less well-delineated spheres of civil society to be self-governing, and resulted in the creation of spheres of mixed state and non-state actors working on governance together. In Australia, the Commonwealth called on the states to join the neoliberal push to deregulate private sector market activity, to sell state government assets to the private sector and to use market mechanisms in novel ways.

Initially, there was a burgeoning of enthusiasm for contract-based purchaser–provider arrangements. Drawing on principal–agent theory (for a discussion see Broadbent et al. 1996), the idea was that because agents – suppliers in a market model, or subordinates in a bureaucratic model of service provision – pursued their own interests, they could not be trusted to pursue the government's ends. To counteract this, they needed to be constrained by contractual obligations – either through a commercial contract or an employment contract linked to a performance agreement – that provided rewards for compliance or punishments for noncompliance with the government's wishes (Yeatman 1995). A recent example has been the Commonwealth's construction of incentives to reduce waiting lists for elective surgery through specific purpose payments to the states.

A major problem for the theory was that, in practice, the transaction costs of specifying the services and measuring performance often outweighed the financial benefit to government of doing business this way (Williamson 1996). In our waiting-list example, states made the effort to manage surgery waiting lists by any technique other than by doing more surgery – imposition of arbitrary rules for removing people from the waiting list, shifting the wait to a delay in the initial consult with the surgeon, and so on. The Commonwealth responded by ever more detailed monitoring and metrics for defining waiting lists. In the broad, these definitional and measurement issues were compounded by the loss of trust engendered by the principal–agent arrangements, and the low-trust relationships of the theory became a self-fulfilling prophecy (e.g. see Boston 1995 on New Zealand).

This led to a maturational evolution of neoliberalism rather than its demise. Trust has been recognised as necessary for effective government. Without it, governments cannot obtain legitimation through the articulation of what they see as the public interest. Trust is also central in an instrumental way to the implementation of government programs. The evolution of MLG arenas in the deepening integration of federal activities since the advent of neoliberalism has, at least over the last decade, been recognised as requiring high levels of trust in order for these arenas to optimise their performance, to avoid lowest common denominator decision-making and achieve highest common factor joint action. So what may be the preconditions and operating requirements for high trust MLG networks?

Taking the liberal conception of society as 'traversed by a variety of self-regulating domains of social interaction, that is, as substantially more than just an artefact of government' (Hindess 2000: 124), MLG creates nexuses of negotiation between various layers of government and the agencies of self-regulation within civil society. As well as the involvement of representative government interests, the population subject to MLG is also engaged through these civil structures. Where liberals imagined that the state should leave civil society to its own devices as much as possible, neoliberals imagine that various self-governing mechanisms (such as the interplay of supply, demand and price in a market) might be the most effective way to organise public sector activities. For example, in the 1980s cleaning government offices was tendered out to the market, followed soon after by selling the government buildings themselves and renting back the space.

Neoliberal governments may have embraced MLG not so much to cede power as to multiply and exercise it at a distance:

> Organizations, actors, and others that were once enmeshed in the complex and bureaucratic lines of force of the social state are to be set free to find their own destiny. Yet, at the same time, they are to be steered politically 'at a distance' through the invention and deployment of a whole range of new 'fidelity techniques' which can shape their actions while apparently enhancing their independence (Rose 2000: 158).

Provincial and national level governments can both do this simultaneously, seeking to harness the resources of the other to their own policy or political ends, on the assumption that an effective nexus of power can work for both of them. The appearance – which may turn out to be an actuality – of ceding power to the new governmental arena may in fact be a precondition for its success. Any electoral kudos generated by such success can then be claimed at a later date.

A dominant theme in the liberal and neoliberal governmental tradition has been the freedom of citizens. This has been expressed in two types of freedom: both a reluctance to curtail existing freedoms and in the creation of specific degrees of freedom within governmental programs

(Berlin 1958). In both its rhetoric and administrative practice, neoliberal governmentality has been principally concerned with coupling state power to the administration of freedom, and the freedom to choose within a market has been a guiding metaphor. As Berlin noted, however, there is a fundamental tension between liberty as an ideal of liberal governments and the actual reliance on control of the means of violence in the legislation, financing and administration of governmental programs. Much of the politicking by sectional interests around the development of specific government programs concerns the preservation of existing freedoms, or the creation of new possibilities for advancement of those interests within the constraints of the program (for a case study see 'Administering Freedom and the Politics of Medicare', Dugdale 2008: 121–28).

While MLG in Australia has also exhibited this concern for freedom, the multi-level context gives a different character to this concern. Because the governance is concerned with things at the intersection of, or in between, the jurisdiction of the different governments involved, the systems of control are often not as well developed. In a uni-governmental arena, such a vacuum would create a tendency to draw upon and elaborate existing powers to strengthen social control over the domain under consideration (Cohen 1985). In multi-level arenas, agents of each government tend to be wary of the expansion of the other government's constraining powers. It could be argued that this dynamic gives more play to the creative rather than constraining use of power. There may be greater interest in crafting policy solutions that create wider spheres of action for the sectional interests of concern to each government in the arena, but that do not expand the application of constraints from one or other government; for example, the construction of new spheres of free action rather than to the administration of freedoms within existing spheres. This creative drive from MLG may be intensified when combined with a high-trust environment, as discussed above.

In modern Western governments, statutory regulators have been actively discouraged from adopting an entrepreneurial mentality, perhaps as a backlash against earlier traditions of abuse by those with statutory power in the Renaissance city-states of Europe, where it was used for enterprising activities that were essentially standover tactics. MLG occurs between the domains of regulation that proliferate within specific governments and must solve problems of diffused authority and power. It can do this through the creation of new spheres for the coordination and regulation of particular fields of endeavour by engaging civil society rather than through the development of statutory regulators in one or other jurisdiction. Such engagement of civil society in the governance of specific activities expresses a traditional liberal orientation. It is also now common for MLG strategies to interweave public sector and civil activities in the neoliberal fashion. In comparison to hierarchical command-and-control–style governance, the MLG of a particular domain may facilitate consensus-building and agreement on practical objectives between the institutions and interests involved. Optimistically, this could nourish a more entrepreneurial style of governance where creation and sharing of information, mustering of resources and coordination of action are the order of the day.

Directions for further analysis

Rose proposes that analysing government can proceed by considering four domains: the regimes of intelligibility within which conduct is governed (i.e. what counts as an interesting policy question, or what would be recognised as a satisfactory policy solution, or what can be accepted as an illuminating data set); the social objects that are governed, or that are constituted in order to govern them; the technical practices of intervention applied to the objects governed; and the way power is exercised in, and shapes, these three things (Rose 2000: 144–47). MLG creates arenas where the activities of the participating governments in each of these domains intersect. If we examine these intersections, we would expect that sometimes national and state perspectives will be harmonious, but that often they will be at odds in one way or another. Let us briefly consider the sorts of interaction within each of these domains that could arise between Commonwealth and state government appointees to an MLG arena.

The regime of intelligibility at the national level of government may differ from that at the provincial level. Consider national data collections, such as those arranged by the Australian Institute of Health and Welfare, a Commonwealth Government–created, statutorily independent institute whose governing board includes Commonwealth, state and independent directors. The institute collects data from state-run services for national collections to allow accountability for Commonwealth-funded programs, performance benchmarking between states, and research by governments, universities and private companies. Consistent definitions across states for each data collection meet a federal objective of highlighting the equity, or lack of it, between regions, but has in some cases been opposed by the provinces with poorer performance that to date has not been a political issue for them.

Achieving consistency in definitions used to measure waiting times for surgery and emergency room treatment is an example. It is much easier to arrange the availability of data within a single level of governance institutions than it is in MLG arenas. For example, Commonwealth Government collections of benefits payment data are complete, well defined (at least statutorily), and cross-correlate with each other. By contrast, health datasets of real interest exist at both state and federal level. The creation of comparable health data across the federation is difficult, takes time and is politically interesting. We can generalise that, compared to single-level institutions, MLG arenas are less well served by data and face high transaction costs in sharing and making sense of data. Participants need to spend a considerable portion of their time negotiating the construction of intelligible, illuminating datasets to inform their work.

The objects to be governed may vary at different levels of government. For example, the national government may be interested in governing cardiovascular risk factors, while the state government may be interested in governing health services for chronic heart failure or procedure rates for coronary artery disease. An intergovernmental forum (such as the National Health Priority Area working group to develop a national service framework for cardiovascular disease) will be subject to both these interests. In this example the strong relationships between the Commonwealth and state interests should offset any antagonism or awkwardness between the contestants.

The techniques of intervention will vary substantially. If we consider the governance of alcohol consumption, the national government has taxation powers that the states have agreed to hand over to the federation. State governments, on the other hand, have detailed regulatory statutes available to them to govern licensing of alcohol outlets and govern opening times and conditions of sale and display that the national government does not have the power to enact, and if it did, may not have the capability to administer.

An MLG arena in each of the three domains just described has the capacity to invent, or negotiate, a rationality, a set of governmental objectives and a series of interventions that are particular (or peculiar) to that arena. In such cases, the arenas generate governing power. This is precisely what the case studies in this book describe.

In this chapter, I have drawn on political theory in the governmentality literature to generate a series of analyses of MLG drawing on my experience as a participant in Australian federal governance arrangements in the health field, and that of colleagues in wider fields in Australia and the United States. My purpose has been to identify mechanisms and observe tendencies, and it is beyond my scope to explore how widespread the mechanisms may be, or how easy to generalise are the trends. In characterising the analysis as an exploration of multi-level governmentality, I hope to have given some coherence – in perspective at least – to my considerations on how multi-level arrangements can bear on the quite disparate issues of the limitations of democracy, the impact of trust and the evolution of liberalism. In the discussion of each of these issues, I have tried to bring out how MLG arrangements can engender creativity and entrepreneurial action involving participating governments, interest groups and citizens. It would be wrong to conclude that MLG has some essential tendency that promotes more creative government. I do think, however, that there is sufficient evidence of such creativity to warrant further exploration of where it is occurring, of the conditions in which it flourishes, and of how multi-level institutions can be designed to facilitate it. Such explorations should be of interest to both researchers and practitioners of the art of governance.

References

Beck, U. (1992). *Risk Society: Towards a New Modernity.* Sage, London.

Berlin, I. (1958). Two Concepts of Liberty. In: Berlin, I. (ed.) *Four Essays on Liberty* (1969). Oxford University Press.

Boston, J. (ed.) (1995). *The State under Contract.* Bridgit Williams Books, Wellington.

Broadbent, J., Dietrich, M. & Laughlin, R. (1996). The Development of Principal–Agent, Contracting and Accountability Relationships in the Public Sector: conceptual and cultural problems. *Critical Perspectives on Accounting*, 7(3): 259–84. doi.org/10.1006/cpac.1996.0033

Burchell, G., Gordon, C. & Miller, P. (1991). *The Foucault Effect: Studies in Governmentality*. University of Chicago Press. doi.org/10.7208/chicago/9780226028811.001.0001

Cohen, S. (1985). *Visions of Social Control: Crime, Punishment and Classification*. Polity.

Daniell, K.A., White, I., Ferrand, N., Ribarova, I.S., Coad, P., Rougier, J.-E., Hare, M., Jones, N.A., Popova, A., Rollin, D., Perez, P. & Burn S. (2010). Co-engineering Participatory Water Management Processes: theory and insights from Australian and Bulgarian interventions. *Ecology and Society*, 15(4): 11. doi.org/10.5751/es-03567-150411

Dean, M. (1999). *Governmentality: Power and Rule in Modern Society*. Sage, London.

Dean, M. & Hindess, B. (1998). *Studies in Contemporary Rationalities of Government*. Cambridge University Press, Cambridge.

Dugdale, P. (1993). Public Management in the Welfare State: Managerialism and Consumer Advocacy in the 1980s. MA Thesis, Faculty of Sociology, ANU, Canberra.

——. (2008). *Doing Public Policy in Australia*. Allen and Unwin, Sydney.

Ericson, R.V. & Stehr, N. (eds) (2000). *Governing Modern Societies*. University of Toronto Press, Toronto.

Fenna, A. (2009). Federalism. In: Rhodes, R.A.W. (ed.) *The Australian Study of Politics*. Palgrave Macmillan, Basingstoke, pp. 146–59. doi.org/10.1057/9780230296848_11

Foucault, M. (1972). *The Archaeology of Knowledge*. Tavistock, London.

——. (2007). *Security, Territory and Population*. Lectures at the College De France 1977–78, Palgrave MacMillan, New York.

Fukuyama, F. (1995). *Trust: The Social Virtues and the Creation of Prosperity*. Free Press, New York.

Goodin, R.E. (1996). *The Theory of Institutional Design*. Cambridge University Press. doi.org/10.1017/CBO9780511558320

Hindess, B. (2000). Divide and Govern. In: Ericson, R.V. & Stehr, N. (eds) *Governing Modern Societies*. University of Toronto Press, pp. 118–40. doi.org/10.3138/9781442675452-008

——. (2002). Deficit by Design. *Australian Journal of Public Administration*, 61(1): 30–38. doi.org/10.1111/1467-8500.00256

Hooghe, L. & Marks, G. (2001). *Multi-level Governance and European Integration*. Rowman and Littlefield, Lanham MD.

Ison, R., Collins, J., Colvin, J., Jiggins, J., Paolo Roggero, P., Seddaiu, G., Steyaert, P., Toderi, M. & Zanolla, C. (2011). Sustainable Catchment Managing in a Climate Changing World: new integrative modalities for connecting policy makers, scientists and other stakeholders. *Water Resources Management*, 25(15): 3977–92. doi.org/10.1007/s11269-011-9880-4

Kluth, A. (2011). The People's Will: democracy in California. Special report. *The Economist*, 23 April 2011.

Lessons from California: the perils of extreme democracy. *The Economist*, 23 April 2011, p. 12.

Luhmann, N. (1985). The Work of Art and the Self-Reproduction of Art. *Thesis Eleven*, 12(1): 4–27. doi.org/10.1177/072551368501200102

Miller, P. & Rose, N. (1990). Governing Economic Life. *Economy and Society*, 19(1): 1–31. doi.org/10.1080/03085149000000001

Offe, C. (1984). *Contradictions of the Welfare State*. Hutchinson, London.

Papadakis, E. & Taylor-Gooby, P. (1987). *The Private Provision of Public Welfare: State, Market and Community*. Wheatsheaf Books, Sussex.

Parsons, T. (1977). *The Social System*. Routledge, New York.

Reynolds, M. & Holwell, S. (eds) (2010). *Systems Approaches to Managing Change: A Practical Guide*. Springer, London.

Rose, N. (1999). *Governing the Soul: The Shaping of the Private Self*. 2nd edn. Free Association Books Ltd, London.

——. (2000). Governing Liberty. In: Ericson, R.V. & Stehr, N. (eds) *Governing Modern Societies*. University of Toronto Press, pp. 141–76. doi.org/10.3138/9781442675452-009

Stehr, N. & Ericson, R.V. (2000). The Ungovernability of Modern Societies: states, democracies, markets, participation, and citizens. In: Ericson, R.V. & Stehr, N. (eds) *Governing Modern Societies*. University of Toronto Press, pp. 3–25. doi.org/10.3138/9781442675452-002

Uhrig, J. (2003). *Review of the Corporate Governance of Statutory Authorities and Office Holders*. Commonwealth of Australia, Canberra 2003, www.finance.gov.au/sites/default/files/Uhrig-Report.pdf   [Accessed: 07/05/17].

Veronesi, G., Harley, K., Dugdale, P. & Short, S.D. (2014). Governance, Transparency and Alignment in the Council of Australian Governments (COAG) 2011 National Health Reform Agreement. *Australian Health Review*, 38(3): 288–94. doi.org/10.1071/AH13078

Williamson, O. (1996). *The Mechanisms of Governance*. Oxford University Press.

Yeatman, A. (1995). Interpreting Contemporary Contractualism. In: Boston, J. (ed.) *The State Under Contract*. Bridgit Williams Books, Wellington.

6

Multi-level Governance as Political Theory

Russell Kerr

Train kept a rollin'

In the 2013 film, *Snowpiercer*, the tiny portion of humanity remaining after a geo-engineering incident triggers a global ice age are confined to a train circumnavigating the earth once a year. Korean director Bong Joon-ho's adaptation of the 1982 French graphic novel, *Le Transperceneige*, can easily be seen, as the comic can be read, as an allegory. But is it an allegory of potential catastrophe – a return to a Hobbesian political state – or is it an allegory of a current political condition?

A case for both readings can be readily made. Like the standard version of Thomas Hobbes's *Leviathan* (1651), outside the train (Commonwealth), life is unendurable: security resides only in the protection of the sovereign. In the film, the train's captain and builder of its 'sacred' engine (compare the Hobbesian state as 'mortal god'), Wilford, could play the role of sovereign.[1] Moreover, just like Hobbes's conception of sovereignty, some

---

1   The film changes character names and alters roles from the graphic novel; e.g. in the comic, Wilford is Forrester, an engineer who is more isolated from the rest of the train than its tyrant (see Lob and Rochette (2014), especially pp. 102–10). The three-volume French original has been translated into a two-volume English-language set.

members of humanity remain in a condition at once inside and outside the state of nature; those confined to the back of the train, where life is indeed 'poor, nasty, brutish and short'.[2]

Alternatively, the train can be seen as an allegory of current conditions of extreme inequality in security, wealth, privilege and distractions in advanced liberal polities. The train (a Scheherazade-like 1001 carriages, each one a story) is a linear hierarchy, with a rigid order separating those at the back ('Know your place, keep your place' threatens a Thatcher-esque bureaucrat) from the middle (classes) and the tyrant alone at the head of the train. Once the film's main character, Curtis, fights his way to the front of the train in the hope of obtaining justice for those at the back, he is offered the tyrant's role. Along the way, those who died in the struggle to advance Curtis turn out to be the numerical sacrifices that Wilford has calculated are needed to maintain the social order (that same bureaucrat announces the exact number of who will die early in the piece).

According to this latter interpretation, political freedom is at issue: Curtis has betrayed the revolution, or the revolution is betrayal. At the same time, the story shares a structure with another tale of money, democratic promise and betrayal: *The Wizard of Oz*. Here, Curtis/Dorothy struggles to make it to the singular place of the master of the machinery (Wilford/ the Wizard), only to be shown that, all along, he/she has the power to realise what he/she sought out power to achieve. The lesson is not only political; it is wrapped in an economic debate. The key here is that, like the distribution and display of wealth and power in the film (and a wicked witch in both), Frank Baum's *The Wonderful Wizard of Oz* (1900) is a tale concerned with value, debt and the insecurity of currency (in the film the main currency is a drug, while it is free silver in Baum's Oz).[3] It would certainly be possible to construct an analogy with current economic circumstances in the European Union (EU).

Which interpretation to choose: the allegory of a return to Hobbes or an allegory of contemporary reality? Must we choose? According to the vast bulk of current social and political writing, we have to choose, because a polity such as the EU cannot be both a Hobbesian state and a contemporary one. My illustration of *Snowpiercer* is meant to suggest

---

2 c.f. Hobbes (1985: 186).
3 For more on late 19th-century American populism, fiat money and the *Wizard of Oz*, see Dighe (ed.) (2002); Rockoff (1990) and Ziaukas (1998).

that, in fact, not only can we not choose between these allegorical images, but also we should not. The remainder of this essay attempts to explain why.

The argument proceeds in three steps. The first step outlines the case for the EU as a move away from sovereignty-centred politics and towards governance. This case involves two dimensions: it is a claim to novelty, or a new conception of politics, and it is a claim to a new conception of 'the people', or at least to a concept of 'variable publics' understood to be at odds with the classical notion of the fixed public defined by its citizen status in a singular state. Combining these two claims, multi-level governance (MLG) may claim to reinvigorate civic engagement and thus potentially redeem the 'democratic promise' (Goodwyn 1976) that has eluded the polities of advanced liberal societies. (This promise can be traced to the American populist political economy to which *The Wizard of Oz* responds.)

The second step is to show that the rhetorical distinctions MLG employs to make its claim to novelty and democratic promise lead to several debilitating results. Adapting a Kantian split between sovereignty and government implies placing some of our contemporaries in the past; as a result, MLG shares with liberal and neoliberal theory a view of the future where no-one's place is certain. Dividing past from future in the name of novelty – and in opposition to sovereignty – also raises questions about MLG's ability to account for how it gets from there to here. The rhetoric of change from a 'world dominated by sovereignty' suggests that governance tends to rely on a non-causal sense of transformation. This non-causal form of reasoning sits uneasily with MLG's dominant idea of political bodies. At the same time, non-causal reasoning is at the centre of Hobbes's argument for sovereignty, and can act as a point of similitude between MLG and sovereignty.

The third step elaborates part of Hobbes's argument for sovereignty. Specifically, an overview of Hobbes's rhetorical re-description of bodies shows that sovereignty does not consist in positing a 'constitutive outside' to the commonwealth in the form either of a state of nature or system of states.[4] On the contrary, Hobbes's political subjects only appear as such in the perpetual instants of crossing boundaries with these outsides.

---

4   c.f. Brown (2005: 61).

Thus, sovereignty is not helpfully understood in opposition to MLG. In this chapter, MLG is treated as a boundary-crossing activity.[5] This activity includes crossing boundaries with sovereignty. But the main innovation I propose, against the grain of long-standing habit, is to treat sovereignty too as a boundary-crossing conception of politics.

Sovereignty vs governance

The sovereignty/governance opposition is most apparent, developed and sharp in analyses of the EU. Take the example of Bob Jessop's rich concepts of 'meta-' and 'multi-scalar' governance. While EU member governments may take on the coordinating role of 'meta-governance', there can be no question of a return to a 'stable equilibrium' of a final form of meta-governance, which would be tantamount to a return to sovereignty as a singular mode of rule and subjection:

> But there is no point at which a final metagovernance instance can be established to coordinate the myriad subordinate forms of governance – this would re-introduce the principle of sovereignty or hierarchy that growing social complexity and globalization now rule out (Jessop 2005: 66).[6]

For some analysts, sovereignty is less a principle than a problematic. Measured according to the standard of Hobbes's classical account of sovereignty as necessarily undivided, Fritz Scharpf (2012) demonstrates well the dilemmas of the EU in conditions of divided sovereignty and crisis. Scharpf (2012: 29–30) points out that governing via the market leads to both an intensification of the euro crisis and a legitimacy crisis. Seen from the vantage point of divided sovereignty (which leads to his salient discussion of 'output legitimacy'), the EU might well be seen in Hobbesian terms as 'facing the constant danger of fragmentation and dissolution' (Hänninen 2014).

---

5   See *Daniell and Kay*.
6   In the MLG literature, this beginning may be prefaced by a quasi-historical account of the fate of the political community from its putative origins in classical Greece (e.g. Cerny 2009), or it may not. In either case, the line drawn between 'the sovereign state' and the varieties of governance supports the legitimation of governance as a conceptual object.

Scharpf's response to this dilemma is to lower the 'political salience' of legitimation issues in times of crisis, essentially by governing through the market less (see also Hänninen 2009). Others, however, begin from an assumption that the Hobbesian paradigm belongs to the past. Consider the conclusion to the influential Hooghe and Marks (2003: 241):

> Political science has had far more to say about <u>how</u> collective decisions can and should be made than about <u>for whom</u> they can and should be made. Answers to the 'how' question have narrowed because there is no legitimate alternative to liberal democracy. Debate centers on the merits of alternative democratic designs. But there is little consensus about jurisdictional design – the 'for whom' question. Central states are shedding authority to supranational and subnational authorities, but what kinds of jurisdictional architecture might emerge?

While granting the centrality of the problem of authority from the outset of their article, Hooghe and Marks (2003) treat the issue as an organisational one throughout, deferring the question of what authorises this treatment. Nonetheless, the authors engage in a practice of temporal differentiation that permits a particular conception of politics to appear as the solution to their future-oriented question.

In their conclusion, the novelty of MLG is not so neatly boxed in a return to the past. After all, their terms are familiar to 19th-century liberal thought,[7] which divides discussion of politics into a matter of politics-as-sphere ('scope') and politics-as-activity ('how'). The division, of course, is enabled by the future-oriented claim of 'no alternative'. The future features a further division between the relative authority of bodies 'above' and 'below' the national. This triple division (and its 'vertical' and 'horizontal' spacing), in turn, permits one available political option: (legitimate) dispute will be over 'who' the people are in a given area of political decision-making. If it is an axiom of contemporary politics that 'the people are always missing' (Deleuze 1993: 220), the picture drawn by Hooghe and Marks goes some distance towards creating an image of the people.

Hooghe and Marks's implicit solution to the political founding problem resonates with discussions in contemporary political theories of federalism,[8] for which the MLG concept can have a particular salience.

---

7   c.f. Palonen (2003: 171).
8   See, for example, Goodin (2008, especially p. 151).

Neither governance nor federalist discourse is inclined to acknowledge its authorising and legitimating work. Nonetheless, the aspiration to identify the *demos* (the people who are constituted to participate in politics) through decision-making authority is a feature shared with sovereignty as a discourse of political founding. The shape of that authority, and the routes it takes (horizontal–vertical / ascending–descending), are the object of a properly topological analysis (see esp. Hänninen 2014).

Hooghe and Marks return to one version of past political theory (19th-century liberalism) to counter another (Hobbes's conception of sovereignty). This return is carried out in the name of a future-oriented conception of the *demos* and democratic design. At the same time, it is an attempt to incorporate a claim to novelty into its design. Such a claim is required not least by MLG's effort to differentiate itself from sovereignty. Nonetheless, claims to novelty are not new: political theory has long worked according to a variety of claims to novelty, and Hobbes's argument for sovereignty is among them.[9]

Similarly, Jessop's acknowledgement of definition by negation (see footnote 9) is another opening to a formulation of governance as novel, particularly in contrast to state and supra-state sovereignty. Jessop goes on to observe that, while the role of governments at all levels in meta-governance may increase state capacity in some dimensions, analysts are witnessing:

> a trend towards the de-statisation of the political system. This involves a shift from government to governance on various territorial scales and across various functional domains (Jessop 2005: 65).[10]

Tellingly, Jessop's 'shift' in the passage above is glossed as 'alternative' in Stephen George's contribution to the same volume:

> Placing multi-level governance in the context of the intergovernmental/supranational debate in EU studies allows an informed understanding of it as an alternative to state-centred perspectives (George 2005: 125).

---

9   Evidence of argumentation from novelty is readily available in the MLG literature. In the case of the EU, Philippe Schmitter (1998: 132) speculates whether 'something qualitatively different' than a sovereign order is emerging. Sharing Schmitter's concern for a conceptual and analytic response, Bob Jessop (2005: 61) observes that, at present, 'it is much clearer what the notion of governance excludes than what it contains' (c.f. Bache and Flinders 2005: 96; see also Jessop 2009).

10   See also Héritier and Rhodes (2011).

My focus here is on the equivalence of 'shift' and 'alternative' in accounts of the difference between 'state-centric' and governance modes. Clearly, the equivalence is a response to conditions under which novelty appears as both a problem and an opportunity. How a shift from government to governance is equivalent to an alternative between them is a question of some theoretical and empirical interest. However, that is not my main concern. Whatever else they may be, as descriptions, these formulae do not serve to further understanding of what has 'shifted' or become an 'alternative' precisely; or how, or under what conditions, or for whom. As explanations amenable to any sort of causal analysis, these characterisations are of little specific value.

Sovereignty off the rails

On the other hand, these distinctions have a strong rhetorical value. The government/governance division can be seen as a question of re-description (c.f. Palonen 2002); that is, as a matter of political rhetoric, such as Quentin Skinner (1996) and Patricia Springborg (2010) find in their different ways within Hobbes's classic work on sovereignty. It could also be judged as an instance of indeterminacy (Hänninen 2014), insofar as the vexed question of the EU as a polity can be approached on a single line of reasoning from both a past-bound ('shift') and future-bound ('alternative') perspective.

Here, the founding acts of governance occur well within the bounds of the distinction –credited to Jean Bodin in the early 17th century (Lee 2013) but found in Hobbes (1651) and still in Immanuel Kant at the end of the 18th century – between sovereignty and government. In Kant's paradigmatic version in his 1795 essay, *Perpetual Peace*, 'the forms of a state (civitas) can be divided either according to the [number of] persons who possess the sovereign power or according to the mode of administration exercised over the people by the chief, whoever he [sic] may be' (Kant 1975: 95).

The first term in this division is sovereignty and, while important, it is far less a matter of concern to the governed. The second, which concerns the exercise the state makes of its power, is the mode of government. Government, Kant goes on to insist, is either republican (where the executive is separated from the legislative) or despotic (where it is not). Democracy, we should note, is for Kant a species of the latter. This is because 'all' (citizens as a single will), who are 'not quite all' (some citizens may disagree), establish an executive power over all. Democracy is thus for Kant in contradiction with freedom (Kant 1975: 96).

It is not difficult from this distinction to see that 'the hierarchical state' in MLG discourse fits Kant's account of sovereignty. In the MLG account, sovereignty is then conflated with government in the state. That is, while Kant's republic corresponds well to what is now meant by representative democracy (a form of government in Kant's terms), the MLG literature sees government as a species of the state, and thus of sovereignty. Once this conflation has been made, governance reappears within the sovereignty/government distinction to fulfil the role that government is no longer adequate to carry out. The distinction, however, lacks one term: sovereignty is subtracted, now relegated to the never (hopefully) to return past. Governance alone remains.

Such an effective logic of founding bears comparison with those of Hobbes, Locke and Rousseau, to name only the most obvious. Three common features of this logic of founding should be noted. First, it proceeds by means of splitting, of making authoritative distinctions, within a spatial domain (the political community). Second, founding invokes a split view of time: some aspects of the present ('sovereignty' in MLG's case) are relegated to the past, others to the present ('government') and some are granted the future ('governance'). Third, the account takes place in the name of an authorised and authorising people ('citizens').

This schematic view of governance as political theory requires, however, a further step. In the discussion above, Kant's distinction between sovereignty and government occurs within the single state. Kant's essay is not often remembered for this distinction, but rather for its attempt to outline the requirement that republican states – which alone promise freedom for their citizens – realise a federation. In other words, there is an 'international' imperative to Kant's project, without which his characterisation of freedom in a single state is without force.

Anthony Pagden, among others, has not hesitated to see in this federation the model for the imposition of a universalist mode of governance that is now familiar in institutions ranging from the International Monetary Fund, World Bank and international non-government organisations to the United Nations human rights regime (Pagden 1998; see also the conclusion to Pagden 2001). There is a considerable cost to this singular universalism, however, and that is a constitutive fracturing of the world populations governed by states into those with a governable future and those for whom this future is doubtful.[11]

These fractures are enabling, and thus can be characterised as temporal and spatial borders that the community of humanity, as a community of state-bound citizens, must cross to realise the future promise of freedom. Borders, in others words, matter. Moreover, they matter 'politically': those contemporaries who embody the past in the present ('medieval Muslims', 'non-modern societies', 'rogue states' etc.) may be legitimately governed by paternalism/coercion until they are ready to accede to the level achieved by states governed through the freedom Kant requires for private property, security of contract and thus 'peaceful commerce' to flourish everywhere (Helliwell and Hindess 2011, 2015).

In developments of some moment for the concept of MLG and its relation to the politics of the market, contemporary political theory has sought to retain Kant's affirmation of peaceful commerce among republics in the widely disputed 'democratic peace thesis'.[12] One means of doing so has been to jettison at least some of Kant's 'metaphysics' in favour of a 'political liberalism'.[13]

But this is where things fall apart. As far as future-oriented politics goes, such a manoeuvre appears self-defeating. As Helliwell and Hindess (2015) have admirably demonstrated, attempts such as Thomas Pogge's effort

---

11 As Helliwell and Hindess (2015) demonstrate, Kant's account of progress towards an ideal political community depends upon placing some members of humanity closer to that future goal, and others (notably 'the Tahitians', who are placed at the developmental level of sheep) more distant from it. Echoing Jessop's implicit division of contemporary global politics into past, present and future, a cosmopolitan vision of humanity as a political constituency operates along a single (developmental) line that consists of fractures:

> Kant is able to bring all of humanity together into a single cosmopolitan progression only by distributing its diverse sections along one developmental ladder. What we have here is a matter of cosmopolitan unification by a no less cosmopolitan differentiation (Helliwell and Hindess 2015).

12 See, for example, Doyle (1983a, 1983b, 1986), Cavallar (2001), MacMillan (2004), Rosato (2003).

13 Most notably in Rawls (1985, 1996, 1999).

to appropriate Kant's cosmopolitan program shorn of its metaphysical foundations result in a view of future politics without guarantee of improvement.[14]

Having placed itself at the apex of time, nothing guarantees that contemporary liberal thought will remain there, or even that this apparently privileged site will remain available. At the same time, the developmental, differential view of humanity underwriting the cosmopolitan vision works unchecked. These twin dynamics challenge modes of political thought that take their bearings from a distinction with sovereignty, even as they attempt acts of founding familiar in style to 'sovereignty-centred' political theory.

The challenge is particularly felt in comparisons of governance and neoliberalism. If an absence of a future guarantee is a dilemma for governance, neoliberalism might appear well placed to profit from this void (which neoliberals gloss as 'anarchy'). For example, Samuel Huntington (2006: 1) begins his 1968 study of 'political order in changing societies' by asserting that the form of government (in the Kantian sense) matters little: what counts is 'effectiveness'. Cognate arguments can be found in Mancur Olson (Olson 1971, 1993; McGuire and Olson 1996), who is well known for his 'collective action problem', as well as in Francis Fukuyama's (2008) review of the Regional Assistance Mission, Solomon Islands (RAMSI).

To the 'failed state' problem of the Solomon Islands, Fukuyama recommends a form of 'shared sovereignty' with more capable states. A 'state-building' project must recognise that the Solomon Islands are emerging from a 'state of nature' (anarchy) requiring the 'helping hand' of properly ordered commonwealths. A profound politics is at work in this shallow formulation. Fukuyama appears to discuss two states, the failed and the capable. But are these two states or one?

---

14   See Pogge (1992, 1994, 2002). The failure of future guarantee follows because Pogge's design:
lacks the original's optimistic teleology. As a consequence, it also lacks [Kant's] belief that
current political ideals are still far from the best they can be; in Pogge's vision contemporary
ideals of freedom and democracy are presented as the ultimate political values to which all
sections of humanity should unquestioningly aspire (Helliwell and Hindess 2015).

The characterisations of 'anarchy' and 'capability' mirror steps in Hobbes's anti-historical tale[15] of the founding of the sovereign state. In Fukuyama, as in the standard view of Hobbes, a movement of necessity to escape disordered violence establishes the link between anarchy and capability. The link between steps can also be reasoned as temporal: 'the condition of anarchy' and its inhabitants constitute the prehistory of the commonwealth. Like Hobbes, for whom American Indians represent a minimal form of self-government in an indefinite European past, Fukuyama defines Melanesian social organisation as belonging to a past that Europeans have surmounted:

> Segmentary societies are a coherent and stable form of social organization, but in Europe they were superceded at a fairly early point by more modern forms of political organization not based on kinship. Segmentary societies could not meet the challenges of large-scale social integration in a region characterized by persistent warfare and expanding trade (Fukuyama 2008: 2).

In a development not dissimilar to the way in which governance can emerge from a splitting of sovereignty and government, in shared sovereignty two states are split and rejoined to conjure one: the singular story of the sovereign state. In part, this conjuring is achieved by replacing definite history with a developmental concept of 'society', buttressed by a hierarchy of capacities. Those capacities are ranged in a temporal order of strength, where capacities located in the past are the weakest. Given these affinities with a rationality of violence in international relations as a practice of founding, MLG's normative urge runs the risk of collapsing into the 'might makes right' counterargument familiar to political theory since Thrasymachus' early challenge to Socrates in Plato's *Republic*.

The discussion above illustrates a critical point: claims to comparative efficiency, capability and capacity for 'learning'[16] may well depend upon a politics of founding whose major feature – a division of populations into states governed according to a division determined suitable for a future invoked as necessary but also impossible – is shared with the classical claims to sovereignty it seeks to avoid.

---

15   Contrary to the view put forward by John Locke, Hobbes did not argue that 'the state of nature' is an historical condition; indeed, he argued against practical history as a means of deducing an enduring commonwealth (see, among others, Sorell (2000: 83–84).

16   c.f. the critical remarks in Dale (2004: 189).

Nowhere in the MLG literature is the legitimating logic of these temporal and spatial divisions more apparent than in debates over the relationship between MLG and its constituency, or its (variable) publics. As a ramification of Kant's conception of freedom, the matter tends to resolve into the question of how, in the EU, democratic governance reflects economic governance, or governing 'in the name of the market' (Hänninen 2013). As a corollary, governing 'in the name of the people' will require authoritative mechanisms for representation in decision-making on multiple levels and at different scales.

As a political logic, one attuned to the need to authorise and legitimate its forms and vocabulary, MLG is challenged by problems associated with 'state-centric' political theories. In as much as MLG claims to depart from 'sovereignty-centred' thinking, a double challenge thus presents itself. Considered as a form of political theory, MLG displays the hallmarks of a practice of founding. Nonetheless, as again the example of Kant suggests, there is considerable doubt as to whether this can be accurately described as a founding in the classical style of the self-sufficient community of the singular state.[17]

Governmental freedom

The absence of a causal founding logic in MLG is not due in the first instance to appeals to complexity and network logic. Some of these accounts may be more or less plausible if – and only if – political bodies are granted an existence prior to their conditions of action, and they are credited as sources of (rational) agency, however 'interdependent' such agency may be pictured.

---

17   In part, the doubt arises because of the tension in liberal thought between republicanism and democracy, formalised by Kant. Multi-level government sits in an uneasy position within this tension. For example, multi-scalar politics remains 'state-centric' insofar as it echoes Robert Dahl's republican effort to rid political thinking of its dependency on notions of classical Greek autonomy and singular sovereignty (c.f. Magnusson 2011: 144). On the other hand, Hooghe and Marks's democratic founding of a potentially 'new form of multi-layered governance without clear lines of demarcated jurisdiction and identity' (Schmitter 1998: 132) resonates with Jessop's idea that no final form of governance is possible or desirable – a conception of 'global politics' traceable to the anti-democratic Kant (c.f. Franke 2001: 150). In sum, a Kantian conception of political community can conjure the people, but quite possibly at the cost of the democratic claims made in their name.

Much governance literature shares international relations' neo-realist illusion that political bodies exist prior to, and independent of, their conditions of action,[18] but with an important twist. Avant et al. (2010) symptomatically invoke both the idea of bodies pre-existing their milieu and the idea that, in the actions of some privileged bodies, borders are merely spatial, and do not otherwise matter: 'For purposes of this inquiry, *global governors are authorities who exercise power across borders for purposes of affecting policy*' (Avant et al. 2010: 2, italics in original). Much can be said about a formulation that restricts governing to its effect on policy. In any case, enough has been said thus far, and much more follows, to indicate that for governance generally, and MLG in particular, crossing borders is a highly political moment.

Discussing the 'rational actor' presumption only in the context of international relations discourse would, however, be incomplete and misleading. Barry Hindess (1991) has argued that the idea of an actor as the locus of desires and beliefs – whose actions follow those desires and beliefs – is rife in 'domestic' democratic discourse. This view of the 'rational actor' has a legitimating rather than explanatory or heuristic role. In its place, Hindess proposes 'a more general model in which the actor is conceived simply as a locus of decision and action' (Hindess 1991: 221).

Rejecting the correlation of freedom and security in sovereignty yields another set of issues for governance.[19] Hindess (2001, 2005) and Helliwell and Hindess (2002) challenge the common defence of liberal government

---

18   Just such a characterisation of political bodies dominates the discipline of international relations, where it can be characterised as neo-realism. The description holds, even across 'schools' that expend much of their energy (intellectual and otherwise, one suspects) attaching labels to rival schools. Thus it is that, despite claims and counter-claims, the 'English school' of constructivism (see Bull 2002; Bull and Watson 1984; Hurrell and Woods 1999) shares with its largely systems-centred counterpart (e.g. Wight 1977; Wendt 1999; Buzan and Waever 2003; Albert et al. 2001) and many 'postmodern' accounts (e.g. Weber 1995) the basic assumptions concerning political bodies that are relevant to this discussion. Variations within and between positions are, of course, expected and found, and this snapshot is scarcely a survey of international relations as a discipline. But it is, for all that, defensible, as an attentive reading of Rob Walker's now-classic *Inside/Outside* (1993) would show. Significant, if partial, exceptions to this account include Larner and Walters (2004), Fry and O'Hagan (2000), Soederberg (2005), Baker et al. (2005), and Hobson (2012).

19   Multi-level governance both confirms and challenges sovereign accounts of political bodies, and thus of freedom. For example, governance thinking on security (e.g. Lavenex 2004; Lavenex and Schimmelfennig 2009) tends to accept the Hobbesian/Westphalian claim that the violence of the state is designed (whatever its practical or policy failings) to protect the population within its remit. Security is thus a matter of 'external relations' in relation to other states, or in what is often called 'external governance'. The danger for governance thinking on security is that it will follow the Hobbesian relation of the self and the state, 'associating individual security (safety) and the security of the state (survival) against external aggression' (Bigo 2008: 106).

as a principled defence of freedom. They show that for certain targets – for example, colonial 'indirect rule', the urban poor, migrants, Indigenous populations, the provision of social services – liberalism finds it practical or necessary to govern coercively; i.e. through unfreedom.[20]

Indeed, as in Kant's developmental division of peoples within a 'world' of states, there is an important sense in which the system of states is *governed*; this, despite the legitimating myth of the Westphalian state (c.f. Hunter 2001; Hobson 2013; Waters 2009), upon which MLG literature depends for its understanding of sovereignty and its transformations. The novelty of the present is not to be found in the application of non-state actors to government, as the concept of governance would have it: evidence of this rule by non-state actors is plentiful in the historical literature.[21]

What is new since at least the end of World War II is a significant challenge in the organisation of Western government to the idea of the state as 'the highest of all' forms of political community (Aristotle's phrase), a challenge that is most clearly made by an extension of governmentality to the system of states (Hindess 2005: 407). Hindess is acutely aware of stretching the Foucauldian concept of governmentality beyond its presumed purview, the national state.[22] What permits this extension is, in part, Foucault's analysis of the 'art of government'.[23] The art in question practises a refusal of Hobbes's reduction of politics to institutions licensed by a singular sovereign authority.

Refusing the ideal of a singular sovereign authority has ambiguous consequences for governance. The tension between two loci of 'the highest' – the state and the system of states – points to a neglected aspect of 'the self-governing community of citizens' as a useful fiction for political theory and practice. In political designs where rule is not simply authoritarian

---

20 Far from expressing hypocrisy (the view of Said 1993) or inconsistency (Pitts 2005) in the application of a principle, in Hindess' view liberalism is better seen in Michel Foucault's terms as 'the work of government'. When viewed in this way, the Foucauldian idea that liberalism 'governs through freedom' (Foucault 2008: 63) can also be tested. The result is that, seen as the work of government, which encompasses many non-state actors, authoritarian rule (the 'government of unfreedom') may well serve the aims of liberalism. Moreover, the work of government is not confined to the 'domestic' sphere.

21 Hindess (2005: 405–06); c.f. Raeff (1975).

22 A political *a priori* many of Foucault's followers forget; see also Walters and Haahr (2005); Walters (2011).

23 For a lucid description, see Magnusson (2011: 91–110).

(as it is in Hobbes), this fiction is in part maintained by another: the fiction of a common culture, such as appears in the Roman republic or in John Locke's law of opinion and reputation (Hindess 1992, 1997).

It is an open question whether governance serves to create a fiction of a common culture for the state/system of states (Pagden's position above), or whether the indeterminacy of this aporetic relation permits acts of political founding that may intimate unforeseen political transformations. Earlier, I suggested the latter possibility in the context of MLG's capacity to at least conceptually redeploy the Kantian sovereignty/ government distinction, and to 'create a people'.

In this creation, freedom is centrally at issue. Foucault's emphasis on the important role of the government of the self in political rationality raises again the question of causality introduced earlier in the discussion of MLG as a form of political theory. Consider Foucault's insistence that the governmental self is not to be treated as a substance (as in the rational actor model), but as a (variable) form.[24] As form, the self ('the subject') may well move in a realm of coercion (i.e. be in some respects amenable to a causal account), but this does not exhaust understanding of what is involved. Lacking an *a priori* substance or nature, the self is 'a practice of freedom', not a self-identity.

The sovereign people

We can now return to the question of the role that non-causal reasoning[25] plays in MLG and in sovereignty. I suggest a connection between the non-causal account of transformation in MLG and the non-causal dimension of the self in freedom as the work of government. Both non-causal elements contribute to the authorisation and legitimation of the people.

Foucault's rejection of Hobbes's classic account of sovereignty has been noted above (see also Foucault 2003; Neal 2004). As we will see below, despite the considerable value of his critique, Foucault has failed – in common with influential liberal scholarship on Hobbes (e.g. Skinner 1996, 2008; Pettit 2008) – to consider the central role of form in Hobbes's

---

24 See Foucault (1997: 290–91); c.f. Veyne (1997).
25 By 'non-causal' I do not refer to Quentin Skinner's neo-Kantian reasoning on speech-act theory; on this aspect of Skinner's work, see Hindess (2014: 48–49).

argument. The cost of this omission in the case of liberal thought, particularly in its republican variety, is a failure to consider the idea of freedom, and thus democracy, as governed by form in the complex of self, state and system of states. Our account of MLG has revealed the centrality of this complex. It has also shown that MLG can be comprehended as a practice of founding, of establishing (authorising and legitimating) a 'people' (a *demos*). Might the non-causal character of MLG's legitimating reasoning be seen as a treatment of boundary-crossing as form?

Indeed it might. In this section I seek to show that Hobbes can also – in fact, should – be read as performing this very action of authorisation and legitimation. I use the example of Richard Tuck's attempt to discern a defence of a certain condition of democracy in Hobbes's authoritarian reasoning. Following Bodin's earlier insistence that sovereignty must be perpetual (uninterrupted) to be at all, Hobbes solves the problem, according to Tuck, of how sovereignty can subsist when the sovereign is unable to give commands, such as when asleep. During this time, the sovereign delegates power to some other body for the duration, taking it back upon waking. 'Just so a people, on the election of a temporary Monarch, retains the right of meeting again at a certain time and place, and on that day resumes its power' (Hobbes in Tuck 2006: 189).

For Tuck, democracy can be called a 'sleeping sovereign' in this sense, handing over administrative power to another authority of whatever sort (say, the US Congress or the Australian parliament) on condition that it has designated a time and place (e.g. elections) to take back that power. Such a Hobbesian form of democracy accords, in Tuck's view, with the constitution of revolutionary France, now 'the standard view of democratic constitutions in the modern world,' but first articulated by Hobbes (Tuck 2006: 189–90).

Tuck's account of Hobbesian democracy relies on Hobbes's *De Cive* (*On the Citizen*, 1647); Tuck's argument may be refined in his forthcoming work, *The Sleeping Sovereign* (2015), especially in light of criticism (e.g. by Hoekstra (2006) in the same volume as Tuck's essay). As an authorisation of representative democracy, Tuck's use of Hobbesian sovereignty is powerful, despite concerns by fellow liberal theorists. But it fails, in my view, as an account of Hobbes's reasoning.

So too does Phillip Pettit's attempt to explain how Hobbes founds a people in his account of the move from 'the state of nature' to the commonwealth and the establishment of sovereignty. Pettit's individual is an assumed, unproblematic category. But 'the people', as such, actually fall short of presence in his account, since they exist only after the sovereign is instituted – and if the multitude cannot authorise anything, then what/who are the 'all individuals, each and every one, that contracts the escape from the state of nature?' (Pettit 2008: 123).

Answers will only be found by attending to the whole of Hobbes's thought. Here, answers concern the ideas of form, freedom and bodies that make sovereignty work. Without this explanation, conceptualising the relation between sovereignty and governance as border-crossing politics remains seriously incomplete.

Acknowledging the inseparability of Hobbes's science of motion and politics (c.f. Slomp 2000; Hänninen 2014), and turning to Hobbes's *Leviathan*'s essential chapters on the self, we find that Hobbes devotes an early section of the text (Chpt. 2, 'Of Imagination') to dreams. There he attempts to demonstrate his view of sense certainty in a distinction between the dreaming and waking state. This distinction is not easily made, Hobbes says, not least because dreams may present more immediate clarity than the decaying sense of distance from sensations experienced while awake. Nonetheless, causal reasoning operates in both; it is simply reversed: 'our Dreams are the reverse of our waking Imaginations; The motion when we are awake, beginning at one end; and when we Dream, at another' (*Leviathan*, Chpt. 2).

What enables this account of motion, cause and sensation is Hobbes's conception of bodies. A summary of the salient points will have to suffice (drawn in part from Kerr 2013). In his view of motion, Hobbes distinguishes between bodies and accidents. For Hobbes, knowledge of cause proceeds from knowledge of parts of bodies, not wholes, since parts are indeed accidents. But what are accidents?

For Hobbes, accidents are parts of a body that together constitute a body's *nature*, though not the actual body.[26] It is a critical mistake[27] to read Hobbes as following Aristotle's claim that the whole is prior to its parts: this easily leads to the illusion of a common culture within a

---

26   c.f. Hobbes (1913: 19–20).
27   e.g. by Bates (2012: 78).

self-sufficient community, criticised above. Actually, Hobbes can be seen to redescribe Aristotle's idea of 'species' (*eidos* or *form*) in a clever criticism of the still-powerful Aristotelian reasoning of his day, in order to account for subject–object relations according to the new dualistic science of Hobbes's contemporary, Galileo. The idea of species includes the concept of *ananke*, or necessity, which is needed to explain knowledge, but is non-causal.

As hypothetical necessity, *ananke* does not govern sequences.[28] Moreover, this view of necessity presupposes freedom, but in a highly conditioned manner: the freedom to do otherwise is faced with a milieu in which no reasonable alternative course of action is available. Such is the *ananke* that requires free and equal subjects in 'meer nature' to recognise its intolerable nature and agree to contract amongst themselves to establish 'a common Power to keep them all in awe' (*Leviathan*, Chpt. 13). Yet, this single necessity cannot suffice, beset as it is by logical problems: if the multitude in meer nature is as thoroughly insecure as Hobbes avers, then contract appears impossible; if it is not, then such a drastic agreement seems unnecessary (Walker 2006: 64).

Hobbes's solution is to project the condition of a here and now in meer nature to his auditors, but as a condition in an indefinite past, there among 'the savage peoples of America':

> It may peradventure be thought, there was never such a time, nor condition of warre as this; and I believe it was never generally so, over all the world: but there are many places, where they live so now. For the savage people in many places of America, except the government of small Families, the concord whereof dependeth on naturall lust, have no government at all; and live at this day in that brutish manner, as I said before (*Leviathan*, Chpt. 13).

This passage establishes the basic divisions of space and time, in which some peoples are not quite in the same time as others, later adapted by Kant. To make these divisions work to authorise sovereignty, Hobbes invokes necessity-in-form. To tell the story of the absence of alternative for a move from meer nature to the commonwealth, Hobbes substitutes a set

---

28   c.f. Balme (1939: 136).

of *accidents* there and then for an imaginary situation here and now. His narrative thus moves backwards, though apparently forwards (from meer nature to the commonwealth), as Rob Walker has brilliantly illustrated.[29]

The reversible causality here is created by *ananke*, as we saw – and shall see again – when Hobbes discusses dreams. This form governs the logic of sovereignty's founding in several ways, across seemingly sharp divisions in time and space. As the accident of the 'Body Politique' (commonwealth), meer nature too can be seen as *ananke*. All this is erased, of course, in treatments of Hobbes which misconstrue meer nature as 'the state of nature' or 'anarchy'.

The Euclidian, geometric logic of ananke at work in *Leviathan* belies Tuck's effort to appeal to a *demos* (citizen–people) within a single state: Hobbes's logic of founding is necessarily at once a matter of consent *and* conquest. Violence and peace are co-terminal in Hobbes's sovereignty – a condition of constant and paradoxical motion required by Hobbes's idea of freedom and necessity. As a consequence of his idea, the realm of the several sovereigns is neither 'anarchistic' (analogous to, or identical with, 'the state of nature') nor potentially a realm of 'international society' (cooperation underwritten by universal norms).[30] Instead, this realm can be understood as Baroque (Hänninen 2014): a realm of 'bare nature' required for the laws of motion governing Hobbes's *demos* to operate. In brief, Hobbes's commonwealth is always excessive – going beyond itself in order to be.

The liberty of crossing borders

Naturally, the title of this section can be taken literally, and some important recent work has been done on border-crossing markets (Callon 2007; Hänninen 2013) and peoples (Bigo 2002; Ragazzi 2009). My point is entirely sympathetic to these analyses but with a different emphasis: these themes can also be seen to play out the roles of freedom and equality in founding Hobbes's commonwealth as a practice of sovereignty.

---

29 esp. Walker (2010: 139–41).
30 Contra Noel Malcolm's (2002: Chpt. 13) reading of 'Hobbes's Theory of International Relations'.

Hobbes's sovereignty is licensed by far more than a definitional sense of a hierarchical authority within a territorial state with a monopoly on the legitimate means of violence (following 20th-century glosses on state sovereignty). As shown above, Hobbes's bodies cross boundaries of space and time, presence and absence, by splitting the form of bodies from their substance. Hobbes's political bodies are thus not 'bounded' in any simple way. By contrast, contemporary liberal theory sees 'the people' as simply unbounded by statist politics, at least as a regulative ideal (Kant), requiring an institutional moulding (new politics) to bring it into being in an appropriate form (see, for example, Abizadeh 2012). I have indicated the risks of this strategy for MLG in the discussion of Hooghe and Marks's attempt to create/locate 'the people' above. I have also indicated, in the context of Kant and governance, that the freedom and equality of the *demos* are not credible claims. In this section I suggest that the salient source for these claims is no less than Hobbes – the very thinker against whom liberal claims to freedom and equality are made.

It is an article of scholarly faith that Hobbes's account of bodies – including the commonwealth he hopes to establish – is deterministic. Most accounts infer from this that liberty must end once obligation is begun. This faith cannot, however, account for Hobbes's reasoning on how consent is established in sovereign domination.

The main target of liberal critiques, and the main point of justification for their versions of liberty, is Hobbes's formulation of sovereignty by institution (consent/contract) and by acquisition (conquest). Like Foucault (2003: 96), these commentators take Hobbes to be arguing that there is no interesting difference between these types of sovereignty. This hasty reading of Hobbes is a fatal mistake if we want to understand how Hobbes's sovereignty works. In Skinner's version, as with Pettit, Hobbes is understood to be arguing for a view of freedom that excludes subjection to rule, leaving the scope for liberty extremely narrow, perhaps no more than the right to the means of self-preservation. Evidence is offered in Hobbes's statement (*Leviathan*, Chpt. 21) that:

> There is written on the Turrets of the city of Luca in great characters at this day, the word LIBERTAS; yet no man can thence inferre, that a particular man has more Libertie, or Immunitie from the service of the Commonwealth there, than in Constantinople. Whether a Common-wealth be Monarchicall, or Popular, the Freedome is still the same.

Explanatory appeals are also made to the silence of the law; that is, Hobbesian liberty consists in whatever the sovereign leaves unsaid. But is this what Hobbes says? He seems to say the opposite: liberty is identical in Constantinople and Luca because the liberty in question is directed 'externally', towards resisting or invading others from outside, as the preceding sentence in the passage (*Leviathan*, Chpt. 21) says:

> The Athenians, and Romanes, were free; that is, free Common-wealths: not that any particular men had the Libertie to resist their own Representative; but that their Representative had the Libertie to resist, or invade other people.

Sovereignty is not silent here, yet it is the condition of the liberty of particular people. Moreover, the passage is drawing a connection between sovereignty by institution and by acquisition, and thus between 'state sovereignty' and relations between sovereigns. How is this achieved?

Sovereignty by acquisition (conquest, or victory) is also a founding, a beginning of sovereignty – a feature commentators oddly ignore. Charles Tarlton (1999) is one of the few to notice that a split takes place in *Leviathan*, where all at once sovereignty as such (the covenant or 'contract') divides into two types, institution and acquisition. The latter includes Despotical dominion (Chpt. 19),

> when the Vanquished, to avoyd the present stroke of death, covenanteth either in expresse words, or by other sufficient signes of the Will, that so long as his life, and the liberty of his body is allowed him, the Victor shall have the use thereof, at his pleasure.

The passage is curious as it is unclear whether the victorious sovereign is a party to the covenant – if the answer is yes, then the basic procedure of 'exit' from Hobbes's meer nature into the commonwealth is no longer applicable. If not, does the covenant still establish a commonwealth – and how could this work with the victorious sovereignty already established? Moreover, the preservation appears to be merely 'bare life', rather less than is promised by Hobbes's initial picture of sovereignty's benefits. Does sovereignty have a different composition under diverse circumstances of founding? Hobbes cannot allow this: sovereignty is identical, and sovereigns are formally equal.

None of these questions are answered by attending to the concept of servitude Hobbes goes on to describe as a result of this covenant. Tarlton is not much interested in these questions either; his claim is that Hobbes is hypocritical. The two forms of sovereignty are very different, and the brute facticity of 'despotical domination' is the truth of the merely hypothetical, verbal concept of sovereignty as covenant and consent offered early in the text.

In addition to charges of hypocrisy, some describe Hobbes's argument as 'paradoxical' (Springborg 2009) and others as 'political, not metaphysical' (Baumgold 2005, 2009) – a procedure we have seen in legitimations of liberalism as a principled defence of freedom, despite its endorsement of authoritarian rule. There is another answer, however: Hobbes's *Leviathan* is an entirely consistent text. The 'magic instant' (Walker 2010) of founding sovereignty is actually always multiple, crossing the borders of subjective knowledge, science, worlds before and after politics, freedom and necessity, and between sovereigns. The last border-crossing is especially important and hard to grasp. Through the ananke of bodies, Hobbes effects the founding of a single sovereignty and relations between sovereignties in a single stroke. The problem for later thinkers of the logical priority of the state or the system of states largely derives from Hobbes's move here.

Like meer nature and the commonwealth, the end is in the beginning at the present stroke of death. But where in the establishment of the commonwealth do the multitude surrender (give up their rights in a mutual covenant) and 'then' submit to the sovereign thus created (all this appears in a single instant, as Rob Walker (2010) stresses)? In the case of conquest, bodies submit 'first', and then surrender. These *appear* equivalent: all that differs, says Hobbes, is the location of fear (it sits among the multitude in the former case, but between the multitude and the sovereign in the latter). Yet, we can, from *Leviathan*'s point of view, explain this by observing that, in a reversal of the founding dream of consent, the dream of conquest demands that the bodies' fear causes an image of the sovereign to appear.

Dreams must have a place, if a sovereign is to be a person(s), and yet be perpetual – in this sense Hobbes's *Leviathan* is a manual for a sovereignty that never sleeps: the dream is written from a waking point of view. Contra Tuck (2006, 2015), dreams do not register a reserve power of 'the people'. If anything, the reversible relation of conquest and consent that establishes sovereignty as simultaneously within a single polity and between them points to an inhuman view of the sovereign people, whose ever-wakefulness knows only a non-dream.

It is significant in this context that William Burroughs precisely describes America not as a utopia or nightmare, but as a non-dream (Burroughs and Odier 1974: 102–08). For all the talk of America as a 'post-sovereign empire', reluctant or otherwise (c.f. Hardt and Negri 2000), Burroughs' insight suggests that this discourse is well off the mark. Yet, if aspects of America resonate with Hobbes's version of sovereign subjectivity, that certainly does not allow it to be contrasted with a 'Kantian Europe'.

In this context it is helpful to be reminded that the inscription of sovereignty in conquest arising from bodies can also be questioned on its claims to universality. Reminding us of the hegemony of a singular conception of freedom and equality in politics, Christine Helliwell (2000) has argued convincingly that the prevalent liberal feminist fear of violence as arising from sexual differences in bodies (which is strikingly similar to the Hobbesian dream that brings forth the conquering sovereign) should not be imposed on societies such as the Gerai of Borneo, who do not dream of sexual difference, nor have nightmares of rape. The more general point is that imagining a people, a way of life or political formation opposed to sovereignty is self-defeating. Sovereign lines of separation do not place things on one side or the other: the founding line has only one side.

Hobbes's dream of conquest in effect turns reason inside-out, rather like the single-sided line of a Möbius strip (c.f. Bigo and Walker 2007): carrying the waking logic of *ananke* into sleep, the dream appears as if exterior to the familiar, daily experience of the commonwealth. As a founding act of reasoning, Hobbes draws lines between the self, the state and the 'several sovereigns' (there is not a world of sovereigns in Hobbes; 'international relations' await Kant, as Walker (2010) recounts) in order to connect them into a single line. That line is the necessity (*ananke*) of establishing a new form of political community, where 'no viable alternative' (c.f. Hooghe and Marks above) is conceivable. As described, these features of political reason are amenable to a topological analysis, just as Sakari Hänninen (esp. 2014) undertakes in exemplary fashion.[31]

---

31 This account of Hobbes's founding argument is, of course, far from complete. There is much more to discuss in the composition of sovereignty than space permits. This is particularly true of Hobbes's reasoning on geometry, domination, movement and 'savages'. Nonetheless, these considerations – which I shall treat extensively elsewhere – support the more limited account given here.

The art of not crossing borders

This essay has examined some dynamics of recent thought on governance in the EU, as seen through Hobbes's discussion of sovereignty. More specifically, it has looked at some claims to political novelty and democratic potential in the burgeoning literature on MLG. The essay makes three claims in relation to this literature. First, MLG's claims to novelty and democratic enhancement are dependent upon opposition to a flawed conception of sovereignty. Second, this oppositional approach turns out to be self-defeating. Locating sovereignty in a past from which governance has declared independence enables a rhetoric of political founding familiar to classical sovereignty thinking. Third, the response urged to this dilemma was to refuse an oppositional approach to politics. To this end, classical sovereignty in its Hobbesian formulation was revisited. Instead of familiar clichés of three worlds, 'the state of nature, the territorial state and system of states', Hobbes's sovereignty works like MLG: as a border-crossing conception of politics.

Far from a relegation to the past or an eternal presence, sovereignty as Hobbes argues it remains a contemporary practice.[32] I have argued that the multiple crossing lines of Hobbesian reasoning appear as one, but we should not be fooled by his authoritarian reasoning. I have also shown that the Hobbesian state is necessarily excessive, going beyond itself: to the 'savages' of the present–past without proper government, to other sovereigns for recognition, and to 'external governance' in the name of 'security and development' (c.f. RAMSI in Fukuyama (2008)). An extended treatment could also examine the excessive state in Hobbes's concern for the welfare of colonies (c.f. *Leviathan*, Chpt. 22) and to the state's topological stretching via money (Hänninen 2014).

As a boundary-crossing activity, MLG continues to draw on the lines of distinction and connection Hobbes first sketched centuries ago. One implication for further research is that MLG too would benefit from a topological analysis. While governmentality can stretch its forms to take in the system of states and its mutations, governance attempts to reach

---

32 On this point I am sympathetic to the efforts of other students of sovereignty, including Neil Walker (2003) and Raia Prokhovnik (1999, 2007), and especially Constantin Fasolt (2003). In other respects, like Rob Walker, I try to show that fundamental aspects of sovereignty – in this chapter the focus is on form – are missed by texts that see 'political' and 'legal' sovereignty as the essential objects of analysis.

'the globe' – not least by crossing its own conceptual borders with state sovereignty and the market. As a future-oriented act of founding political community, reaching for the globe is driven by Hobbes's logic of *ananke* (form): it appears as both necessary and impossible.

The topological problem is especially serious for MLG's conception of 'the people'. On Hobbes's account of sovereignty, the *demos* are on the line of border-crossing – eternally trapped in the necessary movement of crossing boundaries in order to be at all. The work of that movement is the fragile foundation of sovereignty's edifice; without it, sovereignty simply falls into incoherence. Conventional accounts construe Hobbesian sovereignty as either fully present or entirely absent (Walker 1993, 2010). The novelty and salience of governance is indexed by the degree to which the opposition between sovereign presence and absence is no longer credible or desirable. Little attention has been paid to the 'mobile permanence' of the people in Hobbesian sovereignty.

Dualistic portrayals of sovereignty and governance miss the role of dualism in politics, to their cost. For example, the title of this section is a nod to the work of James C. Scott (2009, 2013), who has long argued that the idea of the state captures much less of the imagination of politically organised peoples than the developmental West assumes (see, in particular, his devastating review of Jared Diamond (Scott 2013)). Where I depart from Scott is in the apparent dualism of his (and others') conception of politics: there is freedom, and there is capture. Hobbes's sovereignty is so powerful precisely because it employs a range of nasty, brutish dualisms to cut short the possibility of escape.

MLG is in a position to challenge sovereignty's work not because of its distance from sovereignty but precisely due to its proximity. MLG attempts to create a people in crossing borders between governance and sovereignty, past and future, the state and the system of states. We can now see MLG's rationality as evolved from Hobbes's. The fixed, frozen-in-motion *demos* of Hobbes's violent, statist authorisations has emerged as a fluid, variable border-crossing *demos* of global aspirations.

Nothing guarantees that movements in reverse along the line between sovereignty and governance do not or cannot occur. A reversal is not a return to the past: sovereignty as a boundary-crossing politics is a contemporary practice. The prime virtue of MLG may be its capacity to approach this practice as both dangerous and contingent: as authorising a conception of freedom and equality that confines 'the people' to an oscillation between mobile permanence and permanent mobility; to approach border-crossing as, in other words, politics. This, it seems to me, is a primary challenge faced by attempts to grasp the senses of transformation at work in social life for more than half a century.

As we began with the image of a train, so we might end with one. This is China Miéville's *Iron Council* (2004). In a sense it's the inverse of *Snowpiercer*: a train grown organically with a marvellously heterogeneous group of rebels/marginal/outcasts (i.e. only those inhabiting the rear of Bong's train) fleeing from a ponderously large, violent and corrupt city. As the train returns to the outskirts of the city to meet its historical destiny in a final confrontation with the city's militia, one of the Iron Council's founders, Judah, manages to freeze the train in a 'time golem', somewhat like the 'bug in amber' that Kurt Vonnegut invokes in *Slaughterhouse Five*. Judah (sure, the reference is clear) has saved the train's denizens from perhaps certain death, but he has also stolen their history – as another founder, Ann-Hari, points out before she shoots Judah for his betrayal. In his freezing of the history of the *demos* in its perpetual border-crossing, is Hobbes not playing the role of Judah? Between this theological–humanist betrayal and that of *Snowpiercer*'s 'new world order' (which renews the Genesis myth when the heroes derail the train), what shape of train does governance conduct?

References

Abizadeh, A. (2012). On the Demos and Its Kin: nationalism, democracy, and the boundary problem. *American Political Science Review*, 106(4): 867–82. doi.org/10.1017/S0003055412000421

Albert, M., Jacobson, D. & Lapid, Y. (eds) (2001). *Identities, Borders, Orders: Rethinking International Relations Theory*. University of Minnesota Press, Minneapolis and London.

Arts, B., Lagendijk, A. & van Houtum, H. (eds) (2009). *The Disoriented State: Shifts in Governmentality, Territoriality and Governance*. Springer, Berlin.

Avant, D.D., Finnemore, M. & Sell, S.K. (eds) (2010). *Who Governs the Globe?* Cambridge University Press.

Bache, I. & Flinders M. (2005). Multi-level Governance and British Politics. In: Bache, I. & Flinders M. (eds) *Multi-level Governance*, Oxford University Press. pp. 93–106.

———. (eds) (2005). *Multi-level Governance*. Oxford University Press.

Baker, A., Hudson, D. & Woodward, R. (2005). Conclusions: financial globalization, multi-level governance and IPE. In: Baker, A., Hudson, D. & Woodward, R. (eds) *Governing Financial Globalization: International Political Economy and Multi-level Governance*. Routledge, London and New York, pp. 192–201.

———. (eds) (2005). *Governing Financial Globalization: International Political Economy and Multi-level Governance*. Routledge, London and New York.

Balme, D.M. (1939). Greek Science and Mechanism I. Aristotle on Nature and Chance. *The Classical Quarterly*, 33(July/Oct.): 129–38. doi.org/10.1017/S0009838800022308

Bates, D.W. (2012). *States of War: Enlightenment Origins of the Political*. Columbia University Press, New York.

Baumgold, D. (2005). Hobbes's and Locke's Contract Theories: political not metaphysical. *Critical Review of International Social and Political Philosophy*, 8(3): 289–308. doi.org/10.1080/13698230500187169

———. (2009). Unparadoxical Hobbes: in reply to Springborg. *Political Theory*, 37(5): 689–93. doi.org/10.1177/0090591709340141

Bigo, D. (2002). Security and Immigration: toward a critique of the governmentality of unease. *Alternatives: Global, Local, Political*, 27(Feb.): 63–92. doi.org/10.1177/03043754020270S105

———. (2008). Security: a field left fallow. In: Dillon, M. & Neal. A.W. (eds) *Foucault on Politics, Security and War*. Palgrave MacMillan, Houndmills, pp. 93–114. doi.org/10.1057/9780230229846_5

Bigo, D. & Walker, R.J.B. (2007). Political Sociology and the Problem of the International. *Millennium: Journal of International Studies*, pp. 725–40. doi.org/10.1177/03058298070350030401

Brett, A. & Tully, J. (eds) (2006). *Rethinking the Foundations of Modern Political Thought*. Cambridge University Press.

Brown, W. (2005). *Edgework: Critical Essays on Knowledge and Politics.* Princeton University Press, Princeton and Oxford.

Bull, H. 2002 (1977). *The Anarchical Society: A Study of Order in World Politics.* 3rd edn. Palgrave, Houndmills.

Bull, H. & Watson, A. (eds) (1984). *The Expansion of International Society.* Clarendon Press, Oxford.

Burroughs, W.S. & Odier, D. (1974). *The Job: Interviews with William S. Burroughs.* Rev. edn. Grove Press, New York.

Buzan, B. & Waever, O. (2003). *Regions and Powers: The Structure of International Security.* Cambridge University Press. doi.org/10.1017/CBO9780511491252

Callon, M. (2007). An Essay on the Growing Contribution of Economic Markets to the Proliferation of the Social. *Theory, Culture and Society,* 24(7–8): 139–63. doi.org/10.1177/0263276407084701

Cavallar, G. (2001). Kantian Perspectives on Democratic Peace: alternatives to Doyle. *Review of International Studies,* 27(2): 229–48. doi.org/10.1017/S0260210500002291

Cerny, P.C. (2009). Neoliberalism and Place: deconstructing and reconstructing borders. In: Arts, B., Lagendijk, A. & van Houtum, H. (eds) *The Disoriented State: Shifts in Governmentality, Territoriality and Governance.* Springer, Berlin, pp. 13–40.

Dale, R. (2004). Forms of Governance, Governmentality and the EU's Open Method of Coordination. In: Larner, W. & Walters, W. (eds) *Global Governmentality: Governing International Spaces.* Routledge, London and New York, pp. 174–94.

Deleuze, G. (1993). One Manifesto Less. In: Boundas, C.V. (ed.) *The Deleuze Reader.* Columbia University Press, New York, pp. 204–22.

Dighe, R.S. (ed.) (2002). *The Historian's 'Wizard of Oz': Reading L. Frank Baum's Classic as a Political and Monetary Allegory.* Greenwood Press, Westport, CT.

Doyle, M.W. (1983a). Kant, Liberal Legacies, and Foreign Affairs. *Philosophy and Public Affairs,* 12(Summer): 205–35.

———. (1983b). Kant, Liberal Legacies, and Foreign Affairs, Part 2. *Philosophy and Public Affairs*, 12(Autumn): 323–53.

———. (1986). Liberalism and World Politics. *The American Political Science Review*, 80(4): 1151–69. doi.org/10.1017/S0003055400185041

Fasolt, C. (2003). *The Limits of History*. University of Chicago Press.

Foucault, M. (1997). The Ethics of the Concern for the Self as a Practice of Freedom. In: Foucault, M. *Ethics: Subjectivity and Truth. The Essential Works of Michel Foucault 1954–1984, Volume One*. Rabinow, P. (ed.) The New Press, New York, pp. 281–301.

———. (2003). *Society Must Be Defended: Lectures at the Collège de France, 1975–76*. Macy, D. (trans.) Penguin, London.

———. (2007). *Security, Territory, Population: Lectures at the Collège de France, 1977–1978*. Senellart, M. (ed.), Burchell, G. (trans.) Palgrave MacMillan, Houndmills.

———. (2008). *The Birth of Biopolitics: Lectures at the Collège de France, 1978–1979*. Senellart, M. (ed.), Burchell, G. (trans.) Palgrave MacMillan, Houndmills and New York.

Franke, M.F.N. (2001). *Global Limits: Kant, International Relations and Critique of World Politics*. SUNY, New York.

Fry, G. & O'Hagan, J. (eds) (2000). *Contending Images of World Politics*. MacMillan Press, Houndmills.

Fukuyama, F. (2008). State-Building in the Solomon Islands, *Pacific Economic Bulletin*, 23(3): 18–34.

George, S. (2005) Multi-level Governance and the European Union. In: Bache, I. & Flinders, M. (eds) *Multi-level Governance*. Oxford University Press, pp. 107–26.

Goodin, R.E. (2008). *Innovating Democracy: Democratic Theory and Practice after the Deliberative Turn*. Oxford University Press. doi.org/10.1093/acprof:oso/9780199547944.001.0001

Goodwyn, L. (1976). *Democratic Promise: The Populist Moment in America*. Oxford University Press, London and New York.

Hänninen, S. (2009). Politics of Security in an Age of Anxiety: the double-bind between freedom and control. In: Scheinin, M. (ed) *Law and Security: Facing the Dilemmas*. EUI Working Paper LAW 2009/11. European University Institute, San Domenico di Fiesole, Italy, pp. 7–22.

——. (2013). Neoliberal Politics of the 'Market'. *No Foundations: An Interdisciplinary Journal of Law and Justice*, 10: 40–58, www.helsinki.fi/nofo/NoFo10HANNINEN.html [Accessed: 01/05/2014].

——. (2014). Thomas Hobbes Reading the EU as a Polity. In: Fichera, M., Hänninen, S. & Tuori, K. (eds) *Polity and Crisis: Reflections on the European Odyssey*. Ashgate, Farnham, pp. 111–34.

Hardt, M. & Negri, A. (2000). *Empire*. Harvard University Press, Cambridge, MA, and London.

Helliwell, C. (2000). 'It's only a Penis': rape, feminism, and difference. *Signs*, 25(3): 789–816. doi.org/10.1086/495482

Helliwell, C. & Hindess, B. (2002). The 'Empire of Uniformity' and the Government of Subject Peoples. *Cultural Values*, 6(1): 137–50. doi.org/10.1080/1362517022019784

——. (2011). The Past in the Present. *Australian Journal of Politics and History*, 57(3): 377–88. doi.org/10.1111/j.1467-8497.2011.01603.x

——. (2015). Kantian Cosmopolitanism and Its Limits. *Critical Review of International Social and Political Philosophy*, 18(1): 26–39. doi.org/10.1080/13698230.2014.995499

Héritier, A. & Rhodes, M. (eds) (2011). *New Modes of Governance in Europe: Governing in the Shadow of Hierarchy*. Palgrave MacMillan, Houndmills.

Hindess, B. (1991). Rationality and Modern Society. *Sociological Theory*, 9(2) (Autumn): 216–27. doi.org/10.2307/202085

——. (1992). Power and Rationality: the Western concept of political community. *Alternatives: Global, Local, Political*, 17(2): 149–63. doi.org/10.1177/030437549201700201

——. (1997). *Discourses of Power: From Hobbes to Foucault*. Blackwell, Oxford.

——. (2001). The Liberal Government of Unfreedom. *Alternatives: Global, Local, Political*, 26(2): 93–111. doi.org/ 10.1177/030437540102600201

——. (2002). Neo-Liberal Citizenship. *Citizenship Studies*, 6(2): 127–43. doi.org/10.1080/13621020220142932

——. (2005). Politics as Government: Michel Foucault's analysis of political reason. *Alternatives: Global, Local, Political*, 30(4): 389–413. doi.org/10.1177/030437540503000401

——. (2014). Bringing Metaphysics Back In? *History of European Ideas*, 40(1): 44–49. doi.org/10.1080/01916599.2013.784032

Hobbes, T. (1913). *The Metaphysical System of Hobbes in Twelve Chapters from Elements of Philosophy Concerning Body Together with Briefer Extracts from Human Nature and Leviathan.* Open Court Publishing, Chicago.

——. (1651). *Leviathan.* MacPherson, C.B. (ed. and 'Introduction') (1985). Penguin, London.

——. (1647). *On the Citizen.* Tuck, R. & Silverthorne, M. (ed. and trans.) (2003), Cambridge University Press.

Hobson, J.M. (2012). *The Eurocentric Conception of World Politics: Western International Theory, 1760–2010.* Cambridge University Press. doi.org/10.1017/CBO9781139096829

——. (2013). The Other Side of the Westphalian Frontier. In: Seth, S. (ed.) *Postcolonial Theory and International Relations: A Critical Introduction.* Routledge, London and New York, pp. 32–48.

Hoekstra, K. (2006). A Lion in the House: Hobbes and democracy. In: Brett, A. & Tully, J. (eds) *Rethinking the Foundations of Modern Political Thought.* Cambridge University Press, pp. 191–218. doi.org/ 10.1017/CBO9780511618376.012

Hooghe, L. & Marks, G. (2003). Unravelling the Central State, But How? Types of multi-level governance. *American Political Science Review*, 97(2): 233–43.

Hunter, I. (2001). Westphalia and the Desacralisation of Politics. In: Hindess, B. & Jolly, M. (eds) *Thinking Peace, Making Peace.* Occasional Paper Series 1/2001. Academy of the Social Sciences in Australia, Canberra, pp. 36–44.

Huntington, S.P. (1968). *Political Order in Changing Societies.* (2006). Yale University Press, New Haven.

Hurrell, A. & Woods, N. (eds) (1999). *Inequality, Globalization, and World Politics.* Oxford University Press.

Jessop, B. (2005). Multi-level Governance and Multi-level Metagovernance. In: Bache, I. & Flinders, M. (eds) *Multi-level Governance.* Oxford University Press, pp. 49–74.

———. (2009). From Governance to Governance *Failure* and from Multi-level Governance to *Multi-scalar Meta*-governance. In: Arts, B., Lagendijk, A. & van Houtum, H. (eds) *The Disoriented State: Shifts in Governmentality, Territoriality and Governance.* Springer, Berlin, pp. 79–100. doi.org/10.1007/978-1-4020-9480-4_4

Kant, I. (1975). Perpetual Peace. In: Beck, L.W. (ed.); Beck, L.W., Anchor, R.E. & Fackenheim, E.L. (trans.) *Immanuel Kant. Kant on History.* Bobbs-Merrill, Indianapolis, pp. 85–136.

Kerr, R. (2013). Sovereignty Never Sleeps. Paper presented to the Finnish Political Science Association Annual Conference, 7–8 March, University of Lapland, Rovaniemi, Finland.

Larner, W. & Walters, W. (eds) (2004). *Global Governmentality: Governing International Spaces.* Routledge, London and New York.

Lavenex, S. (2004). EU External Governance in 'Wider Europe'. *Journal of European Public Policy,* 11(4): 680–700. doi.org/10.1080/1350176042000248098

Lavenex, S. & Schimmelfennig, F. (2009). EU Rules beyond EU Borders: theorizing external governance in European politics. *Journal of European Public Policy,* 16(6): 791–812. doi.org/10.1080/13501760903087696

Lee, D. (2013). 'Office Is a Thing Borrowed': Jean Bodin on offices and seigneurial government. *Political Theory,* 41(3): 409–40. doi.org/10.1177/0090591713476050

Lob, J. & Rochette, J.-M. (2014). *Snowpiercer Volume 1: The Escape.* 2014 edn, Selavy, V. (trans.) Titan Comics, London.

MacMillan, J. (2004). Liberalism and the Democratic Peace. *Review of International Studies,* 30(2): 179–200. doi.org/10.1017/s026021050400600x

Magnusson, W. (2011). *Politics of Urbanism: Seeing Like a City.* Routledge, Milton Park.

Malcolm, N. (2002). *Aspects of Hobbes.* Oxford University Press. doi.org/10.1093/0199247145.001.0001

Marks, G., Scharpf, F.W., Schmitter, P.C. & Streeck, W. (eds) (1998). *Governance in the European Union.* Sage Publications, London.

McGuire, M.C. & Olson Jr, M. (1996). The Economics of Autocracy and Majority Rule: the invisible hand and the use of force. *Journal of Economic Literature,* 34(1): 72–96.

Miéville, C. (2004). *The Iron Council.* (2011), Pan Books, London.

Neal, A.W. (2004). Cutting Off the King's Head: Foucault's *Society Must Be Defended* and the problem of sovereignty. *Alternatives: Global, Local, Political,* 29(4): 373–98. doi.org/10.1177/030437540402900401

Olson, M. (1971). *The Logic of Collective Action: Public Goods and the Theory of Groups.* Harvard University Press, Cambridge, MA.

——. (1993). Dictatorship, Democracy, and Development. *American Political Science Review,* 87(3): 567–76. doi.org/10.2307/2938736

Pagden, A. (1998). The Genesis of 'Governance' and Enlightenment Conceptions of the Cosmopolitan World Order. *International Social Science Journal,* 50(Mar.): 7–15. doi.org/10.1111/1468-2451.00105

——. (2001). *Peoples and Empires: A Short History of European Migration, Exploration and Conquest, from Greece to the Present.* The Modern Library, New York.

Palonen, K. (2002). The History of Concepts as a Style of Political Theorizing: Quentin Skinner's and Reinhart Koselleck's subversion of normative political theory. *European Journal of Political Theory,* 1(1): 91–106. doi.org/10.1177/1474885102001001007

——. (2003). Four Times of Politics: policy, polity, politicking, and politicization. *Alternatives: Global, Local, Political*, 28(2): 171–86. doi.org/10.1177/030437540302800202

Pettit, P. (2008). *Made with Words: Hobbes on Language, Mind and Politics*. Princeton University Press.

Pitts, J. (2005). *A Turn to Empire: The Rise of Imperial Liberalism in Britain and France*. Princeton University Press. doi.org/10.1515/9781400826636

Pogge, T.W. (1992). Cosmopolitanism and Sovereignty. *Ethics*, 103(1): 48–75. doi.org/10.1086/293470

——. (1994). An Egalitarian Law of Peoples. *Philosophy and Public Affairs*, 23(Summer): 195–224. doi.org/10.1111/j.1088-4963.1994.tb00011.x

——. (2002). *World Poverty and Human Rights*. Oxford University Press.

Prokhovnik, R. (1999). The State of Liberal Sovereignty. *The British Journal of Politics and International Relations*, 1(1): 63–83. doi.org/10.1111/1467-856X.00004

——. (2007). *Sovereignties: Contemporary Theory and Practice*. Palgrave MacMillan, Basingstoke. doi.org/10.1057/9780230593527

Raeff, M. (1975). The Well-Ordered Police State and the Development of Modernity in Seventeenth- and Eighteenth-Century Europe: an attempt at a comparative approach. *The American Historical Review*, 80(5): 1221–43. doi.org/10.2307/1852058

Ragazzi, F. (2009). Governing Diasporas. *International Political Sociology*, 3(4): 378–97. doi.org/10.1111/j.1749-5687.2009.00082.x

Rawls, J. (1985). Justice as Fairness: political not metaphysical. *Philosophy and Public Affairs*, 14(3): 223–51.

——. (1996). *Political Liberalism*. Columbia University Press, New York.

——. (1999). *The Law of Peoples*. Harvard University Press, Cambridge, MA.

Rockoff, H. (1990). The 'Wizard of Oz' as a Monetary Allegory. *Journal of Political Economy*, 98(4): 739–60. doi.org/10.1086/261704

Rosato, S. (2003). The Flawed Logic of Democratic Peace Theory. *American Political Science Review*, 97(4): 585–602. doi.org/10.1017/S0003055403000893

Said, E.W. (1993). *Culture and Imperialism*. Alfred A. Knopf, New York.

Scharpf, F.W. (2012). *Legitimacy Intermediation in the Multilevel European Polity and Its Collapse in the Euro Crisis*. Max-Planck-Institute für Gesellschaftsforschung Discussion Paper 12/6, October, Cologne.

Schmitter, P.C. (1998). Imagining the Future of the Euro-Polity with the Help of New Concepts. In: Marks, G., Scharpf, F.W., Schmitter, P.C. & Streeck, W. (eds) *Governance in the European Union*. Sage Publications, London, pp. 121–50.

Scott, J.C. (2009). *The Art of Not Being Governed: An Anarchist History of Upland Southeast Asia*. Yale University Press, Chicago.

———. (2013). Crops, Towns, Government (Review of Diamond, J. The World until Yesterday). London Review of Books, 35(22): 13–15, www.lrb.co.uk/v35/n22/james-c-scott/crops-towns-government [Accessed: 15/11/13].

Skinner, Q. (1996). *Reason and Rhetoric in the Philosophy of Hobbes*. Cambridge University Press. doi.org/10.1017/CBO9780511598579

———. (2008). *Hobbes and Republican Liberty*. Cambridge University Press.

Slomp, G. (2000). *Thomas Hobbes and the Political Philosophy of Glory*. St. Martin's Press, New York. doi.org/10.1057/9780333984437

Soederberg, S. (2005). The New International Financial Architecture (NIFA): an emerging multi-level structure of neo-liberal capitalism. In: Baker, A., Hudson, D. & Woodward, R. (eds) *Governing Financial Globalization: International Political Economy and Multi-level Governance*. Routledge, London and New York, pp. 171–89.

Sorell, T. (2000). Hobbes's Uses of the History of Philosophy. In: Rogers, G.A.J. & Sorell, T. (eds) *Hobbes and History*. Routledge, London, pp. 81–95.

Springborg, P. (2009). The Paradoxical Hobbes: a critical response to the Hobbes symposium. *Political Theory*, 37(5): 676–88. doi.org/10.1177/0090591709340140

———. (2010). Liberty Exposed: Quentin Skinner's Hobbes and republican liberty. *British Journal for the History of Philosophy*, 18(1): 139–62. doi.org/10.1080/09608780903339277

Tarlton, C.D. (1999). 'To avoid the present stroke of death': despotical domination, force, and legitimacy in Hobbes' *Leviathan*. *Philosophy*, 74(2): 221–74. doi.org/10.1017/S0031819199000273

Tuck, R. (2006). Hobbes and Democracy. In: Brett, A. & Tully, J. (eds) *Rethinking the Foundations of Modern Political Thought*. Cambridge University Press, pp. 170–90. doi.org/10.1017/cbo97805 11618376.011

———. (2015). *The Sleeping Sovereign*. Cambridge University Press, New York. doi.org/10.1017/CBO9781316417782

Veyne, P. (1997). Foucault Revolutionises History. In: Davidson, A.I. (ed.) *Foucault and His Interlocutors*. University of Chicago Press, Chicago & London, pp. 146–82.

Walker, N. (2003). Late Sovereignty in the European Union. In: Walker, N. (ed.) *Sovereignty in Transition: Essays in European Law*. Hart Publishing, Oxford and Portland, OR, pp. 3–32.

Walker, R.B.J. (1993). *Inside/Outside: International Relations as Political Theory*. Cambridge University Press.

———. (2006). The Doubled Outsides of the Modern International. *Ephemera: Theory & Politics of Organization*, 6(1): 56–69.

———. (2010). *After the Globe, Before the World*. Routledge, New York and Oxford.

Walters, W. (2011). Foucault and Frontiers: notes on the birth of the humanitarian border. In: Bröckling, U., Krassman, S. & Lemke, T. (eds) *Governmentality: Current Issues and Future Challenges*. Routledge, New York and London, pp. 138–64.

Walters, W. & Haahr, J.H. (2005). *Governing Europe: Discourse, Governmentality and European Integration*. Routledge, London and New York. doi.org/10.4324/9780203299722

Waters, T.W. (2009). 'The Momentous Gravity of the State of Things Now Obtaining': annoying Westphalian objections to the idea of global governance. *Indiana Journal of Global Legal Studies*, 16(1): 25–58. doi.org/10.2979/GLS.2009.16.1.25

Weber, C. (1995). *Simulating Sovereignty: Intervention, the State and Symbolic Exchange*. Cambridge University Press.

Wendt, A. (1999). *Social Theory of International Politics*. Cambridge University Press, New York. doi.org/10.1017/CBO9780511612183

Wight, M. (1977). *Systems of States*. Leicester University Press.

Ziaukas, T. (1998). Baum's Wizard of Oz as Gilded Age Public Relations. *Public Relations Quarterly*, 43(3): 7–11.

Part 2: Education and Social Policy

7

Negotiating the Early Childhood Education Revolution: An Exercise in Multi-level Governance

Trish Mercer and Wendy Jarvie

Introduction

When Kevin Rudd's Labor Government came to power in November 2007, state and territory premiers and chief ministers were amongst those most keenly anticipating a 'change of guard' in Canberra. Before the year had ended, the new prime minister had chaired his first Council of Australian Governments (COAG) meeting, an historic all-Labor meeting that agreed to institute 'a new model of cooperation underpinned by more effective working arrangements' and the corresponding development of a new Commonwealth–state financial relations framework.[1] Over the next year, the frenetic activity that took place through COAG's working-group processes produced this new architecture based on a level of cooperation and collaboration that sharply contrasted with the previous decade of conflict and disharmony (Anderson and Parkin 2010: 99).

---

1 COAG Communiqué, 20 December 2007: 1. The outcome of these COAG meetings and others referred to in this paper can be found at: www.coag.gov.au/meeting-outcomes.

The implementation of the Rudd Government's major election commitment to achieve universal access to 15 hours of preschool weekly for all Australian four-year-olds by 2013 was a new reform agenda caught up in these processes. For early childhood education (ECE), this episode in contemporary federal dynamics would be characterised by a number of elements that were more typical of what is termed multi-level governance (MLG) than classic federalist governance approaches to cooperative policymaking. This case study, prepared from our perspective as former Commonwealth education bureaucrats closely involved in implementing this reform, will examine why ECE became a national priority at this time and to what extent the processes of building ECE into COAG's new framework incorporated an MLG orientation.[2]

Early childhood education: The policy challenge

In the opening years of the 21st century, national and international commentators agreed on the complexity of educational offerings in the year before formal schooling for four-year-olds across Australia: preschool[3] was a labyrinth of conflicting terminology, diverse service types, uneven quality, limited funding provision and confusing regulatory environments in both education and community services. The current landscape was the legacy of a divided system, with the growth of state government oversight and funding of preschools following the kindergarten movement in the late 19th century, whereas the Commonwealth had focused its policy and funding support instead on supporting formal child care, building on the private and philanthropic day nurseries from the early 20th century but increasingly provided in private, long day care centres. Significant variations in preschool offerings had developed due to this bifurcation between ECE on the one hand and care on the other.

---

2   This chapter is based on an Australia and New Zealand School of Government (ANZSOG) case study (Mercer 2016).

3   Preschool has been adopted by COAG as the generic term for the education received by children (usually four-year olds) in the year before formal schooling. The diversity of terms employed across Australia is highlighted in an Australian Council for Educational Research report (Dowling and O'Malley 2009: 2–3).

In broad terms, the country was split between two models of preschool provision: across the most populous eastern Australian states of New South Wales, Queensland and Victoria, the state governments subsidised preschool services, which were delivered by non-government organisations; by contrast, in the remaining states and territories, most preschool services were delivered by, as well as funded through, the government education system.[4] This division, however, was complicated by specific jurisdictional variations (for example, New South Wales also funded and delivered a number of government preschools) and by the increasing eagerness of non-government schools to offer school-based preschool. Outside this 'badged' preschool system, moreover, there were also preschool-program offerings of variable quality in many long day care centres. For parents, it was confusing and frustrating to negotiate the early childhood education and care (ECEC) maze – to know, for example, what their long day centre offered beyond safe babysitting; how to balance work and family, especially if they faced the dreaded 'double drop-off' of one child in care and another in sessional preschool; or how to afford the high preschool fees existing in some states, particularly New South Wales.

Given the diversity of preschool delivery, the compilation of any national picture was a fraught exercise. An annual picture, but only of government-provided or subsidised preschool, was provided in the Productivity Commission's Report on Government Services (although this was qualified by data quality issues, such as double counting): for 2007–08, it reported that 69.9 per cent of four-year-old children were enrolled in such preschool services, receiving between 11 and 13 hours of preschool per week.[5] A particular problem, given the critical issue of Aboriginal and Torres Strait Islander disadvantage, was that the only available national figures for the number of Indigenous four-year-olds receiving preschool were collected through the then Commonwealth Department of Science, Education and Training (DEST) for the purpose of Indigenous preschool subsidies. In the years before the Rudd Government's election, such data limitations had a serious impact on policy development, creating a degree of uncertainty in the minds of policymakers as to the extent of preschool coverage, including for key sub-populations.

---

4 These models and the additional variability at state/territory level are outlined in Dowling and O'Malley (2009: 4–5). The Commonwealth Department of Education, Science and Training also had a relatively small allocation (some $13 million) to support the provision of Indigenous preschools across the country.

5 Steering Committee for the Review of Government Services Provision (2009: 3.21–3.23).

Internationally, Australia consistently achieved a bottom ranking (at 30th) on early childhood provision in the annual education report by the Organisation for Economic Co-operation and Development (OECD), with a percentage of GDP (0.1 per cent) for 'pre-primary education' sitting well below the OECD average (0.45 per cent).[6] Data limitations notwithstanding, this was a telling figure in the policy debate, due to the sheer scale of the difference.

Reflecting the Commonwealth's focus on funding child care, early childhood responsibility at the national level (and also in some states) was in 2006 nested in the Families, Community Services and Indigenous Affairs (FaCSIA) portfolio. With no national policy on preschool or an early years curriculum framework, ECE did not feature in mainstream (i.e. schooling) educational debates, such as those on national curriculum and assessment and teacher training standards. Yet, neuroscience in the 1990s discovered the importance of brain development in the early years for later skills formation. Such 'brain science' was transforming the understanding of researchers and policymakers of the importance of ECEC, reflected in initiatives in South Australia and Victoria to review their policies and profile early childhood development. This traditionally 'soft' area of public policy had also acquired a hard edge through the analyses of leading economists (such as Nobel Prize–winning James Heckman) of the impressive investment return from early childhood for human capital development, although the longitudinal studies cited as evidence were targeted to disadvantaged children (Elliott 2006: Sec. 3), rather than universally available.

As the Coalition Government under John Howard approached the end of its final term in 2007, there was increasing lobbying to address Australia's poor record in ECE and its low investment compared to that made in schools. Pressure was also mounting from some jurisdictions to reconsider the separation of care and education and the confusing regulatory roles played by the Commonwealth and states, fuelled in part by the increasing domination of private for-profit providers in long day care provision. On 10 February 2006, COAG made the landmark decision to include early childhood in its agenda for human capital reform, which signalled that this was finally a priority for public policy attention. By early

6   This OECD expenditure was for 2005 on institutions for pre-primary education and did not include Commonwealth expenditure on preschool delivered in child care centres (due to the absence of formally recorded data) and therefore underestimated Australia's spend (OECD 2008: Table B2.2).

2007, however, with Commonwealth–state tensions intensifying in the pre-election period, the decision taken by COAG at its 13 April meeting reflected a relative stalemate on early childhood, with the Commonwealth having restricted reform proposals to the development of a national approach on quality assurance and regulations.[7]

Reforming early childhood education: Labor's election promises

At the start of the election year in January 2007, Kevin Rudd, as the new opposition leader, seized the initiative to profile ECE in the first major policy statement for his promised 'Education Revolution', citing the research into brain science and cost benefits of ECE investment as productivity drivers (McKew 2013: 129–30). 'New Directions for ECE' committed Labor to spend $450 million a year by 2013 on achieving universal access for all Australian four-year-olds to 15 hours preschool weekly, delivered by four-year-degree qualified teachers, in public and private settings. Other early childhood election commitments included three significant workforce initiatives to boost the supply of early childhood teachers and child care workers, a national Early Years Learning (curriculum) Framework, an additional 260 'early learning centres' with integrated education and care, new quality standards for child care, and measuring the school readiness of every five-year-old child through the Australian Early Development Index (AEDI).[8] Labor also promised to implement the OECD's recommendation for integrated, national leadership by transferring responsibility for ECEC to the education portfolio.

Following the election of the Rudd Government in November 2007, the administrative changes put in place in December 2007 duly established an Office of Early Childhood Education and Child Care (OECECC) in the new mega-department of Education, Employment and Workplace Relations (DEEWR), with Julia Gillard (then deputy prime minister) as the portfolio minister and Maxine McKew as parliamentary secretary for ECEC. With such an explicit reform agenda on ECE, there was

---

7   COAG Communiqué, 10 February 2006: 2 and Attachment A p. 2; COAG Communiqué, 13 April 2007: 4.
8   These were not the only election commitments in early childhood. For full details, see Rudd and Macklin (2007).

a clear government expectation that the policy development phase had been undertaken and that the challenge was, therefore, to implement this element of the Education Revolution rather than to explore the implications of adopting this reform approach in such a complex and neglected policy area.

From its first days, the OECECC was immersed in planning for the implementation of universal access to preschool and other ECEC-related election commitments. A five-year expenditure plan of $533.5 million for universal access leading up to full implementation in 2013 was developed, including an early offer of $10 million for state and territory governments to invest immediately to support access to preschool for disadvantaged and Indigenous children. This initial funding was an effective way to begin a major reform process, in terms of exciting interest in ECE, building working relationships and acquiring knowledge of state priorities.

While this initial sweetener opened dialogue with state officials, Labor's election policy flagged two options for delivering the universal access funding: through the traditional route of state grants (known as specific purpose payments or SPPs) or direct Commonwealth grants to providers. Notwithstanding that there was no existing SPP and that ECE was delivered in both government and non-government settings, the universal access and other ECEC election commitments were quickly swept up into the bigger picture of Rudd's federalist reform agenda.

Australian federalism and MLG

In terms of the division of government between national and state/territory (hereafter referred to as 'state') levels, the Commonwealth and states share intermeshed responsibilities in many social policy areas. Since the 1970s, the Commonwealth increasingly exercised its constitutional ability under section 96 to extend its influence by employing 'tied' or conditional grants (the SPPs). By 2000–01, such SPPs covered some 42 per cent of the total grants to states (Vromen et al. 2009: 306; Fenna 2009: 156).

The Howard years of government (1996–2007) were characterised by a strongly interventionist approach from the central government, which was manifest in the extension of conditionality under these SPPs, including to policy issues beyond the core funding rationale. Education was a sphere singled out for such regulatory federalism, with the Commonwealth tying compliance with contentious national policy initiatives to ongoing core funding – a stellar example being the requirement in school grants legislation that the state governments adopt a Commonwealth-approved and standardised form of student performance reporting in their schools (Vromen et al. 2009: 309; Miragliotta et al. 2010: 253).

Such an increasingly assertive Commonwealth approach to intergovernmental relations heightened the long-standing tensions between these two levels of government over the division of policy responsibility and the processes for establishing and maintaining an effective working relationship in common policy areas. As (Fenna 2004: 171) has observed:

> 'cooperative federalism' might have been a prerequisite in this working relationship but it was hardly an accurate description given the conflict and coercion which more often characterized the interactions in these years.

COAG, which had begun in a more cooperative period in 1992, was seen as a mechanism for the Commonwealth to push its policy positions rather than engage with the states in discussion and negotiation (Fenna 2004: 182; Vromen et al. 2009: 309).

The earlier Labor governments of Gough Whitlam, Bob Hawke and Paul Keating had also not been averse to employing tied grants as a vehicle to extend Commonwealth influence in key policy areas. While traditionally Labor governments had opposed federalism as an obstacle to national policymaking, since the 1970s, Labor has 'reconciled itself' to this fundamental characteristic of the political landscape (Galligan and Mardiste quoted in Fenna 2004: 184). Any view of federalism as a somewhat outdated political system had, moreover, been challenged by the emergence of a confederal united Europe and the rising number of federal countries. The new Rudd Government was known to have looked for inspiration to its UK counterpart, and particularly the social reformist policies of the British Government under Tony Blair, which was regarded as pro–European Union (EU) compared to its Conservative predecessors (Miragliotta et al. 2010: 226–27; Bache 2004: 175–77).

It was the creation of the integrated EU that stimulated the development in Europe of MLG as a concept and brought about its pervasiveness not only in academic discourse, but also in bureaucratic circles. While this is not yet the case in Australia, the complexity and level of difficulty of the policy decisions that are increasingly confronting governments demand more flexible and innovative approaches than are usually associated with governance arrangements under cooperative federalism. One of the values of MLG is that it draws our gaze to the adaptations required of governance in responding to this pattern of complex policy challenges, such as the challenge experienced by Commonwealth and state bureaucrats during 2008 of how to embed the Rudd Government's ECE election commitment within the design for the new federal financial relations architecture.

So how does MLG help us to understand Australian federalist processes of policy development in the contemporary environment? A core contribution is that it assists our understanding of how decision-making involving tiers of government occurs: instead of concentrating our attention solely on the vertical interactions between the two levels of government, MLG places a wider focus on governance and the dynamic, flexible and, importantly, more informal processes operating within a particular policymaking episode. This incorporates horizontal as well as vertical relationships, which may be less hierarchical and include the influence of non-government actors. The core MLG characteristic of 'continuous negotiation amongst nested governments at several territorial tiers' was first defined by Marks (1993: 392), one of the leading contributors to MLG literature (Bache and Flinders 2004: 3). MLG is also associated with a climate of cooperation in which mutual agreement and shared authority and responsibility are dominant, in contrast to the discord and competition that can be characteristic of federalism (Stein and Turkewitsch 2008: 14).

A further refinement in the development of MLG has been its subdivision into two types, of which Type I is relevant for this case study. Type I, which assumes many characteristics closely associated with federalism, is focused on power-sharing among governments operating at only a few levels, such as the Australian national government and the tier of states and territories, with their overlapping powers but with distinct boundaries. Such Type I MLG serves an institutional purpose of highlighting how power and sovereignty is divided between national and state levels in order to enable cooperative approaches to policymaking and to avoid overcentralisation of authority. Type II MLG, by contrast, is represented by policy structures that are more fragmented and numerous, and operates with more flexibility and variability (Stein and Turkewitsch 2008: 3, 9, 12; Bache and Flinders 2004: 5).

MLG has been characterised by Kay as a 'label' for a phase of Australian federalism in a globalised economy era (*Kay*). In the face of demanding policy challenges, Australian federalism is seen to have become more fluid and innovative, thereby breaking free from the shackles of its federal design. This is illustrated by the move away from joint decision-making at the intergovernmental level towards majority voting, to avoid the 'joint decision trap' whereby one level of government can retain the status quo by vetoing any change (*Kay*; Stein and Turkewitsch 2008: 3). Painter has examined how majority voting became part of the Australian cross-governmental ministerial council deliberations from the late 1980s, although consensus typically prevails (Painter 1996). While it has no legislative underpinning, COAG has become a central institution for intergovernmental relations and the operation of what is described as 'executive federalism' (Blayden 2013: 58–59). COAG itself is supported by official committees and working groups to progress policy development between meetings, and this aspect of its operations was taken to a heightened level of activity under the Rudd Government.

The ECE dimension of Rudd's COAG reform agenda

During the 2007 election campaign, Rudd signalled his commitment to federalism as the means of progressing policy reform (Anderson and Parkin 2010: 97–98). His government's early determination to adopt a collaborative partnership approach to Commonwealth–state relations and to remove the major source of disharmony by redesigning the federal–financial framework and rationalising the SPPs was, therefore, perceived by the media and academic commentators as a return to cooperative federalism (Miragliotta et al. 2010: 69; Vromen et al. 2009: 31). Yet, in practice, the process that followed the December 2007 COAG meeting and dominated Commonwealth–state governmental interactions through 2008 can arguably be said to have displayed many characteristics associated with MLG in its Type I approach, at least for the ECE element. As one important indicator, in an acknowledged break with previous practice, Commonwealth ministers were to oversee working groups of senior officials covering the seven areas of COAG's 2008 work agenda, including SPP rationalisation, with nominated senior state officials (rather than the corresponding state minister) acting as deputies. Gillard, whom the media dubbed 'Minister for Productivity', chaired the so-called

Productivity Agenda Working Group (PAWG), overseeing reform across early childhood, schools and skills, with Helen Silver (secretary of Victoria's Department of Premier and Cabinet) as her deputy. COAG'S objectives for this working group clearly signalled the new paradigm in that this was expected to involve:

> additional effort, greater collaboration and sharper focus on improving outcomes – starting with the earliest years, and moving through school and into the training system (COAG Communiqué, 20 December, 2007: 6).

Not only was early childhood thus firmly positioned in the productivity agenda, but also the polarisation that had characterised education discussions over the last decade would be a thing of the past.

Just over a year down the track, Gary Banks, the productivity commissioner, would reflect on the 'novel design' of this new working group structure and 'the punishing dictates' for ministers and officials in responding to a tight timetable of four COAG meetings across 2008 (Banks 2009).[9] Anderson and Parkin later described it as a 'quite remarkable innovation' (2010: 100). For officials in central agencies and line departments in Canberra and around the country, it was a gruelling schedule of meetings, pre and post meetings, teleconferences and briefings to support COAG and also the treasurers' ministerial council. To take forward the education and training work program, the PAWG quickly established three subgroups on schools, skills and workforce development and early childhood development (ECD), composed of senior officials from central agencies and line departments.

At the next COAG meeting, on 26 March 2008, COAG affirmed that the review of SPPs was a priority area, to establish 'genuinely collaborative working arrangements, including clearly defined roles and responsibilities and fair and sustainable financial arrangements to facilitate a long-term policy focus and reduce blame shifting' (COAG Communiqué, 26 March 2008). The SPPs would be contained in an intergovernmental agreement, to underpin the reforms. COAG also endorsed the specific aspirations, outcomes, COAG targets, indicative program measures and policy directions identified by the PAWG as the basis for its creation of new generation education SPPs that would, moreover, include implementation

---

9   Banks also referred to the complexity of the human capital agenda in terms of reform delivery and pointedly noted that Heckman's analysis of the benefits of preschool investment was based on programs for disadvantaged children (rather than universal provision).

of federal election commitments.[10] It would, however, take many months of robust discussions and intense negotiations through PAWG and its three subgroups to produce the draft input for the new Intergovernmental Agreement on Federal Financial Relations, which COAG would consider in November.

As the proverbial infant in the COAG Education family, early childhood did not fit easily into these processes. As mentioned previously, ECE had no existing SPP, so discussion seesawed back and forth as to whether it should be included with the schools SPP, given the importance of an effective transition to school, or be an agreement in its own right, given interest in the broader ECD agenda encompassing education, care and health. Under the new Commonwealth–state financial arrangements, there was also the capacity for new national partnership payments to support project delivery or drive reforms of national importance – although this would be a part of the new COAG architecture that was more fluid during the year. Of the three subgroups to PAWG, only that reviewing ECD was chaired by the Commonwealth (DEEWR deputy secretary Wendy Jarvie), which reflected the new and evolving nature of this reform agenda.

There was, however, some frustration around the role for existing ministerial councils and their senior officials' groups, which were sidelined under these new arrangements, adding a further challenging element for Minister Gillard in bridging the two worlds between PAWG and the existing ministerial councils and groups of officials.[11] Again, ECE was in an unusual position, having previously come under the purview of the community services ministers: a new Early Childhood Ministers Committee was now established as a satellite of the Ministerial Council for Education and Training Ministers, so that education and community services ministers with responsibility for early childhood matters could come together.

---

10   COAG Communiqué, 26 March 2008, Supplementary Information to that contained in the Communiqué: 1–2. The Human Capital Framework of the PAWG was later published in the Commonwealth's May Budget papers, as part of a broader communication strategy around the COAG processes (Gillard 2008: 22, 24–25).

11   This also created uncertainty for the role of Maxine McKew, as parliamentary secretary for early childhood, who later recalled that her relationship with Gillard, while 'workable', 'could have been a lot better' (McKew 2013: 122).

As so often happens in reform processes, the early childhood reform agenda quickly expanded into a broader, indeed whole-of-government, agenda before the reality of what was possible in fiscal terms and in an overloaded policy environment impelled a pulling back and creation of parallel processes (see Figure 7.1).

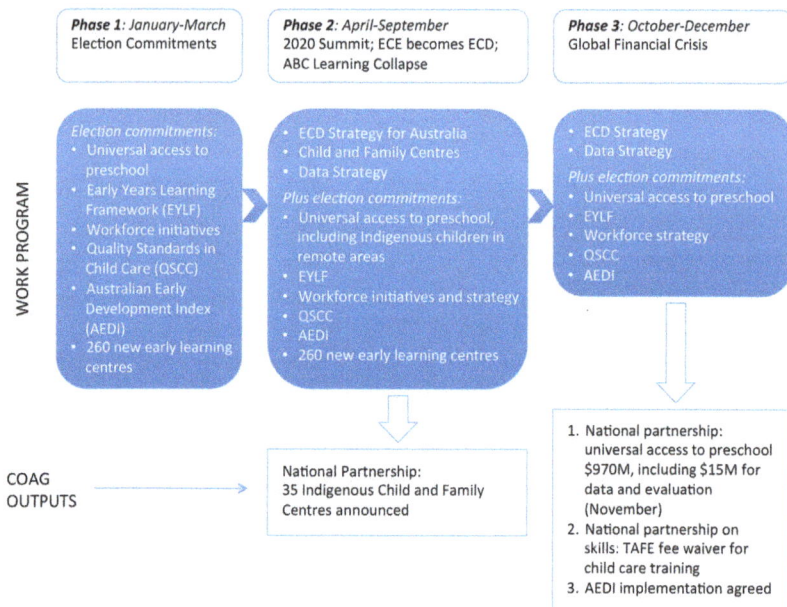

Figure 7.1: The Early Childhood Development (ECD) Subgroup work program, 2008

Source: Trish Mercer and Wendy Jarvie

Prime Minister Rudd, in his powerful 'Sorry' speech delivered to Parliament and the nation in February 2008, committed to providing access within five years to a quality preschool program for all Indigenous four-year-olds in remote communities – this was quickly added as an additional ECE target at the March COAG meeting (COAG Communiqué, 26 March 2008: 7). This meeting also agreed that the ECD program would include the development of quality standards and a rating system for child care and preschool (another election commitment). Given the expansive policy environment, bureaucrats on the ECD subgroup began work on a broad canvas of early child care reform across the interrelated spheres of education, families, health and Indigenous affairs.

The prime minister signalled his interest at his 2020 'Ideas' summit in integrating early childhood interventions through the medium of child and family centres. In July, COAG agreed to the development of a broader national strategy for ECD that would include child and family centres (COAG Communiqué, 3 July 2008: 6). With the map of the new federalism being drawn up concurrently, the ECD subgroup found its task both complex and ambiguous, with changing and sometimes conflicting advice over issues such as whether policy and funding should be dealt with separately and whether it should develop a national agreement with national partnerships hanging off it or begin with just one focused national partnership.

As the year progressed, however, the reform climate became less expansive. In July 2008, under pressure from the states, the Commonwealth formally re-acknowledged that it 'should be responsible for its election commitments' and that 'the legitimate and additional financial implications for the States and Territories' (COAG Communiqués, 28 March and 3 July 2008) would be part of the final determination by treasurers of the new generation SPPs. Politically, the fragile unity of COAG was disrupted when the Labor Government in Western Australia under Premier Alan Carpenter, following a surprise early election, was replaced in September by Colin Barnett's Liberal–National coalition. And, most ominously, governments were beginning to appreciate the intensity and depth of the storm clouds enveloping both developed and developing economies in what became known in Australia as the global financial crisis (GFC).

When COAG met on 29 November, Rudd and Treasurer Wayne Swan engaged in a frenetic day of final bargaining over additional resourcing before leaders emerged to announce that an historic Intergovernmental Agreement on Federal Financial Relations had been signed, rationalising over 90 SPPs down to just five. The communiqué reaffirmed that these new 'cooperative working arrangements' were aimed at improving services by 'reducing Commonwealth prescriptions on service delivery by the States', providing them 'with increased flexibility in the way they deliver services to the Australian people'. This also enabled 'a clearer specification of roles and responsibilities of each level of government and an improved focus on accountability for better outcomes and better service delivery' (COAG Communiqué, 29 November 2008: 2). Performance reporting and analysis (including data quality issues) would be coordinated by an expanded COAG Reform Council and the Productivity Commission would report to the nation's leaders every two to three years on the economic impacts and benefits of this complex reform program. While this new financial arrangement has been recognised as a pro-federalist innovation, the Commonwealth retained a degree of conditionality in certain priority reform areas through the new national partnership payments (Anderson and Parkin 2010: 99, 102–03).

Early childhood undertakings were pared back to fulfilling the core election commitment through one such national partnership payment for ECE – a five-year agreement providing $955 million for states and territories to implement the universal access to preschool commitment by 2013 and $15 million for data development and evaluation.[12] There had been 35 (since expanded to 38) child and family centres already agreed to in the Indigenous Early Childhood Development national partnership signed off in October (see Figure 7.1). Quality standards and a rating system for ECEC and the broader ECD strategy were postponed for future COAG agendas. It was, nevertheless, a singular achievement, recognised externally, that the major building block of universal access had been signed off by all political leaders and that the nation's intergovernmental body now had early childhood integrated into its national reform agenda (Kronemann 2008: 3, 32).

Deborah Brennan, a keen observer and analyst of early childhood policies, later hailed the government's early childhood reform agenda, including this national partnership on ECE, as a considerable achievement, while nevertheless drawing attention to the gaps, weaknesses and inconsistencies that remain in Australia's ECEC approach (Brennan 2011). An associated but unheralded reform has been the structural move, following the Commonwealth's lead, of ECE into the education portfolio in those states and territories where this had been administered in other departments.[13]

---

12 There was also a national partnership developed by the Skills and Workforce Development Subgroup with the assistance of the ECD Subgroup, to deliver the Commonwealth election commitment to fund states for the removal of TAFE fees for diplomas and advanced diplomas of children's services courses.

13 Such machinery of government changes largely took place during 2008, except in New South Wales, where ECEC was finally moved into the education portfolio following the state election in 2011. In Western Australia, child care is still administered in Communities portfolio; in all other jurisdictions, education and care is integrated under education. At the national level, from December 2014 until November 2015, child care was located in the Department of Social Services. It is currently back with the Education and Training Department.

The MLG elements of COAG'S ECE processes

With the intergovernmental agreement signed, it was hardly surprising that the working group structure was disbanded early in 2009, although a National Early Childhood Development strategy group continued to meet to take forward the unfinished agenda. PAWG and its subgroups had been 'fit for purpose' for the chaotic period of drafting the new education agreements, but it was not seen as an ongoing governance arrangement. As a bold experiment in reshaping federal relations, however, its core features appear closer to the MLG concept than to classic federalism, particularly in the case of the new policy agenda that was being rolled out in early childhood, which had the advantage of a relatively low political profile. From the EU experience, MLG is likely to be more evident in 'low politics' issues, where the stakes are less significant and the politics are less fraught (Bache and Flinders 2004: 199).

In another mark of difference, after that first COAG meeting in December 2007, traditional hierarchical processes were overtaken by the degree of urgency for the review of SPPs and the public emphasis on collaborative arrangements between the two tiers of government to produce the desired outcomes. The usual vehicle of ministerial councils working under the aegis of COAG was set aside; senior Commonwealth and state line department officials were instead brought onto PAWG and its subgroups, along with central agency representatives. For state officials, especially those from central agencies, working under the direct oversight of the Commonwealth education portfolio minister to formulate recommendations to COAG, was a unique and somewhat disconcerting experience. The non-involvement of state education ministers unsurprisingly created difficulties for some state officials. A senior state official who sat on both the subgroup and PAWG has confirmed those difficulties and suggested, with hindsight, that they might have been smoothed over if a meeting involving these ministers had been held early in the process.

In the ECD subgroup, this mixed membership came from the departments of Prime Minister and Cabinet, Premier and Cabinet, Treasury, Finance, Education and Community Services, with each jurisdiction determining which agencies would represent them. Such a horizontal dimension played out, moreover, inside the two levels of government outside the subgroup meetings, given the constant need for checking in and reassessing jurisdictional positions on the shifting agenda – particularly in the middle of the year, when the early childhood agenda was broadened to incorporate a wider spectrum of ECD proposals. Within this horizontally structured, more flexible subgroup, continuous negotiation and constant communication were the hallmarks of its operating style, as decisions taken might be quickly superseded by further advice from the central COAG Secretariat, Treasury or COAG itself.

It was, from an insider's perspective, an exhilarating, exhausting, fast-paced and relentless slog, conducted through robust and, at times, heated and even passionate discussions. Speed in negotiation was possible, due to the priority accorded the agenda and the relationships and degree of trust that had developed. This was tested when the Commonwealth decided to ask the group to broaden its already large agenda to develop a proposal for integrated Child and Family Centres: this was agreed to over the phone by jurisdictions in the space of an afternoon and without formal papers.

The first meeting of the subgroup was facilitated and chaired by an external consultant with senior bureaucratic experience, and this innovation helped to break down the normal Commonwealth/state reserve.[14] Following this, frequent and extended subgroup meetings facilitated the development of a significant depth of understanding of jurisdictional challenges and key policy considerations; it built, moreover, a degree of camaraderie as the subgroup explored the dimensions of this new national sphere of social policy. The Commonwealth's early offer of $10 million for the states to invest immediately in universal access projects to help the most disadvantaged children laid the groundwork for a new relationship of working more cooperatively together and learning about state priorities. The Commonwealth was also more transparent with regard to the available funding and distribution methodology. For their part, state representatives were more prepared within the subgroup environment to provide relatively open assessments of their capabilities and challenges in achieving universal preschool coverage.

---

14 This was Mary Ann O'Loughlin, then with The Allen Consulting Group but subsequently appointed as head of the COAG Reform Council. She had been a deputy secretary in the Australian public service and had also worked in Prime Minister Keating's office. Coincidentally, the first meeting was held on the day of Prime Minister Rudd's 'Sorry' speech, which committed the Commonwealth to a new target of quality preschool for all Indigenous four-year-olds in remote communities.

Queensland, for example, was 'coming from behind', having recently added an extra year of formal schooling that was partly achieved by discontinuing their government delivery of sessional preschool.[15] Victoria and South Australia, with high preschool enrolments but some gaps in coverage and hours offered, were keen to shape the national policy debate. New South Wales, on the other hand, where preschool fees and availability were sensitive issues and where the community services portfolio had functional responsibility for ECE, took a lower profile than they did, for example, on the schooling subgroup. Across jurisdictions, the most significant barriers to achieving universal access to preschool, inevitably, were for Indigenous four-year-olds, notably those living in remote and rural areas.

Compared to the tenor of Commonwealth–state meetings in the education sphere over the previous decade, discussions on the ECD subgroup were conducted in a less adversarial and more informal atmosphere. The COAG expectation of a cooperative working arrangement set the tone for discussions in PAWG and, correspondingly, the ECD subgroup. As an emerging issue, early childhood operated to an extent 'under the radar' and, compared to the schools agenda, was not weighed down by the years of polarised debate on sensitive issues. Working on a policy landscape characterised by such diversity, underinvestment by government and variable quality supplied an incentive to consider more innovative solutions to the complex policy problems inherent in the Commonwealth's commitment to achieve universal access to preschool within a comparatively short five-year window. Greater collaboration, innovation and relative informality frequently are characteristic features of an MLG approach.

Two significant reforms incorporated into the national partnership agreement on ECE underlined the power of these more collaborative and, at times, innovative discussions in the ECD subgroup. The first, which was specifically acknowledged in the agreement, was the adoption of differential funding for the first four years, in order to provide a greater share to Queensland and the Northern Territory, which had further to go to reach the universal access goal, including the specific target for

---

15 In September 2008, this major gap in preschool access was addressed when Premier Anna Bligh announced a six-year plan for Queensland to reintroduce preschool, utilising the community and private sector for delivery, backed by a $300 million infrastructure program for new kindergarten services (Queensland Premier 2008).

Indigenous children living in remote areas. In the debates in the subgroup, the recognition that some jurisdictions faced a greater challenge and also the internal data analysis and funding options developed by the DEEWR representatives had enabled an informed discussion on the impact of differential funding in the initial period to meet the target of universal access to preschool by 2013 across the country.[16]

The second reform initiative, which was also indicated in the agreement, was to reserve central funding of $15 million for data development and evaluation to enable development and implementation of a national performance information strategy – a recognition of the need to work together on data quality issues. This was not replicated in the other education agreements and can be attributed both to the 'low politics' of ECE and the inescapable need to invest in data improvements. Working towards the achievement of nationally consistent data would enable reporting on progress against the performance indicators in the agreement and for the broader public accountability signed off by COAG as a key element of the new federal financial relations.

Given the fast and furious nature of the development of the COAG reform package in 2008, this negotiation was a continuous process conducted largely in-house between the two tiers of government. It was a non-transparent 'top-down' decision-making process with broader stakeholder engagement largely conducted through formalised, 'talking head' consultations at key points across the year (Kronemann 2008: 4). Indeed, a criticism levelled at COAG processes more broadly concerns the limited public information that is available on outcomes and the underpinning rationale for decisions (Blayden 2013: 56). Given the sensitivity of the child care market, a notable exception was the deeper consultative processes conducted around the development of quality standards and a national early years learning framework (EYLF) for ECEC. This limited role for non-government actors reinforced the principally Type I MLG nature of these COAG processes for developing the intergovernmental agreement.

---

16   This was confirmed by a senior state representative on the subgroup, who described the acceptance of differential funding as 'quite remarkable', and put it down to the fact that everyone in the subgroup understood the data and the 'black hole' in Queensland, and that some states had to get more than others if universal access was to be achieved.

Lessons learnt

The emphasis by COAG on collaborative working relations did not prove to be long-lived; Anderson and Parkin have observed that, following the first two years, the Rudd Government was more often seen to be attacking the states 'as impediments to the national achievement of a more effective, consistent and effective policy reform' (Anderson and Parkin 2010: 97).[17] Indeed, in June 2011, Terry Moran (one of the architects of this agreement in his role as head of Prime Minister and Cabinet), described the intergovernmental agreement as a 'radical, yet poorly understood reform', whose promise, moreover, 'has so far not been fully realized' (Moran 2011).[18] The archetypal MLG elements evident in this exercise may, however, be replicable in other policy development processes, albeit with adjustments for the differing circumstances and authorising environments. Potentially transferrable practices that worked for the ECD subgroup can be represented in four areas of learnings: the structural arrangements, supporting processes, skill sets and behaviours of the participants, and negotiating style (see Table 7.1).

Table 7.1: COAG Early Childhood Development Subgroup 2008: What worked – at a glance

Issue/action	Why important?
Structures	
Fit for purpose committees – Productivity Agenda Working Group; ECD subgroup	Clarity – tasks were clear, role of members was clear
Membership of ECD subgroup included central agencies (e.g. Premier and Cabinet, Treasuries) as well as line agencies	Increased understanding of issues and options sped up decision-making within governments
Subgroup reported directly to the deputy prime minister as chair of PAWG	Created a strong authorising environment
Overlapping membership of ECD subgroup and PAWG	Improved PAWG understanding of issues sped up decision-making

---

17   In 2011, the Business Council of Australia, in its submission to a joint parliamentary committee inquiring into federal–state funding agreements, warned that the Commonwealth was moving back to the 'old system' and that there was a proliferation of new agreements since 2008 that reinstated Commonwealth direction over funding (*Australian*, 3 June 2011: 8).

18   Moran attributed this to some state line departments who were taking time to adapt to this reform, although they had willingly accepted the funding increase, and also noted that some Commonwealth line departments had been slow to adapt to the spirit of the agreement.

Issue/action	Why important?
Processes	
First meeting – use of independent ECE expert as facilitator	Built collaborative atmosphere from the beginning
Extensive meetings (usually monthly); intensive meetings (often two days in length)	Allowed sufficient time to develop a common understanding of issues and sufficient opportunity to form relationships
Relatively informal, free-flowing discussion in meetings, flexible agenda, round-the-table summaries	Avoided perception that one jurisdiction was controlling agenda; ensured all voices heard – big and small jurisdictional views captured
Skills and behaviours	
Members held a mix of expertise in ECE and/or government funding and processes	Key issues and problems across all aspects of the agenda were identified quickly and this enabled rapid two-way education of members
Collaborative behaviour, particularly by the Commonwealth; regular use of 'we' meant the Commonwealth was seen to be listening and learning from the states	Promoted greater trust, avoided perception that Commonwealth was imposing its agenda
Negotiation	
Tactic: work on a big vision of ECD while developing options for implementing Commonwealth election commitments	Something for everyone, created a sense of opportunity and a 'blank slate'
Work on developing trust and building relationships	Created a greater willingness to find solutions to problems, and avoided adoption of entrenched positions; more possible on 'low politics' issues
Learn as much as possible about different situation in each jurisdiction	Developed common understanding of issues, particularly the different starting positions on universal access to preschool

Firstly, the *structural arrangements* facilitated policy decision-making in an environment of urgency – which tends to characterise much of public policy development in Australia. Both the overarching PAWG and its offshoot, the ECD subgroup, were structured around a horizontal and senior membership that enabled fast decision-making when required; for the subgroup, a degree of overlapping membership with the PAWG (as the chair and some state representatives attended both), kept a strong linkage with the working group's directions and imperatives – that is, with the authorising environment. The direct lines of reporting from PAWG to COAG bypassed the traditional vertical layer of ministerial councils and accelerated the provision of policy advice to COAG and its key senior officials committee. For the ECD subgroup, these structural arrangements were complemented by *supporting processes* emphasising an energetic, more dynamic operating approach that resulted in relatively informal, free-flowing discussions on the difficult elements of the ECE agenda. The pattern was one of meeting often and for lengthy periods to grapple with the fast-moving agenda and diverse work program. Through such intensive meetings, there was greater capacity to develop a common understanding of the policy challenges at both jurisdictional and national levels and the key elements of a vision for improved ECE services. It is unusual for time-pressured senior bureaucrats to have such an opportunity to interact intensively around a new policy agenda, especially an area such as ECE, which excites strong and passionate views.

Undoubtedly the mix of *skill sets and behaviours* fostered in the subgroup served to create a more positive environment for negotiation of the most difficult issues. Expertise around the table incorporated subject matter experts; those with broader education and community services sectoral understandings, including Indigenous service delivery; and those more attuned to intergovernmental relations and funding vehicles. The collaborative behaviours auspiced by COAG were manifested in such features as the inclusive language adopted ('we' and 'us') and the specific practice of using 'around the table' views to enable the perspectives of small and large jurisdictions to be captured. Certainly, from a Commonwealth perspective, the political alignment at the ministerial level and deliberate focus on cooperation enabled a more open and frank relationship with state counterparts to be developed after several years of more cautious dealings.

The negotiating style for key decisions adopted in the subgroup, informed by such close engagement with the issues, was based on the need to bring all parties together on central issues – while avoiding the 'joint decision-making trap' as far as possible. This helped to offset the disadvantage inherent in being provided with the 'one' solution of universal access to preschool, rather than having been able to debate openly the range of potential solutions to Australia's fragmented ECE delivery and policies. The focus on an idealistic 'big picture' for how early childhood services could be enhanced and strengthened tended to offset and make more acceptable the Commonwealth's inevitable preoccupation with delivery of the government's early childhood election commitments. For state officials, a strength of the subgroup was the fact that the Commonwealth was seen to be listening to, and learning from, them.

Of course, this is not to downplay that there were significant tensions, given the diversity of policy approaches and the time pressures that foreshortened debate on some key issues. Most importantly, with the narrowing of the process to a focus on universal access delivery, there was no agreement on a coherent national policy framework for ECE, and the work of the subgroup became more of a 'slog'. The details of how the states would deliver universal access to preschool within five years and how they would involve the non-government sectors in this delivery were left for resolution in the development of state bilateral plans in the next year. The broader National Early Childhood Development strategy had a bumpy ride and was not agreed and released by COAG (in a very 'light touch' form), until 2 July 2009. Collecting data on every child in their first year of school for the AEDI was not agreed until the Commonwealth government found more money to cover teacher costs.

In addition, when the GFC hit and the Commonwealth pulled back from the proposed child and family centres and the 260 early childhood centres, there was an uneasy period of reassessing the policy directions, given that an important opportunity to create a new and integrated delivery landscape had been lost. In particular, the states that had not received many or any of the first tranche of 38 centres, and who now missed out, had some disappointment to swallow. Nevertheless, the ECD subgroup showed that it is possible for the two tiers of government to work together closely to achieve mutually agreed objectives in a more collaborative environment, exemplifying a broader trend under COAG to encourage the growth of 'new bureaucratic networks across State borders' (Anderson quoted in Blayden 2013: 59).

The key players inside government during 2008 would not have described or recognised the exercise they were immersed in as an example of MLG; if pressed, they might have pragmatically labelled it as an instance of Australian federalism adapting to the exigencies of the contemporary environment, with its emphasis on increasing productivity and investing in human capital. At the same time, they were aware that they were engaged in something new and different – a 'fascinating process' as one state official described it, which was 'bold and unusual' but 'offered something good and worthwhile'. It was characterised by a new and less traditionally hierarchical way of working together, a novel design in structural arrangements, a new focus on objectives and outcomes over inputs, and a new emphasis on accountability and monitoring as the trade-off for the removal of restrictive conditions in the Commonwealth's grants. The novelty of these year-long, less than perfect discussions was captured by Russell Ayres, branch manager in OECECC, who was closely involved in the ECD subgroup:

> What we had created in the National Partnership for Early Childhood Education was all new. It was new (and major) funding; it was a new form of intergovernmental agreement; and it was a new way for government to work with the early childhood education and care sector (at least at the national level).

This episode of working through a new policy agenda confirmed that an MLG approach can deliver results, notwithstanding that ECE reform remained a work in progress at the end of 2008. But this approach was reliant on a fragile balance of power in Commonwealth–state relations that was dependent on the Commonwealth's willingness to cede power. This supportive environment appears to have dissipated in subsequent years, as the Commonwealth shifted its focus towards greater centralisation, amid tension in what was once again a politically divided federation.

References

Anderson, G. & Parkin, A. (2010). Federalism: A fork in the road? In: Aulich, C. & Evans, M. (eds) *The Rudd Government: Australian Commonwealth Administration 2007–2010*. ANU E Press, Canberra.

Bache, I. (2004). Multi-level Governance and European Union Regional Policy. In: Bache, I. & Flinders, M. (eds) *Multi-level Governance*. Oxford University Press. doi.org/10.1093/0199259259.003.0010

Bache, I. & Flinders, M. (eds) (2004). *Multi-level Governance*. Oxford University Press. doi.org/10.1093/0199259259.003.0012

Banks, G. (2009). Evidence-Based Policy Making: What is it? How do we get it? Australia and New Zealand School of Government. ANU Public Lecture Series, Canberra, 4 February 2009.

Blayden, L. (2013). *COAG Briefing Paper No 6/2013*. NSW Parliamentary Research Service, Sydney, July 2013.

Brennan, D. (2011). 'Investing in Childhood: The Progress and the Pitfalls'. *Inside Story: Current Affairs and Culture from Australia and Beyond*. Swinburne Institute for Social Research, 25 August 2011, insidestory.org.au/investing-in-childhood-the-progress-and-the-pitfalls/ [Accessed: 10/05/2017].

COAG Communiqués (2006–09). webarchive.nla.gov.au/gov/20070829 161008/http://coag.gov.au/meetings/archive.htm; www.coag.gov.au/coagmeetingoutcomes/index.cfm [Accessed: 13/12/2014].

Dowling, A. & O'Malley, K. (2009). *Preschool Education in Australia*. Australian Council for Educational Research, Melbourne.

Elliott, A. (2006). Early Childhood Education Pathways to Quality and Equity for All Children. *Australia Education Review*. Australian Council for Educational Research, Melbourne.

Fenna, A. (2004). *Australian Public Policy*. 2nd edn. Pearson Longman, Frenchs Forest, NSW.

——. (2009). Federalism. In: Rhodes, R.A.W. (ed.) *The Australian Study of Politic*. Palgrave Macmillan, Chippenham and Eastbourne. doi.org/10.1057/9780230296848_11

Gillard, The Honourable J. (2008). Ministerial Statement 13 May 2008. *Commonwealth Budget Education Revolution 2008–09*. Commonwealth Government, Canberra.

Kronemann, M. (2008). *Aboriginal and Torres Strait Islander Children and the National Early Childhood Agenda. An Initial Discussion Paper*. Dusseldorp Skills Forum, Melbourne.

Marks, G. (1993). Structural Policy and Multilevel Governance in the EC. In: Cafruny, A. & Rosenthal, G. (eds) *The State of the European Community Vol. 2: The Maastricht Debates and Beyond*. Longman, Harlow, pp. 391–410.

McKew, M. (2013). *Tales from the Political Trenches*. Melbourne University Press, Carlton, Victoria.

Mercer, T. (2016). 'Universal Preschool: The rocky path to policy change'. ANZSOG case study, www.anzsog.edu.au/resource-library/case-library/universal-preschool-the-rocky-path-to-policy-change-2016-176-1 [Accessed 11/10/17].

Miragliotta, N., Errington, W. & Barry, N. (2010). *The Australian Political System in Action*. Oxford University Press, South Melbourne.

Moran, T. (2011). Speech to Eidos Institute, An Australian public policy think tank. Brisbane. 8 June.

OECD (2008). *Education at a Glance 2008*. Organisation for Economic Co-operation and Development, Paris.

Painter, M. (1996). The Council of Australian Governments and Intergovernmental Relations: A case of cooperative federalism. *Publius: The journal of federalism* 26(2) (Spring).

Queensland Premier (2008). Message from Queensland Premier, TowardQ2, September, cabinet.qld.gov.au/documents/2009/jun/ toward%20q2%20qld%20next%20steps/Attachments/Q2%20 Summary.pdf [Accessed: 15/12/14].

Rudd, K. & Macklin, J. (2007). New Directions for Early Childhood Education. Universal access to early learning for 4 year olds. Australian Labor Party, January 2007.

Steering Committee for the Review of Government Services Provision (2009). *Report on Government Services 2009*. Vol. 1. Melbourne.

Stein, M. & Turkewitsch, L. (2008). The Concept of Multi-level Governance in Studies of Federalism. Paper Presented at the 2008 International Political Science Association International Conference, Concordia University, Montreal, Quebec, Canada.

Vromen, A., Gelber, A. & Gauja, A. (2009). *Powerscape Contemporary Australian Politics*. Allen and Unwin, Crows Nest, NSW.

8

The Deployment of an Epistemic Model of Multi-level Governance: A Study of Differences in Hearing

Anthony Hogan

Medicine is not the only player upon the stage of what Michel Foucault called 'bio-politics' (Osborne 1996).

The current disability support system is underfunded, unfair, fragmented, and inefficient. It gives people with a disability little choice, no certainty of access to appropriate supports and little scope to participate in the community. People with disabilities, their carers, service providers, workers in the industry and governments all want change (Productivity Commission 2011).

Introduction

The governance of human communication has been a matter of contention over millennia, particularly for Deaf people, and the lives of those who hear differently from others (henceforth the *governance of differences in hearing*, since most acquire a change in hearing status rather than being born with it and most retain some experience of hearing). In addition, while there have been multiple players in the shaping of these governmental processes, for the most part people who hear differently from others have been the subject of, rather than the author of, such processes. I assert this position, noting two important exceptions: members of the linguistically oriented Deaf Community – the signing world – have often shaped the terms of their own governance, albeit they have often been marginalised from the more dominant phono-centric culture as a result (see, for example, Corker 1998); second, the involvement of deafened people within their own self-help movements such as Self Help for Hard of Hearing (SHHH) and Better Hearing Australia (BHA). From within this group, I note two distinct positions: a smaller cohort who seek to shape their lives according to their own lights; and a second, more common group whose lives and the services they use, be they children, the children's parents or deafened adults, have been the subject of governance processes and concerted efforts of subjectification for over 150 years. It is this latter, most numerate group to which this chapter gives most attention as it considers the development and breadth of governmental processes in this space.

I approach this discussion in several ways. First, the analytical lens provided within Lukes's (1974) theory of the three faces of power enables the framing of a number of important questions about the governance of hearing difference and subsequent social participation. The application of this lens enables questions to emerge that are concerned with why it is that differences in hearing (and disability, more generally) have been a site of governance for so long. Moreover, it enables one to consider the nature of the social agenda around differences in hearing participative capacity and the kinds of interests that have driven it to given ends. Such a lens raises questions about who gets to decide these issues and how such decision-making processes secure sufficient legitimacy, so they can be progressed. It is a study of who wins the battle of ideas and, in turn, is able to secure resources to shape processes that subjugate large numbers of people. While I value Lukes's insight that the third face of power is concerned with the shaping of personal preferences, I have found the analytical lens that can be shaped from Michel Foucault's (1988) approach to the technologies of the self, taking into account more recent modifications to that framework (Akram and Hogan 2015), to be most useful in articulating how governmental structures can be developed and deployed in such a way so as to shape the 'conduct of conduct'.

The core of this framework is straightforward. Certainly, the battle for ideas is constant and enduring, but some ideas find dominance and legitimacy in given places at given times. The social processes that legitimise the emergence of dominance stem from securing what Foucault refers to as the 'the interests of the interested', a more recent variation of Karl Marx's insight that the ideas of the ruling class are, in each and every epoch, the ruling culture. Foucault asserts that symbols and meaning systems emerge that are legitimised by the convergence of the interests of the interested. In turn, this process legitimates some practices and beliefs over others, setting in place three additional processes: (i) the funding and formation of institutions and technologies that can be used to shape beliefs and behaviour; (ii) the training of practitioners and the development of techniques of subjugation; and (iii) the application of such techniques on, and by, willing individuals on themselves as they engage in taken-for-granted processes of the formation of the self.

Contrary to the deterministic argument (e.g. Hay and Wincott 1998), individuals can and do have a say over their formation as individuals. It is not the case that people cannot pursue alternatives, just that few have either the courage or the resources, certainly within the deafness milieu, to pursue such alternatives. The Deaf Community is a case in point. Social Scientist Hal Colebatch (University of New South Wales) remarked, following his receipt of a cochlear implant, that the dominant group in deafness, the oralist movement (see Winefield 1987 for further detail),[1] as they are known, have been so successful in their mission that they are the 'only show in town'. For over 100 years they have been able to shape the agenda, dominating the distribution of funding by ensuring that the policy lens is solely focused on the issues that they wish to see progressed.

It is not the purpose of this chapter to detail how the oralists achieved this position. Rather, the central concern of this chapter is with the governance of hearing difference. Such a governmental arrangement cannot, however, be understood outside the socio-historical context within which it emerged – the milieu from within which the dominant systems of meaning and symbolism grew and found legitimacy. To this end, I first summarise the key arguments of the body of work I have developed over the past 20 years, referring the reader to more detailed studies where further substantiation of the arguments is sought. While from one perspective it could be argued that this is a multi-level approach to governance, it is also epistemic, in that what is most interesting about this approach to governance has been the capacity of the oralist movement to kill off notions of hearing difference, the other, and of alternate ontologies and epistemes of the body (de Sousa

---

1   The oralist movement took the position that it is a hearing world and that a person should participate in it on the terms of hearing people. A similar argument was taken by patriarchal society with regards the social position of women.

Santos 2014), and that it serves as its first master the needs of a phono-centric, market-oriented society. It is epistemic (de Sousa Santos 2014), not because of what it bans but for the fact that only some processes of people-formation gain social support, including resources, while those that exist outside this structure are left to wither, as it were, on the vine.

This is a social issue not only because this process systematically extinguishes difference, but also because the movement, whose methods are inherently expensive,[2] has failed to deliver on its promise that people, by enrolling in such processes, would enjoy equitable participation in society (Hogan and Phillips 2014). In this vein, I document the development of a legitimated capacity to govern the difference in hearing before concluding the chapter with a consideration of what an alternative frame of governance could look like.

The shaping of the habitus surrounding deafness and disability

Summarising the work of Hogan (1997), it is apparent that, over several hundred years, a variety of community, medical, educational and social interests have been concerned with the governance of hearing difference. Notably, that body of work highlighted the emerging discourse of dependency/independence centred on forms of communication (e.g. sign language verses oral communication) (Winefield 1987) and, in turn, framed the governance of hearing and disability issues generally. This controversy, while driven by concerns focused on securing a given form of social relations amidst a broader threat of social disruption, largely centred on the politics of meaning and symbolism surrounding deafness with regard to supporting the broader functioning of 19th-century Western society. In the case of deafness, people such as Alexander Graham Bell took up this cause with earnest.

Bell observed that devotees of the methods he proposed were even prepared to die for the cause, if it meant that people could be saved from the perils of a deaf world (Winefield 1987; Bruce 1973). In addition to his work on the education of deaf children, Bell also developed an early form

---

2   Many thanks to Michelle Barry, Executive Officer, Better Hearing Australia, Melbourne, for this insight.

of an audiometer (a machine that is used to measure hearing impairment). While the institutional and professional arrangements that underpin modern hearing services only began in earnest following World War II, they did, however, draw upon the ontological assumptions underpinning deaf education. As Winefield (1987: 22) observed:

> Normal society, Bell maintained, consisted of people who could speak and hear and make use of the English language. The job of educators, therefore, was to prepare deaf children to make their way in the world by being able to communicate in English by speaking and reading lips.

Bell conceived of deafness as disconnecting individuals from a phono-centric society, and that it was the place of hearing services to restore people to participation in such a society. The problem with Bell's conception of speech-based (rather than sign language or augmented forms of communication) social inclusion and participation was that his model sought to eliminate, rather than encompass, difference.

Harlan Lane (1993), a major critic of the bureaucratic implementation of this process, identified the issue at stake as being one of bio-politics, where power is exercised in the lives of people with disability. On the one hand, Lane argues that the governance of deafness results from individualising processes legitimated by formal modes of government. To a certain extent, he also recognises that the governance of Deaf people (that is, members of the signing Deaf Community) is situated within a broader system of governance concerned with the regulation of disabled people and others whose social status came to be considered marginal. Lane stops short, however, from describing how such a process of governance came into being, leaving the reader with the sense that people who design and run hearing services, as an example, simply had the power to make it all happen. As such, Lane's position could unintentionally suggest a more simplistic understanding of how power is deployed, as though power could be possessed like a side gun slung across the waist band. Foucault's understanding of power is far more complex:

> Power is not something that is acquired, seized, or shared, something that one holds on to or allows to slip away; power is exercised from innumerable points, in the interplay of non-egalitarian and mobile relations (Foucault 1978: 94).

If Foucault's insights on the social processes of the formation of the self are correct, then one ought to be able to document how power comes to be exercised and focused on the formation of people who hear differently from others. At issue within such an analysis is that governance processes are based on the seemingly legitimate, taken-for-granted, unquestionable commonsense way in which things get done, such that one way of acting would seem the only way one would act in a given circumstance. It is this taken-for-grantedness about the deficits of hearing difference and its inherent threat to broader society, along with assumptions about the validity of phono-centricism, that underpin the emergence of a multifaceted approach to the governance of hearing difference. Such an approach resulted from the collaboration of institutions and professions, situated within a social context shaped by these specific meanings and economic relations, and came into being in such an unexceptional process that technologies and specific techniques of self-formation could be brought to bear on given groups of individuals in such a way as to seek to influence the behaviour of those people in ways that seem self-evident.

This chapter, then, examines the developments of such modern hearing services, considering as it does the models of individual formation that were, in turn, brought to bear on the person who hears differently from others, while acknowledging the dominance of one form of governance over others. Moreover, this chapter seeks to make apparent the fact that it is possible for individual and institutional actors to deploy a governmental process not only without the consent or involvement of those most affected, but also because of processes of personal formation and socialisation that result in people enrolling themselves in procedures and using technologies despite the fact that they may not improve their social position.

The development of publicly funded hearing services in Australia

Publicly provided hearing rehabilitation services commenced in earnest in America following the World War II, with service provision focused on veterans (Gaeth 1979). Interestingly, the early development of hearing services was centred on a medical model of the body that focused services on an integrated model of delivery concerned with the wellbeing of the whole person (Gaeth 1979). Given the notable limitations of the hearing devices available at that time, concern existed that the medical model over-promised on the extent to which the offered interventions (such as surgery, hearing aids, lip-reading training) could meet the needs of returning veterans. Notably, the service model saw that a 'man is more important than his ears' (Gaeth 1979: 6). The service model was centred on two principles: the positive and negative of hearing loss. With regards to the positive, the program sought to equip the person with *normal* functioning using hearing aids, speech reading and related tools. As such, a foundational step in the development of this service model was the taken-for-granted acceptance of a deficit model of hearing, remediated, as it were, by hearing aids and supplementary training designed to maximise the benefits the device could offer. Interestingly, though, the model acknowledged the limitations of the devices at that time.

The negative approach to the program was constructed as follows:

> The rehabilitee must learn new ways of getting along in a world that is dependent on communication. If he wears a hearing aid, he must learn to think and act like a person who wears a hearing aid, not like a person who is perfectly normal but cannot hear well. He must prepare himself to meet the thoughtless attempts of others to communicate with him (Gaeth 1979: 6).

Central to the negative approach was the taken-for-granted acceptance of the ontology underpinning communicative relations – it is a hearing world and one must learn to live in it as a hearing person. Similarly, it was taken for granted that, from an interactional point of view, the person whose hearing was different from others would adapt themselves to the needs of dominant society, despite the fact that such a process could be difficult and/or stigmatising.

In Australia, the resulting, Commonwealth-funded service-delivery model was based on a military style of teaching that was matter of fact, if not somewhat confrontational; services were concerned with delivering help 'which lays the cards on the table and gives help on how to cope' (Gaeth 1979: 5). In addition, hearing services were not voluntary, but rather soldiers were 'sent' for rehabilitation (Gaeth 1979). As military personnel, the participant's job was to be in the program. The power to compel people to participate in hearing services also serves to underpin the command-and-control values at the centre of many hearing services today. Within the audiological sector, there is an evident culture of annoyance with people who will not take appropriate action to manage their hearing loss or use their hearing aids, as though they were somehow disobeying orders.

Setting aside the values that guided the delivery of services, the idea of providing people with access to assistive listening devices as well as support in managing everyday interactions was considered to be a form of audiological Camelot[3] (Ross 1997). Some of the values underpinning the service model also foreshadowed the emergence of the social model of disability (Oliver 1996). Henoch (1979) argued that services for older people who heard differently needed to address the social aspects of hearing by working with families and people who regularly interacted with the person to enable them to participate in those interactions. These models of intervention similarly did not question the assumption about the primacy of the taken-for-granted rules of phono-centric communication. Rather, a supportive, adherence-centred model was put in place where people who heard differently were offered support while they learnt to fit in with others and the way that taken-for-granted phono-centric communication took place.

Like all fairy tales, the days of Camelot were numbered. Within barely a decade the then *comprehensive approach* to the delivery of hearing services was abandoned. This appears to have occurred as a result of three intersecting factors: the resource demands placed on the field by the rubella epidemic (which I discuss further below), the resulting reduced clinical time available to work with adults and the subsequent over-reliance on the technical competencies of hearing aids.

The then Commonwealth government–run National Acoustic Laboratory (NAL) (now Australian Hearing), was the primary institutional mechanism through which hearing services were deployed at the societal level. Cordell's (1978) history on the development of this service model highlights several important points. Cordell affirms that hearing services in Australia, as elsewhere, were developed in response to the needs of deafened veterans returning from the war.[4] From a 'public health' perspective, the need for the service was at an epidemic level, given the number of veterans with hearing loss. The service model was deficit based and focused on the provision of hearing aids as well as communicative support and training provided by what became known as adult aural rehabilitation specialists. The outcomes that could be delivered by hearing aids were also limited, however, and, as such, communication training and support services were developed by the community sector, on a voluntary basis, with little financial support. It was in this context that the community organisation BHA emerged, providing

---

3   A utopian notion that this was the ideal form of hearing services consisting of the provision of devices and psycho-social support.

4   See also tinyurl.com/hearingservices [Accessed: 17/12/2014].

further support and communication training on a voluntary basis. This service particularly taught people to lip-read and to develop their social skills, and it provided a much-needed source of social support. Even today, those older adults who do not fare so well with cochlear implants often seek support from BHA.

The epidemic of war-related hearing problems was followed by the rubella epidemic (Upfold and Isepy 1982), which had a serious impact on NAL resources, which needed to be focused on this new and pressing service need. Increasingly, resources that were used to provide in-depth services for adults were replaced with expert services concentrated on children with fairer hearing. Cordell (1978) shows that again NAL essentially focused on the provision of hearing aids; but child aural rehabilitation specialists also emerged as a form of service provider with NAL. Services concerned with communication training were, again, time intensive – more so for children who were, as yet, to fully establish language, complete school or attain marketable employment skills. Cordell (1978) points out that, in time, NAL continued to focus on the delivery of hearing aids while state-funded schools for deaf children delivered the more time-intensive programs of communication training. In subsequent decades, government-funded services for people who hear differently from others were extended to certain groups of eligible aged pensioners in Australia.

Summarising this section, we see then that hearing services were based on a taken-for-granted medical, phono-centric, deficit model of the body. They deferred to the dominant communicative culture and worked to enable people with impaired hearing to participate in society on that basis. Its focus was on fitting devices and not on the social emancipation of people who hear differently from others.

Workers compensation hearing services

The postwar period also saw the development of primarily state-based hearing services for workers whose hearing was changed as a result of sustained exposure to loud noise at work.[5] Services for this group became an issue in the 1950s and 1960s (*Milne v International Combustion Australia Ltd* [1953] WCR 80). A particular problem in law was that

---

5   Comcare is a Commonwealth agency with responsibility for workers compensation services for Commonwealth employees, including people in the armed services.

industrial deafness (as it was called) did not result in an incapacity to work and not having an incapacity to work meant that the worker, in this case Mr Milne, did not have a date of incapacity. This legal problem 'came to a head' in *Commissioner for Railways v Coates* (1960) WCR 88 in the NSW Supreme Court, which provided a simple statutory formula for determining the date of injury; that is, the date of the worker's application is deemed to be the date of onset of the disease.

The fact that the worker did not have incapacity to work, however, also by inference meant that the worker did not have an incapacity that required intervention for the purpose of restoring their ability to work. In law, such interventions are defined as reasonably necessary treatments, a definition that is also applied to Australia's recent National Disability Insurance Scheme (NDIS). In the case of industrial deafness, treatment for the resulting disability fell through a gap since the person could work and thereby retain earning capacity. Treatment and rehabilitation services concerned with equipping the person for work were not designed to address the implications of an industrial injury that resulted in the person having a disability but not necessarily an impediment to work. As Bohle et al. (1991: 281) argue, the broad objective of workers compensation legislation is for 'the provision of income security to injured workers, requiring employers to fund such benefits, enhancing and facilitating the rehabilitation of injured workers'. Similarly, Luntz (1975: 65–66) points out that compensation relates primarily to a loss of earning capacity: 'the impairment [a] the ability of that person to engage in work that is useful or gainful; or [b] the wellbeing of that person, or both'.

An interesting point of contrast exists between this model and other models of hearing services. For people with other forms of acquired hearing impairment, services were designed to fit the person back into society. Within the workers compensation system, the reverse applied. Since the worker continued to fit in at work, no service was required, irrespective of the impact of impaired hearing on the worker or their family.

During the late 1980s, Australian Government departments adopted the policy that the government should not provide a public service that could as readily be provided by the market. This policy took effect in hearing services in 1996 with the introduction of a voucher system that would enable 'greater private sector involvement in the provision of government funded services'.[6] The Office of Hearing Services (OHS) was,

---

6   tinyurl.com/hearingservices [Accessed: 17/12/2014].

in turn, established within the Commonwealth Department of Health and Ageing (DOHA) to administer this program. As at December 2013, there were 2,637 accredited service outlets in Australia where the hearing-services model could be accessed. Assuming an Australian population of four million people who hear differently from others, this represents one hearing-services outlet for approximately every 1,500 people. As such, this model of service delivery is pervasive in Australia but, nonetheless, it is essentially a broadly developed infrastructure for the deployment of hearing aids.

In addition, while the nation has a highly developed infrastructure for the deployment of hearing aids, persistent concerns have been held about the adequacy of this service model or the practical utility of hearing aids. In response to consistent complaints from the community sector about the limits of hearing aids, the expense of delivering such a program and the inadequacy of the service model vis-à-vis social outcomes, the OHS introduced a Rehabilitation Plus program in 2008. While this program was sold as being put in place to address some of the social issues facing people who hear differently, its primary aim was to get people to use the hearing aids with which they had been provided. Non-use of hearing devices remains a contentious issue. For example, OHS reported that its data showed about 30 per cent of people who received hearing aids did not use them.[7] Soon after, they reported to the Australian Senate that 10–13 per cent of people with devices did not use them. This was in contrast to data reported in *Lancet* (Smeeth et al. 2002) that about 40 per cent of people with hearing aids do not use them. The most recent Australian data (produced by the research company *instinct and reason*) shows an average rate of device non-usage at 28 per cent.

Despite the privatisation of adult hearing services in Australia, the current Australian Government provider, Australian Hearing (previously NAL), remains the dominant player in hearing services and the funding of the majority of hearing services is federally controlled. Moreover, across the spectrum of hearing-service providers in Australia, there are few practising audiologists who did not complete their initial postgraduate service with either NAL or Australian Hearing. Indeed, these institutions have served as the developmental ground for much of the profession and, as such, serve as the key institutions that shape and reinforce the service-delivery values of Australia's hearing services.

---

7   OHS, personal communication, 7 December 2011.

A review of their respective websites is informative. The NAL website[8] promotes its product development and range of research projects. Its research is concerned with:

1. assessing hearing loss; e.g. techniques and technologies
2. rehabilitation procedures; e.g. the relationship between speech perception and production with linguistic, educational and social outcomes; developing prescriptive procedures to enable the combination of acoustic and electric stimulation; the relationship between frequency compression; and educational outcomes
3. rehabilitation devices – research into hearing aids, self-fitting hearing aids, cochlear implants and the barriers to people accepting hearing aids
4. engineering technologies; e.g. the development of an automatic auditory brain response (ABR) audiometer.

In short, NAL researches hearing aids and related technologies and is concerned with the impacts and outcomes associated with these products. The website of Australian Hearing[9] prominently promotes the use of a wide range of hearing aids and devices. It provides its services to people who are eligible for support under the Australian Government's Hearing Services Program, including Pensioner Concession Card holders, veterans, Indigenous people and people under 25 years of age. The website makes it clear that Australian Hearing essentially offers hearing testing and a device-fitting service.

The extensive range of private service providers that are accessible in Australia can be found on the OHS website. Similar to Australian Hearing, the range of services provided by the private providers is inherently consistent with the scope of works funded by OHS. Without doubt, there are exceptions to the rule, with some providers offering an approach more informed by social- and citizen-based models of disability; fewer still, however, engage in emancipatory processes. The evidence in support of the view that the scope of service delivery remains narrow is borne out in OHS's published budget papers, which demonstrate that less than 5 per cent of eligible clients have been provided with access to alternate models of service.[10]

---

8   www.nal.gov.au [Accessed: 20/03/2014].
9   www.hearing.com.au/category/hearingsolutions/ [Accessed: 20/03/2014].
10   See for example www.health.gov.au/internet/budget/publishing.nsf/Content/2011-2012_Health_PBS [Accessed: 23/03/2012].

Adding the *multi* to the levels of governance of hearing services

We have seen so far that, from the audiological perspective and irrespective of governmental processes, Camelot existed in the golden days of the postwar period. Looking back at this period, one can see that the initial hearing services were comprehensive, providing both hearing devices as well as social support. At the same time, the service design was steeped in taken-for-granted assumptions that underpinned the medical, phono-centric model of the body, while the service model was based on an authoritarian, hierarchical medico–military culture. Socially, a compliance model was put in place wherein people were provided with skills development in coping with discriminatory and stigmatising behaviours. In time, the marginalisation of the provision of non–device based services occurred. Certainly, by the mid-1960s, questions were raised about the credibility of audiologists engaged in the provision of client-support services, commonly referred to then as aural rehabilitation:

> The drift from aural rehabilitation has been so extensive that it represents a change in the basic direction of the field … The audiologist who voluntarily chooses the role of rehabilitation worker must be truly dedicated, for he runs the danger of being considered incompetent for other functions by his peers (Rosen 1967, cited in Ross 1997).

Despite such marginalisation, a range of people-centred, non-device and often community-based service models continued to be developed and delivered within pockets of excellence across the world (Pengilley 1975; Plant 1976, 1977; Anderson 1991; Hetu and Getty 1991; Getty and Hetu 1991; Hogan et al. 1994; Erdman et al. 1994; Sherbourne and White 1997; Westcott and Kato 1998).

Beyond models of service such as those offered by BHA, community-based service delivery models, although poorly resourced and few in number, also began to emerge in Australia in the 1970s. The most notable service model in Australia was founded by the Victorian Hearservice. Their program identified three main aims (Pengilley 1975):

1. alleviate anxiety in the individual who has the problem, and assist him [sic] to achieve better communication skills
2. assist the individual's family and his human environment
3. educate the public through a HEAR Promotion Program.

The program sought to address both the social as well as individual, family-based aspects of living with impaired hearing. By the 1980s, the state-based Hearservice offered two courses: Coping Skills I and II. These courses were offered in small groups, essentially for older people with impaired hearing. The programs were offered over a series of weeks and focused on developing people's skills through the use of a range of communication tactics. The 1980s also saw collective groups emerging, such as a national consumer peak group then known as the Australian Deafness Council, which, in time, was renamed, at the insistence of the Commonwealth, as the Deafness Forum of Australia. On various occasions, this peak group has attempted to launch a series of social education programs aimed at improving social participation and reducing the stigmatisation of people who hear differently from others. Since their funding base is less than that of your average neighbourhood centre, however, it is reasonably given that their capacity to be effective is severely constrained. As Jordan and Halpin (2006) state, given that the dispensing of hearing aids and devices is the primary policy for hearing services in Australia, any other form of service delivery is unlikely to receive much support.

Some of the early service models (e.g. Plant 1976, 1977; Westcott and Kato 1998) had their origins within government-based hearing services programs. Plant, for example (1976: 15–19), remarks that the NAL recognised 'that the mere fitting of a hearing aid is not a satisfactory solution to the many problems confronting' people who hear differently from others. While Plant argued that group-based and individual follow-up programs were necessary, his perspective was framed in phono-centric values, since he saw the purpose of such support as giving people 'a realistic attitude' to managing their difficulties.

In the late 1990s, the then Australian Hearing Services offered *seriously deafened adults* access to intensive communication training and support via residential workshops (Westcott and Kato 1998). Participants in cochlea implant programs were also beginning to take part in group-based interventions. At the time, similar programs could be found in other countries across the world, such as Denmark, which, in turn, influenced the development of the service base offered within Australia (Anderson 1991: 51–57). However, unlike most countries, the Danish programs tended to be offered to any person with *impaired hearing*, not just those with more severe degrees of impairment. Anderson (1991) reported that, in the Danish program, following hearing aid–fitting, allocated individuals were then 'slotted' directly into a group program consisting of two hours one week followed by a one-hour session the following week. Participants requiring further assistance could return at any time. Those requiring further help could be offered two other courses of eight two-hour small group sessions. As per Anderson's (1991) description of the program, they too were highly phono-centric in nature. She notes that the first course aimed to:

- give participants insight and knowledge of their handicap and acceptance of hearing loss
- cover basic anatomy, physiology and pathology of the ear, diagnosis, audiograms (including recruitment and tinnitus), hearing tactics, lip reading and relaxation techniques.

The second course aimed to enhance:

- auditory and visual awareness
- lip-reading and body-language reading skills
- skills in natural signing and gestures, mimicry, acceptance of hearing disability
- ability to manage stress.

Reports of similarly designed programs (e.g. Kirby and Rogan 1981; Della Valle 1988) can be found in the literature of the time. At an individual level, such programs are well and good as they equip people to cope with unfavourable social interactions. They are, however, not without their limits because they do not address the social relations of hearing. Rather, they promote a message of accept, adapt and comply with the demands of the phono-centric society.

This results in two problematic outcomes. First, people who hear differently from others are rightly reluctant to use such tactics, as they risk further stigmatising themselves. Second, because the need for interactive change has not been socially legitimated, the capacity at the individual level to leverage change is limited. As one person remarks:

> I might add that some of my friends, even knowing of my hearing difficulties, still talk to my back or with faces turned away and then wonder why I don't answer them (Letter to the Editor, *The Senior*, February 2012).

And another person writing to the same newspaper remarked:

> People constantly laugh when I repeat what I heard as it bears no resemblance to what they are saying. While I appreciate the humour of the situation, it can be embarrassing. I just smile and don't respond (Letter to the Editor, *The Senior*, February 2012).

Today, a fledging infrastructure of community-based hearing services still exists in Australia. The design of such services confused by their seeking to address the needs of Deaf people as well as people who hear differently from others, as though, yet again, their social, cultural and communicative needs were all alike. Most services retain a strong focus on accessing technology and some remain tightly enmeshed within the medical model of service delivery.

The governance of other community-based hearing services

The historical development of hearing services in Australia is anomalous to the structuring of the nation's other disability services. Most disability services in Australia came under the auspices of the then National Disability Agreement (Council of Australian Governments 2009) and were funded either through the then Commonwealth Department of Family and Community Services (now the Department of Social Services) and Indigenous Affairs (FaHCSIA) (and presently within the Prime Minister's department), or through community service departments found within state government departments. The annexation of hearing services within the medical model in health has had profound consequences for the development of alternative forms of service delivery. Unlike services for the Deaf Community (see, for example, detail of services funded in this sector in Access Economics (2006)), which are, for example, widely funded as disability services, comparatively few alternative service models exist for people who hear differently from others, as funded under the NDA. Moreover, since the development of Australia's NDIS in 2013, the majority of hearing services have remained annexed within health services. While attempts have been made to shift hearing services for those with severe to profound impairment to the NDIS, the movement of children's services, in particular, has been fiercely resisted by service providers. Their resistance centres on the extent to which a highly decentralised model of service provision that requires a 'high level of expertise' can be delivered by generalist providers of disability services. At the time of writing, these policy disputes have not been resolved. It would appear, however, that services for adults with hearing impairment that is severe or 'worse' and aged less than 65 years will be provided under the NDIS.

The community-based services that do exist operate under a number of structures. Some service models closely align themselves with the medical model, having medical specialists as their patrons, and work to continue to address the support needs of people that cannot be addressed by hearing devices. A variety of community-based services have followed aspects of the British model, where centres provide people with access to assistive listening devices other than hearing aids. While these services address an important need, they similarly reinforce a value that depicts the participation needs of people who hear differently from others as being those that can be addressed through the provision of technology alone, without addressing the structuring of the social relations of hearing.

A small group of service providers have developed communication-training programs that equip people to more cleverly manage the everyday challenges of communicating in adverse settings. While generally I am supportive of these kinds of interventions, since they equip people to better manage potentially stigmatising social situations, my support for them is qualified by the extent to which such services also work to change the structuring of communication at the societal level and address the social position of people who hear differently. For the most part, these kinds of services receive little, if any, funding support. Some children's services receive funding from the Department of Social Services under the Better Start program.[11]

Taken altogether, there are very few alternative support models available to people who hear differently that do not fall within the medical, phono-centric, device-based model. Considering the Foucauldian model of personal formation that I presented earlier, I contend that hearing services at the institutional, technological and practitioner level are focused on the formation of individuals so that they adhere to the dominant structuring of an existing, albeit unfair, hearing society and are based on an ablest model of social relations. Notably, a good proportion of people who hear differently are dissatisfied with this model of service delivery (Chisolm et

---

11   www.dss.gov.au/our-responsibilities/disability-and-carers/program-services/for-people-with-disability/better-start-for-children-with-disability-initiative [Accessed: 12/12/14].

al. 2007; Smeeth et al. 2002). The individualising nature of the service model and the imbalance in power relations, however, maintain the status quo. One person who hears differently remarks on this experience:

> Over the past 20 years I have had 5 sets of hearing aids, some of them with remote controls but none of them very satisfactory as all they do is amplify all the noises around us, including the ones we don't want to hear such as background noise/music. When having new hearing aids fitted recently I was told I needed to concentrate better. (Letter to the Editor, *The Senior*, 9 February 2012)

Central to the problems with hearing services that are identified in this chapter is the narrowly constructed base for the governance of these services where, for the most part, end users have little, if any, input into service design and where consumer groups are routinely excluded from funded service models. The rationale and strategy for funding services for people who hear differently needs to be reviewed so that the narrow focus on needs and outcomes presently embodied within a device-centric system may be expanded in keeping with the principles of the co-design of disability services. Specifically, the primary focus of funded services for people who hear differently needs to address the basis upon which people can participate in community life by having equal access to enabling social processes and being able to enjoy a level of socio-economic wellbeing similar to all other citizens. Within such services, the need for social change and achieving social outcomes is given priority over assessments and prescriptive services.

Governing governance

One model of hearing services, then, takes dominance over alternative models of service delivery and support – the device-centred medical model, underpinned as it is by its logic of accept, adapt and comply. This model of hearing services sits within a governance structure that is focused on the reproduction of the individual as a hearing person. The service model is based on:

- unexamined assumptions about the negativity of the experience of disability
- the privileging of input, device-based interventions over social position and social outcomes

- the absence of any endeavours to change the social relations of hearing, including the social structuring of communication or addressing the acoustic accessibility of built environments
- a particular form of governance of people with disability.

The benefits of device-based interventions in their own right, as beneficial technologies, are not contested. Indeed, elsewhere I have demonstrated the benefits such technologies can have in the lives of people who hear differently from others (see, for example, Hogan 2001; Hogan et al. 2009). What is disputed is the process of governance that focuses social pressure upon people who hear differently from others to adopt one way of managing hearing over viable alternatives. From the social perspective, people who hear differently from others have become an object of processes of subjectification. This process of governance shapes the meaning of deafness and implicitly links it with the longer-standing discourse on disability that is concerned with the threat disability poses to liberal economy through constructed, indeed privileged, notions of social and economic dependency.

Over the past 70 years, institutional processes encompassing formal government, industry, the academy and charity-based services have gradually been formed into an organised system that channels the opportunities offered to the person with impaired hearing, with a view to promoting the formation of the self into a being who is socially and economically independent. The ethical responsibility for personal reformation falls to the individual who, in turn, may attempt to conform to the demands placed upon him/her.

When confronted with this dilemma, the individual may readily accept the situational assessment and remedies offered within the existing process of governance and willingly seek to reform themselves as hearing people. To the extent that such self-subjugation works, this intervention and its consequences enable the individual to maintain his/her social attachments and provide a strategy for living within the hearing world. Opportunities for humanising the process do exist but individuals generally need access to people or processes that validate their actions. Nonetheless, most people do not reach this point of decision-making. Rather, services engage the individual into specific processes of self-reformation before he/she has had the opportunity:

- to critique the social meanings attributed to deafness
- to be informed about all the options that are available to him/her

- to consider the consequences of pursuing such options
- to talk through such processes with well-informed, non-tokenistic peer advocates who have already been through such processes
- to negotiate this process with his/her family from an equal position of power.

If meaningful social outcomes are to be achieved by people who hear differently, then service providers need to work with, rather than on, disabled people (Oliver 1996). Hearing services are centred on a value base that, if it was ever right, is long overdue for a review. Within the historical milieu underpinning hearing services, it was deemed acceptable for professionals to determine the range and nature of services to be offered to, or provided to, people who hear differently. Things have changed. The social impact of various social movements over the past 30 years has seen patriarchy, science and medicine lose much of their privileged positions in broader society. The interests and legitimacy of oppressed groups, such as people of colour, minority ethnic communities, women, and gay and lesbian people, have gradually received recognition, as has the politics of difference in general and the social model of disability in particular. Throughout the world, disability groups are contesting the medicalisation of disability and the marginalisation of disabled people. While the Deaf Community has been at the forefront of such social change, people with impaired hearing have been less willing to align themselves with what many consider to be a stigmatised identity.

Acknowledgement

A preliminary version of this paper appeared in *ENT and Audiology News* (United Kingdom), May 2009.

References

Access Economics (2006). *Listen Hear! The Economic Impact and Cost of Hearing Loss in Australia*. CRC for Cochlear Implant and Hearing Aid Innovation and Vicdeaf, Melbourne.

Akram, S. & Hogan, A. (2015). On Reflexivity and Breaches to the Routinisation of Everyday Life. *British Journal of Sociology*, 66(4): 606–25. doi.org/10.1111/1468-4446.1215

Anderson, M. (1991). Services For Hearing Impaired People and Training for Health Workers in Denmark. *Auration* No. 1, National Acoustic Laboratory, Chatswood.

Bohle, P., James, C. & Quinlan, M. (1991). Occupational Health and Safety Law: Workers' compensation, rehabilitation and injury impacts. In: Quinlan, M. & Bohle, P. (eds) *Managing Occupational Health and Safety in Australia: A Multidisciplinary Approach*. Macmillan Education Australia, South Melbourne, pp. 243–83.

Bruce, R.V. (1973). *Bell: Alexander Graham Bell and the Conquest of Solitude*. Cornell University Press, Ithaca.

Chisolm, T.H., Johnson, C.E., Danhauer, J.L., Portz, L.J., Abrams, H.B., Lesner, S., McCarthy, P.A. & Newman, C.W. (2007). A Systematic Review of Health-Related Quality of Life and Hearing Aids: Final report of the American Academy of Audiology Task Force on the health-related quality of life benefits of amplification in adults. *Journal of the American Academy of Audiology*, 18: 151–83. doi.org/10.3766/jaaa.18.2.7

Cordell, J. (1978). *Early History of National Acoustic Laboratories*. Internal Report No 6. National Acoustic Laboratories, Australian Department of Health, Millers Point, Sydney.

Corker, M. (1998). *Deaf and Disabled, or Deafness Disabled? Towards a Human Rights Perspective*. Open University Press, Buckingham.

Council of Australian Governments (2009). *The National Disability Agreement*. Canberra, www.federalfinancialrelations.gov.au/content/npa/national_agreements/national-disability-agreement.pdf

Della Valle, E. (1988). Aural Rehabilitation for the Elderly. MA Thesis, Macquarie University, 1988.

de Sousa Santos, B. (2014). *Epistemologies of the South – Justice against Epistemicide*. Paradigm Publishers, Boulder.

Erdman, S.A. (2009). Therapeutic Factors in Group Counseling: Implications for audiologic rehabilitation. *Perspectives on Aural Rehabilitation and Its Instrumentation*, 16(1): 15–28. doi.org/10.1044/arii16.1.15

Erdman, S.S., Wark, D.J. & Montano, J.J. (1994). Implications of Service Delivery Models in Audiology. *Journal of the Academy of Rehabilitative Audiology.* 27: 45–60.

Foucault, M. (1978). *The History of Sexuality Volume One – An Introduction.* Penguin, London.

——. (1988). Technologies of the Self. In: Martin, L., Gutman, H. & Hutton, P.H. (eds) *Technologies of the Self – A Seminar with Michel Foucault.* Tavistock, London, pp. 16–49.

Gaeth, J.H. (1979). A History of Aural Rehabilitation. In: Henoch, M.A. (ed.) *Aural Rehabilitation for the Elderly.* Grune and Stratton Inc., New York, pp. 1–21.

Getty, L. & Hetu, R. (1991). Development of a Rehabilitation Program for People Affected with Occupational Hearing Loss. 2: Results from group intervention with 48 workers and their spouses, *International Journal of Audiology*, 30(6): 317–29. doi.org/10.3109/00206099109072894

Hay, C. & Wincott, D. (1998). Structure, Agency and Historical Institutionalism. *Political studies*, 46(5): 951–57. doi.org/10.1111/1467-9248.00177

Henoch, M.A. (ed.) (1979). *Aural Rehabilitation for the Elderly*, Grune & Stratton, New York.

Hetu, R. & Getty, L. (1991). Development of a Rehabilitation Program for People Affected with Occupational Hearing Loss: A new paradigm. *International Journal of Audiology*, 30(6): 305–16. doi.org/10.3109/00206099109072893

Hogan, A. (1997). Issues Impacting on the Governance of Deafened Adults. *Disability And Society*, 12(5): 793–805. doi.org/10.1080/09687599727056

——. (2001). *Hearing Rehabilitation for Deafened Adults – A Psycho-social Approach.* Wiley (Whurr) Publishers Ltd, London.

Hogan, A., Ewan, C., Noble, W.G. & Munnerley, G. (1994). Coping with Occupational Hearing Loss: The University of Montreal Acoustics Group Rehabilitation Programme. An Evaluation Study. *Journal of Occupational Health & Safety – Australia and New Zealand*, 10(2): 107–18.

Hogan, A., O'Loughlin, K. & Kendig, H. (2009). The Impact of Hearing Loss on Personal Health – A Threshold Effect Model. *Journal of Ageing and Health*, 21: 1098–111. doi.org/10.1177/0898264309347821

Hogan, A. & Phillips, R. (2014). *(We Want) a Fairer Hearing*. University of Canberra.

Jordan, G. & Halpin, D. (2006). The Political Costs of Policy Coherence: Constructing a rural policy for Scotland. *Journal of Public Policy*, 26(1): 21. doi.org/10.1017/s0143814x06000456

Kirby, V.M. & Rogan, S.D. (1981). A Four Week Group Communication Training Programme for Adults. *Journal of the Aural Rehabilitation Association*, 14(Fall): 8–16.

Lane, H. (1993). *The Mask of Benevolence. Disabling the Deaf Community.* Vintage Books, Random House, New York.

Lukes, S. (1974). *Power – A Radical View.* Macmillan Press, London. doi.org/10.1007/978-1-349-02248-9

Luntz, H. (1975). *Compensation and Rehabilitation.* Butterworths, Sydney.

Oliver, M. (1996). *Understanding Disability – From Theory to Practice.* Macmillan, London. doi.org/10.1007/978-1-349-24269-6

Osborne, T. (1996). Security and Vitality: Drains, liberalism and power in the nineteenth century. In: Barry, A., Osborne, T. & Rose, N. (eds) *Foucault and Political Reason – Liberalism, Neo-liberalism and Rationalities of Government.* University of Chicago Press, pp. 99–121.

Pengilley, P. (1975). *Aural Rehabilitation – Churchill Fellowship Report.* Victorian Hear Service, Jolimont.

Plant, G.L. (1976). Aural Rehabilitation Programmes For Deafened Adults. *Australian Journal of Human Communication Disorders*, 4(1): 15–19. doi.org/10.3109/asl2.1976.4.issue-1.04

——. (1977). *Adult Aural Rehabilitation – A Report On World Health Organisation Fellowship.* National Acoustic Laboratory, Sydney.

Productivity Commission (2011). *Disability Care and Support Report*, No. 54, July 31. Canberra, Australia.

Ross, M. (1997). A Retrospective Look at the Future of Aural Rehabilitation. *Journal of the Academy of Rehabilitative Audiology*, 30: 11–28.

Sherbourne, K. & White, L. (1997). An Evaluation of the Impact of Rehabilitation Courses for Deafened Adults Run by the Link Centre for Deafened People. Manuscript.

Smeeth, L., Fletcher, A.E., Ng, E.S., Stirling, S., Nunes, M., Breeze, E., Bulpitt, C.J., Jones, D. & Tulloch, A. (2002). Reduced Hearing, Ownership and Use of Hearing Aids in Elderly People in the UK – the MRC Trail of the Assessment and Management of Older People in the Community: A cross sectional survey. *Lancet*, 359: 1466–70. doi.org/10.1016/S0140-6736(02)08433-7

Upfold, L.J. & Isepy, J. (1982). Childhood Deafness in Australia. Incidence and Maternal Rubella, 1949–1980. *The Medical Journal of Australia*, 2(7): 323–26.

Westcott, S. & Kato, J. (1998). 'Living with Deafness': A residential workshop to improve communication for deafened clients and partners. 13th Annual Conference, Australian Audiological Society, Novotel Hotel, Sydney.

Winefield, R. (1987). *Never the Twain Shall Meet – The Communications Debate.* Gallaudet University Press, Washington.

9

Multi-level Governance in Aboriginal Community Development: Structures, Processes and Skills for Working across Boundaries

Wendy Jarvie and Jenny Stewart

Introduction

As a federal nation, Australia has had long experience with multi-level governance (MLG). In most policy fields, federal and state governments share powers, producing complex and often intricate intergovernmental structures and processes (Galligan et al. 1991; Painter 1998). As policy and management challenges have grown in complexity, interest has increased in finding new ways of working that transcend these traditional arrangements (Edwards and Langford 2002). 'Working across boundaries' represents an emergent form of MLG, as policymakers have sought to address the challenges of complex, fluid and overlapping jurisdictions (Bache and Flinders 2004: 5).

Policymaking for Indigenous Australians exemplifies these challenges to a high degree. The failure of governments to work together and with communities has, arguably, been a fundamental factor in producing poor outcomes and mutual frustration. During the early 2000s, the government under Prime Minister John Howard, in its third term of office, decided that the status quo was not an option and a 'quiet revolution' was needed (Vanstone 2005). Together with the states and territories, they decided to trial new ways of working to tackle Indigenous disadvantage. The results were the Council of Australian Governments (COAG) trials of 2003–07, which were an attempt by governments (state, federal and local) to embrace the possibilities of cross-boundary working, and to learn from the results: a practical experiment in MLG in the Australian context.

In this chapter, we focus on the structures, processes and skills that were deployed and developed in the most successful COAG trial site, in the Murdi Paaki region of western New South Wales (ANAO 2008). Our aim is to elucidate the ways in which actors (particularly government and community actors) addressed the challenges of cross-boundary working in an environment of considerable jurisdictional flux and ambiguity, and to identify, from the case study, some guiding principles for bureaucratic action.

Background

Improving outcomes for Indigenous Australians has long been considered one of the most difficult problems in Australian public policy. On most indicators of wellbeing, Aboriginal people continue to lag significantly behind the rest of the Australian population, although, in recent years, the gap has narrowed in relation to some indicators (SCRGSP 2016).

The policy context is generally considered to be complex, conflicted and multi-layered. Policy values have oscillated dramatically over the past 40 years, reflecting the outcomes of fierce ideological battles, the actions and efforts of activists and (often) the consequences of disappointing experience.

Within this environment of swirling contestation, there have been, beginning in the mid-1990s and gathering strength in the 2000s, a number of attempts by governments to approach these difficult problems in new ways, and to learn from the resulting experience. Many of these new approaches emanated from COAG and included an increasing emphasis on intra-governmental cooperation and on partnerships between Aboriginal people and governments (see COAG 2004; Gray and Sanders 2006).

In 2002, COAG announced trials of these new approaches at eight sites across Australia, one in each state and territory (COAG 2002). Murdi Paaki was the site chosen for New South Wales.

The Murdi Paaki region was a governance region under the *Aboriginal and Torres Strait Islander Commission Act 1989*. It included 16 communities ranging from Broken Hill, Wilcannia, Menindee, Dareton-Wentworth and Ivanhoe in the south-west, to Brewarrina, Bourke, Lightning Ridge, and Walgett in the north and Cobar in the centre. Gullargambone, Collarenebri, Goodooga, Enngonia, Weilmoringle and Coonamble completed the set.

In 2005, the Indigenous Australian population of Murdi Paaki was around 7,500 people, representing 14 per cent of the total population of the region. The region is the most disadvantaged in New South Wales, with significant problems of health, employment, housing, education and crime. At the time of the trial, these were exacerbated by a long period of drought with few agricultural jobs, and flow-on impacts on villages and towns. Further detail is in Jarvie and Stewart (2011).

Design features

Type II MLG is characterised by fluidity, often manifesting as a patchwork of overlapping jurisdictions, arising in response to particular governance challenges (*Kay*; Hooghe and Marks 2003). While the COAG trials exhibited many of these features, it is important to acknowledge that, at least in their initial forms, they were acts of deliberate administrative creation, rather than emergent forms of activity. The trial objectives included tailoring government action to identified community needs and aspirations, encouraging innovation, cutting red tape, working to build the capacity of Aboriginal people so that they could negotiate as genuine partners with government, building the capacity of government employees so they could work in the new way with Indigenous communities, and the negotiation of agreed outcomes and benchmarks for measuring progress (Morgan Disney 2006). These design features provided an institutional underpinning (and impetus) to the cross-jurisdictional framework for governance.

Lead agencies

For each trial site there was a lead Commonwealth agency and a lead state government agency that were expected to liaise and coordinate with relevant agencies within their jurisdictions, as well as with their state counterparts and the Aboriginal communities. In Murdi Paaki, the lead Commonwealth agency was the Department of Education, Science and Training (DEST), and the NSW Department of Education and Training (DET) was the lead for the NSW Government.

Shared responsibility agreements in Murdi Paaki

Shared responsibility agreements, at both community and regional level, represented a key part of the original program logic because they established a basis for mutual commitments to outcomes. They were particularly prominent in the Murdi Paaki context. In 2003, a shared responsibility agreement was signed between the Commonwealth Government (represented by DEST), the NSW Government (represented by DET) and the Murdi Paaki Regional Council. This document established regional objectives to be addressed by partnership-based working arrangements. As well as this overarching agreement, agreements were signed in relation to a number of specific activities. In all, 29 shared responsibility agreements were signed across the region

Flexible funding

Significant staff and project-funding resources were needed, and creative approaches to financing by participating agencies were required. Because projects were to be identified by communities, and could cross existing government and program boundaries, flexible funding arrangements were necessary to support them. Within the Commonwealth, the Office of Indigenous Policy Coordination in the Department of Immigration and Indigenous Affairs (DIMIA) set up a flexible funding pool to support all the COAG sites, and lead agencies could bid for funds. To increase the speed of finding funds for Murdi Paaki, the Minister for DEST, Brendan Nelson, agreed in 2003 for uncommitted funds from the Indigenous Education Strategies program to be set aside to meet education elements of projects. Later in 2006–07, DEST established a fund that drew from across the department as a whole.

Actual delivery and funding of projects was undertaken by a number of different agencies. For example, funding of consultants to help to develop the action plans was provided by Family and Community Services (FaCS), while secretariat support for the working parties was funded from the Department of Employment and Workplace Relations' (DEWR) Indigenous programs, with training provided by NSW TAFE. Facilitators were funded by the NSW Premier's Department, the Commonwealth's flexible funding pool and DEST. The Commonwealth Department of Health and Ageing (DOHA) funded a drug and alcohol network. In reality, the bulk of the funding was found by the Commonwealth, particularly DEST, who not only funded four staff positions for Aboriginal officers in Dubbo and a support section in Canberra, but contributed an estimated $2.1 million to projects funded under shared-responsibility agreements.

Structures

Structures are important in MLG because they provide occasions, arenas and spaces for interaction. In the Murdi Paaki trial, the sheer number of actors required structures that transcended 'top-down' and horizontal divides and were robust enough to be enduring and meaningful but were also sufficiently flexible to give participants room to move.

Intergovernmental networks

Within the Commonwealth Government, the key agencies were the lead agency, DEST, FaCS, Families, Community Services and Indigenous Affairs (FaCSIA) after 2005, and the Aboriginal and Torres Strait Islander Services (ATSIS) (2003–04). Later, DOHA became a significant player at a project level. Within DEST, officers engaged in supporting the trial were located in Canberra, Sydney and Dubbo, and the complex information flows and coordinated action were managed through the formation of a Murdi Paaki Coordination Group. Because state managers of Australian Government departments were responsible for Commonwealth service delivery in New South Wales, these officers were actively engaged as well. In addition, the Secretary of DEST was a member of a Commonwealth Government committee composed of the Secretaries from the lead agencies of the eight trials, as well as the head of Prime Minister and Cabinet and ATSIS.[1]

---

1   A detailed description of the arrangements of the Commonwealth secretaries, and how this changed over time, can be found in Gray and Sanders (2006), p. 5.

From the NSW Government side, key players were DET (the lead agency), the NSW Department of Aboriginal Affairs (DAA), and the NSW Premier's Department. DEST, DET and DAA provided officers for the action team, which was located in Dubbo. DET used the existing NSW Government Regional Coordination Management Group to coordinate across NSW Government agencies. The NSW Government had a stable Indigenous Australian engagement philosophy – Two Ways Together[2] – over the course of the trial, which enabled them to engage in a steady and systematic way with Murdi Paaki, although, like many state governments, they had limited flexible funding to contribute to community priorities. Local government was not a significant player in the trial, except in a couple of communities.

In addition, there were a large number of organisations that engaged in different ways and at different times over the trial, including the Barwon Darling Alliance, various chambers of commerce, Aboriginal organisations, such as land councils, medical services, community development employment projects, and the Murdi Paaki Regional Enterprise Corporation.

Government–community networks

The action team was the focus of day-to-day interaction between government and community and their experience on the ground gave them the insight to be the most critical officials. Meetings involving higher levels of government opened with reports from the action team and, indeed, discussions and decision-making were characterised by lack of hierarchy – no single agency controlled the agenda; it was set mutually. Overall guidance for the trial was provided by a joint community, NSW Government and Commonwealth Government steering committee. The chair was rotated between the three lead partners – Sam Jeffries as the chair of the Regional Council and then the Murdi Paaki Regional Assembly, and deputy secretaries from DEST and DET. The committee met regularly, no less than four to five times a year to the end of 2007, generally in Sydney but also, when it could be organised, within the region. Four regional thematic subgroups were developed late in the trial: education and employment, culture and heritage, health, and crime and justice. Developed in response to the 16 community working party action

---

2   Two Ways Together – Partnerships: a new way of doing business with Aboriginal people, NSW Aboriginal Affairs Plan 2003–12. See NSW Auditor-General (2011).

plans and the realisation that many priorities were best handled through a regional approach, subgroups included representatives of Aboriginal communities and Commonwealth and NSW government agencies.

The action team in Dubbo ensured that the communities were the focus of action and attention. Supporting a simple interface, however, required a high level of government complexity. As one interviewee explained 'this level of complexity was needed to produce simplicity on the ground'. Figure 9.1 shows some of the key Murdi Paaki communication and coordination structures as they existed in 2006.

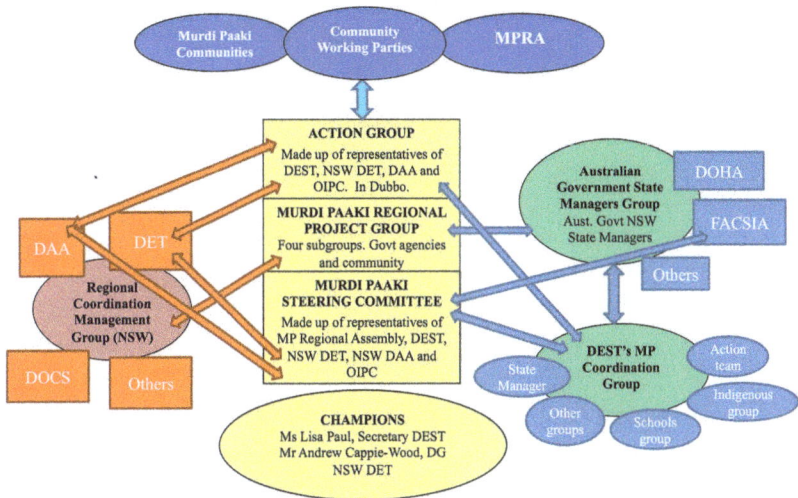

Figure 9.1: Bureaucratic complexity: Murdi Paaki governance structures 2006

Source: Wendy Jarvie and Jenny Stewart

Community

Two main structures within the Aboriginal community engaged with government through the trial. The first, the Murdi Paaki Regional Assembly – a new form of the previous Murdi Paaki Regional Council – proved to be a significant actor. Chaired by Indigenous Australian leader, Sam Jeffries, and meeting regularly throughout the period, the assembly comprised the chair together with chairs of 16 Murdi Paaki community working parties. At its meetings, the assembly discussed priorities, progress and plans for the region as a whole. It was also a prime point of contact for government agencies (state and federal) to interact with the communities.

The second was the community working parties. Formed under the auspices of the regional council in the late 1990s, their prime role was then to coordinate action in relation to housing. In the Murdi Paaki trial, these working parties were refreshed and/or created and acted as the key intersection point between the action team, agencies and the communities themselves. Each working party was constructed differently and reflected the characteristics of the local community, although they worked under a common operational framework. The working parties were not formal corporate bodies and membership was open to everyone in the Indigenous community in each town. Leadership was determined by a voting process or, in the smaller communities, more informally. In practice, the majority of chairs were men although, over time, a larger number of women began to assume leadership roles.

Processes

Peters and Pierre (2004) stress that, whatever the degree to which its analysis is institutionally directed, MLG is fundamentally about process. As they put it, 'multi-level governance refers to connected processes of governance incorporating both public and private actors in contextually defined forms of exchange and collaboration' (Peters and Pierre 2004: 76). It follows, therefore, that managing MLG requires attention, not just to structures, but also to the ways in which these structures are articulated through inter-agency and interpersonal relationships. In the next section we detail the processes that built and maintained these relationships.

Negotiation

Continuous negotiation, though not emphasised in the original trial documents, turned out to be at the heart of the COAG trials. Effective partnership between governments required constant negotiation – particularly around galvanising resources, but also to join up government agencies' action, such as in health or education, and to ensure they were adopting the same approach. Partnership with Aboriginal communities also required intense negotiation – particularly in identifying community priorities and methods of project financing and management, as well as in the precise wording of shared responsibility agreements. Indeed, as the Murdi Paaki case makes clear, the process of negotiation was an important mechanism for building trust and for developing a common understanding of issues and the best way to address them. In most locations there were also intensive negotiations, if not disputes, between Aboriginal community members, families and clans as they identified priorities and jockeyed for influence with governments.

Where the negotiations were successful, projects could be identified and presented to government. Where unsuccessful, paralysis set in. When dysfunction set in in Bourke, the action team held firm and rejected offers to make deals outside the community working party. Some Bourke community members saw that this assisted their existing leadership to re-establish consensus. Indeed, for some community members, the working party and the governance it represented were important disciplines in themselves: 'Proposals had to come before the working party – there were no separate deals.'[3]

Planning

Given the importance of working to address community priorities, the steering committee agreed that each community working party would be supported to develop an action plan. These set out the community vision and priority actions for dealing with particular problems. The majority of action plans were completed in 2005, but a number were not finalised until May 2006, when the trial had only 18 months left to run. Given concern over government impatience with progress, the steering committee agreed to try to develop some shared responsibility agreements with the most advanced communities. The first agreements with Bourke and Brewarrina were signed in December 2004, two years into the trial but before the action plan for Brewarrina was finalised. It was soon found that communities were struggling to relate to government and, in late 2005, facilitators were recruited to provide professional and technical help for the communities.

Building trust

Trust with Aboriginal communities was built through keeping commitments, continuous engagement and negotiation. The continuous engagement was important as it showed that public servants were listening seriously and were prepared to enter into debate, rather than make

---

3   Bourke community member interviewee.

arbitrary decisions. They didn't always satisfy community expectations, but they were prepared to spend time to get an outcome everyone was happy with. This was very different from the kind of 'consultation' in which government officials listen politely and then leave. A particularly important feature was the preparedness of the action team to support small projects that built Aboriginal culture, such as the refurbishment of a cemetery or the holding of a culturally significant festival. But it required a cultural change: 'We had to leave our ego at the door if we wanted to engage with the communities ... Also to build trust with NSW (government), we had to avoid the stereotype that we were the heavy handed Commonwealth, using our money to bully.'[4]

Supporting community governance

Particularly important were the six-monthly governance workshops for the chairs of community working parties and secretariats, mentoring for chairs and a youth leadership program. Where communities were fractured, the Dubbo-based action team attempted to help them move forward by 'refreshing' the membership of the community working party. The working parties were supported by paid secretaries and, from 2005, by facilitators who played a brokerage role, progressing matters between meetings and engaging with other groups in order to advance particular projects.

Prioritising

Community priorities were identified in the 16 community action plans and supported through shared responsibility agreements, occasionally involving local government as well as state and Commonwealth governments. Local agreements covered environmental health, community and family wellbeing, the engagement of young people in community life and education, and crime prevention (Urbis Keys Young 2006). For example, these agreements supported a night patrol, a culturally significant festival and early childhood education (Bourke); an oval (Enngonia); refurbishing a cemetery (Collarenebri); and supporting Aboriginal community–controlled organisations and aged-care provision (Brewarrina).

---

4   DEST public servant interviewee.

Regional priorities were developed by the Murdi Paaki Regional Assembly or the regional subgroups, and included professional technical support; air conditioning in homes; health, education and employment; crime; community capacity and leadership; and regional cultural and heritage. These were frequently responded to through regional shared responsibility agreements. A particular subset of this was government-led initiatives that were derived from community or assembly priorities but not funded through formal agreements with the assembly or communities. Two examples are from education and health:

1. The Learning to Read, Reading to Learn initiative (Koop 2008)

   This program was the major contributor to the rapidly rising literacy scores in Murdi Paaki that occurred during the trial (Jarvie 2008). It was supported by strategies such as school principals discussing the school plan with the local community working party, a mentoring program for school principals and workshops and conferences for principals and schools under the Commonwealth Government 'Dare to Lead' program. The agreement reached between the federal department and its NSW partner was critical here, with DEST supplying the funds from its flexible funding bucket.

2. The Drug and Alcohol network

   The NSW Health Department, working with Commonwealth Government support and funding, was able to develop a number of useful health strategies, with the federal department drawing on its experience working in communities in Queensland. A systematic approach was adopted, with a consultant scrutinising community action plans for health-related priorities and validating findings through discussion with 10 communities. Five key themes were identified, including mental health and substance abuse, youth issues, chronic disease, family wellbeing and environmental health. A partnership between the Commonwealth Office of Aboriginal and Torres Strait Island Health (part of DOHA), the Greater Western Area Health Service, the Outback Division of General Practice, the Royal Flying Doctor Service and The Lyndon Community in Orange was created, and funding, including $1.22 million recurrent funding from DOHA, was found to establish a drug and alcohol network. The network, based on partnership principles of the trial, has heavy engagement with Aboriginal medical services, community working parties and regular reporting to the Regional Assembly.

Skills

The 'people side' of MLG is insufficiently appreciated. Skills are not only demanded – they are also developed through this way of working. From the perspective of Indigenous Australian leadership, the most important outcome was their personal development, in particular the growth of skills and confidence, not only in dealing with government, but also in engaging with other Aboriginal leaders and within their own community.[5] The 2006 evaluation (Urbis Keys Young 2006: ii) identified that governance capacity had improved and continues to improve and that communities 'appear better able to articulate their priorities to government in constructive fashion'. Interviewees noted the increased visibility of Aboriginal people in some communities, such as Cobar. For many of the smaller communities, this was the first time they felt they 'had a voice' and government attention, which also contributed to their confidence.

One of the unexpected successes of the Murdi Paaki trial was the releasing of bureaucratic energy. The high-level impetus and flexible structure of the trial enabled public servants to carry out work that they would otherwise have found difficult to get support for and to fund, as exemplified by the education and health initiatives. The public servants involved in those projects, when interviewed in 2010, retained strong memories of the sense of opportunity and excitement of the time. Bureaucratic energy and initiative was liberated by the trial, which was a result of support 'from the top' and flexible ways of working that the trial legitimated. A number of Indigenous Australian members of the Dubbo staff also thought that it was the best job they had ever had. They appreciated the autonomy and the responsibility: 'I knew when I said I would do something I would have to do it. I knew I would be going back to the community.' In some ways, the impact on the public servants involved in the education and health departments remains one of the most sustained outcomes of the Murdi Paaki trial.

---

5   Feedback from meeting with Murdi Paaki Regional Assembly October 2009.

Leadership

The importance of leadership in individual communities has already been mentioned. The leadership provided by Sam Jeffries was also critical, not only in his pragmatic support to continue the trial despite the abolition of the Aboriginal and Torres Strait Islander Commission in 2005 but also his work to create the Regional Assembly, which provided an essential infrastructure for capacity-building and negotiation with government (Jeffries & Menham 2011). There are few regions in Australia where leadership by Indigenous Australians is so relatively uncontested, or so effective.

Leadership in government was important as well. It was leadership that focused on providing structure and support for those 'on the ground' in a way that was appropriate for the design of the trial. This meant communicating the necessity for role flexibility. As one senior public servant said: 'Everyone was a leader at times, a partner at times and a follower at times.' The calibre of the leaders of the action team and the continuity of the team's personnel was a significant ingredient, as their role required consistent engagement and negotiation with Aboriginal communities and with government officials of many agencies and at all levels. Public servants saw the culture and leadership of the government agencies as critical – 'everyone respected each other, despite our differences'; 'we had a principle – to deliver on all commitments' and 'we knew we had support from the top'.

When negotiating with communities, collaborative leadership could be difficult for public servants who were used to assuming control and dispensing money from defined sources. Already divided communities could be further fractured in the face of the more traditional bureaucratic approach.

Listening

All actions were underpinned by the need to build and maintain trust and this necessity permeated everything governments did. If there was no trust between governments, and between Aboriginal communities and government, the trial would fail. The first essential was learning how to listen. 'Stop talking and start listening' was the first request made by Indigenous Australian leaders at a meeting in 2003. Delivering early on some small but important projects, such as a community garden and a cemetery makeover, was important, as was delivering on commitments, including holding to agreed processes, despite occasional setbacks.

Joining up the dots

Bureaucratic (and community) silos mean that people who should be communicating with each other frequently do not. Successful community brokers recognise these informational blockages and do something about them – 'joining up the dots', as one experienced broker termed the process. Joining up the dots also meant identifying opportunities as they emerged, and working with events as they happened, rather than trying to engineer outcomes. This 'administrative bricolage' saw the Bourke facilitator use an emergent crisis about juvenile crime to further the community's case for improved holiday programs and after-school care.

Obstacles and challenges

The bureaucratic politics of MLG are incessant and exigent. Change is inevitable and is often the result of impatience with the slowness of transaction-intensive policymaking. If MLG is not only an inevitable and desirable phenomenon, these obstacles (which derive from friction points with more conventional ways of working) require attention.

Instability in the authorising environment

The COAG trials were to last five years, which is a relatively long time by Commonwealth Government standards. There was, however, considerable turbulence in the Commonwealth policy environment. First, in July 2003, the Aboriginal and Torres Strait Island Commission's (ATSIC) program functions were dispersed to mainstream government agencies and its coordination role was handed to ATSIS, a new executive agency in the immigration and multicultural affairs portfolio. This was followed in 2004 by the abolition of ATSIS and the absorption of its functions into DIMIA, and the announcement that Commonwealth Indigenous programs would be coordinated on the ground from 29 Indigenous Coordination Centres. The abolition of ATSIC, including the ATSIC regional councils, followed in 2005 and, in January 2006, Indigenous policy coordination was transferred to the expanded FaCSIA. Finally, in 2007, in the last year of the trials, the Commonwealth Government announced the Northern Territory emergency intervention, which was a major practical and philosophic shift away from partnership with Aboriginal communities to direct action and control.

Meanwhile, in late 2005, six of the eight Commonwealth departmental secretaries relinquished their lead agency roles to the Office of Indigenous Policy Coordination, part of DIMIA and, later, FaCSIA. Many had found progress in negotiating with Aboriginal communities to be slow and some of the problems intractable (Gray and Sanders 2006). The Commonwealth was also negotiating bilateral agreements with state governments that, in some states, subsumed the trial activities. In many trials, the handover of leadership within the Commonwealth to the Office of Indigenous Policy Coordination in 2005 led to the effective end of the trial as the approach was merged into new delivery arrangements through the Indigenous Coordination Centres. When Commonwealth interest in the trials waned and resources dried up, with few exceptions, state agencies also lost focus. An evaluation was published in 2006 but, by then, activity had ceased.

Instability in communities

The community working parties that we examined in detail found the work of consensus-formation and action planning to be extremely difficult. The work was demanding and time-consuming and required considerable diplomatic skills to overcome divisions in the community. All the working parties had periods of instability, and one withdrew from the trial for a period. Six of the working parties did not sign shared-responsibility agreements during the trial, apart from the regional agreements. Personalities and leadership factors played a key role here. Family-based factions formed in several communities and there was competition for power and resources that swirled in and around the community working parties. Governments and the action team faced difficulties in this situation. There were no obvious tools that they could use to help, apart from refreshing the working party membership or supporting the facilitators and the chair to find a way through.

Working 'under the political radar'

As instability in the Commonwealth policy framework increased, senior bureaucrats in DEST and DET agreed that they would try and work 'under the political radar' to keep faith with the original aims of the trials, and the Aboriginal leadership in Murdi Paaki. Indeed, they saw that any change in approach would undermine the level of trust they had built up with the Regional Assembly and Sam Jeffries. Relationships remained good between DET and DEST, so much so that officials who were only engaged at the end of the trial took the good relationship as a given. But working 'under the radar' has its risks for public servants because maintaining good relationships with the hierarchy remains essential.

Coordination

The original (and emergent) intergovernmental design was based on networking. The Howard Government and FaCSIA, however, were intent on a harder-edged approach. Announced in 2004, Indigenous Coordination Centres were supposed to achieve formal coordination of Commonwealth Indigenous programs at a regional level. As already described, most of the Commonwealth secretaries eventually handed their lead responsibilities to the Office of Indigenous Policy Coordination. This did not happen in Murdi Paaki, as Sam Jeffries made it clear that the Aboriginal communities wanted DEST and DET to stay involved in the trial. This complex situation was nominally solved by making the head of the Bourke Indigenous Coordination Centre a member of the action team and requiring all shared-responsibility agreements to continue to be approved by the Murdi Paaki steering committee.

With the transfer of Indigenous policy coordination to FaCSIA in 2006, the trial entered an extremely difficult phase. The manager of the Indigenous Coordination Centre was in the uncomfortable position of reporting to his own hierarchy, with its priorities and philosophy of Indigenous coordination, while another Commonwealth agency was leading the trial. This might have worked if everyone supported the philosophies and principles of the trial, however, the FaCSIA minister, Mal Brough, was promoting the government's belief in the efficacy of a more directive approach to Indigenous Australian development. Unlike the previous minister for Indigenous affairs, Amanda Vanstone, his approach was less consensual and more 'carrot and stick'. Brough wanted shared-responsibility agreements with individuals and clans, not communities. Indeed, by 2005, the emphasis in these agreements changed from partnership, to 'the community meeting its obligations' in return for government funding.

This philosophic approach better suited FaCSIA officials, who found the 'community-led' approach to priority setting in the Murdi Paaki trial to be too slow and too engaged with developing representative structures and not enough on delivering outcomes (Stewart and Jarvie 2015). For the last two years of the trial, much lead agency time and energy was spent negotiating with FaCSIA. Two particularly difficult items were finding ongoing support for the Regional Assembly (seen by FaCSIA as a representative structure that was not focused on outcomes) and the fact that the 2006 independent evaluation of the Murdi Paaki trial was seen by FaCSIA officials as exaggerating its achievements. From a DEST official's perspective, the philosophic differences were one of the biggest hurdles the trial faced and an important cause of the lack of sustainability of some aspects.

Resources

The additional cost of the trials, beyond normal government expenditure, is not known. By mid-2005, however, it was clear that the simple concept behind the trials was, when put into practice, costing more in time, resources and effort than had ever been envisaged by the COAG architects in 2002. Continuous negotiation was time-intensive and staff in Dubbo were stretched meeting its demands. The aim was to have a member of the Dubbo team at every community working party monthly meeting. This involved attendance at 16 monthly meetings spread across thousands of kilometres. This was in addition to assisting with working party problems, negotiating projects with communities and funding agencies, briefing hierarchy and organising six-monthly governance workshops and consultations with the Regional Assembly. Justifying these costs in terms of hard outcomes was a difficult task.

Conclusion

There is no manual for public servants operating in environments where achieving objectives requires working in cooperative, non-hierarchical ways. New public management, with its emphasis on outputs and outcomes, provides little guidance. The Murdi Paaki experience suggests a number of 'do's' that bear repeating here:

1. build trust
2. start small
3. be flexible
4. negotiate
5. develop collaborative leadership
6. allow time to pass.

More broadly, the Murdi Paaki trial showed that governments find it difficult to sustain working in 'light touch' ways, particularly in a contested policy space such as Indigenous Australian development and in situations where there is a lack of cohesion. Public servants and ministers, impatient for outcomes in the key areas of measurable disadvantage – education, health and crime – have little patience with actions that are not, to them, directly linked to those outcomes, such as maintenance of cultural heritage, visibility in a community and having structures that enable their voice to be heard. Trust requires action and communication – through explanation, argument and negotiation. This is easy to characterise as time wasting.

The COAG trials suggest that MLG, to be successful in Indigenous Australian development, requires acceptance by community, governments, business, media and public servants that the focus on 'getting things done' must be moderated to include actions associated with building trust and creating consensus, including ensuring the stability of philosophy and policy, allowing sufficient time and valuing public servants who can embrace and undertake this new way of working.

References

ANAO (2008). *Whole of Government Indigenous Service Delivery Arrangements*. Performance Audit, Report no. 10. Australian National Audit Office, Canberra.

Bache, I. & Flinders, M. (2004). Themes and Issues in Multi-level Governance. In: Bache, I. & Flinders, M. (eds) *Multi-level Governance*. Oxford University Press, pp. 1–14. doi.org/10.1093/0199259259.003.0001

COAG (2002). *COAG Reconciliation Framework: Report on Progress in 2001*, Council of Australian Governments, webarchive.nla.gov.au/gov/20070829162314/http://coag.gov.au/meetings/050402/index.htm

——. (2004). *National Framework of Principles for Delivering Services to Indigenous Australians*. Council of Australian Governments, Canberra.

Edwards, M. & Langford, J. (2002). *New Players, Partners and Processes: A Public Sector without Boundaries?* National Institute for Governance, Canberra.

Galligan, G., Hughes, O. & Walsh, C. (eds) (1991). *Intergovernmental Relations and Public Policy*. Allen and Unwin, North Sydney.

Gray, W. & Sanders, W.G. (2006). *Views from the Top of the 'Quiet Revolution': Secretarial Perspectives on the New Arrangements in Indigenous Affairs*. CAEPR Discussion Paper No. 282/2006, ANU, Canberra.

Hooghe, L. & Marks, G. (2003). Unraveling the Central State, But How? Types of Multi-level Governance. *American Political Science Review*, 97(2): 233–43.

Jarvie, W. (2008). Working Differently to Make a Difference in Indigenous Communities. *Public Administration Today*, 14(Jan–Mar): 5–12.

Jarvie, W. & Stewart, J. (2011). Working with Complexity: Murdi Paaki and the COAG Trial 2002–2007. *Australian Journal of Public Administration*, 70(3): 259–74. doi.org/10.1111/j.1467-8500.2011.00734.x

Jeffries, S. & Menham, G. (2011). 'The Murdi Paaki Regional Assembly and Government Reform', *Journal of Indigenous Policy*, 46: 41–45, www.austlii.edu.au/au/journals/JlIndigP/2011/9.html

Koop, C. (2008). Reading to Learn in Murdi Paaki: Changing outcomes for indigenous students. *Literacy Learning: the Middle Years*, 16(1): 41–46.

Morgan Disney (2006). *Synopsis Review of the COAG Trial Evaluations: Report to the Office of Indigenous Policy Coordination*. Morgan Disney and Associates, November.

NSW Auditor-General (2011). *Performance Audit. Two Ways Together – NSW Aboriginal Affairs Plan,* www.audit.nsw.gov.au/ArticleDocuments/143/213_Two_Way_Together_Aboriginal_Affairs.pdf.aspx?Embed=Y [Accessed: 17/12/2014].

NSW Government (2006). *Two Ways Together Regional Report: Murdi Paaki.* Department of Aboriginal Affairs, Sydney.

Painter, M. (1998). *Collaborative Federalism: Economic Reform in Australia in the 1990s.* Cambridge University Press, Melbourne. doi.org/10.1017/CBO9780511552236

Peters, B.J. & Pierre, J. (2004). Multi-level Governance and Democracy: A 'Faustian bargain'? In: Bache, I. & Flinders, M. (eds) *Multi-level Governance.* Oxford University Press, pp. 75–89. doi.org/10.1093/0199259259.003.0005

SCRGSP (2016). *Overcoming Indigenous Disadvantage: Key Indicators 2016.* Steering Committee for the Review of Government Service Provision, Productivity Commission, Canberra.

Stewart, J. & Jarvie, W. (2015). Haven't We Been This Way Before? Evaluation and the Impediments to Policy Learning. *Australian Journal of Public Administration.* 74(2): 114–27. doi.org/10.1111/1467-8500.12140

Urbis Keys Young (2006). *Evaluation of the Murdi Paaki COAG Trial.* Prepared for the Office of Indigenous Policy Coordination, www.dss.gov.au/sites/default/files/documents/05_2012/coag_nsw.pdf [Accessed 21/12/2014].

Vanstone, A. (2005). Address to the National Press Club. 23 February, www.kooriweb.org/foley/news/vanstone1.html [Accessed: 02/06/2014].

Part 3: Spatial and Planning Policy

10

Multi-level Housing Policy in Australia

Patrick Troy

Introduction

Since settlement in 1788, housing policy in Australia has always been subjected to several levels of regulation and control exercised by different levels of authority. For a broader discussion of multi-level governance (MLG) of urban development see Stilwell and Troy (2000).

Initially, regulations governing housing were introduced by the central colonial administration in London, although early governors had a high degree of discretion over urban regulations, including control over aspects of housing. Later, a degree of devolution of responsibility for aspects of housing occurred as the realities of centralised administration overwhelmed the central administration in each colony. The vehicle chosen for the devolution of responsibility varied between the colonies. For example, the *Police Land Act 1833* in the NSW colony was used to enforce compliance with building safety and health regulations in NSW until 1837 with the promulgation of the *Building Act* (Troy 1988).

Housing policy responsibilities and issues before federation

Local government was created in NSW (Larcombe 1961) as the creature of colonial, later state, administration and was given responsibility for administering central policy and building regulations – especially over housing. Local government was created in the other colonies at different stages in their development and with different responsibilities. There was, however, a wide disparity between and within the colonies in relation to the development of accommodation standards and their enforcement. By and large, the colonial administrations were happy to 'live and let live' as long as there was no 'disaster' resulting in injury or loss of life. The quality of accommodation was essentially determined by the strength of demand and regulations governing housing were enforced in an almost 'accidental' way.

As local governments matured and their urban centres grew, the larger of them sought more engagement in aspects of housing policy beyond the structural, health and fire safety regulations introduced by the respective colonial administrations.

The larger urban centres sought to take more enlightened approaches to the quality of urban spaces and the dwellings in them, frequently initiating campaigns for the improvement of various aspects of the accommodation in their areas. These initiatives did not always win the approval of colonial administrations. At times, colonial administrations had larger ambitions than the local authorities, and vice versa. But at all times, the underlying issue was more a reflection of differing ambitions about the extent to which local communities – many of which were forced to accept responsibility to establish local government to provide local services – could decide what they wanted, how much and the standards that should apply to developments in their area.

Local communities could make a case for 'local exceptionalism', arguing that they knew what they wanted and were unhappy about being required to comply, initially with colonial, later state, policies and standards. Enforcement of colony-wide policies and associated regulations over local ambitions could become the avenue of political expression and opposition to the central administration. Central administrations were often accused of being 'out of touch'.

The early years of federation

The advent of statehood that came with federation in 1901 did not increase the powers of local governments and left undisturbed the wide range of responsibilities and standards relating to the construction and operation of dwellings that were formerly held by the colonial administrations. In the delineation of responsibilities between the states and the Commonwealth, there were significant differences between the states of the new nation in relation to many aspects of housing, and the Commonwealth had virtually no authority in the area.

Throughout the early years of the Commonwealth, each state pursued housing policies with little regard to what others were doing.

These differences had little effect for much of the early period of federation. The range of climatic conditions, the differences in economic development and the locally available building materials, together with the differing scale and nature of urbanisation, meant that the states were under little pressure to pursue standardisation of building regulations or to explore issues of equitable access to accommodation. This inevitably meant that there were significant differences between them in the reach and detail of housing regulation. Commencing in 1910, Queensland led the states in addressing the affordability of housing for low-income households by introducing a Workers Dwelling Scheme under which low-income households could have an advance to build a home on a site they owned.

Other states followed suit with variations that included, in South Australia from 1910, being able to buy a house and land through the State Bank of South Australia. Western Australia chose in 1912 to establish a Housing Board with the power to build a house on land already owned by an applicant. In 1912 in NSW, a local authority, the Sydney Corporation, was empowered to build dwellings for rent. Victoria in 1914 extended the involvement of local government in housing by giving it the power to borrow to buy land and build dwellings for leasing. The Victorian scheme failed because ratepayers were reluctant to support ventures into municipal housing.

Intergovernment relationships and responsibility sharing

In short, although housing issues had long engaged colonial and state governments as well as their local government authorities, the history of the relationship between the two levels of government was not propitious. The power of colonial administrations and, later, the state governments, meant that they could establish regulations relating to the structural and fire safety aspects of housing and ensure that elemental aspects of health, especially for ventilation and sanitation, were taken into account in building new housing. Once reticulated water services were developed, states also defined the conditions applying to their provision. The further development of water-based sanitation systems was followed by articulation of regulations governing their provision. Local authorities, however, had the responsibility of administering the policies. State administrations had limited abilities to enforce compliance. In many areas, local authorities simply 'ran dead' on issues of quality, not only because they believed housing standards were too high but also because they had limited resources to address them. State and local administrations basically ignored issues of access to accommodation and paid little attention what might be termed the equity aspects of housing provision.

As evidence emerged of the inadequate slum housing in which large proportions of the population lived in the older, inner areas of the major settlements, the limited abilities of local authorities to ameliorate them became more obvious.

The Commonwealth had no interest or experience in administration of such matters, although it was to have responsibilities in such matters once it began the process in 1912 of building the nation's capital, Canberra, in what was essentially a 'greenfield site' (note that the Commonwealth retained responsibility for control of development of Canberra until 1988 when the Australian Capital Territory was given a large degree of administrative independence). As the Commonwealth slowly evolved and grew in confidence, it acquired the obligation for the accommodation of its officers. This meant that it had to ensure that they enjoyed housing of comparable quality irrespective of the location in which they served. In accepting this obligation, the Commonwealth began the process of developing standards and regulations, which meant that it often adopted the standards of the 'leading states'.

Housing issues in the inter-war years

Following World War I, the Commonwealth, in 1919, enacted the *War Service Homes Act* to provide houses for sale to ex-servicemen. The houses were expected to comply with the relevant state regulations so their construction did not entail competition between levels of government over housing standards.

Apart from accepting, in 1928, its responsibility for housing of the residents of the new national capital, Commonwealth initiatives were restricted, in the same year, to permitting the Commonwealth Savings Bank to advance funds to state authorities and the private sector to increase the funds available for home purchase. The scheme was directed at middle-income households and founded on the notion that the housing would comply with state regulations. Little housing was financed under the scheme. A proposal by conservative Prime Minister Joseph Lyons in the 1934 election to introduce a national housing scheme under which low-cost housing would be provided in association with state and local government and include a slum clearance program was aborted following the election by Robert Menzies as attorney-general (later to become prime minister), who argued that the Commonwealth did not have the constitutional power to do so.

Increasing social concerns

Deterioration of the state housing situation continued during the 1930s Depression and was accompanied by rising concern among social activist groups over the health and social consequences of the slum conditions under which significant proportions of the population lived. The regulatory framework devised by state governments and administered by local authorities seemed impotent in responding to the situation.

By the 1940s, there was increasing concern over the housing experience of large proportions of the population. Rents were high and, although home ownership had nationally reached 50 per cent by 1911, the level of home ownership in the major cities was significantly lower (Troy 2012). There was an unacceptable level of homelessness and overcrowding was common, in spite of state and local regulations drawn up to reduce the challenges to health that overcrowding brought. Reviews of housing conditions undertaken by various state agencies and religious and political reformist groups revealed the parlous conditions under which many low-income households lived.

The growing case for national intervention in housing policy

Early in World War II, concern was expressed about the social welfare of the lower income members of society, leading to the creation in 1941 by the conservative government in the Commonwealth parliament of a Joint Parliamentary Review of Social Security that revealed the crisis in social welfare and, in particular, the conditions under which a large minority of the community was housed. This was the first national review of housing undertaken by a national government in Australia. Following a recommendation of the Joint Parliamentary Review of Social Security and a change to a Labor government, the Commonwealth created the Commonwealth Housing Commission, which was charged with the obligation to:

> inquire into and report [on] matters in relation to the public safety and defence of the Commonwealth: the present housing position in Australia; and the housing requirements of Australia during the post-war period (CHC 1944).

Each state had a shortage of accommodation due to the low level of building activity in the 1920s and 1930s that was exacerbated by wartime limitations on domestic construction. There was, in addition, rising concern in the larger cities, especially Sydney and Melbourne, over the slum housing conditions under which low-income households lived. Menzies, however, used the opportunity in his May 1942 speech, 'The Forgotten People' – while claiming that there was no class war – to set out in considerable detail his view of the middle class, which he saw as the national backbone. He argued that the middle class had a 'stake in the country', the material aspect of which he averred found concrete expression in the habits of frugality and saving:

> for a home of our own ... one of the best instincts in us is that induces us to have one little piece of earth with a house and a garden which is ours: to which we can withdraw, in which we can be among friends, into which no stranger may come against our will.

He also took the view that the wealthy could look out for themselves and that those 'at the other end of the scale was the mass of unskilled people who were almost invariably well organized and with their wages and conditions safeguarded by popular law' (Menzies 1943). Like the 1928 initiative, he saw the opportunity for the Commonwealth to improve the housing conditions of the middle class by increasing opportunities for them to acquire their own home.

In making its report to the Commonwealth, the CHC took a larger view than that adumbrated by Menzies in asserting: 'We consider that a *dwelling of good standard and equipment is not only the need but the right of every citizen*' (CHC 1944, emphasis in original).

The CHC made a number of recommendations commenting on housing design, estate development, the need for better planning and on the development of a housing program under which households would not be required to pay more than 20 per cent of household income on rent.

Outcomes of Commonwealth–state negotiations

The 'National picture' that emerged from negotiations over the proposed Commonwealth–state Housing Agreements (CSHA) revealed widely divergent views about the need for, and nature of, a housing program. In response to the CHC's proposal that advances be made to the states to enable them to acquire land for urban development and to construct housing on the condition that the states each establish town planning processes and schemes, the states adopted different positions. At the 1944 meeting of premiers to discuss the details of the Commonwealth's proposal for the creation of a research-based planning system, the states resisted. The most assertive was Queensland whose premier, Frank Cooper (Labor), announced his opposition to the proposal saying:

> while the exigencies of the war demanded sacrifices of Queensland so that Australia might be served, after the war Queensland would consider her claims as paramount.[1]

The premier of Victoria, Albert Dunstan (Country Party), who had earlier agreed on the need for a scientific basis for town planning, declined to participate, saying his government had already submitted its own legislation to parliament and there was no need to go over the same ground.

---

1   From the record of 1944 meetings between Commonwealth and states (AA A9816/4 1943/1423 Part 1).

The Commonwealth had also proposed that, initially, housing built under a Commonwealth-funded program would be for rental, with ex-servicemen being given preference until the shortage of housing was addressed. Here states also revealed their opposition, with Queensland and Tasmania saying that those given access to housing had to be able to acquire it. The two states displayed little preparedness to depart from strongly held ideological views about the approach to be adopted in relation to the creation and ownership of housing. This was paradoxical because both were Labor states directly challenging and refusing to participate in a scheme that the national Labor Government proposed. This was mildly embarrassing because a conservative government in South Australia, which had mounted an imaginative, large scale and successful public rental housing scheme since 1936, refused to 'sign up' for fear that they might have to compromise on what it held was a superior scheme. It was able to use its state bank to facilitate home purchase and ensure that the site planning and development of estates was of a high order, enjoying a high reputation as a consequence. South Australia took the view that its housing program was superior to that proposed by the Commonwealth and did not 'sign up' to the CSHA until 1956.

In the postwar period, the states also agreed to continue the uniform income-taxation provisions they had agreed to fund the war effort. This initiative profoundly affected the distribution of power between the Commonwealth and states, significantly increasing the power of the former and reducing that of the latter. The central control, especially over the raising of loans to fund infrastructure investment, materially affected the capacity of the states to provide the water services and transport infrastructure needed to foster and direct housing development to accommodate burgeoning population pressures resulting from Commonwealth migration programs.

The Commonwealth–state Housing Agreements

The CSHAs under which funds were advanced to each state for the construction of housing (initially for rent) ran for an agreed but extendable period initially of five years.

The first agreement ran from 1946 to 1956. There was considerable philosophical disagreement over the role of the state in housing, with some reluctance on the part of Commonwealth ministers and officials to pursue the program. The program was developed by a federal Labor administration on the assumption that it was for 'public housing'. Although the sale of such housing was not excluded, it was assumed that, until the housing crisis was 'solved', housing built under the agreement should be for rent. Two states, Queensland and Tasmania, both Labor states, argued strongly that housing should be able to be sold to sitting tenants and refused to 'sign up'.

The Commonwealth undertook to share the burden of any losses incurred under the program but insisted that economic rents should be struck to recoup outgoings on dwellings and that rents should not exceed 20 per cent of income.

Some elements within the Commonwealth administration opposed the idea of a public housing program, arguing that it was outside the Commonwealth's powers, and also out of a belief that government ought not be involved in such matters. How much such views influenced the Commonwealth approach to negotiations with states it is impossible to say. Suffice it to note that the Commonwealth Treasury took a restricted view of the purposes to which Commonwealth funds for a housing program could be applied. The 'triumph' of the Commonwealth's limited views on such matters is the proximate reason why the great majority of Commonwealth-funded housing projects were developed with almost no community facilities, thus making them less attractive as places in which to live and which ultimately helped foster the stigmatisation of households who lived in them.

The postwar period

Housing, although a basic need, elicits a wide range of responses. The Commonwealth clearly responded to the objective conditions that existed in the mid-1940s by constructing a program to alleviate them. There was an obvious ideological dimension to the initiative. In the view of the major proponents of the public housing program, the 'market system' had failed and the solution was to try to create an alternative set of rights in relation to housing.

The Commonwealth's engagement in housing always had a degree of ideological tension to it that affected the way in which CSHAs were negotiated and administered. Sometimes the tension was between the Commonwealth and various states; on other occasions, the tensions were within the Commonwealth or within one or more states.

The sale of public housing

Although the Commonwealth's involvement in housing was not high on Menzies' agenda, once he regained office as prime minister in 1949 he did not move to change the direction of the public housing program until 1954 when, during an election campaign, he announced that housing built by the states under the CSHA could be sold to sitting tenants. The initiative, reflected in the CSHA negotiated in 1956 when the Commonwealth allowed public housing to be sold on concessional terms using funds granted to permanent building societies, effectively undermined the intention and development of the public housing program. The initiative was entirely consistent with Menzies' 'Forgotten People' speech (Menzies 1943) and began the process of destruction of the CSHA.

Home ownership

The public housing program under the CSHA was successful and popular but, in pursuit of the objective of increasing home ownership and withdrawing from housing provision through the states, several Commonwealth ministers sought to limit the program and all sought ways of influencing development decisions. Part of their response in 1964 was to make home ownership more attractive by developing a Home Savings Grant Scheme under which households that saved through an approved lending institution for a specified period could be awarded a grant to be used to increase their deposit on a dwelling. At the same time, Minister Leslie Bury sought to dramatically restructure the Commonwealth's approach to housing and was appointed the first minister for housing. Bury sought to increase direct Commonwealth control over housing programs and, like his predecessor, William Spooner, minister for national development, was concerned that too much of the kudos associated with housing resided with the states.

It is important to recall that the level of 'owner building' – that is, houses built by individuals for themselves – exceeded the level of housing built under the CSHA or by registered builders, significantly increasing the level of owner occupation (Troy 2012) and, in an important sense, was a strong measure of the instinct to which Menzies (1943) had referred. The level of owner building was entirely a response within the states, although Commonwealth control over the supply of building materials indirectly affected the rate of completion of houses.

Commonwealth politics and policy responses to slum housing

Slum housing had attracted the attention of social reformers and its existence was a major reason that the federal government became involved in improving the housing stock. During the first 20 years of the CSHAs, the Commonwealth did not see slum clearance as the most important housing initiative so did not pursue the issue with great energy. Senator Annabelle Rankin, who replaced Bury in 1966 as housing minister, was determined to eliminate slum housing and to develop a research base to housing policy articulation and program development. She argued for a slum-clearance program, with the resulting vacant inner-city land being made available for higher income housing on the grounds that it was too valuable to be used to accommodate low-income households. In this she was at odds with Spooner, who had argued that low-income households should be accommodated at high density in inner-city areas that traditionally voted Labor. In proposing such a policy, Spooner was suggesting concentrating low-income households in inner electorates and, in so doing, ensuring that Labor voters would not become a 'problem' in suburban areas that returned conservative representatives. More conservative ministers proposed that the Commonwealth should not be engaged in housing programs for low-income earners at all but, nonetheless, argued that it should have more direct control over how the housing program was developed and administered.

Although the Commonwealth formally eschewed direct responsibility for the details of housing developments, several ministers sought to encourage slum-clearance projects in inner areas out of a belief that, by committing themselves to such (expensive) projects, the states would have fewer resources available for construction of traditional houses in the suburbs that were perceived to be a threat to conservative electorates. The series of slum-clearance projects that were undertaken in Melbourne and Sydney were important recognition of the need to be seen to be eliminating substandard accommodation. The fact that the replacement housing was built in such a way that it was difficult to sell separately was to some extent a defensive response of the states to ensure that they retained control over a stock of housing for low-income households.

Late 20th-century reforms

The Labor administration from December 1972 to December 1975 gave confused signals over its approach to housing issues. It wanted to maintain a public housing program delivered through the states but also wanted to make it easier for low-income households to purchase their houses. The CSHA of 1973 increased the targeting of low-income households.

Commonwealth provision of housing

Legal advice tendered to the Commonwealth in the early 1970s indicated that it had the power directly to provide housing to the majority of the population for whom it provided social benefits (pensions, child welfare etc.) or employed (including in the armed services) by extending its activities to include other citizens. This advice provided the justification for the Commonwealth to undertake a major housing project in inner Sydney (the Glebe Estate) under which housing was acquired, renovated and new housing built to provide a significant increase in public housing in the area.

In 1975, it also created the Australian Housing Corporation to enable it to directly deliver housing. In its creation the Commonwealth was trying to build on its powers to deliver housing to ex-servicemen. The change of government at the end of 1975 led to the abolition of the Australian Housing Corporation before it had developed any programs in the states. The Commonwealth, in 1976, reintroduced the Home Savings Grant Scheme that had been phased out in 1972.

From public to welfare housing

Following a review of the CSHA, the Commonwealth Government under Malcolm Fraser decided in 1978 to change the basis of the agreement with the states to three years by changing the focus of program from a public housing program to a welfare-housing program under which the states were to provide matching funds. To further sharpen the focus, the Commonwealth stipulated that the basis of rents was to be changed from 'economic rents' to market rents (reduced in negotiations to 'market-related rents'). The ambition to charge market rents rather than economic rents was to reduce the Commonwealth obligation to underwrite the program by reducing the demand for public housing.

The changes to the administration of the CSHA in 1978 completed the change of the original housing ambition from a public housing program to a welfare program and, once the introduction of the policy of market-related rents took effect, to a residual social-housing program. The final stage of conversion to a residual social-housing program was accompanied by the demonisation/stigmatisation of residents in such housing estates as they became concentrations of households of multiple disadvantage – the consequences of the Commonwealth's strictures on what could be funded under the CSHA meant that the lack of facilities and poor access to employment accentuated the social disadvantage such households experienced.

To reduce the burden on the Commonwealth and the level of public housing, the Commonwealth also decided in 1979 to increase the proportion of funds devoted to welfare housing by increasing the funding for pensioner housing and for housing Indigenous Australian communities. The Commonwealth was positioning itself to vacate the field. The 1978 CSHA was due to run out in mid-1981. A strong group of Liberal ministers wanted to terminate the agreement but the minister, Tom McVeigh, a traditional Country Party man from Queensland, supported continuation of the agreement and succeeded in getting the Commonwealth to agree to another three years.[2] Although he was impressed by the project, he was less successful in preventing the sale of the Glebe Estate to the NSW Government in 1981. The Commonwealth also directly boosted home ownership in 1982 by reintroducing taxation deductions for mortgages for home owners, radically changing the controls over trading banks' lending limits and relaxing the regulations under which savings banks operated, and introducing a mortgage- and rent-relief scheme.

The segmentation of welfare housing and Commonwealth independent action

The Commonwealth again changed tack on housing with the election of a Labor Government under Bob Hawke in 1983. The new CSHA that was negotiated in 1984 extended the segmentation of welfare housing to

---

2   Tom McVeigh, personal communication, 2013.

additional identified groups within the community. The Commonwealth also removed further controls over both trading and savings banks, setting in train the massive increases in house prices that followed.

The Commonwealth's decisions in the 1980s accorded preferential treatment of capital gains on housing. In particular, its decision not to tax capital gains on the 'family home' and to permit negative gearing on investment by home owners in additional dwellings introduced distortions in the housing market that affected the ability of states to secure planned developments.

The non-taxation of capital gains in their houses encouraged home owners to 'over invest' in their dwelling, leading to the development of 'McMansions' in the expectation that, when they retired, they would be able to sell their homes and 'downsize', leaving them with a significant capital sum they could use to fund their retirement. The negative gearing of second dwellings enabled high-income households to claim the 'loss' incurred in raising a mortgage on its purchase as an offset on their income tax. This was highly inequitable in its effects.

21st-century issues and reforms

The 'experiment' with public housing through the CSHA came to an end as the Commonwealth increased the focus on housing as part of the social security system and further segmented the provision of housing to specific groups. The proportion of the stock of housing held as public housing fell to 4 per cent by the national census of 2006. Home ownership, which had been the emphasis of Commonwealth policy, had reached 70 per cent by 1966 and has slowly declined since. The last CSHA was signed in 2003 and, in 2009, was replaced by the National Australian Housing Assistance plan.

Discussion of the MLG Australian housing policy system

The history of responses of state and Commonwealth governments to the housing crisis in 1945 was one of contestation between the two levels of government. In the early period, the Commonwealth acted as though it was unsure of its constitutional authority in housing. Its confidence grew with its increasing command over national economic policy. States were limited by a lack of financial resources from providing infrastructure. The massive increase in urban populations, stimulated largely by Commonwealth immigration programs and by the migration of rural dwellers to the city as rationalisation/modernisation of primary production proceeded, created increasing demands for urban housing. The growing demand for housing was accompanied by the population's rising expectations of housing quality and home ownership. The massive surge in owner building, together with the ability from 1956 to buy houses built under the CSHA, lifted owner occupancy rates.

Commonwealth governments, especially of the more conservative cast, were concerned that the kudos from housing programs funded under the CSHAs fell largely to the states. Commonwealth officers and political leaders sought increasing direct control over what housing was built where. States were required to provide detailed proposals of their programs. The Commonwealth was asserting power over the states in areas that it had formerly claimed to have no responsibility.

Throughout the life of the Commonwealth initiative to create a public housing system in which households could exercise a choice to buy their own home or elect to rent accommodation in well-planned and well-located housing, the problems of MLG were starkly revealed. The difficulties that emerged in trying to establish continuities and consistency within and between the Commonwealth and state administrations proved to be insuperable. The time taken to design and construct housing and to establish communities was long but could be subverted by lack of consistency or continuity in policy development. States could enter into programs designed to secure long-run housing programs to produce efficient and equitable urban development with confidence, only to find that the Commonwealth adopted policies driven by a contrasting ideological agenda with little or no consultation with them and that undermined their activities.

Shared public and private responsibility over housing

One of the paradoxes that exists in Australia is that there is now a significant disjunction between the approaches by Commonwealth and state governments over who bears the responsibility for areas of social policy such as housing. Households may experience difficulties in securing adequate housing of an acceptable standard but be unsure as to which level of government might be able to resolve those difficulties. The level of government with the greatest capacity to provide them with the level of ontological security they desire is undoubtedly the Commonwealth. The Commonwealth's power over income tax and its ability to construct favourable financial conditions enables it to make promises to help households secure home ownership that inevitably comes closest to their ambitions. State governments have never had access to comparable levels of resources.

Local government rarely had resources sufficient to embark on housing programs. Although they notionally had the power to affect the quality, scale and type of housing provided in their area, local governments were increasingly made to understand that they were creatures of state governments as they were required to adhere to state-determined housing targets. The independence of local government promised by state governments was limited by state decisions seemingly more responsive to pressure from developer interests to reduce the influence of local governments over development control plans.

The promise of the programs constructed under the CSHA was founded on notions of stability and on equitable treatment between states and between different groups within them. While for a moment it seemed that there was sufficient shared experience to warrant a 'national' response to the accommodation needs of the population, it soon unravelled. The ambitions of Queensland and Tasmania, who wanted residents of housing built under a public scheme to be able to buy it, and the decision by South Australia to stay out of the Commonwealth scheme are evidence of the fragility of the idea of national purpose.

The propensity of Commonwealth ministers (and their departments) to directly shape the contours of housing policy compounded the difficulties that multi-level government administration of housing programs confronted. Much of this contestation came from the fundamentally different ideological origins of the definition of the boundaries within which housing programs were developed and delivered. The initial Commonwealth proposals were developed out of a notion of the welfare state that evolved out of the experiences of the Depression enriched by radical views about social justice. Some states (and, indeed, at the Commonwealth level) held to a more robust view that reliance on 'the market' would produce an acceptable, (and in this view) desirable, outcome.

There was always a tension between Commonwealth and state agencies that advised on housing programs. The state agencies were staffed by people who had direct experience of developing housing and of administering it and were consequently immediately aware of the human dimensions of the policies and programs. The Commonwealth agencies had few staff with direct experience. These differences could be observed in meetings between Commonwealth and state ministers and officers. The state housing agencies were often led by officers with long experience in delivering housing and who were committed to the ideals of public housing. The Commonwealth was staffed by few officers with direct experience and their careers were not necessarily bound up in quite the same way with the program's success.

The initial CSHAs were developed out of a shared understanding between the Commonwealth and the states over the accommodation needs of the population. There was always a determination that, as far as possible, those needs would be equitably met. The differences between Commonwealth and state administrations and their ideological preferences, however, meant that MLG issues were magnified at each level by inconsistency of commitment due to internal tensions, such as differences between them in the approach to home ownership. Conservative Commonwealth governments tended to emphasise home ownership. Labor governments acknowledged the attractions of home ownership but were more concerned over the need to secure equitable treatment for all groups in society. The distribution of rights in housing was seen as a strong indicator of the balance in society.

When only one-third of households were owner-occupiers, two-thirds were sensitive about the quality of their housing and their security and could respond to Commonwealth initiatives to acknowledge their concerns. By the time two-thirds of households were owner-occupiers or were given significant advantages in investment in housing and the Commonwealth had successfully 'split' the 'welfare' lobbyists by ensuring religious and charity activists had resources to provide accommodation, housing had receded as a national concern and was transformed into a concern over the private financing of the debt incurred in home ownership. The lifting of controls over banks requiring them to hold a certain proportion of their investment portfolios in housing and to limit the level of housing mortgages to a set maximum proportion of household income was followed by a rapid inflation in house prices. The developer industry and associated financial interests, including the major banks, which enjoyed

Commonwealth government 'protection', were increasingly influential in controlling decisions affecting the scale and nature of development, including the level and nature of infrastructure provision, further reducing the ability of local governments to protect or promote the nature of developments.

Although states agreed to establish planning authorities to provide urban development plans and strategies as a condition of obtaining Commonwealth funds under the CSHA schemes, they took no initiatives to prevent rent-seeking by existing land owners. Consequently, state and local governments had little influence over the price, amount or nature of accommodation. The nature of the housing industry changed, with large-scale land and housing developers being able to exert pressure on state and local governments to influence the types of dwellings permitted and the nature and mix of infrastructure to support them.

The Commonwealth–state model of delivery of housing that was built on notions of acknowledging differences between the states, especially in relation to the lower income members of society, failed. The last agreement in 2003 was final evidence of the consequences of trying to address their needs without broad consensus and continuity of commitment. The dominance of the push for home ownership that was achieved by the Commonwealth delivering significant subsidies to achieve that ownership, which was undertaken with little consultation with the states, ensured that state governments were always at a political disadvantage in exploring/ responding to housing challenges. The failure was also, no doubt, due to the increasing influence of the centralising approach adopted by Council of Australian Governments (COAG).

The conservative reaches of the Commonwealth succeeded in reducing its commitment to public housing. It had swept up a range of programs designed to address the accommodation needs of specific groups by recasting them as state responsibilities. There was no common commitment among the states to a public housing program. The 'agreements' between the states and Commonwealth provided for states to arrive at their own programs. National housing objectives were broadly defined in the new National Affordable Housing Agreement (COAG 2009). The agreement was innovative because it directly acknowledged the role of local government in the provision of housing, albeit in its role to endorse and apply state regulations in relation to building approval processes and local planning and development approval. That is, it accorded local government little direct involvement in housing policy but provided the excuse that housing costs were high because of local approval processes and administrative and operational charges that were vaguely described as 'charges that influence housing affordability'. It was also innovative because it set out a description of the responsibilities of the Commonwealth and the states and territories in achieving a number of outcomes. The rhetoric of the agreement was acceptable but provided no level of resources on which the states could rely to develop or manage programs to produce the desired outcomes.

Addressing MLG challenges of the future in housing policy

The new landscape of housing policy was recognised in the way in which housing was dealt with under the developing COAG. Created in 1992, COAG was designed to achieve national standards in delivery of services, including housing, and to give more confidence to state administration in the development of their programs. It was also designed to reduce pressure on Commonwealth administration.

The housing 'crisis' that was manifested in the 1990s and early 2000s was revealed in increasing concern over affordability of housing. The Commonwealth's policies in relation to housing finance, including its preferment of investment in rental housing, created speculation in rental housing and its reduction of funding for state housing programs led to the 'crisis'. Although the crisis was real, Commonwealth reluctance to embark on an ameliorative program was consistent with its view that housing issues were essentially the responsibility of the states. The influence of neo-liberalist philosophy, which saw the outcomes as a 'natural' part of the playing out of the market, also led to a Commonwealth response designed only to deal with the consequences of extreme market outcomes that were socially unacceptable. Although the Commonwealth held to a view that it had vestigial responsibility for some welfare housing issues, its basic position was that, in providing the control of the major elements of the economy, it was doing all that was necessary to provide for Commonwealth involvement in the governance of housing. This was reflected in the fact that to the extent that the Commonwealth accepted some responsibility for housing, it was administered through the Department of Social Security from 1996–98 and the Department of Families and Community Services after 1998.

Milligan and Pinnegar (2010) provide a useful exploration of the origins of the 2009 Commonwealth housing initiative, including identification of the limits of the National Affordable Housing Agreement program, pointing out that it does not address 'the absence of a long term investment plan sufficient to enable social housing to grow and to be reconfigured to better match current and projected needs' (338).

The sorry history of Commonwealth engagement in housing policy and programs is outlined by Milligan and Tiernan (2011). The history focuses on direct program delivery but eschews exploration of the effects of the suite of initiatives directed at taxation, preferential financing or cash grants for owner-occupiers and the 1978 introduction of market-related rents for public housing, all of which have profoundly affected the shape and nature of the supply and demand for housing. Save for the 1978 changes to the rents to be paid for public housing under the CSHA, few of these initiatives were the administrative responsibility of housing portfolios but were designed and delivered through central 'economic' agencies.

State housing authorities have never been high in the administrative ranking in the states. By and large they have been, and are, agencies charged with responsibility to deliver real accommodation services to real people. Over the last 60 years, the greater part of the resources available to them for housing came from the Commonwealth, so they were never dependent to a high degree on the vagaries of state budgets. The changing climate and framework within which they operate under COAG, whilst being described as an agreement reached between state and Commonwealth governments to deliver greater flexibility, now places the states in a more precarious position on housing issues. The assurances that prevail so long as the states annually make progress on Commonwealth-set performance indicators simply presage contestation between the two levels of government.

The risk is that, rather than reducing the levels of conflict, the multi-level governance of housing now in place will invite the Commonwealth to be more interventionist but, in doing so, it will be less focused on delivery of accommodation than on attempting to structure the financing of housing.

Taking the long view suggests that the housing crisis experienced up to the end of World War II was due directly to the failure of the market to deliver socially acceptable outcomes. There was no national approach to, or consideration of, housing issues; consequently, the fragmentation of responses from each state could not be expected to produce an even outcome. For a while after World War II there was an agreed view that there should be a national approach to housing. The states had some responsibilities to deliver appropriate amounts and quality of housing. Local governments had little say in the quality or quantity of housing produced. For the last 50 years, as its control over the economy has increased, the Commonwealth has inexorably retreated from direct influence over the quality or quantity of housing. It has been content to use its powers over interest rates and monetary policy to influence supply. To some degree, it has tempered its commitment to the efficacy of 'the market' by making contributions to the accommodation needs of selected minorities, such as its support for the 'welfare' housing provided by churches and other groups that work for 'good causes', such as aged citizens and housing for Aboriginal communities, but eschewed opportunities to see housing as a right of citizens.

References

CHC (1944). Final Report, 25 August 1944 Ministry of Post-War Reconstruction, Commonwealth Housing Commission, Sydney.

COAG (2009). *National Affordable Housing Agreement: Intergovernmental Agreement on Federal Financial Relations*, www.federalfinancialrelations. gov.au/content/npa/national_agreements/national-housing-agree ment.pdf [Accessed: 21/12/2014].

Larcombe, F. (1961). *The Development of Local Government in New South Wales*. Cheshire, Melbourne.

Menzies, R.G. (1943). *The Forgotten People and Other Studies in Democracy*. Angus and Robertson, Sydney.

Milligan, V. & Pinnegar, S. (2010). The Comeback of National Housing Policy in Australia: First reflections. *International Journal of Housing Policy*, 10(3): 325–44. doi.org/10.1080/14616718.2010.506747

Milligan, V. & Tiernan, A. (2011). No Home for Housing: the situation of the Commonwealth's housing policy advisory function. *Australian Journal of Public Administration*, 70(4): 391–407. doi.org/10.1111/j.1467-8500.2011.00746.x

Stilwell, F. & Troy, P. (2000). Multilevel Governance and Urban Development in Australia. *Urban Studies*, 37: 909. doi.org/10.1080/00420980050011154

Troy, P. (1988). Government Housing Policy in New South Wales 1788–1900. *Housing Studies*, 3(1): 20–30. doi.org/10.1080/02673038808720611

——. (2012). *Accommodating Australians: Commonwealth Government Involvement in Housing*. Federation Press, Sydney.

11

Multi-level Governance in Integrated Land Use and Natural Resource Planning on the Urban Fringe: A Case Study of Processes and Structures for Governing across Boundaries

Iris Iwanicki, Kathryn Bellette and Stephen Smith

Introduction

The southern and eastern rural–urban fringe of metropolitan Adelaide provides a case study of different governance systems across three levels of government – federal, state and local – dealing with urban development and water resources management. As *Kay* observes in his chapter, multi-level governance (MLG), while over 20 years old, is a relatively little acknowledged process 'creating cross-jurisdictional policy capacity in Australia, across and between different governance jurisdictions to match the territorial scale that is functional for effective policy response'. The subject of this chapter provides a demonstration that the MLG concept (see also Hooghe and Marks 2001) can contribute to outcomes involving land-use planning, natural resource management and different levels of governance structured around water management. This MLG case study is of formal, institutionalised MLG with a hierarchy of governance determined by legislation. The MLG is horizontal between state government portfolios and amongst local governments, vertical between state government and local government, and ultimately driven by water reforms required by the federal government. Interwoven governance frameworks in this case study shifted over two decades during the 1990s and 2000s, and required simultaneous consideration of numerous and varied interests.

During this period, legislative, governance structures and geographical boundaries changed, primarily through implementation of the South Australian *Water Resources Act (SA) 1997*. The ability to integrate across the planning processes outlined in the *Water Resources Act* and the South Australian *Development Act 1993* was an opportunity for the implementation of consistent policy across the three levels of governance responsible for development and water resources management. Integration also involved optimising benefits and costs for the many different parties to arrive at an agreed outcome.

This chapter is structured in three sections. The first describes the role of one of the five local councils within the southern region in facilitating integration of natural resource management (NRM) and urban development in the Willunga Basin within the case study area. The Willunga Basin is a geographic area that, at the time, lay partly within four council areas.[1] The second section outlines how the concept was progressed at the catchment level by the Onkaparinga Catchment Water Management Board. Legislation, policies and governing the management of water-resource sustainability and urban development are discussed as well as how the process involved broad levels of public, local and state government consultation and information exchange – driven by the desire to effectively integrate policies consistently across all governance levels. Third, lessons learnt from the processes are identified and discussed.

---

1   Namely, Willunga, Adelaide Hills, Noarlunga, Happy Valley, Yankalilla councils prior to amalgamation of the Willunga, Happy Valley and Onkaparinga councils in 1998.

Historical context – integrated planning of the Willunga Basin

In the early 1990s, the southern-most metropolitan council, the District Council of Willunga (Willunga DC), incorporated small pockets of urban settlements within a predominantly rural area and coastal housing. McLaren Vale, renowned for its quality wines, was within the Willunga Basin, which also included magnificent coastal beaches and the Aldinga Scrub – the largest metropolitan remnant of historic coastal vegetation and plains bordered by the Willunga hills. It was close to city markets, despite high levels of unemployment compared to the rest of the metropolitan area. By the 1990s, vineyards had predominantly replaced the almond orchards of Willunga and the area was declared a water protection area due to concerns over the quantity and quality of groundwater in the basin.[2]

The council area's landscape of orchards, grain-growing and vineyards with small local wineries was viewed by the council and some sections of the community as an agricultural resource. It is bordered to the north by coastal housing, which is poised to expand in response to metropolitan population growth.

During the 1990s, the Willunga DC area increasingly came under pressure for urban development by land speculators, despite lacking social and physical infrastructure. Owners of crop lands, troubled by the impact of expanding suburban life and facing retirement, anticipated the sale of their land as a form of superannuation. The state viewed the Willunga council area as predominantly deferred urban in nature, with state population projections of 70,000 – an increase from 7,000 – through continued suburbanisation of the land. As a result, the community within the Willunga Basin was divided on future choices (Figure 11.1).[3]

---

2   SA Government Gazette, 24 December 1998; see also Iwanicki (1994, 1995).

3   The DC of Willunga and the South Australian Government signed a memorandum of understanding to jointly undertake a process of strategic planning to identify where urban development could occur. Funded by the federal Better Cities Program, the process included intensive community discussion, peer review by a reference group and regular council endorsement of each stage of the process (Iwanicki 1994, 1995).

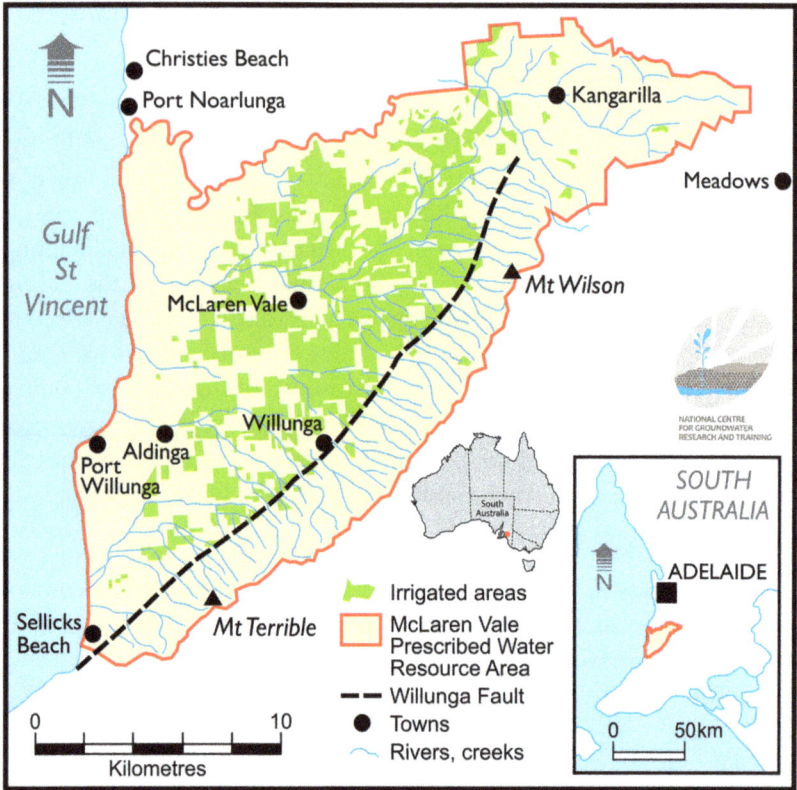

Figure 11.1: Willunga Basin – a geographic area, the majority of which was in the District Council of Willunga prior to 1997, and subsequently Onkaparinga Council, which amalgamated the councils of Happy Valley, Noarlunga and Willunga

Source: Harrington and Cook (2012: 11)

Aided by the Building Better Cities program funding (1991–96), established under the federal government of Paul Keating, the Willunga Council entered into a memorandum of understanding with the state planning minister in 1994 to undertake a strategic-planning process for the wider Willunga Basin area. Part of the process was to communicate and regularly inform the Adelaide Hills, Happy Valley and Noarlunga council planners of the progress of investigations concerning their areas within the Willunga Basin.

Accepting that large parcels of land along the coast had been purchased by the state's then Urban Land Trust for future housing development, Willunga Council's strategic-planning process supported the McHarg (1969) planning approach[4] and sought to identify an urban form along the coastal area with reference to land capability (PAS 1993), water sustainability (Cresswell 1994) and landscape values (Woodhead Firth Lee 1994). To this end, the council commissioned a land-capability assessment that extensively mapped the soils, climate, rainfall and groundwater in order to review the future of the Willunga Basin.

Investigations also included an economic study of the Willunga Basin, a landscape values analysis and an urban-form and water-resources study. As the water resource was considered a key planning issue of the process, each consultant team undertaking the urban-form, economic and water-resources studies worked collaboratively. Findings of the investigations established:

- potential for small-scale value-adding industries and enterprises aided by the establishment of economic incubators while conserving suitable land for viticulture and horticulture
- there was ample water from natural rainfall for horticulture, but winter storage and retention needed to be achieved possibly through groundwater injection and utilisation of treated waste water
- urban development to be contained along the coastal area in the form of high-density 'nodal' villages serviced by a dual reticulation – non-contact water being supplied by sewage treatment plants servicing each village in order to minimise impacts on the marine environment and manage water sustainably
- land-based disposal of treated water from waste treatment plants.

The outcome of the strategic-planning process was the completion of a Willunga Basin planning strategy accompanied by a budgeted five-year plan, reviewable each year. During the preparation of the strategic plan, constituent neighbouring councils of Happy Valley, Adelaide Hills and Noarlunga were consulted.

---

4   McHarg criticised a 'cookie cutter' approach to postwar suburban subdivisions and espoused a philosophy of landscape analysis so that new development could respond to landscape values through design approaches based on a comprehensive analysis of geology, typography, weather, landscape values and soil profiles. He worked and taught primarily in the United States.

Consecutively, a plan amendment report was prepared to establish a District Council of Willunga Interim Structure Plan, which broadly identified a rural enterprise/conservation zone east of the Main South Road and a historic Port Willunga/Aldinga policy area within an overall coastal area west of Main South Road that was designated for future investigations into the recommended urban form.

Amalgamation of the then Happy Valley, Noarlunga and Willunga councils to form the City of Onkaparinga in 1997 resulted in the Willunga Basin strategic plan not being implemented.[5]

Building on the development of the Willunga Basin Strategic Plan pertaining to the southern portion of the Onkaparinga Catchment Water Management Board's area, the board sought to bring the land use–planning and catchment-planning systems into synchronicity across a wider region, which was enabled by the provisions of the *Water Resources Act* relating to catchment planning from 1998–2005. This was facilitated by the water reform process and this new legislation.

A new legislative context

The national water reform agenda and the South Australian *Water Resources Act 1997*

In the mid–late 1990s, the process of water-resource management change in South Australia was driven by the Council of Australian Governments (COAG) national water reform agenda (COAG 1994) and the reforms agreed to under the agenda by each Australian state were to provide an integrated, total catchment approach to water-resource management throughout the country. Funding by the federal system has favoured

---

5   Ongoing community pressure concerning the protection of rural land and water management, however, ultimately resulted in separate legislation to retain the rural character of McLaren Vale in the south, and the Barossa Valley north of metropolitan Adelaide in 2012 via the *Character Preservation (McLaren Vale) Act 2012* and the *Character Preservation (Barossa Valley) Act 2012*. Ostrom (2008) emphasises the importance of community actions in the model of polycentric governance. In this case, organised community lobbying led to the drafting of the 2012 Act which maintained rural land and water resources capable of future food production close to the city – a major objective for sustainability first identified in the Willunga Planning Strategy of 1997. The role of local community groups seeking greater assurance of the retention of rural land within the Willunga Basin exemplifies the concept of local advocacy in sustainable water and land uses.

regions and been linked to ongoing reforms by each state. The water resources legislation established catchment water management boards, with a dual responsibility to prepare and implement a catchment water management plan and a water allocation plan for prescribed areas, which the Onkaparinga Catchment Water Management Board (OCWMB) undertook in 1999 and 2000 (see OCWMB 2000a; 2000b). The catchment boards were statutory bodies of the state government responsible for regional catchment scale management.

The area for which the OCWMB was responsible covers 920 square kilometres, partly within the Adelaide Hills Council, the cities of Marion and Onkaparinga, and the District Councils of Mount Barker and Yankalilla (Figure 11.2).

The McLaren Vale prescribed wells area is within the catchment, as well as a number of watercourses. Apart from the Onkaparinga River, all the watercourses have ephemeral flows within the catchment area (OCWMB 2000a).

Under s 92(7) of the *Water Resources Act*, the catchment water management plans were required to be in keeping with the following South Australian state legislation:

- *Coast Protection Act 1972*
- *Development Act 1993*
- *Environment Protection Act 1993*
- *National Parks and Wildlife Act 1972*
- *Soil Conservation and Land Care Act 1989*
- *Native Vegetation Act 1991*
- any other guideline, plans or policies as prescribed by regulation.

Importantly, the primary legislation in South Australia governing land-use planning, the *Development Act 1993* and Regulations, and the then *Water Resources Act 1997*, made reference to each other in regard to consistency of respective state- and local-level plans.

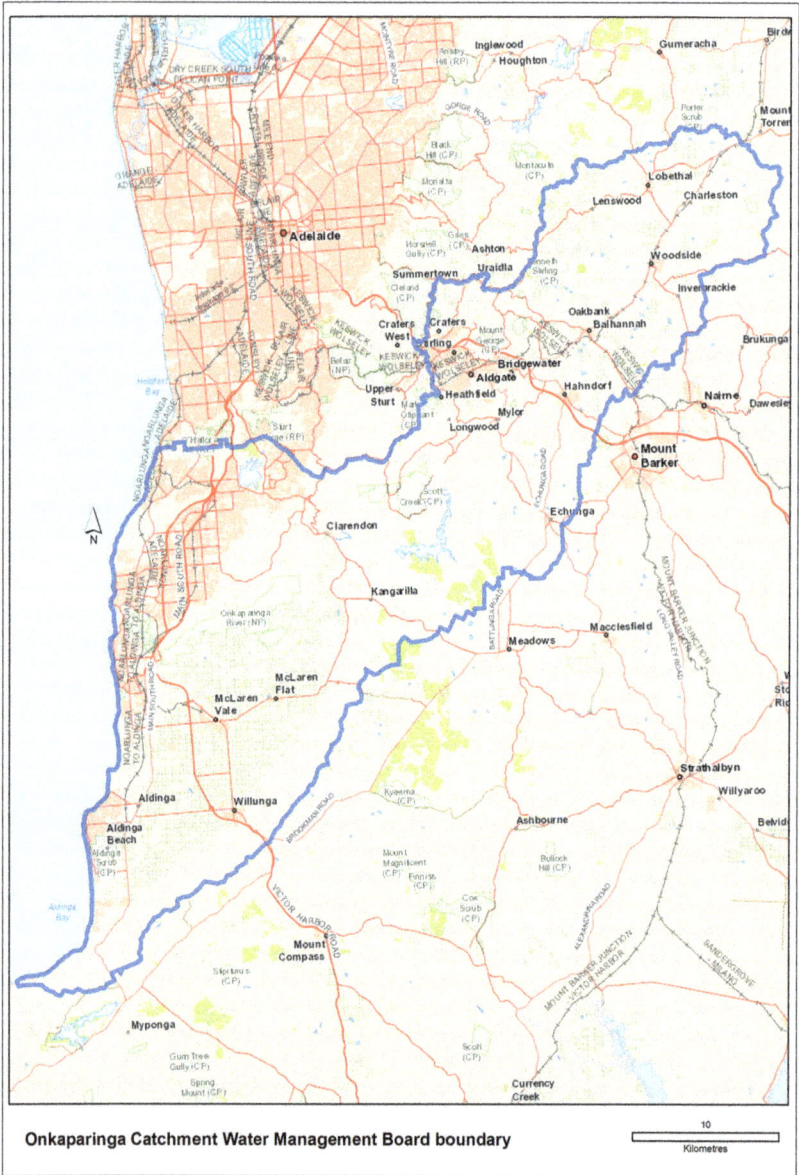

Onkaparinga Catchment Water Management Board boundary

Figure 11.2: The Onkaparinga Catchment Water Management Board
Area – showing council boundaries
Source: OCWMB (2000a: 10)

The Onkaparinga Catchment Water Management Plan (Catchment Plan) (OCWMB 2000a) was in keeping with all of the above legislation. It was deemed by the OCWMB, however, that the development plans of constituent local councils – the primary tool of land-use planning under the *Development Act* – could be amended to better achieve the objectives contained in the Catchment Plan. The 'joined up legislation' meant one of two things at the time: first, the Catchment Plan and/or its implementation would be constrained by a number of policies that differed within the development plans of the five local councils; second, a catchment board could seek to utilise policies of a catchment plan as a trigger to amend the relevant development plans to meet the aim of achieving integration between the key policy documents relevant to the five councils and the state government by planning processes outlined in the water resource legislation. This second option would meet the aim of integrating key policy documents and legislation relating to land-use planning and water resources. The opportunity provided by the *Water Resources Act* up until the commencement in 2004 of the *Natural Resources Management Act* [6] actively sought integration at a legislative level between the Development and Water Resources Acts.

The players

Federal, state and local governments were involved as a consequence of COAG's national water reform agenda and agreed reform. Local councils within catchment areas became key players in the reform process because of their responsibility for public spaces and obligations under the *Development Act 1993*. Under the *Development Act*, development plans provide a framework for managing new 'development', namely any change in land use, land division, the construction of dams and the location and design of new buildings or alteration of existing buildings, all of which impacted upon water catchment management to some degree.

---

6   The *Water Resources Act 1997* was replaced by the *Natural Resources Management Act 2004*, which brought together legislation relating to water resources, soil conservation, pest plant and animal control. This reform replaced the catchment boards, soil conservation boards and animal and plant control boards with NRM boards. The geographic reach dealt with a regionally based area rather than catchment-based areas, incidentally changing the dynamics, nature and capacity of community engagement by the replacement body. It is of note that, when the provisions of the *Water Resources Act* were carried over to the *Natural Resources Management Act*, almost all provisions were transferred; however, the provision to enable catchment boards to change constituent council's development plans was omitted.

At the state level, Planning SA was the key state government department reporting to the planning minister and in charge of residential and industrial development (e.g. Planning SA 1998, 1999). In relation to catchment management, there were several structural and administrative iterations of the Department of Environment and Heritage/Natural Resources and Department of Water reporting to the minister for the environment and/or water on matters relating to coastal areas, native vegetation, biodiversity and/or water resources management. In addition, other closely related agencies included the Environment Protection Authority (EPA), responsible for pollution prevention and management, and Primary Industries SA, responsible for sustainable agriculture. The catchment boards reported to the minister for environment and natural resources and, subsequently, the newly designated minister for water resources. The OCWMB area encompassed primary water catchments supplying metropolitan Adelaide.

The five constituent councils within the OCWMB boundary were geographically varied, ranging from urban to rural production and from hills to coast. Onkaparinga is the largest urban council in the Adelaide metropolitan area, resulting from the amalgamation of Happy Valley, Willunga and Noarlunga Councils, as outlined above.

The *Development Act* and *Water Resources Act* planning processes

At the state level, the peak planning documents are the State Planning Strategy (South Australian Government 2000), which is required under the *Development Act*, and State Water Resources Plan (South Australian Government 1999), required under the *Water Resources Act*.[7] Nested within the State Planning Strategy and State Water Resources Plan respectively are local council development plans and catchment water management plans. All amendments to council and minister-initiated development plans within the council areas must be consistent with the State Planning Strategy.[8] Plan amendments are made via a series of steps

---

7   The *Water Resources Act* established catchment water management boards. The six South Australian catchment boards were Northern Adelaide and Barossa Catchment Water Management Board, Onkaparinga Catchment Water Management Board, Patawalonga Catchment Water Management Board, River Murray Catchment Water Management Board, South East Catchment Water Management Board and the Torrens Catchment Water Management Board.

8   *Development Act (SA) 1993.*

that generally take between three to five years to progress to endorsement by the state government. During the negotiated process of amendment, broad-based community consultation is required, including with state agencies. Section 30 of the *Development Act* requires a review of council development plans every three to five years. The planning minister may also amend development plans, consistent with the State Planning Strategy.

Similarly, the OCWMB was responsible for providing and reviewing a rolling five-year catchment water management plan to guide water-resource management within its area. The first Onkaparinga Catchment Plan was adopted by the then minister for water resources on 1 December 2000. The relationship between the two pieces of legislation and plans are depicted in Figure 11.3.

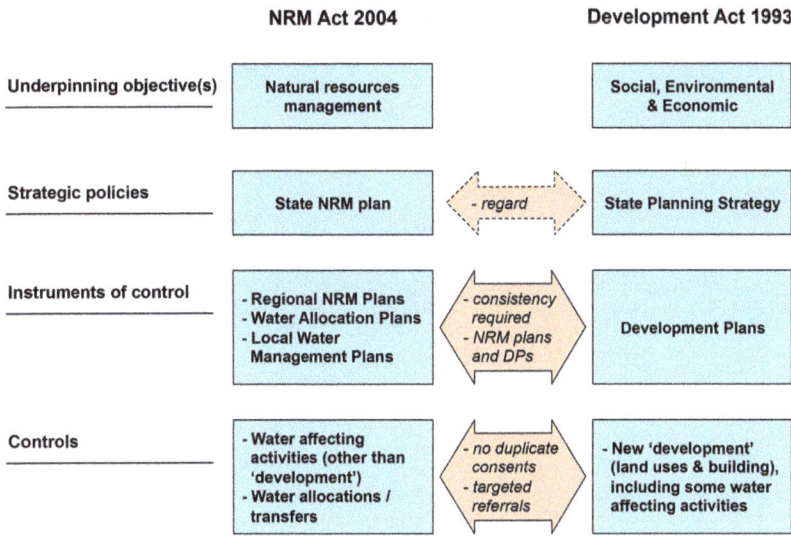

	NRM Act 2004		**Development Act 1993**
Underpinning objective(s)	Natural resources management		Social, Environmental & Economic
Strategic policies	State NRM plan	- regard	State Planning Strategy
Instruments of control	- Regional NRM Plans - Water Allocation Plans - Local Water Management Plans	- consistency required - NRM plans and DPs	Development Plans
Controls	- Water affecting activities (other than 'development') - Water allocations / transfers	- no duplicate consents - targeted referrals	- New 'development' (land uses & building), including some water affecting activities

Figure 11.3: The relationship between the *Development Act, Water Resources Act* and state and local government roles

Source: Author's construction in conjunction with R. Teague, Planning SA, Department of Transport and Urban Planning (Bellette 2004)

In looking at the sustainable use of water as part of investigations for the Catchment Plan, the OCWMB estimated that the available water resources within the board's area comprise urban and rural surface flows (105,000 ML per annum (ML/a)), groundwater (18,000 ML/a) and effluents from wastewater treatment plants (12,400 ML/a). Supplementing this included imported water from the River Murray via the Onkaparinga pipeline (24.000 ML/a) and from Myponga Reservoir. Of the 160,000 ML/a available water, about one-third is used within the catchment area, with 47,500 ML exported to Adelaide and about 35 per cent out to the marine environment. Beginning with this equation, sustainable water use would involve:

1. Increasing the use of stormwater and wastewaters which are presently unused and which have an undesirable impact on their environments, resulting from or related to their non-use

2. Using waters to augment or replace waters taken from existing sources, in so far as investigations show the economic practicality and relative long term benefits of so doing

3. Increasing the efficiency of using existing and new water sources and systems

4. Identifying more clearly the water needs of ecosystems (environmental flows etc.) and allocating water of adequate quantity and quality to meet those needs

5. Working with other Boards and agencies to reduce dependence of Adelaide on River Murray water and any associated, non-essential diversion of this water into and out of the catchment in the light of findings on the feasibility and benefits of using, and / or increasing, the efficiency of using existing and new water sources and systems

6. Aquifer storage and recovery opportunities (OCWMB 2000a).

Table 4.1 of the Catchment Plan (OCWMB 2000a) identifies where planning is relevant to key issues:

1. Limited use of water sensitive design, and land management. The reasons for this include the fact that the housing industry is slow to provide smart new development, the low use of stormwater and lack of integrated design. It is desirable to incorporate policies into Development Plans to encourage water sensitive design at household, community and regional levels while acknowledging that local councils in the process of managing the public environment can establish best practice in stormwater treatment, including the design of public reserves, streets and drainage systems.

2. Minimum standards for housing development are desirable, including on-site rainwater storage and re-use, and the provision of dual systems where non-contact water can be provided from rainwater collection (e.g. plumbing into laundry and toilet directly from a rainwater tank) as part of a minimum standard for development. Ideally, new housing

areas should be required to incorporate local stormwater treatment systems and a set of dual reticulation pipes required for new homes to further reduce the demand for potable water.

3. The impact of dams on surface water flows in the McLaren Vale Prescribed Wells Area and the Mt Lofty Ranges Watershed and policies for development of new dams that address the need to maintain low flows during low rainfall periods for maintenance of watercourse environmental health.

4. Managing Growth – new urban infrastructure targeting land and industrial water re-use options, with an informed urban population and behavioural changes to less waste, improved biodiversity, enhanced sense of relevance and commitment to sustainable water use, and increased awareness of water 'processes'.

Integrating catchment management within the planning system

In the closing years of the 1990s there were two options for the OCWMB to integrate policies from the Catchment Plan with local government development plans:

1. The *Water Resources Act* s 96 allowed the state water resources minister, in consultation with the state planning minister, to identify the need for an amendment of a development plan of a constituent council/s via the catchment plans. The Minister for Planning must also approve the Plan Amendment Report, i.e. consensus between both ministers is required.

2. The Development Act allows councils, authorised by the state planning minister, to amend Council Development Plans.

In aiming to have all development plans of councils within the catchment support the catchment water management plan, the OCWMB did not request the minister for water resources to authorise amendment of the relevant development plans. For a newly formed board, this option was deemed unlikely to be well received by councils. Instead, the board aimed to work with their councils collaboratively by funding and coordinating an integrated development plan amendment on behalf of councils for approval by the planning minister (Bellette 2001).

Moreover, one of the stated goals of the OCWMB was to integrate resource management through coordinated policies 'and effective partnerships between stakeholders' (OCWMB 2000: v).

The OCWMB then began negotiation with councils, with a view to undertaking, on behalf of councils, the preparation of a catchment-wide development plan amendment based upon a review of each development plan, for approval of the planning minister. The development plans are council-based, which meant each development plan had to be separately reviewed as part of an integrated development plan amendment. Afterwards, the board approached the individual councils and obtained their agreement to the amendment of each council plan to incorporate catchment management principles. The OCWMB appointed a consultant planner to firstly prepare a standard draft set of objectives and principles and review each development plan within the catchment. The exercise was aimed at encouraging development mindful of catchment care from 'site to sea'.

The first phase of obtaining the agreement of local councils within the catchment to participate was followed by formulating a statement of intent (SOI) to which the participating councils jointly signed for ministerial consent to proceed. Once the planning minister's support was granted, an intensive process of reviewing each existing development plan to crosscheck existing policies in the individual council plans that impinged on water management processes was undertaken, incorporating consultation with council planners on a regular basis.

The OCWMB endorsed draft development plan amendment provisions to address minimisation of erosion, siltation and urban design standards conducive to sustainable water use. As a draft, the Catchment Plan Amendment Report (Catchment PAR) addressed issues such as requirements for water-sensitive design for new development and encouraged aquifer storage recovery of treated wastewater and stormwater.

A steering committee comprising senior planners of each council, planner representatives from Planning SA, the Water Resources Department and OCWMB members was formed with oversight of the Catchment PAR process. Each stage of the Catchment PAR process, including the SOI that outlines the scope of the proposed Catchment PAR, was signed off by all councils, and subsequently the state planning minister.

In the process, it was possible to position water catchment issues in a proactive manner into the 'mainstream' land-use planning system, rather than the catchment policies being outside this framework and therefore in a reactive position (see also Smith and Iwanicki 2004). It was believed by the OCWMB that, as much as possible, catchment management issues should be internalised into the daily management framework of state and local governance in recognition of water as a basic need (Bellette 2000).

In addition to the Development Act activities, the OCWMB utilised provisions under the *Native Vegetation Act 1991* to move to incorporate a refund of the Division 2 levy (via s 140 of the Act)[9] into its Catchment Plan for landholders holding a Native Vegetation Heritage Agreement over their land. The agreements are made under the *Native Vegetation Act* and require property owners to maintain and manage native vegetation in perpetuity, in return for in-kind assistance from the Department of Environment and Heritage. In doing so, the board recognised that the preferred land use in a catchment where water quality is the primary objective is undisturbed native vegetation and this sends positive reinforcing messages to the community about the value of good catchment management (Bellette 2001).

What and who were driving the negotiations?

The aim of the board was to ensure that each development plan contained policies that enabled those in the catchment water management plan.

The project was initiated by the OCWMB. The entry point to the process was informal approaches by the OCWMB general manager to the heads of planning from each of the five local government councils to discuss the likely interest of each council at large, including elected members. Upon receiving positive feedback, the OCWMB developed a written proposal and presented this to each council. Each council then agreed that the OCWMB would engage a consultant to develop a catchment-wide plan

---

9   The *Water Resources Act* Division 2 s 135 allows for councils to contribute to catchment water management boards whereby catchment water management plans specify an amount to be contributed by each council based on their proportionate share of the catchment. This levy is passed on by councils to landholders under s 138. Section 140 allows catchment boards to refund levies paid by landholders who undertake land- or water-management practices designed to conserve water or maintain or improve water quality or provide other benefits.

amendment report on their collective behalf covering each of the five councils to ensure consistency of policies across the councils that enabled relevant catchment plan policies listed above.

The process from July 2000 to December 2005 involved the following legislative steps required by the then current provisions of the *Development Act* for amending a development plan. The SOI was endorsed by councils.

1. SOI was submitted to Planning SA for ministerial approval. The SOI envisaged a timeframe for the minister to consider the amendments to the development plan(s) for adoption in November 2002.
2. The SOI was approved by the minister for planning.
3. Councils were provided with draft plan amendments for endorsement.
4. The draft for consultation was agreed to by all councils (except Yankalilla Council). At this time Yankalilla withdrew, as the proportion of the DC Yankalilla within the boundaries of the OCWMB was considered insignificant.
5. Draft plan amendments were submitted to Planning SA for ministerial approval to commence consultation. Ministerial approval was granted.
6. Consultation on the draft OCWMB PAR took place, with two public hearings.
7. Submissions were summarised and addressed in a report for OCWMB.
8. The final plan was presented to councils for endorsement. The cities of Onkaparinga, Marion and Mt Barker supported endorsement.
9. Planning SA was requested to endorse amendment for Onkaparinga, Marion and Mt Barker.
10. The EPA and the Adelaide Hills Council had raised concerns.
11. Concerns were addressed – development plans for these councils were then submitted to Planning SA and received ministerial authorisation.

Different geographically grounded issues between councils resulted in some councils accepting the water-sensitive planning policies more readily than others (See Figure 11.4).

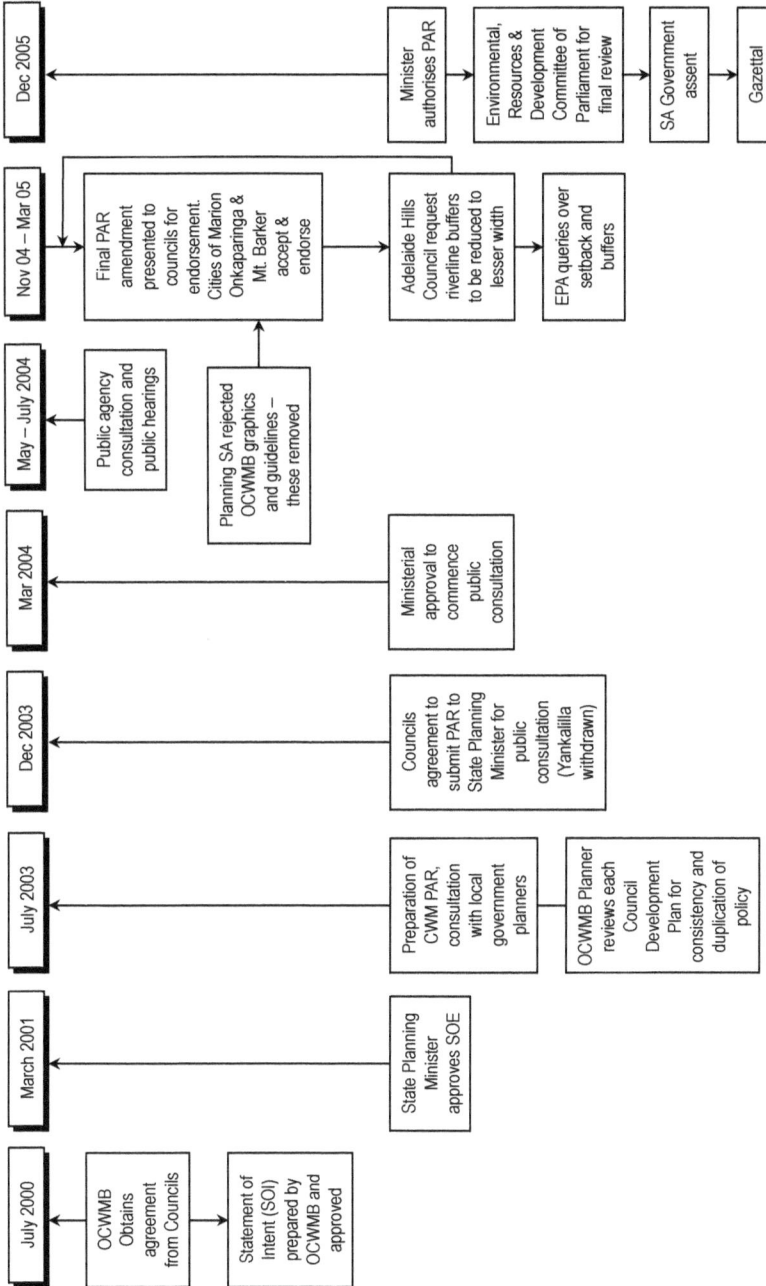

Figure 11.4: Multi-level governance reform – the development plan amendment

Source: Iris Iwanicki

Matters raised during the process

The predominantly rural Adelaide Hills Council requested buffers to be no greater than 5 metres because of the perceived economic loss due to land being removed from production via wider buffers. The state EPA, however, indicated it wanted buffer provisions of 50 metres to be consistent with existing setback requirements, which dealt with septic tank installations near watercourses. The provisions were changed by the OCWMB to meet the requirements of the Adelaide Hills Council. The OCWMB also clarified with the EPA the nature of buffers as opposed to setback distances.

Planning SA was supportive of the amendment but, since the commencement of the catchment PAR, they started developing modular topic-based templates of policy principles in order to provide consistency across council development plans within the state. While the Catchment Plan review process sought to provide relevant guidelines and examples in one legislative document, Planning SA considered that much of the content of the amendment was more suitable for a guideline than a PAR, including the diagrams and design techniques developed. The OCWMB was concerned, however, that without incorporation in the development plan the information would be difficult to require from applicants. Ultimately, Planning SA endorsed the amendment following the excision of the graphic material originally provided.

Despite the various issues raised by different agencies and levels of government, and given the complexity of changing legislation, local government structures and state agency approaches, the process of integrating development planning with catchment planning was enabled by a number of factors discussed in the following sections.

The importance of individuals

The OCWMB and staff had a pre-existing relationship with the five councils and staff and worked closely with them on the drafting of the Catchment Plan. Councils, therefore, had a level of ownership of the Catchment Plan. Furthermore, part of the implementation of the plan was to ensure consistency with each council's development plan; hence, they already had a level of 'buy in' to the Catchment PAR.

In addition, representation of the two major councils within the catchment on the OCWMB sustained earlier commitment to the process. The two councils collectively comprised the majority of the board's area: one board member was an elected member of the Adelaide Hills Council, and one member was the CEO of the Onkaparinga City Council. Although both the *Development Act* and *Water Resources Act* had provisions for ensuring that catchment and development plans were consistent, no Catchment Board at the time had considered or triggered the process through either Act.

The integration process was initiated by the general manager and subsequently followed through by the board's land-use planner, who could both see the significance of the opportunities, importantly to the benefit of both land-use planning and catchment management. The general manager had worked in both land-use planning and natural resource management and environment protection, and promoted communication and integration across the disciplines and relevant government bodies.

The OCWMB played a role by recognising the significance of land-use planning to enable some aspects of the board's Catchment Plan, and therefore made a significant investment to employ a land-use planner (the only catchment board in South Australia to do so). The catchment planner was previously employed by the Adelaide Hills Council, one of the five councils involved in the PAR.

The planning consultant chosen to undertake the joint five-council PAR was previously the environmental services manager and strategic planner in the former Willunga Council, now amalgamated into the Onkaparinga Council. One of the significant enablers in the PAR process was the work history, local knowledge and networks provided by these two planners.

In summary, the project was driven by three people – initially the general manager of the OCWMB, then the OCWMB land-use planner and the planning consultant.

Timelines and resources

The total length of time from initial floating of the concept to PAR approval was in the order of five to six years, as shown in Figure 11.4. Issues raised by different participants at different stages of the amendment process involved negotiation prior to final drafting, but at no stage was the outcome at risk.

Has the process succeeded and why?

The process of incorporating catchment planning and land-use development planning policies was successful, given the commitment and resources from the board staff and consultant planner and significant in-kind contribution from the five constituent councils. In addition, the process was aided by:

- having representatives of the Adelaide Hills Council (ex-mayor and then current councillor) and the CEO of the Onkaparinga Council as board members, who were supportive of the catchment program
- the board recognising the significance of land-use planning to enable some aspects of the OCWMB's catchment plan and therefore employing a land-use planner
- the continuity of commitment and drive of the three employees responsible for the various stages of the Catchment PAR.

For its part, the OCWMB pursued integration of policies by taking responsibility for:

- funding the PAR so the review and amendment process of council development plans were cost-free to local government (councils, apart from in-kind contributions through participating in discussions on the content and approach to the PAR, did not have to undertake the review directly)
- taking responsibility for shepherding the passage of the PAR through state government processes, again, a cost-free process for local councils
- not proceeding at any stage of the amendment unless first obtaining approval from each council
- establishing strong community links and support for the project
- acting as a facilitator between state and local government
- having an already established relationship between the OCWMB and constituent councils through engagement on drafting the catchment water management plan and subsequently funding on-ground catchment projects within councils.

Among the observations and lessons learnt from this MLG case study was the frequent complaint by developers and the public that development plans provide little guidance for applicants. During the process, board planners discussed the need for more guidance, including illustrative examples to provide clarity of policy. The desirability of achieving water-sensitive design in all new development provided a basis for drafting illustrative principles that addressed the following:

- site management – prior to, and during, construction of buildings, sites to be managed in order to prevent excess erosion and siltation following clearance and management of litter/waste during construction
- building design, car parks
- stormwater systems
- on-site rainwater retention and re-use.

The illustrative guidelines were subsequently discarded when it was clear that not all councils concerned, nor the state, were supportive of this approach. Similarly, the maximisation of water re-use through planning policies was also approached with caution by government. It appears that, despite the rhetoric of catchment management, implementation is difficult and slow. The use of topic-based modules with standardised text and the requirements for consistency in preparing amendments did not encourage creativity in the drafting of development plans.

Some of the reasons for success or otherwise are based on the process and the governance level at which amendments to planning policies are attempted. It is clear that policies alone will not result in change and need to be accompanied by extensive education of practitioners on desirable design and management for water sustainability. As there was limited understanding amongst council staff and elected members regarding catchment management, there is a need to provide more education on the consequence of actions, particularly around land-use planning. Also, catchment management, while a priority for the OCWMB, was not necessarily a priority for councils and therefore difficult to get on council agendas. Staff shuffling throughout councils and Planning SA meant that experienced council staff were lost from the process. At a state level, ongoing review of the planning system focused on simplifying development plans and thereby improving processing times and expediting development. The specific nature of zoning for individual councils in response to local conditions is consequently often problematic to development plan reform.

Education of the planning profession tends to focus on development. In a broader sense, planners generally lack the capacity to integrate and apply NRM policies. Ongoing professional development for planners should involve:

- an understanding of the resource implications of urban growth
- an understanding of the usefulness of on-site rainwater collection and incentives to the building industry/building owners to incorporate rainwater tanks of adequate capacity in the planning and design of buildings
- incentives and obligations placed upon the design and building industries to begin to provide the consumer with water-sensitive design choices.

For councils/state levels, adoption of the following (which have since become more commonly applied) should involve:

- best practice in council's management of public spaces and stormwater systems
- insistence that new developments score a total of points for environmentally and economically sustainable features in the design of new buildings before being granted development approval
- linking with local suppliers/industries to promote products that conserve water in the household
- incentives for infrastructure systems to provide for water of non-potable quality for watering gardens, flushing toilets and other acceptable uses
- a state campaign of promoting water-sensitive design through publicity, legislation and accreditation procedures to provide consumers with better housing/building choices
- state encouragement and support for the revival of state and local Agenda 21 planning that addresses social, economic and environmental aspects of the community and their environment
- follow-up inspections during construction to ensure that site management systems are being implemented.

Conclusion

The OCWMB was the first catchment board in South Australia to undertake a process of integration of its Catchment Plan with constituent council development plans. The Northern Adelaide Barossa Catchment Water Management Board later followed the process.

Given the above lessons and observations, the success of the process demonstrated that having key 'champions' who had the persistence to collectively steer what was a lengthy process through the many changes in policy and government structures at multi-government levels was vital. The success was also partly achieved by the fact that the catchment boards were associated with specific communities within a defined catchment area, focused on a specific issue (water) and facilitated involvement of many different community groups. Community awareness of the issues involved in catchment care was well established when the reviewed PAR was put on public exhibition. Much of that awareness was encouraged by a well-focused program of public involvement, specifically in catchment issues and reinforcing the shared nature of water resources throughout a catchment area in terms of sustainable water use, water-based biodiversity, and pollution impacts downstream and upon the marine environment. With the larger geographic areas covered by respective NRM boards, the same level of community involvement and engagement does not appear to have been achieved.

The specific legislative reference to linking the development plan and catchment planning processes at regional level was lost with the amendment of the *Water Resources Act* when it became part of a broader piece of legislation via the *Natural Resources Management Act*.[10] Although a planning pathway for synchronising regional NRM plans and council development plans remains possible via the *Development Act*,[11] the emphasis within the *Natural Resource Management Act* and *Development Act* is on gaining concurrence with state-level plans, rather than at both the state and local/catchment levels.

In conclusion, certainly the intent of the relevant legislation was to achieve MLG, both horizontally between the state government portfolios and across local governments located geographically within catchments, and vertically between local and state governments. The changes to state government administrative structures and methods for standardising

---

10   Nevertheless, s 74(4) of the (current) *Natural Resources Management Act 2004* does require the state NRM plan to take into account the provisions of the Planning Strategy and may identify changes (if any) considered by the NRM Council to be desirable to the State Planning Strategy. The reciprocal provisions in the *Development Act*, however, although similar in intent, are not so specific. Section 22(3) requires that the Planning Strategy may incorporate documents, plans, policy statements, proposals and other material designed to facilitate strategic planning and coordinated action on a state-wide, regional or local level.

11   In fact, as outlined above, this was the pathway chosen by the OCWMB for the catchment-wide development plan amendment via the Catchment PAR.

planning guidelines during the MLG integration process undertaken by the OCWMB, however, made the process undertaken to achieve this very protracted. Ultimately, the success achieved in integration across and within levels of government was short lived due to the amalgamation of boards under the *Natural Resources Management Act 2004*. To date, under the NRM regime, application of the processes available to integrate land-use planning and natural resources planning has not been undertaken comprehensively at state level, nor at the regional level.

The exercise and lessons could consequently be seen as somewhat historical but, nevertheless, instructive as a demonstration of the innovation potential arising from integrated MLG planning systems.

References

Bellette, K. (2000). The Water Resources Act 1997 – A Quantum Leap in Funding for Sustainability. Paper presented to the Water Law Seminar. Hydrological Society of SA and the National Environmental Law Society (SA), October 2000, Adelaide.

——. (2001). Legislation and Policy – One Sixth of the Equation for Sustainable Water Resource Management. Paper presented to the Third Australasian Natural Resources Law and Policy Conference (focus on water), Adelaide.

——. (2004). The Role of Planning in Advocating the Use of Alternative Water sources in the Urban Environment. Presentation at the Enviro04 Conference and Exhibition, March 2004, Sydney.

COAG (1994). *Council of Australian Governments' Water Reform Strategic Framework*. 25 February 1994, Council of Australian Governments Communiqué, Hobart, www.environment.gov.au/system/files/resources/6caa5879-8ebc-46ab-8f97-4219b8ffdd98/files/policyframework.pdf, [Accessed: 22/12/2014].

Cresswell, D.J. (1994). *Willunga Basin Integrated Water Resources Study*. Department of Housing and Urban Development/Department of Environment and Natural Resources, DC of Willunga, South Australia.

Harrington, N. & Cook, P. (2012). *Willunga Research Update, October 2012*. National Centre for Groundwater Research and Training, Adelaide.

Hooghe, L. & Marks, G. (2001). Types of Multi-level Governance. *European Integration online Papers (EIoP)*, 5(11), eiop.or.at/eiop/pdf/2001-011.pdf [Accessed: 22/12/2014].

Iwanicki, I. (1994). Rural/Urban Fringe Planning in Adelaide, South Australia. Paper presented at the Global Forum, Manchester, England.

——. (1995). Seeking Sustainability in the Rural/Urban Fringe – An Overview of the Willunga Basin. Paper presented at Portraits in Planning Conference. October 1995, Adelaide.

McHarg, I. (1969). *Design with Nature*. Garden City Press, NY.

OCWMB (2000a). *Onkaparinga Catchment Water Management Plan*. Onkaparinga Catchment Water Management Board, Adelaide.

——. (2000b). *Water Allocation Plan, McLaren Vale Prescribed Wells Area*. Government of South Australia, Adelaide.

Ostrom, E. (2008). *Polycentric Systems as One Approach for Solving Collective-Action Problems*, dlc.dlib.indiana.edu/dlc/bitstream/handle/10535/4417/W08-6_Ostrom_DLC.pdf [Accessed: 22/12/2014].

PAS (1993). *Willunga Basin Land Capability Study – Final Report*. Planning Advisory Services/Eco Management Services, South Australian Office of Planning and Urban Development and Willunga District Council, Adelaide.

Planning SA (1998). *Planning Bulletin, Industrial Development*. Adelaide.

——. (1999). *Good Residential Design SA*. Adelaide.

——. (2004). Slide from a generic presentation on the State Planning Strategy. Department of Transport and Urban Planning. Adelaide.

PPK (2000a). *Onkaparinga Catchment Water Management Plan – Local Government and Development Plans*. Technical Paper 3. PPK Environment and Infrastructure, Adelaide.

——. (2000b). *Onkaparinga Catchment Water Management Plan – Land Capability and Land Use*. Technical Paper 5. PPK Environment and Infrastructure, Adelaide.

Smith, S. & Iwanicki, I. (2004). The Good, the Bad and the Ugly – Integrating Catchment Management and Development Planning. In: *Proceedings of 'WSUD 2004: Cities as Catchments' International Conference on Water Sensitive Urban Design*. Engineers Australia, Barton, ACT, pp. 721–28.

South Australian Government (1993). Development Regulations. Adelaide, www.legislation.sa.gov.au/LZ/C/R/Development%20 Regulations%201993.aspx

——. (1999). State Water Plan. Adelaide.

——. (2000). *Planning Strategy for Metropolitan Adelaide*. Department of Transport and Urban Planning, Adelaide.

Woodhead Firth Lee (1994). *Willunga Basin Urban Form and Landscape Study*. Deptartment of Housing and Urban Development, District Council of Willunga, South Australia.

12

Regional Solutions for Multi-level Governance Challenges in Australian Coastal and Climate Change Planning

Barbara Norman and Nicole Gurran

Introduction

Australia is one of the most urbanised nations in the world and the location of its urban growth is predominantly in the coastal zone. The 2009 Australian parliamentary report, *Managing our Coastal Zone in a Changing Climate: The Time to Act is Now*, raised critical issues in relation to managing coastal urban growth in the context of climate change (Australian Parliament 2009; Thom 2010). In particular, it concluded that a more adaptive and systems approach to coastal planning will be required to plan for increasing coastal risk and uncertainty, together with meaningful and ongoing community engagement.

This chapter explores the experience of regional alliances in identifying what strategies could provide the foundations for more sustainable coastal planning and the implications for multi-level governance (DCC 2009; DCCEE 2010; Gurran et al. 2011). With reference to the international literature and research on multi-level governance and climate change policy (e.g. Richardson et al. 2011), the chapter suggests that a national policy framework for sustainable cities and regions should underpin long-term regional arrangements for a more sustainable and resilient coastal future. Furthermore, integrated regional planning presents a critical strategic policy instrument for better coordination, integration and implementation in coastal Australia.

The first part of the chapter outlines the policy context surrounding planning for coastal climate change at the national, state and local government levels. Key issues for the coastal communities and the coastal environment include managing urban growth, potential risks and liabilities in response to climate change, financing and governing the transition and a significant gap in skills for implementing a low carbon and more resilient built environment (Norman 2010). The intersection of increased coastal urban growth and the projected impacts of coastal climate change (DCC 2009; Steffen 2009) will require a coordinated response by coastal planning and emergency management to minimise the level of risk to coastal communities (Gurran et al. 2011; Norman 2009).

The establishment of the National Coastal and Climate Change Council in 2010 signalled national recognition of the critical issues involved in sustainable coastal planning (DCCEE 2010). The second part of the chapter discusses this national policy context of managing coastal urban growth and climate change. It discusses the major recommendations of national inquiries and the council, as well as the current policy framework and highlights specific strengths and weaknesses. This is followed by the case for regional-level intervention to tackle the complex or 'wicked' problems associated with overlapping jurisdictional responsibilities, agendas and interests influencing planning and management of the coastal zone.

To address such challenges, and to better connect urban and regional planning, infrastructure development and environmental science, including the impacts of climate change, groups of coastal councils are increasingly forming regional alliances. The third part of the chapter focuses on this regional dimension, which expands beyond a single municipality while remaining closer to the community than higher levels of government (Norman 2010; Smith et al. 2010). The discussion refers to five examples of voluntary regional coastal groupings in different parts of coastal Australia, including the Sydney Coastal Councils Group (SCCG) (a metropolitan coastal region within the nation's largest state capital city, New South Wales), the Peron Naturaliste Partnership (the nine coastal councils on the south coast of Western Australia), the G21 Geelong regional alliance (five councils on the industrial city of Geelong's urban edge, Victoria), Dhimurru Sea Country Plan (in remote north-east Arnhem Land, Northern Territory) and South East Coastal Adaptation (SECA, a research collaboration in the increasingly populated area of south-east Australia, far south New South Wales and eastern Victoria). These partnerships/collaborations at the local and regional level are explored to gain a deeper appreciation of the drivers, opportunities and potential barriers to achieving a more sustainable regional approach to urban growth and climate change.

The final section of the chapter will consider the potential contributions of regional planning to managing urban growth and climate change and the implications for multi-governance. Coastal planning is inherently complex, dealing with multi-governance across landscapes in the catchment-to-coast-to-marine continuum. The regional case studies point to some key principles that should underpin more sustainable coastal governance and planning in Australia.

Coastal management: A matter of national interest

National, state and local levels of government, including community and private sector organisations, are substantially involved in the Australian urban and regional planning system in which coastal management is embedded. This section outlines the key dimensions of coastal management and discusses it in the context of sustainability and climate change. It outlines the key issues in planning for coastal climate change and discusses the implications for the broader outcome of sustainable coasts.

Coastal planning in Australia is primarily based on the concept of integrated coastal management, which is recognised and adopted globally (United Nations, European Commission, South Pacific Forum, the United States and New Zealand). In this chapter, integrated coastal management is defined as:

> The integrated planning and management of coastal resources and environments in a manner that is based on the physical socio-economic, and political interconnections both within and among the dynamic coastal systems, which when aggregated together, define a coastal zone (Sorensen 1997).

All three levels of government in Australia undertake distinct roles in relation to coastal planning and management. The Commonwealth has played an important policy development role, with a series of national-level inquiries since the 1970s drawing attention to the risks of coastal urbanisation: the Australian Advisory Committee on the Environment (AACE 1975), the Standing Committee on Environment and Conservation (1980), and the Resource Assessment Commission (1993). More recently, attention has shifted to the risks associated with climate change in coastal areas, with a significant parliamentary enquiry conducted in 2008 (discussed below).

The federal government has also played an important role in funding support for coastal initiatives, particularly in relation to information such as mapping and coastal data, with a more recent focus on coastal adaptation. Coastal funding programs have included programs such as Caring for our Coasts and Coastal Adaptation Decision Pathways at the regional and local level. The national government, therefore, plays a role of policy development, support and facilitation in coastal planning and management, rather than a direct one of regulation. The *Environment Protection and Biodiversity Conservation Act 1999* (EPBC Act) provides a mechanism of referral to the Commonwealth on matters of national environmental significance and has been triggered in the coastal environment. In one of only two EPBC Act refusals, Minister Peter Garrett refused a proposed development of 730 lots in the vicinity of Booderee National Park, Jervis Bay, on the NSW South Coast, because of the impact on nationally listed threatened species and the ecological integrity of the Commonwealth-managed park, which is dependent on connection to surrounding areas via important wildlife corridors (DEWHA 2009). While it is more common for proposals to be amended rather than refused as a result of Commonwealth referral under the EPBC Act, the legislation has added a layer of additional scrutiny to the existing environmental impact assessment processes conducted by the states.

More recently, the federal government has also used the EPBC Act to undertake 'strategic assessments' in high-growth regions across Australia (e.g. Perth and Peel region in Western Australia, and the Great Barrier Reef in far north Queensland). This means that, rather than subjecting individual development proposals to additional environmental impact assessment by the Commonwealth, detailed examination of ecological risks and parameters for development can be undertaken upfront, providing greater clarity for landowners and communities (SEWPAC 2013). Finally, the Regional Development Australia network of 55 committees under the

Labor governments headed by Kevin Rudd and Julia Gillard required the preparation of regional plans for high-growth coastal regions from Mandurah in Western Australia to south-east Queensland (DRALGAS 2012).

The state and territory governments hold the statutory responsibilities for the development and use of the coastal zone, and these are usually administered through land-use planning legislation or, in some cases, separate coastal management legislation (for instance, the Victorian *Coastal Management Act 1995* and the NSW *Coastal Protection Act 1979*). The state legislation provides the framework and powers for local government action and other relevant public bodies (e.g. regional coastal councils in Victoria) involved in managing the coastal environment (Australian Parliament 2009: Appendix 1). State ministers retain powers on major strategic decisions, such as rezoning of coastal lands from 'greenfield' rural land to urban land available for development, although these actions are often triggered and informed by local government planning processes. Local government is largely responsible for applying the legislation in local planning and development decisions within the policy framework set by higher levels of government. Significant decision-making occurs at the local level, which, although often relatively small in scale, can have a cumulative environmental impact on the coast.

After 2009, the Gillard Government became more active in the development of national coastal policy after being influenced by a series of reports, including *Managing our Coastal Zone in a Changing Climate*, known as the George Inquiry (Australian Parliament 2009); the report to the minister from the national Coasts and Climate Change Council (2011); the Productivity Commission report *Barriers to Effective Climate Change Adaptation* (2012); *Climate Change Risks to Australia's Coast: A First Pass National Assessment* (DCC 2009); and *The Critical Decade* by the Climate Commission (Steffen and Hughes 2013). During the same period (2009–13), a considerable body of research was undertaken into the impacts of climate change on the coast through the National Climate Change Adaptation Research Facility (e.g. NCCARF 2013; Norman et al. 2013). The Department of Climate Change (DCC 2009) report established some initial baseline data on sea-level rise and implications for coastal vulnerability, paving the way for more detailed work to follow. Research findings included that:

> Up to $63 billion (replacement value) of existing residential buildings are potentially at risk of inundation from a 1.1 metre sea-level rise, with a lower and upper estimate of risk identified for between 157,000 and 247,600 individual buildings (DCC 2009: 7).

There have been 25 national inquiries and reports over the last 30 years (Norman 2009), of which the George Inquiry is the latest. This House of Representatives committee report, chaired by the Hon. Jenny George, involved comprehensive engagement of coastal community interests in forming its 47 final recommendations. The recommendations were wide-ranging and included specific actions on coastal governance, emphasising the need for a national approach: 'One clear message emerged – and that is the need for national leadership in managing our precious coastal zone in the context of climate change' (Australian Parliament 2009: ix).

Other key recommendations emerging from the George Inquiry in relation to coastal governance were that an intergovernmental coastal zone agreement should be established (recommendation 44); a national coastal zone policy and strategy should be adopted, setting out the principles, objectives and actions that must be undertaken to address the challenges of integrated coastal zone management for Australia (recommendation 45); and a national coastal advisory council should be convened (recommendation 46). The committee recommended that the intergovernmental coastal zone agreement should:

- define the roles and responsibilities of the three tiers of government – federal, state and local – involved in coastal zone management
- include a formal mechanism for community consultation; incorporate principles based on strategic regional coastal planning and landscape-scale/ecosystem-based coastal zone management
- include an effective implementation plan with resources allocated to ensure that objectives are realised
- be overseen by a new coastal zone ministerial council
- be made public (recommendation 44: 290).

Following the George Inquiry report, the national Coasts and Climate Change Council established in late 2009 (initially chaired by renowned scientist Tim Flannery, followed by coastal management expert Bruce Thom) reported to the minister for climate change and provided two reports during its two-year term: an interim report in December 2010 and a final report in December 2011. In its final report, the council made recommendations in five key areas for action on climate change adaptation: 1) climate-risk protection to guide planning and investment, 2) improving decision-making through better science and information, 3) coastal policy and regulatory reform, 4) on-ground adaptation tackling 'hotspots', and

5) integrating climate change into national agendas. The council also commissioned an important report on the legal implications arising from coastal climate change (Gibbs and Hill 2011).

During 2011, the Gillard Government also established a Climate Change Select Committee comprising ministerial representatives of the states and the Northern Territory. A particular focus was to outline the roles and responsibilities for all three levels of government and the private sector in relation to climate adaptation, as follows:

> The basic principle of the management of climate change risk should be as follows:
>
> Private parties should be responsible for managing risks to private assets and incomes. Governments – on behalf of the community – should primarily be responsible for managing risks to public goods and assets (including the natural environment) and Government service delivery and creating an institutional, market and regulatory environment that supports and promotes private adaptation (Select Council on Climate Change 16 November 2012).

The Select Committee concluded that the federal government's role is to 'provide national science and information; manage Commonwealth assets and programs; provide leadership on national adaptation reform; maintain a strong, flexible economy and a well-targeted social safety net' (Select Committee of Climate Change 2012: 1–3). The state and territory roles are much the same but, at the sub-national level, they have a focus on 'encouraging climate resilience and adaptive capacity'. Local government generally focuses on regional and local impacts and ensuring climate change is considered in decision-making (Select Committee of Climate Change 2012: 3–6).

Despite the above national reports and recommendations, more recent evidence suggests a 'winding back' of environment and planning policy on coasts and climate change at the sub-national level. During 2012/13, the Queensland state 'suspended' its coastal plan, the NSW Government devolved its sea-level rise policies back to local government and announced the end of catchment management, and the Victorian Government softened planning regulations (Norman 2013). The rhetoric of 'cutting the green tape' emerged and grew stronger during the 2013 federal election campaign. To add to the mix, the Australian Local Government Association at its 2013 general assembly resolved:

> That the National General Assembly call on the Australian Government to initiate a coordinated national approach, involving all three levels of Government, for planning and managing the Australian Coast for the benefit of future generations (ALGA 2013).

Despite this fairly extensive national-level policy framework to support climate change adaptation in coastal areas, actual progress at the local scale has been patchy at best (Gurran et al. 2013). A practice audit (involving an internet survey, in-depth interviews and focus groups with planners and councillors) from 47 coastal councils of non-metropolitan Australia found high levels of awareness about climate risks to their communities, particularly in relation to sea-level rise, shoreline loss, storm surge and coastal erosion, and concern that development continues in vulnerable locations, exacerbating future risk. Study participants also reported levels of community anxiety about climate risk. As well as storm surge and inundation, new risks associated with changed climatic conditions, such as increased likelihood of bushfires, concerned local residents. Respondents were also aware of a level of resident anxiety about the impact of perceived climate effects and associated development restrictions on property values.

Despite this evident awareness of, and concern for, climate risks, few local councils have moved far beyond the stage of vulnerability assessment, although many had begun the process of updating infrastructure and asset management strategies, and revising planning controls. This work depends on local political support, with some councils in the study undertaking no climate-related action at all, while others, such as the Cairns City Council in far north Queensland and Lake Macquarie in New South Wales, have developed comprehensive frameworks for climate change adaptation. Councils that have begun to move forward on climate adaptation typically received funding support from Commonwealth or state sources. Such funding is usually provided on a competitive basis, rather than allocated to all coastal councils on the basis of climate risk and need for assistance. Therefore, in reviewing levels of progress towards climate adaptation, a strong bias towards larger, better-resourced councils, governed by committed political leaders, was apparent.

Even these councils, however, reported difficulties associated with gaining community acceptance of the need for action, with some wealthy property owners prepared to mount expensive challenges to preserve development entitlements and to enact private defensive measures, such as seawalls. Others described increasing 'push back' from climate sceptics.

Overall, there was strong criticism for perceived weaknesses in state policy and laws, aside from the identification of sea-level rise benchmarks for land-use planning purposes in most states. Victoria, South Australia, New South Wales, Queensland and Western Australia all had benchmarks at the time the study was carried out, although New South Wales has subsequently amended policy in favour of voluntary local determination. Regulations and development controls governing inundation, building and infrastructure standards for climate resilience were all regarded as inadequate by respondents. Furthermore, new work to improve local planning frameworks was stymied by a lack of reliable and fine-grained spatial data and insufficient resources to commission the necessary studies. This has become a particular issue in New South Wales, where the rescinding of state-mandated sea-level rise benchmarks places the onus on local councils to develop thresholds for planning purposes.

In summary, federal government leadership in the governance of Australia's coastal zone is elusive. As outlined above, there has been a consistent call for a national coastal policy on coastal planning and management to provide a framework for decision-making at the sub-national, regional and local levels. This has been supported by further nationally funded research in the context of climate change. The evidence also indicates, however, that despite national interest, action on coastal management and climate change at the state and local level is unchanged or in some cases diminishing. The only sustained area of activity appears to be at the regional level through voluntary collaboration, as discussed below.

Regional collaborations for more sustainable coasts

Regional organisations have long been part of Australian coastal governance. Statutory regional coastal planning authorities of the 1970s, such as the Westernport Regional Planning Authority and the Geelong Regional Commission, provided significant coastal protection measures for coastal lands facing development. The 1990s saw various iterations of regional coastal and catchment committees with a strong emphasis on collaboration (for example, within Victoria and NSW) and, more recently, the nesting of regional coastal plans in the planning system (Western Australia). This section discusses five voluntary regional collaborations involving a range of stakeholders in different parts of the Australian coastline:

- Sydney Coastal Councils – a coastal alliance of 15 urban councils within Australia's largest capital city in New South Wales
- Peron Naturaliste Partnership – a coastal alliance of nine coastal councils on the south coast of regional Western Australia
- G21 Geelong regional alliance – a coastal alliance of five councils on the urban edge of an expanding metropolis in Victoria
- Dhimurru Sea Country Plan – a coastal alliance of Indigenous land owners in north-east Arnhem Land, Northern Territory
- South East Coastal Adaptation – a research collaboration involving local and regional organisations in south-east Australia involving two states (NSW and Victoria).

These case studies explore regional collaboration across a range of coastal landscapes and jurisdictions, providing insight into emerging responses to coastal planning and management in Australia. Information is drawn from a synthesis of material previously published by the authors and additional primary fieldwork (Norman 2009; Gurran et al. 2008, 2013). The discussion here is not intended to be comprehensive but, rather, to highlight leading practice models in relation to a range of regional partnerships, providing insights into their formation and implications for future coastal governance.

Sydney Coastal Councils Group

The Sydney Coastal Councils Group Inc. (SCCG) is an alliance of 15 coastal councils that has been running since 1989. Established under the *Local Government Act 1993*, its councils flank coast and estuaries north and south of Sydney. The SCCG has developed over time into an effective voice for coastal concerns supported by a considerable body of research (Smith et al. 2008; SCCG 2012). The mission of the SCCG is 'to provide leadership through a coordinated approach to sustainable coastal management' and the aim is 'to promote cooperation between, and coordination of actions by, Member Councils on issues of regional significance concerning the sustainable management of the urban coastal environment' (SCCG 2013: 1). SCCG represents a coastal alliance surrounding a major capital city facing urban growth pressures and large investment decisions on urban-coastal infrastructure, including the location of new airports.

The governance structure of the SCCG is that of a voluntary organisation and is managed by representatives from member councils supported by a smaller executive group and technical and working groups (SCCG 2011). Funding is provided by council contributions based on a flat rate plus 'a further supplementary contribution, calculated on a population basis for each member council' (SCCG 2011: 16.3). The SCCG Strategic Plan 2010–14 outlines the 'guiding principles' for this alliance:

- protection of the environment and cultural values
- integrated planning and decision-making
- sustainable use of natural coastal resources
- appropriate and meaningful public participation (SCCG 2010: 12).

Over 23 years, the SCCG has delivered significant outcomes, including dealing with storm water run-off, protecting Sydney's wetlands, coastal management and sand nourishment. More recent projects have included regional climate change adaptation strategies, community involvement programs and decision-making frameworks for seawall structures (SCCG 2013). Its longevity in continuing as an organisation, involving several councils with diverse agendas, is a hallmark of the SCCG strength as a model of regional collaboration.

Peron Naturaliste Partnership – a west coast regional partnership

The vision of the Peron Naturaliste Partnership is to empower a resilient regional community to reduce risks and optimize opportunities presented by climate change (PNP 2013a: 3).

The Peron Naturaliste Partnership (PNP) is a regional collaboration between nine local councils in south-west Western Australia (Bunbury, Busselton, Capel, Dardanup, Harvey, Mandurah, Murray, Rockingham and Waroona). This covers the coastal region from Cape Peron to Cape Naturaliste. The governance arrangements for this regional initiative rest in a voluntary memorandum of agreement (2011, updated 2013–15). The objectives of the partnership are to:

- demonstrate regional leadership to support effective advocacy at all levels of government;
- facilitate access to data and information relevant to the Peron Naturaliste coast, including estuarine areas

- adopt a regional approach to the preparation of applications for grants and other submissions to support timely adaptation responses to climate change
- promote consistent information to coastal communities and decision-makers about vulnerability and risk and adaptation strategies
- share local knowledge and experience to support and inform innovative and effective adaptation responses
- collaborate over the management implications of the risk to life and property caused by climate change
- identify and address current and potential coastal including estuarine hazards through research and project development (PNP 2013a: 3).

The focus is on regional leadership, access and sharing of data and knowledge, collaboration over funding initiatives and managing risk to people and place. It is a voluntary non-binding agreement to work together on complex coastal issues in the context of climate change.

The motivation to collaborate in this region stemmed from the initial findings in the Department of Climate Change's first pass assessment report (DCC 2009) that indicated that the coastline in the PNP region contained over 60 per cent of residential buildings at risk from coastal inundation in Western Australia, with an estimated replacement value ranging between $2.9 billion and $4.62 billion (DCC 2009: 115; PNP 2013a: 4). Following this, preliminary research that was funded by all three levels of government indicated that, until 2100 in the Peron Naturaliste region, 'erosion is a far more pervasive issue than flooding' (DCC 2009). Around 800 hectares of urban and commercial land are thought to be at risk of increased flooding, and erosion threatens a 200-metre-wide strip along much of the coastline. In economic terms, assets likely to be lost amount to approximately $1.2 billion in value, while around $1.1 billion could be protected at an estimated cost of $120 million (PNP 2013b: 4).

The PNP is funded by contributions from each council on the basis of rates and employs two part-time officers located at Mandurah City Council. The partnership's business plan outlines short-, medium- and long-term goals that will facilitate knowledge and communication to reduce risk to communities and the environment. The emphasis for the PNP in 2013–15 was on communications to build awareness and understanding in the regional community on the risks from climate change and pathways forward.

G21 Geelong regional alliance

G21 is a platform for the councils to engage with business, industry, state and federal government and other agencies on issues of mutual benefit to the region (G21 2013b: 1).

The G21 Geelong regional alliance was established as a community initiative calling for more regional cooperation on matters of mutual interest to five local government areas (Geelong, Colac, Golden Plains, Queenscliff and Surf Coast). The Geelong region has a significant history of active regional organisations dating back to the 1970s. G21 commenced from a community meeting during 2002 and has grown to be a strong regional organisation recognised and supported by all three levels of government (Norman 2009).

G21 is a local government alliance that flanks the south-west coast east of Geelong. It comprises members from four coastal councils and one inland neighbouring council and it is governed by representatives appointed from those councils and elected representatives from its wider membership. G21 is different from a local government alliance in that its membership is diverse and open to statutory authorities, proprietary companies, public companies, local government, cooperatives, incorporated associations, state government departments and authorities, and federal government departments and authorities (G21 2012: 4).

The G21 organises itself around eight 'pillars' – sport and recreation, environment, transport, health and wellbeing, planning and services, education and training, economic development and arts and culture (G21 2012: 6–7). These pillars are underpinned by the G21 Regional Plan, which articulates five key directions: Direction 1 – Protection and Enhance Our Environment, Direction 2 – Create Sustainable Settlements, Direction 3 – Strengthening our Communities, Direction 4 – Refocus our Economy, and Direction 5 – Collaborating to Make it Happen (G21 2013a: 5).

G21 is different from the other regional alliances discussed here because it has a wider focus than the immediate coastline and a more comprehensive regional approach to policy initiatives and actions. This regional collaboration has been particularly successful in identifying priorities for the region derived from its regional plan and subsequently attracting major funding from all levels of government for implementing its program. It appears likely that the collaboration's triple bottom line approach and collaborative governance arrangements underpin its long-run and continuing success. G21 builds on a lineage of regional plans for Geelong region, using 'regional planning' as the tool for integrating a wide range of considerations in managing the multiple pressures facing a large, growing coastal region.

Dhimurru Yolŋuwu Moṉuk Gapu Wäŋa – Sea Country Plan, north-east Arnhem Land

> This plan is an opportunity for us to speak for our sea country in our own way and to do this at a scale that is culturally and geographically appropriate. Our plan provides the framework for a detailed dialogue with the other main stakeholders in Yolnu Sea Country. We look forward to this discussion and exploring ways of implementing this plan to manage Yolnu Sea Country (Dhimurru 2006: 17).

The north coast of Australia is now largely managed by Aboriginal land councils. *Yolŋuwu Moṉuk Gapu Wäŋa Sea Country Plan: A Yolŋu Vision and Plan for Sea Country Management in North-east Arnhem Land, Northern Territory* (Dhimurru 2006; DEWHA 2008) is an integrated coastal plan that represents a regional approach by traditional owners to managing 'sea country', which is defined as both land and sea. The approach is similar to G21 in using a strategic coastal plan to provide the framework for decision-making that respects traditional and community values. It expresses the vision and a plan for the sea country and is underpinned by seven principles that are based on rights, transparent and adaptive decision-making processes and long-term sustainability:

> Seven Yolŋu principles for managing sea country:
>
> 1. We have a basic right and central right to maintain our traditional ownership and management of our sea country using both our traditions and the tools and practices available to us as citizens of contemporary Australia.
>
> 2. We are interested in the long-term benefit of our sea country to Yolŋu people. We are interested in making sure that conservation and management of our sea country brings long-term human wellbeing and benefit to Yolŋu people and to other users who have interests and values there. That is, they believe in and practise cultural, ecological, social and economic sustainability.
>
> 3. We are interested in everybody being clear and transparent about their rights and responsibilities to our sea country.
>
> 4. The best way to conserve and manage our sea country is by drawing on the Yolŋu customary and contemporary knowledge traditions.

5. We need to build on our knowledge of sea country and life forms if we are to manage them sustainably.

6. We should err on the side of caution when considering proposals and options for use of our sea country, especially in the absence of a full understanding of their risks and consequences.

7. We will need to be flexible and adaptable in our responses to caring for and managing our sea country, especially in a world where circumstances can change rapidly (Dhimurru 2006: 11–12).

The principles above also incorporate a precautionary approach to coastal management in the face of environmental risks and recognise that coastal land and waters are a continuum that require an integrated approach to planning and management. Most importantly, the principles provide a possible guide to leading practice in 'collaboration' for environmental management (Hoffman et al. 2012).

South East Coastal Adaptation – a coastal regional research alliance

What is evident is that to be climate-adapted, a community requires effective planning, decision-making and implementation of responses to current and emerging climate change impacts and risks – effective governance with an adaptive decision-making process to planning for climate change (Norman et al. 2013: 4).

The South East Coastal Adaptation (SECA) alliance is a more recent collaboration between three universities (University of Canberra, The Australian National University and University of Wollongong). During 2012/13, a national research project, Coastal Urban Climate Futures in south-east Australia from Wollongong to Lakes Entrance, was undertaken involving regional organisations and relevant local councils. The focus of the research was coastal adaptation. An interdisciplinary team examined coastal urban futures in the context of sustainability and climate change. This regional collaboration builds on a wider regional initiative, Canberra Urban and Regional Futures (CURF) (Norman and Steffen 2011).

A key outcome of the research was the development of seven key principles, devised specifically for coastal towns facing climate change in south-east Australia, but which might resonate more widely:

1. an integrated approach should be adopted for sustainable regional and local planning (social, economic, environmental and cultural)

2. a precautionary principle should be applied to decision-making regarding the location of new and redeveloped urban settlement and infrastructure and other relevant decisions

3. risk management approaches should be incorporated into local and regional strategies for coastal settlements

4. appropriate forums should be established at the regional level to enable collaboration

5. there should be an ongoing process of community engagement

6. the skills and knowledge of regional and local communities should be connected

7. a process of continuing monitoring, evaluation and reporting of adaptation actions should be implemented (summary of Norman et al. 2013: 7).

The research also concluded that a collaborative intergovernmental approach was fundamental to a 'well adapted' community in the future. This is consistent with the key governance recommendations of the George Report, discussed earlier. In other words, the process of decision-making is critical in determining how a community adapts to change (social, economic and environmental). Support and coordination from higher levels is important to ensure that there is a consistent approach to decisions for multi-use coastal zones. It is interesting that the seven principles developed in two separate processes – Yolŋu people in north-east Arnhem land and on the south-east coast New South Wales and Victoria – share approaches to adaptive decision-making processes, take a long-term view, adopt a precautionary approach and a confirm commitment to sharing knowledge.

The SECA collaboration continues under the umbrella of CURF, strengthening partnerships between coastal planning and environmental science and a further collaboration with the ANU School of Art field studies program. This has provided a platform for long-term collaboration on coastal planning and management with regional and local coastal communities in south-east Australia.

National collaborative coastal alliances

The National Sea Change Taskforce (NSTF) was established in response to rapid growth of coastal towns.[1] It is a coalition of coastal local governments concerned with the impacts of growth pressures and consequent demands on infrastructure and services. The taskforce has also been concerned with the impacts of climate change on coastal environments (Gurran et al. 2008, 2011). During April 2006, the taskforce launched a *Sustainability Charter – A Collaborative National Response to Sea Change Growth* (NSTF 2006). The charter aimed to gain support from federal, state and local governments for more sustainable coastal planning that considers social, economic and environmental impacts; to develop innovative and best practice strategic planning at regional and local levels; to preserve local character and sense of place; for the timely provision of resources to meet the needs of high-growth communities for infrastructure and services; to integrate coastal management and conservation objectives with economic development; to support community wellbeing; and to ensure community ownership and participation in key planning decisions affecting the coast (NSTF 2006: 1).

The taskforce has built on this charter through an annual national conference, by commissioned research to inform its policy development and via regular representations to government on the pressures facing coastal communities.

In the context of a looming federal election in 2013, the taskforce joined with allied groups to form the Australian Coastal Advocacy Alliance (ACAA) to advocate for a more coordinated approach to coastal planning in Australia. This groundswell of coastal interests builds on the formative work of the taskforce and presents a considerable coastal coalition with an agreed mandate from local councils and communities. The inaugural membership comprised the NSTF, Association of Bayside Municipalities (Victoria), Australian Coastal Society, Metropolitan Seaside Councils Committee (South Australia), Queensland Regional Natural Resource Management Groups Collective, Surf Life Saving Australia, Surfrider Foundation and SCCG. The ACAA is focused on three key platforms:

> a collaborative national response to coastal planning and management involving all three tiers of government; an intergovernmental agreement defining the roles and responsibilities of each tier of government in

---

1 The National Sea Change Taskforce has now reformed as the Australian Coastal Council Alliance.

relation to the coastal zone; and a national coastal policy that addresses the challenges facing the coast zone through a national coastal commission and accompanying Act (ACAA 2013a).

The ACAA policy platform reflects the key elements of the George Report and the key messages from the regional collaborations and coastal research discussed above – coordination, collaboration and the engagement of all levels of government are critical to effective integrated coastal management. The ACAA actively lobbied the key political parties during the 2013 federal election for support for a national coastal policy (ACAA 2013b).

Discussion

The collaborative regional alliances outlined in this chapter have developed in a range of coastal landscapes and demonstrate potential foundations for more sustainable and integrated coastal planning and management. They point to a series of important principles for coastal governance at regional and local levels, including respect for local and Indigenous Australian knowledge, a focus on adaptation to future climate risk, integrated management across the land and sea continuum, transparency in decision-making and ongoing application of the precautionary principle. In short, despite the continuing gap between the projected impacts of climate change on Australian coasts and action at the state and local level, regional organisations are becoming an important and effective governance mechanism for coastal management for regions experiencing global and climate change.

Table 12.1 highlights some key governance characteristics shared by the case studies. Voluntary collaboration is a common characteristic that is often supported by some form of contract, such as a memorandum of understanding. It is difficult to conclude whether the 'voluntary' nature is by choice or simply a response to the absence of a more formal structure or both. It is clear, however, that these alliances have delivered some leading practice in coastal planning and management throughout Australia. The second key characteristic is the apparent preparedness of local councils to work together on critical issues that cross local government boundaries – in this case, regional climate change and coastal change. This includes local councils on the west, north, south and east coast. The third key characteristic is that there is no long-term security to funding, which is dependent on continuing contributions by participants. This places a heavy reliance on a continuing long-term commitment to a shared interest beyond short-term politics.

Table 12.1: Governance of regional coastal collaborations

Case study	Organisation	Membership	Funding	Outcomes
Sydney Coastal Councils Group (NSW)	Voluntary alliance governed by a constitution	15 local coastal councils	Local council members	Coastal management, regional climate change and sand nourishment
Peron Naturaliste Partnership (WA)	Voluntary alliance established through a memorandum of understanding	Nine local coastal councils	Local council members	Regional leadership, economic impact of climate change, community awareness
G21 Geelong regional alliance	Voluntary alliance governed by a constitution	Five local councils and elected members from wider membership	Local council members	G21 regional plan, significant government grants, wide support from government and industry
Dhimurru (NT)	Community-based Dhimurru Aboriginal Corporation (north-east Arnhem Land)	Clans with estates and interests in the Dhimurru Indigenous Protected Area (IPA)	Wide range of government and research organisations and related industries	Implementing the Dhimurru Sea Country Plan (seven principles), undertaking coastal and marine management and research
SECA (NSW and Vic)	Voluntary research and policy collaboration	University of Canberra, The Australian National University, University of Wollongong collaborating with seven local coastal councils	Universities, research organisations, public agencies and related industries	Coastal adaptation research (seven principles), community engagement on climate change, education

The impacts of climate change will be significant in Australia (IPCC 2014). The extent of these impacts may mean shifting from incremental change to transformational adaptation with implications for institutional and governance arrangements; for example, no development in high-risk coastal areas. The case studies discussed in this chapter provide an insight into some of the governance characteristics of regional alliances and the organic nature of their resilience as organisations facing complex issues of environmental change.

Conclusion

This chapter focuses on the multi-governance challenge of integrated coastal management around Australia and its application by governments in different jurisdictions. Despite a plethora of national- and state-level coastal inquiries and reports over 40 years since the mid-1970s, Australia still lacks a national coastal policy. National-level efforts have, however, undoubtedly informed, and in some cases propelled, activities at lower levels of government. In particular, regional collaboration has provided a mechanism for cutting across jurisdictional boundaries and facilitating innovation. The largely voluntary nature of the collaborations is considered a strength, in contrast with the more rigid nature of the three-tiered federal system, but it also potentially exposes the models to risk if resourcing is reduced.

Managing the long-term environmental sustainability of the Australian coast is a complex multi-governance challenge. Urban growth, the influence of demographic and global change and the impacts of climate change will only increase the pressures on our coastal environment and communities. Regional collaboration, if supported by Commonwealth and state governments, may offer a positive pathway towards an integrated approach for more sustainable coasts in the context of climate change.

References

AACE (1975). *Coastal Land.* Australian Advisory Committee on the Environment, Australian Government Publishing Service, Canberra.

ACAA (2013a). *National Coastal Policy Initiative.* Australian Coastal Advocacy Alliance, coastalcouncils.org.au/ [Accessed: 23/12/2014].

———. (2013b). *Support for a National Coastal Policy.* Letter to Federal Secretary of the Liberal Party of Australia, 7 August. Australian Coastal Advocacy Alliance.

ALGA (2013). Resolutions from the 2013 National General Assembly of Local Government, 16–19 June. Australian Local Government Association, alga.asn.au/site/misc/alga/downloads/events/2013NGA/Resolutions2013.pdf [Accessed: 21/12/2014].

Australian Parliament (2009). *Managing our Coastal Zone in a Changing Climate – The Time to Act is Now*. House of Representatives Standing Committee on Climate Change, Water, Environment and the Arts, Canberra.

Coasts and Climate Change Council (2011). *Summary of Council Recommendations to the Australian Government*. Department of Industry, Innovation, Climate Change, Science, Research and Tertiary Education, Canberra.

DCC (2009). *Climate Change Risks to Australia's Coast: A First Pass National Assessment*. Department of Climate Change, Australian Government, Canberra.

DCCEE (2010). *Developing a National Coastal Aadaptation Agenda: A Report on the National Coastal Climate Change Forum*. Department of Climate Change and Energy Efficiency, Canberra.

DEWHA (2008). *Dhimurru Arnhem Land Northern Territory*. Department of Environment, Water, Heritage and the Arts, Canberra.

——. (2009). *Decision to Refuse Action, Heritage Estates Rezoning and Public Infrastructure Works*. Facilitating Development of 730 Lots, Worrowing Heights, NSW (EPBC 2007/3448). Department of Environment, Water, Heritage and the Arts, Canberra.

Dhimurru (2006). *Yolŋuwu Moṉuk Gapu Wäŋa Sea Country Plan: A Yolŋu Vision and Plan for Sea Country Management in North-east Arnhem Land, Northern Territory*. Dhimurru Land Management Aboriginal Corporation, Nhulunbuy, Northern Territory.

DRALGAS (2012). *Annual Report 2011–02*. Department of Regional Australia, Local Government, Arts and Sport, Canberra.

G21 (2012). *Report to the Region 2012*, www.g21.com.au/g21-report-region-2012 [Accessed: 9/11/2017].

——. (2013a). *Priority Projects G21 Regional Plan Implementation*, www.g21.com.au/priority-projects [Accessed: 9/11/2017].

——. (2013b). *The G21 Municipalities*, www.g21.com.au/g21-municipalities [Accessed: 24/8/2013].

Gibbs, M. & Hill, T. (2011). *Coastal Climate Change Risk – Legal and Policy Responses in Australia*. Report prepared for the Department of Climate Change and Energy Efficiency, Commonwealth of Australia, Canberra.

Gurran, N., Hamin, E. & Norman, B. (2008). *Planning for Climate Change: Leading Practice Principles and Models for Sea Change Communities in Coastal Australia*. Prepared for the National Sea Change Taskforce, Planning Research Centre, University of Sydney.

Gurran, N., Norman, B., Gilbert, C. & Hamin, E. (2011). *Planning for Climate Change Adaptation in Coastal Australia: State of Practice*. Report No. 4 for the National Sea Change Taskforce, Faculty of Architecture, Design and Planning, University of Sydney.

Gurran, N., Norman, B. & Hamin, E. (2013). Climate Change Adaptation in Coastal Australia: An audit of planning practice. *Ocean & Coastal Management*, 86: 100–09. doi.org/10.1016/j.ocecoaman.2012.10.014

Hoffmann, B.D., Roeger, S., Wise, P., Dermer, J., Yunupingu, B., Lacey, D., Yunupingu, D., Marika, B., Marika, M. & Panton, B. (2012). Achieving Highly Successful Multiple Agency Collaborations in a Cross-Cultural Environment: Experiences and lessons from Dhimurru Aboriginal Corporation and partners. *Ecological Management and Restoration*, 13(1): 42–50. doi.org/10.1111/j.1442-8903.2011.00630.x

IPCC (2014). *Working Group II (WGII) Contribution to the Fifth Assessment Report on Impacts, Adaptation and Vulnerability*. Intergovernmental Panel on Climate Change, Yokohama, Japan, 31 March 2014.

NCCARF (2013). *National Climate Change Adaptation Research Facility*. Griffith University, Queensland, www.nccarf.edu.au [Accessed: 23/12/2014].

Norman, B. (2009). Principles for an intergovernmental agreement for coastal planning and climate change in Australia. *Habitat International*, 33(3): 293–99. doi.org/10.1016/j.habitatint.2008.10.002

——. (2010). *Sustainable Coastal Planning for Urban Growth and Climate Change*. NSW Coastal Conference, Batemans Bay.

——. (2013). Smart planning for urban growth can minimise flood risks. *The Drum*, ABC, 31 January 2013, www.abc.net.au/unleashed/4492512.html [Accessed: 23/12/2014].

Norman, B. & Steffen, W. (2011). *Canberra Urban & Regional Futures – An Innovative Regional Platform for Building Resilience.* CURF paper no. 1, Canberra.

Norman, B., Steffen, W., Webb, R., Capon, A., Maher, W., Woodroffe, C., Rogers, K., Tanton, R., Viddyattama, Y., Lavis, J., Sinclair, H. & Weir, B. (2013). *South East Coastal Adaptation (SECA): Coastal urban climate futures in SE Australia from Wollongong to Lakes Entrance.* National Climate Change Adaptation Research Facility, Gold Coast, pp. 130.

NSTF (2006). *Sustainability Charter – A Collaborative National Response to Sea Change Growth.* National Sea Change Taskforce, Sydney, coastalcouncils.org.au/

PNP (2013a). *Business Plan 2013–2015.* Peron Naturaliste Partnership, Mandurah, WA.

———. (2013b). *Coastal Adaptation Decision Pathways Project, Developing Flexible Adaptation Pathways for the Peron Naturaliste Coastal Region of WA.* Peron Naturaliste Partnership, Mandurah, WA.

Productivity Commission (2012). *Barriers to Effective Climate Change Adaptation.* Report 59. Final Inquiry Report, Canberra.

Resource Assessment Commission (1993). *Coastal Zone Inquiry: Final Report Overview.* Australian Government, Canberra.

Richardson, K., Steffen, W. & Liverman, D. (eds) (2011). *Climate Change: Global Risks, Challenges and Decisions.* Cambridge University Press.

SCCG (2010). *Strategic Plan 2010–2014.* Sydney Coastal Councils Group.

———. (2011). *Constitution.* Sydney Coastal Councils Group.

———. (2012). *Prioritising Coastal Adaptation Development Options for Local Development, Project Summary Report.* Sydney Coastal Councils Group.

———. (2013). *About the Sydney Coastal Councils Group,* www.sydney coastalcouncils.com.au/About_SCCG [Accessed: 23/12/2014].

Select Council on Climate Change (2012). *Roles and Responsibilities for Climate Change in Australia*. Paper released at the second meeting of the Select Council on Climate Change, 16 November 2012, Canberra.

SEWPAC (2013). *Strategic Assessments*. Department of Sustainability, Environment, Water, Population and Communities, Canberra, www.environment.gov.au/epbc/assessments/strategic.html [Accessed: 23/12/2014].

Smith, I., Dodson, J., Gleeson, B. & Burton, P. (2010). *Growing Adaptively: Responding to Climate Change through Regional Spatial Planning in England and Australia*. Urban Research Program, Research Paper 31, Griffith University, Brisbane.

Smith, T., Brooke, C., Measham, T., Preston, B., Gorddard, R., Withycombe, G., Beveridge, B. & Morrison, C. (2008). *Case Studies of Adaptive Capacity: Systems Approach to Regional Climate Change Adaptation Strategies in Metropolises*. University of Sunshine Coast, CSIRO Marine and Atmospheric Research, CSIRO Sustainable Ecosystems, WWF Australia, Sydney Coastal Councils Group, Sydney.

Sorensen, J. (1997). National and International Efforts at Integrated Coastal Management: Definitions, achievements, and lessons. *Coastal management*, 25(1): 3–41. doi.org/10.1080/08920759709362308

Standing Committee on Environment and Conservation (1980). *Australian Coastal Zone Management*. Report from the House of Representatives Standing Committee on Environment and Conservation. March 1980, Australian Government Publishing Service, Canberra.

Steffen, W. (2009). *Climate Change 2009 — Faster Change and More Serious Risks*. Prepared for the Department of Climate Change, Canberra.

Steffen, W. & Hughes, L. (2013). *The Critical Decade: Climate Change Science, Risks and Response*. Report for the Climate Commission. Department of Industry, Innovation, Climate Change, Science, Research and Tertiary Education, Canberra.

Thom, B. (2010). *National Coastal Reform—2010 and Beyond*. Keynote speech to the National Coastal Conference, Adelaide.

13

Multi-level Governance in the Lake Eyre Basin: Meeting in the Middle?

Kate Andrews

Introduction

Scale is inescapable in natural resource management (NRM), which operates up and down geographical scales and levels of governance – from paddock to river basin, land manager to federal politician and local to federal government, and all within a complex and constantly changing social–ecological system.

The community-based Lake Eyre Basin (LEB) catchment management framework (1995–2002) and the government-based Lake Eyre Basin Intergovernmental Agreement (2001–ongoing) are examples of collaborative multi-level governance (MLG) in a multi-actor, multi-level system. Both demonstrate two elements of MLG: establishing the vertical and horizontal links between scales and levels and involving a diversity of players, including communities, governments and industry stakeholders. Comparing the government and the non-government models, however, reveals several differences between them, including scope and integration of issues, level of involvement of non-government actors and hierarchy, control and distribution of power. Analysing these two processes leads to a number of questions, including should we expect more of MLG mechanisms than vertical connection between scales and a diversity of players? As discussed by Bache and Flinders (2004), perhaps MLG should represent models that create new forms of accountability and empowered relationships between people and their institutions.

The benefits of MLG have been documented and have particular relevance to NRM:

> From a management perspective, evidence is accumulating that supports the hypothesis that those systems that more consciously address scale issues and the dynamic linkages across levels are more successful at (1) assessing problems and (2) finding solutions that are more politically and ecologically sustainable (Cash et al. 2006).

This paper introduces the LEB community initiative and the intergovernmental agreement, explaining how they sit within the national NRM framework. It describes changes and challenges for the processes over time, compares the characteristics of the two initiatives and, finally, questions how and whether both constitute actual MLG.

Lake Eyre is a huge, ephemeral salt lake in the centre of Australia. Its catchment, the internally draining LEB, stretches across more than 1.2 million square kilometres (Smith 1998), a larger area than France and Germany combined, and contains fewer than 60,000 people, making it one of the most sparsely populated areas in the world. The basin is a biophysically defined region that covers a large portion of central Australia, including substantial chunks of Queensland, South Australia, the Northern Territory and a small area of New South Wales. It cuts across multiple political and administrative jurisdictions and socially defined regions, at many levels. As a result, any NRM process contends with the differences between state legislation, structures, policy and cultures.

The size of the basin, its diverse landscape and values, and the multiple political jurisdictions that it covers, guarantee that its management must incorporate a multitude of different needs and perspectives including pastoralists on family- or company-owned properties; Aboriginal communities and individuals with historical and/or traditional connections to the land; conservationists and the organisations that they work for, such as the Australian Conservation Foundation; the mining and petroleum industries, from individuals engaged in Wild West–style opal mining to the huge, high-tech operations of BHP Billiton and Santos; residents of small and remote towns who work for local councils or are involved in the tourism industry; scientists from many disciplines and institutions;

three layers of government in four major jurisdictions and multiple local governments and state agencies; and landcare and industry groups. This incomplete list captures the confusion of players with a stake in the future of the LEB.

Proposed World Heritage listing by the Australian Government in the early 1990s generated passion and controversy between these groups and, although listing did not proceed and the Australian Government decided that community efforts could best protect the basin, the battle left a gulf between people who had lost trust in each other.

The Lake Eyre Basin Community Initiative, 1995–2002

The LEB initiative began in 1995 at a public meeting in Birdsville, Queensland, a one-pub town on the edge of the Simpson Desert. Concerned by conflict between different groups and the potential for World Heritage listing, community members wanted to bring together these different interests to work towards sustainable use and management of the natural resources in the basin.

A cross-section of interest groups was invited to this first public meeting and many different organisations and individuals attended, including government officers and community members. A lot of work went into this pre-negotiation – deciding upon the relevant players, making the contacts, encouraging attendance, employing a professional facilitator and planning the meeting. This preparation ensured that participants were able to agree to move to a next stage. A steering group was formed representing all the different interests, with a two-year sunset clause and no *fait accompli* to continue in any form after that. The steering group was established to explore the issues and future management options of the LEB, particularly through the lens of catchment management, and then to hold another public workshop in 1997 to make a decision as to whether and how to proceed.

As an indication of their commitment to this decision, various organisations and industries contributed start-up funds. Subsequent funding was provided from the Commonwealth Government and the South Australian and Queensland state governments.

As the first meeting was organised by LEB community members (albeit with government agency support), the elected steering group and the subsequent consultation process was less frequently seen as being an imposition from 'outside' or 'government', which is regularly an important concern in the independent culture of the outback. Having the steering group comprised of the various stakeholders created ownership and credibility within the region and encouraged diverse stakeholders to support, rather than undermine, the process. Individuals and various interest groups had a chance to be involved in listening, learning and determining the outcomes.

Given the unusual and extreme natural and geographic characteristics of the basin, it was obvious that it would not be successful to import or impose a framework from anywhere else. Even establishing an organisation was not without difficulties – the terms of reference for the steering group were to explore future options rather than to take concrete steps. It was necessary for the group to first design an appropriate framework to give participants an opportunity to learn about catchment management and collaborative decision-making, and to think through whether and how those process could be used in the LEB to encourage ownership and the implementation of any decision that resulted.

In 1996, while employed as the project officer working for the diverse community steering group, I embarked upon a process of basin-wide consultation, asking people questions like 'What are the major natural resource management issues in the basin?' and 'If catchment management was to work in the basin what would it look like?' Over 20 workshops were held across the basin, along with countless smaller meetings and conversations – over kitchen tables or campfires, tea or beer. People designed their ideal regional community structure for the basin, addressing the challenges and issues of the region and the pros and cons of catchment management. From this, a draft options paper was produced and, after further input and feedback (much of it verbal and derived from the informal conversations that suited some of the stakeholder groups), a final options paper of people's opinions and organisational designs was distributed (LEBSG 1997a). The steering group also produced an issues paper exploring some of the key concerns that had been raised during the consultation: managing pest animals and weeds, management and use of our natural river systems, floodplain grazing and conserving biological diversity (LEBSG 1997b).

Much to the surprise of many, given the bullish independence and individualism that defines outback culture, in 1997 the steering group's final public workshop in Birdsville successfully negotiated to establish a basin-wide integrated catchment management organisation. The potential structure was thrashed out again in detail at the workshop and a mix-and-match version of the designs that had been presented in the options paper was developed (LEBSG 1997a). A transition group was appointed to manage the establishment of the organisation that once again included all stakeholders. The Commonwealth minister of the environment was on hand to announce substantial funding from his government's Natural Heritage Trust.

Participants agreed upon a number of key principles for the catchment process, which would have been unlikely without the previous year of participation, relationship-building and negotiation. First and foremost was inclusiveness. Participants agreed to all stakeholders being involved, from outback pastoralists to urban conservationists, mining companies to Indigenous Australian communities, and scientists to bureaucrats. Likewise, it was agreed that the organisation should address the management of all natural resources and, where possible, the links to economic and social issues. The logic of the biophysical boundaries was seen to supersede the political and administrative borders. It was agreed that the political and administrative borders should be ignored so as to bring together communities and governments of all levels (local, state and federal) within the basin in a multi-state organisation. As a local pastoralist commented in one workshop, 'Water doesn't stop at the state border and nor do feral pigs'. The process of designing and establishing the LEB organisation began as a consultative process and evolved into a participatory one (Andrews 2000, 2003a).

Moving from an idealised and abstract structure on paper to a living, breathing organisation was the next make-or-break stage. Establishing participatory and fair catchment committees over enormous and diverse catchments and then the overarching Lake Eyre Basin Coordinating Group (LEBCG) raised many challenges and tensions, including at one public meeting a request from a local government participant to vote on whether we should run the meeting by consensus or not (we did not vote, and the meeting, as all others, was consensus based). Just as it is counterproductive to artificially divide people from the town where they shop, the catchment/sub-catchment committee boundaries were defined to take into account social catchments with the biophysical (Andrews 2003b).

The basin-wide group and the two first cross-border catchment committees then worked to develop long-term strategies, build partnerships and find funding for on-ground work, such as cross-border pig culls.

From uncertain beginnings as a widely scattered steering group in 1995, by 2000 the LEBCG, of which I was the first CEO, was an incorporated body with an office and staff based in Longreach, Queensland; substantial community involvement; catchment-wide management strategies; and the role of community advisory committee to the newly formed Lake Eyre Basin Ministerial Forum, which was established by an intergovernmental agreement signed between the Australian, South Australian and Queensland governments (Andrews 2003a).

The Lake Eyre Basin Intergovernmental Agreement, 1995–2013

While the above process was underway, the stakeholders in the community initiative were also providing input to a government negotiation to establish an agreement between the Commonwealth, Queensland and South Australian governments to cooperatively manage the major internal river systems that flow from Queensland to South Australia. A heads of agreement was signed by these three governments in 1997 to provide for the development of an intergovernmental agreement. Further consultation occurred in parallel with the development of the community initiative, and further governmental negotiation, and the LEB Intergovernmental Agreement was signed in 2000 in Birdsville, with the launch of the community initiative's first LEB strategy, and Cooper and Georgina–Diamantina catchment plans.

Once ratified by the three governments, the agreement came into effect in 2001, with the Northern Territory Government joining and signing the agreement in 2004. The agreement established the ministerial forum and a senior officers group with two associated advisory committees – the community advisory committee and the scientific advisory panel.

The LEB community initiative, through the steering group and then the LEB coordinating group, encouraged this agreement for a number of years. A regular request from people throughout the process was to link the community structure directly to formal government processes, such as providing a community committee with direct access to the highest political decision-makers through a ministerial forum. This was achieved in 2000 with the agreement that the LEBCG, as the overarching community group, performs the role of a community advisory committee to the ministerial forum. The coordinating group performed this role until late 2002, at which point regional NRM arrangements changed across the country. In late 2003, the ministerial forum appointed members to the community advisory committee.

The Lake Eyre Basin Intergovernmental Agreement
(LEB Intergovernmental Agreement 2000):

> provides for the sustainable management of the water and related natural resources associated with cross-border river systems in the Lake Eyre Basin to avoid downstream impacts on associated environmental, economic and social values (3).

The purpose of the agreement is:

> to provide for the development or adoption, and implementation of Policies and Strategies concerning water and related natural resources in the Lake Eyre Basin Agreement Area to avoid or eliminate so far as reasonably practicable adverse cross-border impacts (6).

The ministerial forum is also required to review the condition of all watercourses and catchments within the LEB agreement area.

The ninth and 10th principles of the agreement state:

> that the collective local knowledge and experience of the Lake Eyre Basin Agreement Area communities are of significant value; and that decisions need to be based on the best available scientific and technical information together with the collective local knowledge and experience of communities within the Lake Eyre Basin Agreement Area (7).

Part Four of the agreement addresses the 'Roles of the parties', outlining the responsibilities and interests first of the Commonwealth and then of the states. Interests or stakeholders other than governments, not being signatories to the agreement, are not addressed. A section, however, does address 'Community advice and representation', stating that 'the Ministerial

Forum will ensure that it has satisfactory access to community advice in relation to matters relevant to this Agreement' (LEB Intergovernmental Agreement 2000: 9), illustrating how the arrangements maintain the existing power balance. Advice can be provided by the scientific and community committees to the ministerial forum; however, they do not formally participate in the decision-making. Additionally, as the states and territory have statutory responsibilities for NRM, the agreement relies upon their cooperation and commitment to function. A state has no obligation to do so.

The borders are back: Establishing state-based regional organisations, 2002–13

In the early 2000s, Australia embarked upon regionalisation of NRM across the country, building upon the statutory-based catchment management bodies that already existed in some states. This constituted a substantial change and established a markedly different regime. Boundaries for each of the 56 regions were established in agreements between the Commonwealth, state and territory governments between December 2002 and June 2004, and bilateral agreements were signed as part of the second phase of the Natural Heritage Trust. Where there were no existing state-based arrangements, non-government organisations – mainly incorporated associations – were established. In the cases where non-government regional organisations already existed, such as the Blackwood Catchment Group in Western Australia or the LEBCG, they were bypassed or subsumed within the new arrangements.

These nationally supported regional arrangements continued through a change of federal government in 2007 and the establishment of a new national program, Caring for our Country. The bilateral arrangements between the states/territories and the Australian Government ceased with the new program; however, the Australian Government continued to fund regional bodies directly and through open competitive arrangements. Regional bodies and their collective or legislative arrangements continue to evolve differently in different jurisdictions.

Figure 13.1 summarises the roles of the various levels of government, regional bodies and community groups as they existed in 2011.

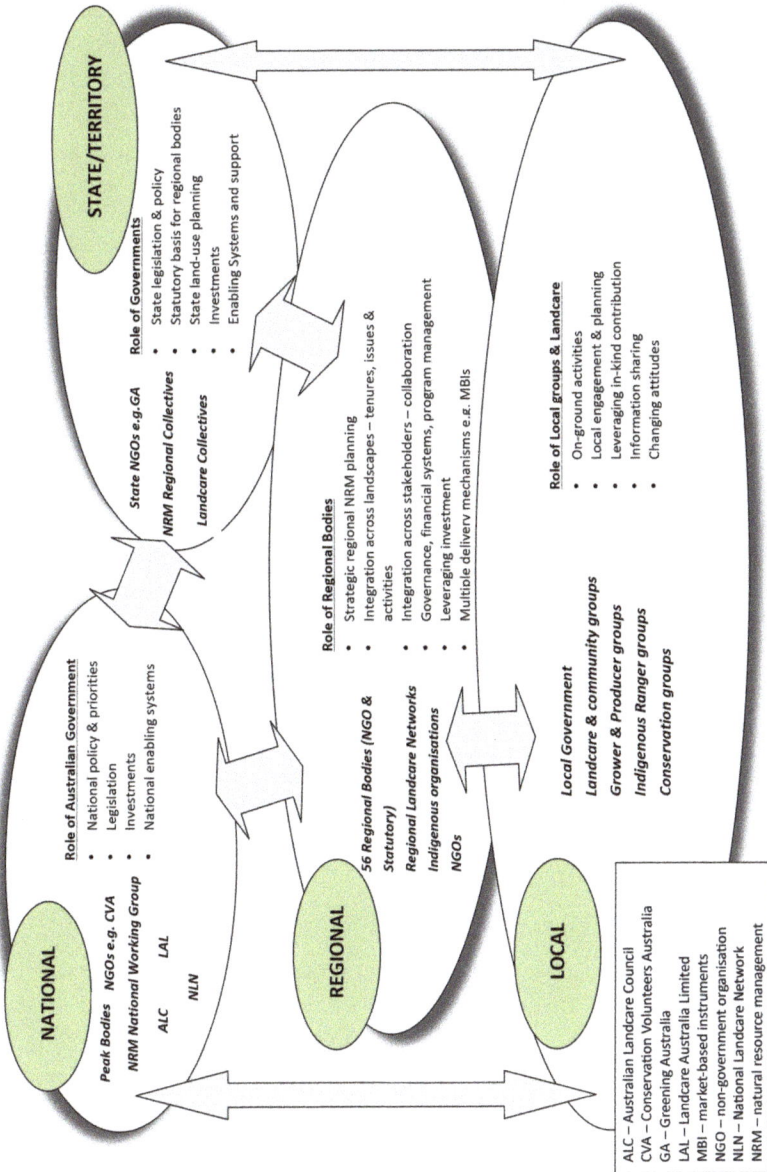

Figure 13.1: NRM MLG structures and roles in 2011

Source: Andrews (2011)

In the case of the LEB, support for the cross-border community organisation of the LEBCG finished and state-based regional bodies were formed – Desert Channels in the LEB portion of Queensland, the SA Arid Lands regional body in north-east South Australia and the Territory Natural Resource Management Board in the Northern Territory.

As a result of these changes, the LEBCG no longer performed the role of community advisory committee for the intergovernmental agreement; rather, the committee was separately constituted by government. Given the small pool of available people, however, it retained some of the original participants. Rather than the committee membership being derived from a process of community consultation, they were ministerial appointments. The two cross-border catchment groups continued to exist under the auspices of Desert Channels Queensland; however, there was little material or logistical support for them and they had no explicit role in the new arrangements. For example, five years after writing the original catchment plan, the Georgina–Diamantina Catchment Committee revisited their plan at a meeting in Boulia. Having no coordinator and no logistical support, the plan was not distributed beforehand and the Desert Channels representative was unable to advise the committee as to what, if any, of the actions and targets had been achieved. The group ended by re-endorsing the plan, which they wholeheartedly supported, but were left in limbo as to what was happening with suggested actions (I was, coincidentally, present at the meeting). It seems likely that the catchment committees will become less and less engaged or relevant as they struggle on with little support.

In the five-year review of the Lake Eyre Basin Agreement (URS 2007), it was recognised that the state-based regional bodies were conspicuous by their absence in the arrangements. Recommendations were made to involve representatives of regional bodies in the community advisory committee. The committee is now constituted of a prescribed range of interests including those of Indigenous Australian communities, pastoral and conservation, and the regional bodies nominate for a number of the positions and hold a position as board members. While chair of Territory Natural Resource Management, I was the board's representative on the committee.

Comparing the community initiative and the intergovernmental agreement

Table 13.1 outlines and compares the major characteristics of the two processes described above.

Table 13.1: Comparison of the Lake Eyre Basin Intergovernmental Agreement and community initiative

Characteristics	LEB Intergovernmental Agreement	LEB community initiative
Geographical coverage	Initially limited to the Georgina–Diamantina and Cooper Creek river systems in Queensland and South Australia, ending at Lake Eyre (signed in 2000); the NT portion of the basin included from 2004	Working to encompass the entirety of the basin, including the western rivers of Lake Eyre in South Australia and the NSW portion
Who initiated, participated and funded	Initiated by governments, negotiated between governments, government consultation of stakeholders and communities	Initiated by local residents, negotiated between stakeholders with participation of governments, initial cash and in kind contribution from industries, local government and individuals, ongoing majority of funding from governments and in kind from individuals and some companies
Initial motivation or governance challenge	Cross-border water management – proposed water developments in the Queensland portion of the basin that would impact upon South Australia, such as the proposal to grow cotton at Currareva near Windorah	Originally, the proposed World Heritage Listing of the LEB, then the proposed irrigation development for the cultivation of cotton at Currareva on the Cooper
Structure and levels	The ministerial forum consists of the Australian Government and three state and territory governments, a senior officer's group and two groups to advise the ministerial forum – the community advisory committee and the scientific advisory panel	Three nested levels: basin-wide coordinating group, catchment management groups, and sub-catchment or working groups as required (determined by local residents or participants)
Status or rules	Legislatively based	A non-government organisation established as an incorporated association with objectives, principles and 'rules' established in a participatory, consensus-based process for each level

Characteristics	LEB Intergovernmental Agreement	LEB community initiative
Scope of issues and policy	Emphasis on water – the agreement provides for the sustainable management of the water and related natural resources associated with cross-border river systems in the Lake Eyre Basin, the scope and interpretation has broadened over time	Emphasis on integrated catchment management (all natural resources and social and economic factors), basin-wide and catchment management strategies addressing NRM issues
Objectives	The purpose of the agreement is to provide for the development or adoption, and implementation, of policies and strategies concerning water and related natural resources in the Lake Eyre Basin agreement area to avoid or eliminate, so far as reasonably practicable, adverse cross-border impacts; under the agreement, the Lake Eyre Basin Ministerial Forum is required to review the condition of all watercourses and catchments within the Lake Eyre Basin agreement area	Coordinating group: to promote ecological and economic sustainability in the basin, develop and communicate a shared strategic vision across the basin, provide a forum for basin-wide issues, provide a communication channel with governments, integrate priorities for action plans and funding, facilitate knowledge flow and development for the basin, represent the catchments on a national level

Catchment committees: to maintain a focus on the catchment perspective; work for ecological, economic and social sustainability within the catchment; develop and maintain a strategic planning process, including compilation, implementation and monitoring; provide a forum for differing opinions on issues within the catchment, followed by a decision-making process based on best available information; represent the catchment perspective on a basin level; involve the catchment community |

Characteristics	LEB Intergovernmental Agreement	LEB community initiative
Participants and role	Ministerial forum: relevant minister from each jurisdiction, meets once a year Community advisory committee: to provide community advice to government on water and related natural resource issues in the Lake Eyre Basin; appointed by the ministerial forum; 17 members representing community stakeholders in the LEB, including from regional NRM bodies, Indigenous interests, pastoral, petroleum and mining; meets twice a year face-to-face Scientific advisory panel: to provide scientific advice to the ministerial forum relevant to the management of water and related natural resources, in particular on monitoring the condition of rivers and catchments; appointed by the ministerial forum Senior officers group: senior government officers from relevant agencies in each jurisdiction, – provides advice to the ministerial forum and implements its decisions LEB Aboriginal forum: held every two years to promote the input of Indigenous Australians into policies devised by the ministerial forum	Catchment/regional committees based upon biophysical and social catchments and which include sub-catchment committees or local groups; these provided membership to the overarching Lake Eyre Basin Coordinating Group, which also included skills-based members and government observers; the Lake Eyre Basin Coordinating Group acted as the community advisory committee until late 2002

Both processes demonstrate the two most obvious elements of MLG: establishing the vertical and horizontal links between scales and levels, and involving a diversity of players, including communities, governments and industry stakeholders.

A comparison also raises several differences between the processes as they relate to MLG, including the scope and integration of issues; level and type of involvement of non-government actors; and the hierarchy, control and distribution of power.

Scope refers to both the physical area and the issues covered. An obvious difference between the two processes addressing the management of LEB was their geographic scope. The intergovernmental agreement originally captured what was the main government concern at the time – the rivers that flowed (occasionally) from Queensland to South Australia. As documented above, however, the geographical area covered by the agreement has increased over time so as to better reflect the river basin as a whole. There was also an initial difference between the scope of the issues addressed by the two MLG processes in that the intergovernmental agreement focused on water management while the community process sought to integrate all natural resource issues and acknowledge the related social and economic factors.

Over time, the intergovernmental agreement has experienced 'scope creep' in that the development of the LEB Rivers Assessment Implementation Plan proposes a strategic adaptive management process that begins with developing a 'desired state of LEB landscape condition'. The second step in the plan narrows in again to riverine landscape condition and then, in later steps, broadens out to encompass LEB landscape form and function (Price et al. 2009). The implementation plan has developed from focusing on river health to a broader, more holistic landscape approach – which goes some way to being an integrated NRM approach (the intent of the community initiative) where natural resources, such as water or vegetation or soil, are not dealt with in isolation but are understood as parts of a whole system. The approach of the LEB community initiative was to integrate catchment management (LEBSG 1997a; Andrews 1999a, 1999b, 2003a) and to ensure that people were an acknowledged part of the equation. The rivers assessment plan has been accepted in a modified form (a smaller budget) by the ministerial forum.

Equally as important as the scope of the MLG processes area and issues is the scope of its decisions. What decisions can the process address and by whom is this determined? Are these decisions relevant to non-government participants?

The level of community involvement is a characteristic that differs significantly between the intergovernmental agreement structure and the community initiative. With the disconnection between the intergovernmental agreement and the LEBCG, the participatory and nested community processes that supported the community advisory committee ceased. Currently, the LEB advisory committee meets twice a year. Social capital and networks that developed through the establishment of the LEB community catchment initiative mean there are individuals willing and able to participate, and strong connections between sectoral players and across jurisdictional borders. Some of the individuals participating in the advisory committee are those who helped design and establish the coordinating group and catchment committees. This continuity has underpinned the existing arrangement. As the inevitable occurs and members change, it will be interesting to see how the formal arrangements work without the same level of ongoing investment of social capital and relationships.

How does the contribution of individuals through an advisory committee become community involvement? How are those individuals supported to broader processes? In theory, formally involving the regional NRM bodies, as occurred in response to the URS review (2007), should achieve this; however, such involvement is hindered by a number of factors. The boundaries of the regional bodies are different and generally larger than the LEB alone, and regional priorities are set within this larger context. Regional bodies predominantly rely on government funding through a national NRM program that is separate to, and generally disconnected from, the LEB process. Funding priorities for that program are set at a national level. As the finances and activities of regional bodies are tied to the requirements of government funding and priorities, this restricts their ability to determine the location and focus of their projects. Thus, maintaining engagement and commitment is a constant challenge, particularly in the Northern Territory, where the regional body covers the entire jurisdiction, of which the LEB is only a small portion. Additionally, regional bodies have varied mechanisms, priorities and capacity for involving their stakeholders.

As the current regional model evolves, cooperative cross-border models are emerging, such as the Rangelands Alliance, which is the most relevant example to the LEB. Once again, though, the boundaries of the alliance stretch beyond the LEB and incorporate a large swathe of the rangelands, including the WA rangelands stretching right to the north-western coastline. Internally to the basin, cross-border catchment committees are continuing but with apparently little support and less relevance.

The LEB Community Advisory Committee and the Scientific Advisory Panel are advisory committees only; they do not have decision-making power. Sitting on a representative advisory committee with no decision-making power and a limited budget is a stark contrast to participating in a non-government organisation with the power to initiate projects and allocate funds. The LEB community initiative's nested processes helped create diverse community input, which resulted in a deeper and supported structure. While ministers hold ultimate decision-making power, the senior officers group has influence through managing the information that reaches ministers, including the framing of briefs and recommendations, the control of budgets and the running of the agreement process, and through the implementation of decisions, either via the secretariat or the relevant government agencies. There is a clear hierarchy and, less clear and overt, distribution of power and influence.

In the case of the LEB, is it possible to determine the influence of this circle of non-state actors who have participated in the process? What has resulted from their influence? Have the Lake Eyre Basin MLG processes resulted in outcomes that have differed from what would otherwise have been the case?

Is it MLG?

The ceding of state authority to non-democratically accountable processes has been discussed as a possible negative consequence of MLG (Termeer et al. 2010). This concern presupposes some redistribution of power away from elected representative government, either through direct decision-making or through influence, which raises the question of how much decision-making power is being redistributed, either up or down the levels of governance or to the non-state players. Once the talking is done, who actually makes the decisions? Bache and Flinders sum this up: 'a distinction must be drawn between multi-level governance and multi-level participation, where the latter notion signals greater involvement without effective influence', going on to say that this failure 'to address the continuing existence of structural inequalities' (2004: 204) may be a weakness in MLG that can perhaps be dealt with through clearer expectations of actors' influence as well as participation. Where does the power to make decisions lie in the structure or system? When Termeer et al. (2010: 29) say that 'the nature of multi-level governance is that it will conflict with existing norms of democratic legitimacy because it will go beyond the control of elected politicians or state executives', they provide a simple benchmark or criteria for determining whether the LEB Intergovernmental Agreement, a multi-level mechanism, is also MLG. In the case of the LEB Intergovernmental Agreement, the decision-making power resides with the ministerial forum and the senior officers group that advises the forum.

Using Peters and Pierre's (2004) description of MLG as a basis on which to compare the LEB mechanisms reveals stark difference. They suggest four characteristics as defining MLG: a wide and diverse set of actors; non-hierarchical and not controlled from above; unconstrained by formal agreements or rules, so informal bargaining is as important as formal power; and largely ignores structure, focusing on process and outcomes. Of these descriptors, the community initiative accords with each while the intergovernmental agreement is only consistent with the first.

Both Termeer's and Peters and Pierre's work provide a basis for introductory discussion as to whether the two processes described in this paper are, in fact, MLG. Although they both established vertical and horizontal links between scales and levels, and involve a diversity of players, there was disparity in the participation of the non-government sector and in the way power was distributed. Evolving MLG, according to Bache and Flinders, needs 'new forms and models of accountability' that build new conduits between the public and institutions. This may involve reappraisal of democracy and the role of representative institutions. However, 'participation does not equate to power and the emergence of multi-level governance does not necessarily enhance the position of weaker social groups' (Bache and Flinders 2004: 205). Should we expect more of MLG mechanisms than vertical connection between scales and a diversity of players? Perhaps MLG should now represent models that create new forms of accountability and empowered relationships between people and their institutions.

References

Andrews, K. (1999a). *Rivers in the Rangelands – What's Happening in the Lake Eyre Basin*. Second Australian Stream Management Conference, 8–11 February, Adelaide, South Australia, pp. 15–20.

——. (1999b). The Lake Eyre Basin Regional Initiative. In: *Sustainable Regional Development – Final Report*. Dore and Woodhill, Greening Australia Ltd.

——. (2000). Case Study 6 – The Lake Eyre Basin Regional Initiative. In: Buchy, M., Ross, H. & Proctor, W. (eds) *Enhancing the Information Base on Participatory Approaches in Australian Natural Resource Management*. Commissioned research under the Land and Water Resources Research and Development Corporation's Social and Institutional Research Program, Canberra.

——. (2003a). Negotiating a Future in the Lake Eyre Basin. Paper for the *International Biennale on Negotiation*, Negocia, Paris.

——. (2003b). Pelicans, Pubs and Politics – plenty of them all in the Lake Eyre Basin. In: *Beef in the Outback – Planning for Profit*. Proceedings of the 8th National Workshop of the Beef Improvement Association of Australia Ltd.

——. (2011). *Levels and Roles within the Natural Resource Management Regional Model*. Working paper for Territory Natural Resource Management.

Bache, I. & Flinders, M. (eds) (2004). *Multi-level Governance*. Oxford University Press. doi.org/10.1093/0199259259.001.0001

Cash, D.W., Adger, W., Berkes, F., Garden, P., Lebel, L., Olsson, P., Pritchard, L. & Young, O. (2006). Scale and Cross-Scale Dynamics: governance and information in a multilevel world. *Ecology and Society*, 11(2): 8. doi.org/10.5751/ES-01759-110208

LEBCG (2000). *A Future for All. Strategic Plans for the Lake Eyre Basin*. Lake Eyre Basin Coordinating Group, Longreach, Queensland.

LEB Intergovernmental Agreement (2000). lakeeyrebasin.gov.au/sitecollectionimages/71d27602-9826-4d4f-9004-fbc30cde225b/files/leb-intergovernmental-agreement.pdf [Accessed: 9/11/2017].

LEBSG (1997a). *Issues Paper*. Lake Eyre Basin Steering Group, Longreach, Queensland.

——. (1997b). *Options Paper*. Lake Eyre Basin Steering Group, Longreach, Queensland.

Peters, G.B. & Pierre, J. (2004). Multi-level Governance and Democracy: a 'Faustian bargain'? In: Bache, I. & Flinders, M. (eds) *Multi-level Governance*. Oxford University Press. doi.org/10.1093/0199259259.003.0005

Price, R., Thoms, M., Capon, S. & Watkins, D. (2009). *Lake Eyre Basin Rivers Assessment Implementation Plan Project Final Report*. Lake Eyre Basin Ministerial Forum, www.lakeeyrebasin.gov.au/resources/publications [Accessed: 22/1/2015].

Smith, D.I. (1998). *Water in Australia: Resources and Management.* Oxford University Press, Melbourne.

Termeer, C.J.A.M., Dewulf, A. & van Lieshout, M. (2010). Disentangling Scale Approaches in Governance Research: comparing monocentric, multilevel, and adaptive governance. *Ecology and Society*, 15(4): 29. doi.org/10.5751/es-03798-150429

URS (2007). *Review of the Lake Eyre Basin Intergovernmental Agreement.* Prepared for the Commonwealth Department of Environment and Water Resources, Canberra, www.lakeeyrebasin. gov.au/sitecollectionimages/resources/2ab8837c-e4aa-48a0-ab67-586004b57be5/files/review-final-report.pdf [Accessed: 20/10/17].

Part 4: Environmental and Agricultural Policy

14

Natural Resource Management as a Form of Multi-level Governance: The Impact of Reform in Queensland and Tasmania

Allan Dale, Sarah Ryan and Kathleen Broderick

Introduction

Australia's multi-level system for the governance of natural resources has changed significantly in the last 40 years. In this context, we refer to multiple levels of governance across spatial scales (as per Cash et al. 2006). We also refer to the 'governance system' to describe the complex array of multiple players (from organisations to individuals) and the decision-making and influence they exert within and across different spatial levels from the site to the global level. While Parker and Braithwaite (2003) refer to governance as the 'intentional shaping of the flow of events so as to realise desired public good', we consider that the shaping is done in both the public and private sectors, and that both public and private outcomes might be achieved through our nation's governance system.

It is important to note that, as a definable part of the nation's wider governance system, no single individual or organisation is in charge of Australia's natural resource governance system. It is the interactions between many independent decision-makers and the decisions they make that determine the nation's natural resource outcomes. While we also cannot forget the interactions between the nation's (social and economic) governance systems and our natural resource governance system, these are not the focus of this chapter. Equally, global-level governance also has significant implications for natural resource outcomes in Australia, though, again, we do not specifically consider the influence of governance at the global level in this chapter.

Natural resources comprise the wide range of biotic and abiotic features provided by nature and used by human society as ecosystem services. These services underpin our social and economic wellbeing as a species. Key natural resources include assets like water, air, soil, minerals, energy, plants and animals and the ecosystem processes that result from interactions between them. Humans value these resources in different, and sometimes competing, ways. These values range from specific utilitarian uses of economic import to a wide range of social, cultural and spiritual values. It should be stressed, however, that these resources also have intrinsic value and many would argue that society has additional, non-anthropocentric stewardship responsibilities for supporting their existence.

Poor natural resource health limits the human potential of Australian society, as natural resources underpin our economy. Consequently, to manage the sustainable use of these resources and to balance competing natural resource values, several reviews and changing governance arrangements have emerged at national, state, regional, local and property levels over the past three decades (e.g. Commonwealth of Australia 1999; Keogh et al. 2006; Australian Government 2011a). More explicit alignment of planning and delivery efforts within these arrangements and between these levels has also been emerging. In this context, this chapter does not repeat the backgrounding to multi-level governance (MLG) concepts outlined in the introductory chapter in this book, but explores and enriches them in a case example.

At the regional level, regional natural resource management (NRM) bodies play a particularly important, but not an exclusive or independent role, in integrating decision-making. There are 56 such bodies across the nation. They are constituted by a variety of methods (usually statutory or community-based) and their core roles include the development and monitoring of regional NRM plans and the collaborative development and implementation of major delivery programs. The emergence of regional NRM bodies over the last 20 years has sparked much more national, regional and local debate about how aspects of NRM governance in Australia work and how they could be continuously improved.

In 2010, the collective of regional NRM bodies (NRM Regions Australia) drew attention to the fact that no one body or institution monitors the health of the Australian NRM governance system as a whole, or takes responsibility for developing a clear vision and driving reforms that would improve its performance. Governance changes at different levels often occur without reference to a broader systemic context. Operating between large governments and small communities, regional NRM bodies are particularly affected by changes both above and below them in scalar terms.

In this chapter, we take as a starting point a recommended set of NRM governance principles that emerged from research undertaken by NRM Regions Australia (Ryan et al. 2010). We then relate the history of changes to the Australian system over the last 30 years or so, and assess the revealed trajectories in terms of these identified principles. The impact of those trajectories on regional NRM bodies is explored in two case regions – Queensland's Wet Tropics and southern Tasmania – enabling us to explore systemic reforms that would enhance our multi-level NRM system.

While the ideas considered in this chapter have emerged from discussions amongst regional NRM bodies and other stakeholders in the NRM system, the views expressed are those of the authors alone. We hope that these thoughts may spark wider academic, government and community discussion about the future of Australia's broader multi-level NRM governance system, as this system underpins the capacity of the nation to secure its longer-term economic and social sustainability.

Principles for a healthy multi-level NRM governance system

The principles that form the starting basis for our analysis were developed by taking a complex systems approach to the governance of natural resources in Australia. By drawing on an extensive literature from research and practice, Ryan et al. (2010) deduced 10 principles that could be used to assess the functional health of our multi-layered system and guide future system changes.

The basis for analysing NRM governance in Australia as a system came from the concepts and theory of complex systems behaviour and the observation that NRM governance has many characteristics of such systems. Principally, these systems have many interconnected and multi-layered component parts and their behaviour as a whole is shaped largely by interactions between layers and components within layers. Cause and effect relationships are not linear, and outcomes cannot be confidently predicted from knowledge of the component parts. Simple interventions often do not work. In the context of NRM governance, the system as a whole includes both the social system (the source of governance) and the natural resource system (the target of governance). In such a systemic context, natural resource governance was considered to be inclusive of the many ways in which decisions that influence natural resources are made: from government policies, legislation and funded implementation programs, to community, industry, traditional owner and farmer actions.

An insight from taking an Australia-wide systems view of NRM governance was that the interconnections between components of the governance system (particularly at different levels) are sometimes weak. There are many organisations involved but they often make decisions independently, with relatively little regard for how the outcomes of that decision will interact in the decision space of others. Another consequence of framing NRM governance as a multi-level system reveals that no single organisation takes responsibility for the design/integrated working of all the components as a whole.

The principles for good health of the NRM governance system were found to be:

- **Continuity:** the need to maintain an enduring country-wide planning and delivery infrastructure based on local skills and social capital that is stable in the medium term, but supported to change and adapt in the longer term.

- **Subsidiarity:** the need to devolve decision-making to the lowest capable level for achieving the job required in order to better engage people, but also to preserve strong roles for governments in providing direction, standards, guidelines, incentives and sanctions.

- **Integration:** the need for alignment of different organisational goals up, down and across levels to ensure they account for interactions in ecosystem processes and trade-offs between ecosystem services.

- **Holism:** the need to place all activities within an holistic context (e.g. not undertaking water planning in isolation from biodiversity planning).

- **System-orientation:** the need to match governance mechanisms to the systemic complexity of the social–ecological system under consideration. Simpler mechanisms can be used where linkages between cause and effect are clear. More nuanced and adaptive mechanisms need to be applied in more complex situations. Additionally, the time scale for change in different contexts needs to be matched to social capacity to absorb change.

- **Relationship orientation:** the need for recognition that relationships between organisations and individuals are important in harnessing synergies across the system.

- **Resilience:** the need to manage for resilience of ecosystems and communities. This requires the use of knowledge of ecosystem dynamics to better target investments to the slow controlling variables that determine ecosystem structure and function.

- **Knowledge and innovation:** the need to equip the governance system with skills, capacity and knowledge and encourage innovation, including in the governance system itself.

- **Accountability:** the need to ensure accountability of key players at all levels in the system based on sound systems data, knowledge and effective reporting.

- **Adaptability:** the whole Australian NRM governance system needs regular review/adaptation.

Articulating these system principles provides us with some theoretical logic in the following section for exploring and analysing the health of Australia's NRM governance system from a regional perspective between 2010 and 2015. We then provide a case study analysis of how decisions at higher levels impact on NRM outcomes in regions. This enables us to consider potential national reforms to the current MLG system that might assist the Australian Government to continue to strengthen the system at national level, while being conscious of the multi-level nature of the system.

Evolution of Australia's national NRM governance system

The foundations of MLG for integrated NRM have been steadily building across Australia over the last four decades. Before the 1970s, state/territory governments, local governments, industries and landholders took the majority of natural resource decisions with little attention to some of the key principles for systemic health such as integration, holism and systems orientation. In particular, the limited systemic focus resulted in undesired environmental impacts arising from poor NRM, producing key pressure points within Australian society.

Consequently, from the 1970s on, when environmental issues (particularly water and air pollution) began to have a higher profile, the predominant state/territory government response to NRM problems was to introduce compliance-oriented regulation (Gunningham 2009). Over the same period, landholders (the people managing most of the nation's natural resources) began to come together at the local scale to embrace a new, or to articulate an existing, ethic of local stewardship (Lockie and Vanclay 1997). This became known as the nation's Landcare movement.

With respect to the relative balance between regulatory, market-based and voluntary efforts, most state/territory governments and the Australian Government have primarily used regulation to address key NRM problems such as soil degradation, excessive land clearing and the overallocation of water. While this has achieved many sound environmental outcomes, it has come at an economic and social cost to the rural and remote communities that manage these resources (Productivity Commission 2003). While achieving environmental outcomes, regulating tree clearing in previously undeveloped but productive areas, for example, can and does impact on future economic development opportunities for particular landholders and communities. In the long term, however, the future of extensive biodiversity, water management and landscape-scale biosequestration/ greenhouse gas abatement activities in Australia will largely depend on the role of privately managed lands. Effective management of these lands, in turn, depends on landholders valuing and managing multiple ecosystem services in the landscape (Commonwealth of Australia 2009; Ostrom and Cox 2010).

Additionally, regulatory protection of the landscape alone does not generate the financial resources needed to manage and restore natural systems and their ecosystem services. State-based legislation to protect vegetation from clearing, for example, does little at the local scale to prevent biodiversity decline resulting from poor grazing practices, weed encroachment, altered fire regimes and feral animal pests (van de Koppel and Reitkerk 2000). In a sense, as a blunt tool, regulation itself has tended to become the baseline for management, providing little incentive for improved practices. Theoretically, using regulation in this way has been seen as a panacea: the application of a single solution to a multi-dimensional problem with potentially unsuccessful and socially divisive results (Ostrom and Cox 2010). This again highlights the importance of the systems and relationship-orientation principles.

Some sense of regional or catchment-scale coordination of emerging regulatory and/or voluntary activities began developing separately in individual states from the 1980s via the birth of diverse types of integrated catchment management groups. A key theme within these groups was the development and implementation of integrated catchment management plans, developed with strong community input and encompassing strategies and support for coordinated on-ground action. This formalised fledgling initiatives within different layers in the system (e.g. at national, state and local levels) and established the foundations for some limited continuity in the relationship between these layers. At this stage, governments across the nation increasingly applied some program-based funding to support integrated catchment management and grassroots landcare delivery.

The fragmented foundations of strong regulatory and weak grants-based approaches in the 1980s and 1990s, however, failed to stem public exposure of several latent natural resource crises, including the insidious creep of dryland salinity and its impacts on infrastructure and agricultural productivity (Australian Government 2001), the collapsing health of Australia's most productive river (MDBA 2010) and the increasing threat of poor water quality in the Great Barrier Reef lagoon (Australian Government and Queensland Government 2009). State-based regulatory approaches to several landscape-scale issues, such as tree clearing, also triggered vocal rural resistance and declining community trust in governments (e.g. see Productivity Commission 2003).

High-profile policy problems of this kind exposed the need for Australia to pay more attention to bigger-picture (holistic) strategic and integrative issues facing the sustainability of the nation's rural and remote landscapes. This led to a distinct shift in thinking about natural resource governance about 20 years ago (Commonwealth of Australia 1999). The combined result was that, from around the turn of this century, the then federal Coalition Government began to be more involved in NRM in agricultural and more remote Indigenous landscapes. The shift aimed to secure a move from a geopolitically (e.g. state by state) and sectorally (e.g. water versus biodiversity) fragmented approach towards a more systemic and integrated national framework, albeit one informed by emerging approaches to integrated catchment management in the states (Dale et al. 2008). This new approach aimed to improve aspects of the nation's natural resource governance system (McDonald and Weston 2004) by focusing on enhancing connectivity among decision-makers (i.e. the relationship principle) and improving the knowledge use, capacity-building and organisational health within organisations (at different levels) to strengthen planning, implementation, monitoring and evaluation (i.e. subsidiarity).

By the early 2000s, the new thinking was formalised through bilateral arrangements between state/territory and Australian governments regarding the delivery of the Natural Heritage Trust and National Action Plan for Salinity and Water Quality. These formally negotiated federal–state government arrangements spearheaded important reforms in the delivery of community-based NRM through strategic investment at a regional scale where regional NRM bodies (i.e. groups that could demonstrably represent viewpoints from across their communities) would develop regional NRM plans. The planning process required securing regional consensus on aspirational and resource condition targets across a wide range of natural assets and community sectors (including agricultural, conservation and Indigenous).

NRM bodies were largely governed by boards with broad combinations of skills that reflected the viewpoints of these different regional sectors. Regional investment strategies developed by the community focused on motivating and engaging landholders to avoid further damage, repair past mistakes and to continuously improve their management practices. Programs and projects were delivered by a variety of complementary partner organisations, such as landcare groups, industry bodies, non-government organisations, traditional owners, state/territory governments, local councils or consultants (often via complex and durable partnerships). Landholders and managers often elected to become part of the NRM process through voluntary extension or incentive programs. Collaborative local projects were encouraged and resources provided to implement priority actions.

Regions, in the context of these new arrangements, generally referred to a sub-provincial geopolitical scale considered appropriate to the effective landscape-scale management of natural resources. Some 56 such regions were defined, mostly based on definable agro-ecological regions that formed a sensible management scale in biophysical, social and administrative terms. There was also often some synergy with biogeographic boundaries (Commonwealth of Australia 2004). Others were based on significant catchments (e.g. the Fitzroy Basin) or sub-catchments (e.g. the Condamine region) or even political–administrative units (e.g. the Northern Territory or the Australian Capital Territory).

Under these community-based arrangements, regional NRM bodies were designated by state, territory and federal governments on the basis of their emerging capacity to deliver effective natural resource programs and to engage the majority of the regional community's interests in the development and implementation of regional NRM plans. Regional NRM plans were jointly accredited by state, territory and federal governments and comprised scientifically informed, but regionally negotiated, targets and priorities. These targets comprised time-bound 'resource condition targets' (e.g. halt and reverse the decline of water quality into the Barrier Reef Lagoon by 2020) and associated 'management action targets' (e.g. rehabilitate 25 kilometres of a region's riparian zone by 2015). These plans reflected nationally consistent priorities (e.g. water-quality improvement) and common approaches to target-setting, but focused their attention on addressing regional priorities. Once accredited by federal and state/territory government agencies, plans formed the basis for investment in identified strategic actions from governments, local government, the community and private sectors.

Essentially, NRM carried out at the regional scale and using NRM planning processes that sought consensus and alignment of effort aimed to contribute to sustainable regional and rural development by integrating environmental policies through on-ground implementation (Williams et al. 2005). The regional NRM bodies, with varying degrees of capacity, developed the deep reach into the catchment, local government, landcare and landholder-based delivery systems required to achieve complex project management and on-the-ground outcomes. There remained also the potential for regions to be able to report on progress on the achievement of targets in a nationally consistent way. Integration with wider regional economic and social development and land-use planning processes was also encouraged.

In the early years, the transition to the new structures and processes posed difficulties in some regions (Farrelly 2005). Implementation of this new national framework had varying strengths and weaknesses across different regions (Lane et al. 2009). Generally, however, it resulted in a shift towards more devolved regional approaches that achieved more integrated NRM (i.e. the application of the subsidiarity principle). With respect to the other governance systems principles articulated earlier, broad themes in systemic improvements that arose from this new approach have included:

- strengthening the scientific basis for decision-making at regional scale, including the integration of the social, economic and environmental sciences (knowledge and innovation)
- experimentation with the establishment of a clear bilateral framework between federal and state/territory governments to mobilise this national approach and to share investment (relationship orientation)
- an increasing level of cross-sectoral collaboration in determining strategic purpose and the alignment and mobilisation of the efforts of multiple parties (relationship orientation)
- progress towards clearer national targets with respect to securing the health of natural resources and a strong focus on monitoring longer-term condition and trend in the health of natural resources, reflecting an outcomes-based approach to investment (accountability)
- increasing the adaptive and longer-term capacity for decision-making of all sectors with a role to play in planning and delivering NRM outcomes (adaptability)
- continuous improvement through joint accreditation of the target-based regional NRM plans and joint designation (an authority to act) of NRM bodies to guide the management of national and state/territory investment at regional scale (adaptability and accountability).

The key role of regional NRM bodies that emerged from these new national governance mechanisms included an increase in coordinated and collaborative action between sectors to resolve local and regional natural resource problems. This played out through enhanced:

- facilitation of local conflict resolution between the agricultural sector and other key sectors such as conservation, urban, mining, tourism, local government and Indigenous interests
- collective planning to review and jointly understand the available natural resource science and the development of jointly agreed targets for improving resource condition and trend
- development of collaborative projects aimed at securing agreed targets
- collective monitoring of resource condition and trend over time.

By and large, the increase in decentralisation of decision-making closer to the local and regional community increased Australia's adaptive capacity to manage natural resources by matching the scale of governance required with the scale of ecological and social processes that need to be mobilised (see Folke et al. 2010). Not all sectors experienced an even distribution of devolved power or appropriate resources, however – for example, the Indigenous sector or the central Australian region. To achieve such an outcome would require a longer-term, target-focused, landscape-scale effort across the nation (e.g. consider the continuity principle). The general national move towards a more nuanced and multi-layered approach, however, in comparison to the blunt and fragmented regulatory resource-use regimes of the past, was a significant governance advance. An integrated NRM framework of this kind, because it was to be focused over long time frames, could be seen to be more resilient in the face of change and shocks compared to remotely managed and fragmented programs (e.g. Folke et al. 2010).

Despite these advances, however, in 2007 a newly elected federal Labor Government, through its new Caring for Our Country program, retreated from a policy-oriented bilateral approach with state and territory governments. It also moved away from fostering the progressive development and continuous improvement of regional NRM plans and longer-term investment based on regional approaches that were continuously refined through outcomes-focused monitoring, evaluation and review. While it did adopt more devolved approaches in Indigenous domains and in some priority regions (e.g. within Great Barrier Reef catchments), and refocused the geographic distribution of resources, it generally moved towards setting short-term national targets via an annual Caring for Our Country Business Plan and running linked competitive grant funding programs to support cross-regional, regional and local initiatives that could deliver on the national priorities. These changes in direction, in part, resulted from Australian Government responses to:

- pressure from various national interests in the conservation sector to alter the approach
- the high transaction costs associated with policy-oriented bilateral negotiations with state and territory governments
- the findings of the Australian National Audit Office that reporting from the key programs was 'insufficient to make an informed judgment as to the progress of the programs towards either outcomes or intermediate outcomes' (ANAO 2008).

Across the nation, many regional NRM bodies concurred with the findings of ANAO (2008) and, indeed, had long been contending that more outcomes-focused (both nationally coordinated and regionally informed) monitoring systems were required. This chapter's case studies, however, suggest that those changes in the nation's governance system have had significant implications for the effectiveness of NRM governance at the regional scale and that systemic, MLG principles were not applied in the policy redesign phase.

Cumulatively across the decades, however, progressive Australia-wide reforms in our natural resource governance system have coincidentally established a good foundation for guiding tradable markets in ecosystem services and emerging markets in terrestrial carbon biosequestration for greenhouse gas abatement (van Oosterzee et al. 2010). Consequently, new developments in reform in the nation's multi-level NRM governance system in 2010 included the then federal Labor Government reviewing the role of regional NRM plans and recognising them as a plank within its recently announced Clean Energy Future initiative. The initiative included a wide range of activities that support not only the reduction of emissions and new renewable technologies, but also the harnessing of old and new ways of thinking about securing landscape resilience and managing/storing carbon in our landscapes. In particular, the initiative allocated $1.7 billion to facilitate land-sector abatement, including $44 million to revitalise the nation's regional NRM plans, with the view that they support landscape-scale adaptation and guide the emergence of the nation's land sector–based carbon market.[1] The then government also made it clear that reinvigorated NRM planning necessarily would need to sit within a wider national framework for both regional development and NRM management.

Since the election of the federal Coalition Government in late 2013, there are early signs of a shift back towards more devolved approaches to NRM. Hence, the balance of this paper focuses its analytical attention and reform-based conclusions on the governance system as it operated up to that time. This means that our analysis may offer some considered guidance with regard to an emerging new phase of reform in the national governance system.

Regional roles in the Australian NRM governance system: Perspectives from Queensland's Wet Tropics and southern Tasmania

To explore how these systemic health principles might or might not have been working in late 2013 from a regional perspective within Australia's multi-level NRM governance system, we used two cases: one from Queensland's Wet Tropics and one from Tasmania's southern region. These case study lessons have drawn largely from the experience and observations of two of the authors. In the Wet Tropics case, Allan Dale has previously operated both as the state government co-chair of the Commonwealth/state government joint NRM steering committee (2001–05) and as CEO of Terrain NRM, the regional NRM body for the Wet Tropics (2005–10). With respect to the Tasmanian case study, Kathleen Broderick has previously operated as the CEO of NRM South since 2009. Additionally, through the interaction of all three authors with the National Chairs Working Group and the national group of CEOs of regional NRM bodies, we believe our findings are largely in accord with those of other regions across the nation.

---

1   See for example: www.climatechange.gov.au/reducing-carbon/carbon-farming-initiative/carbon-farming-initiative-handbook/clean-energy-future [Accessed: 24/12/2014].

Queensland's Wet Tropics region

This region, of about 2 million hectares, comprises conservation, tropical agriculture, urban, tourism, rural residential development and Indigenous land uses (see Dale et al. 2008). Traditional owners (including some 18 different tribal groups) have a mix of historical, cultural and legal interests in all lands in the region. The most productive land is privately owned, while the more rugged parts are mainly leasehold, state forest or national park. Most of the forest in these areas is contained and protected within the Wet Tropics World Heritage Area. Agriculture is the main productive land use with nearly 130,000 hectares under sugar cane, about 25,000 hectares under horticulture, 20,000 hectares under dairy and 700,000 hectares under extensive pastoralism. Improved pastures for grazing account for about 65,000 hectares. In the coastal areas, the main crops are sugar cane and bananas. Extensive grazing is the main land use in the drier, western parts of the region. Forestry has declined in recent times, although rainforest vegetation covers about 95,000 hectares of freehold land. The main land-use trends include ongoing sugar farming and horticultural activities (e.g. bananas and tropical fruits), livestock intensification, private forestry, aquaculture and urban and peri-urban expansion. The balance between the region's primary crops fluctuates over time depending on commodity prices (McDonald and Weston 2004).

The region incorporates most of Queensland's Wet Tropics World Heritage Area (around 1.2 million hectares) and all catchments in the Wet Tropics also flow into the lagoon of the Great Barrier Reef, another world heritage asset of international significance. Consequently, tourism, based on the integrity of the region's world heritage assets and rural landscape, ensures an active regional debate about the need for integrated management of multiple ecosystem services. Losses of agricultural sediments, nutrients and pesticides, apart from diminishing productivity, reduce the resilience of reef ecosystems, while clearing for agricultural expansion competes with the protection of terrestrial world heritage values and the viability of economically important and iconic species, such as the cassowary.

In the last two decades, there has been a particular Queensland Government focus on regulating land management practices to reduce nutrient, sediment and chemical run-off into the reef. Vegetation management has also been heavily regulated. From 2001 onwards, however, the region's NRM plan set agreed foundations for resource condition targets being achieved through a wider range of management actions, particularly landholder-driven practice changes and incentive-driven approaches, largely coordinated and supported by the region's NRM body, Terrain NRM.

It is expected that, in the coming decade, many of those activities conducted by landholders that are consistent with the regional NRM plan's management action targets could also further drive the achievement of resource condition targets through greenhouse gas (biosequestration and abatement) trading, earning investment for the landholders undertaking best practice activities within the landscape. In turn, this market-based incentive would contribute to reducing deforestation and soil and water degradation, increasing reforestation and improving agricultural community and industry uptake of best-management practices. Wider adoption of these practices would enhance the capacity of the region to secure the resource condition targets agreed to in the regional NRM plan.

Southern Tasmanian region

The southern Tasmanian NRM region covers some 2.5 million hectares and comprises diverse ecosystems, from rugged coastlines and offshore islands to mountainous terrain, powerful river systems, highlands, forests and grasslands. The region includes five Interim Biogeographic Regionalisation of Australia regions and three Ramsar wetlands. These varied and significant ecosystems provide habitat for many endemic species, such as the swift parrot and the iconic Tasmanian devil. It is a region renowned for its natural values in that they support productive horticulture, fine wool, lamb production and sought-after nature- and culture-based tourism opportunities.

The region's population of approximately 250,000 is centred on Hobart, the state capital, and is also distributed in small towns and hamlets. There are 12 local government areas in southern Tasmania and many of these councils are key partners in NRM delivery.

Southern Tasmanians are active volunteers and there are over 100 local community groups caring for bushland, coastal areas and cultural heritage in the region. Local community groups are also active advocates for the conservation of natural resources. The Indigenous community is actively involved in land management and cultural interpretation of the landscape. Much of the region is protected in reserves, including the Tasmanian

Wilderness World Heritage area, Macquarie Island World Heritage Area, seven national parks and six marine reserves. Significantly, just 5 per cent of the region's land managers manage 75 per cent of the productive land.

Trends in natural resource–based economic activity include increasing lamb production, increased cherry and wine production and increased horticulture and aquaculture. In addition, there has been recent investment in the expansion of existing irrigation schemes and the development of new irrigation areas in Tasmania. While forestry in Tasmania has been a highly politicised issue, and the industry has recently been in decline, it is likely to continue into the future as an important part of the region's economy. Increasingly, residential development and subdivisions on the east coast threaten natural values, as do the effects of climate change, including increasing storm frequency, sea-level rise and associated coastal erosion. Southern Tasmania is a 'hot spot' for climate change effects and the region has benefited from the extensive science community located there. Natural resource managers are increasingly also seeking to adapt to changing conditions and make the most of biosequestration opportunities.

The regional NRM approach has been adopted in Tasmania more recently than elsewhere in Australia, with three statutory NRM regions being established in 2002. The regions work closely with federal, state and local governments to deliver coordinated NRM. The first regional strategy for southern Tasmania was developed in 2005 and was subsequently reviewed in 2010.

Continuity, subsidiarity and integration: Long-term commitments to continuous improvement

In 2013, regional NRM bodies in both case study regions were a key point of long-term integrated NRM planning, coordinated effort alignment and delivery coordination, and they played an important role in the adaptive management of those more intractable natural resource problems that rely on institutional stability for their progressive resolution (e.g. halting and reversing biodiversity decline or improving water quality). The Australian Government's 2007 retreat from a longer-term systemic approach to the introduction of the more annualised and output-focused Caring for Our Country program initially heralded great financial uncertainty for regional bodies *and* delivery partners in both regions. This was only partially resolved by the Australian Government eventually committing some 60 per cent of stable pre-2007 investment as guaranteed funding via regional NRM bodies and their delivery partners.

The swing in Australian Government support away from (and now back towards) integrated regionalism and continuously improving regional NRM arrangements over the previous five years temporarily reduced institutional stability and increased financial and policy uncertainty in the short- to medium-term in both regions. In the Wet Tropics, while Terrain NRM fared well under the new national competitive system under the Caring for Our Country program (e.g. securing significant Reef Rescue funding), from 2007 there was a parallel short-term collapse in stable investment for other key areas (e.g. biodiversity, pest management and Indigenous land and sea management). It is also worth noting that the region's capacity to secure Reef Rescue funds was, in part, a legacy from the stable institutional arrangements operating pre–Caring for Our Country.

Additionally, in both states, the Australian Government's shift away from bilateralism had the potential to leave the regions more vulnerable to shifting policy environments within the state government.

In the Wet Tropics, introduction of the Caring for Our Country program also stalled progressive improvements in the development of regionally cohesive delivery systems in local government, the conservation sector, in Indigenous and the landcare and catchment management sectors. On the other hand, time-bound programmatic funding (with a specific investment horizon) via the Reef Rescue Program improved capability in the agricultural sector. This gain in capacity could, however, suffer setbacks in the absence of more modest and longer-term regional attention to improving delivery arrangements post–Reef Rescue, even though significantly improving reef water quality will be a multi-decadal enterprise.

In both regions, continued state government support for regional NRM has acted as a buffer against the changes to Australian Government programs. The commitment to regions and regional planning, while only minimally resourced by the states, provided some continuity. This, however, is not a uniform national picture, with some states stepping back from the regional model.

In solving longer-term natural resource problems, Australia's NRM governance arrangements will need to more reliably apply the subsidiarity principle, avoiding the 'roller-coaster' effect in investment in key assets and the 'lucky dip' effect in investment between different asset areas. Indeed, a longer-term, albeit modest, commitment to a holistic, regionally driven and bilaterally mobilised NRM framework would be needed to progress the delivery of the wider range of management actions required to achieve the national outcomes envisaged under programs like Caring For Our Country.

Holism, system orientation, relationship orientation and resilience: The national value of regional NRM plan development, coordination and effort mobilisation

Perhaps one of the greatest regional implications of the federal Labor Government departing from structured bilateralism and the support for continuous improvement in regional NRM plan development and accreditation has been the significant retraction of the resources levered from other investors on the basis of the Australian Government's regional investment. This has reduced the purchasing power of federal and state government dollars for NRM action because local in-kind and cash investment became more difficult to attract and to retain in short-term and *ad hoc* projects. The shift to a nationally competitive grants-based approach (albeit with strategic regional guidance) diminished collaborative approaches in both regions and made strong priority-setting processes and the development of durable delivery systems less effective.

Under Caring for Our Country, the importance of regional NRM plans was diminished. Consequently, this diminished the influence of regional communities in setting federal and state government investment priorities in both case regions. The decline of federal/state bilateralism saw the Queensland Government withdraw significant investment from regional NRM, retreating to much narrower annual financial commitments. Towards the end of 2013, the implications in both regions had included:

- less alignment between state and federal government policy and investment priorities
- reduced state government investment via regional NRM bodies

- diminished alignment of local government, industry and community investment against agreed targets and government investment
- declining collaborative effort among major regional institutions, including state agencies, regional NRM bodies, statutory authorities, research institutions and voluntary regional organisations of councils. Increased competition increased the transaction costs facing all parties in securing investment, with no consequent increase in funding availability
- declining delivery capability within many NRM players involved in planning and delivery.

In the Wet Tropics and in southern Tasmania, for example, a retreat from bilateralism and coordinated regionalism significantly increased the overall transaction costs within regional communities, with multiple parties in all sectors having to spend considerable resources on developing project proposals with low success ratios. The transaction cost for communities developing multiple, poorly coordinated proposals increased, thereby reducing the cost-effectiveness of investment in the region.

From a Wet Tropics perspective, project decision-making became highly centralised, resulting in far less efficient decision-making and poorer regional-scale integration of multiple investments. The capacity of the regional NRM bodies in both regions to align strategic state government effort declined as a result. Cross-departmental coordination of effort (previously arranged through the state's regional coordination groups) evaporated, further marginalising the influence of regional institutions in policymaking.

Reforms in 2010/11 under the Clean Energy Futures framework were of great significance, as they had the potential to result in ecosystem service markets and products of international standing. It was envisaged that enhancing and updating the regional NRM plans had the potential to attract and guide these emerging ecosystem service markets, and that these in turn could become transformative in the way that they could support the agricultural and land-use sectors to trade in greenhouse gas abatement and other complimentary ecosystem services (like biodiversity) within their enterprises. Importantly, enabling mitigation and abatement activities to become ecosystem service commodities would have also allowed the regional model to adjust to climate change and its impacts rather than letting these highly vulnerable regions be overwhelmed by it. Consequently, under the current federal Coalition Government, regional

NRM plans in both regions have been upgraded and revitalised in recent years as a regionalised framework for guiding investment under the nation's currently unfolding Carbon Farming Initiative (see van Oosterzee et al. 2012).

In both regions, potential biosequestration and greenhouse gas abatement activities (most securing a range of multiple ecosystem service benefits) include avoided deforestation, avoided degradation, reforestation using native species and agricultural land management through increasing soil carbon, pasture cover and fertiliser-use reduction. Using an enhanced regional NRM plan (with spatially specific, regional priorities for action and practice improvement) that meets standards agreed at the national and state level is expected to provide a strategic framework for the aggregation of carbon sequestration activities for the market. This will enable the delivery of complementary biodiversity, agriculture, water quality and community benefits (Wentworth Group 2008). Ongoing and adaptive refinement of the regional NRM plan over time will further enhance its efficacy in guiding the market. Next generation NRM plans, for example, will need greater spatial detail. As such a cohesive national and state commitment to continuous improvement in regional NRM is required now more than ever.

Innovation and accountability: Collaborative research and knowledge management

Without systemic knowledge brokerage and collaborative regional research frameworks, federal government and state investment in NRM research and development tends to be strongly researcher or funding agency driven. This reduces the regional impact of research and its ability to be strategically applied to long-term natural resource decision-making. From 2006 to 2010, the Wet Tropics region was well supported by a cohesive research program run through the Reef and Rainforest Research Corporation (RRRC), an independent research broker funded through the Australian Government's Marine and Tropical Sciences Research Facility. The RRRC's governance arrangements effectively represented and involved both researchers *and* regional end-users. Under these arrangements, the RRRC involved regional end-users in determining research priorities, selecting priority projects, project oversight and uptake. Indeed, as a precursor to the RRRC model, the region's original

Rainforest Cooperative Research Centre informed the regional NRM planning process. The arrangements were crucial in the development and implementation of major investments, such as the Reef Rescue Program.

After 2010, the federal Labor Government tended to centralise control and management of significant regional NRM and environment research programs, although broad regional consultation arrangements did remain in place. In the experience of the Far North Queensland region's four NRM bodies, this new approach focused more on better informing the Australian Government with regard to the operation of the *Environment Protection and Biodiversity Conservation Act 1999*. As a result, these regions consider that this represented a shift from well-negotiated and more regionalised program-based partnerships towards more fragmented and centralised project end-user relationships. In their view, this created higher transaction costs for regional communities, and regional NRM bodies were consequently less able to inform the development and monitoring of their internal programs with well-engaged science management arrangements. They also considered that this approach had reduced the capacity of their regional communities to influence policy and investment decisions affecting NRM in the north. Such observations concerning the importance of regionalised and localised knowledge brokerage arrangements are reflected in the findings of Petit et al. (2011) with regard to NRM approaches in Victoria.

Adaptability: Environmental accounts, reporting and adaptive management

The value of establishing a clear national framework for measuring (and responding to) the actual regional (resource condition) outcomes from NRM policy and investment is one of the foundations needed for adaptive management of the nation's natural resources. A national framework could easily be informed, in a consistent way, by aligned approaches across all states and territories and, in turn, across all regions. Apart from such an approach enabling consistent and adaptive regional management systems, it would ensure a high-quality information base for national decision-making.

In the Wet Tropics, by 2013, regional NRM body effort towards reporting on resource condition was affected by the declining policy influence of regional NRM plans, the withdrawal of strategic funding and a government focus on monitoring and evaluating project-level outputs (Australian Government 2011b).

Tasmanian regions had not stopped planning and reporting on their regional strategies and the three Tasmanian regions reviewed and renewed their strategies in 2010. These strategies, however, were developed in the absence of a national accounting system and before the identification of greenhouse gas abatement opportunities required updating to accommodate the expanded role.

From a regional perspective, making and maintaining a cohesive, science-driven and evidence-based argument about the condition and trend of critical natural resources greatly empowers the capacity of regions to devise effective solutions that might enable a policy change or investment response from governments. It also helps mobilise the inherent efforts of the region's key land managers.

Between 2007 and 2010, there was a shift away from building a nationally integrated resource condition monitoring framework that has clear mechanisms for influencing policy and investment. National monitoring frameworks for key assets were progressing (e.g. water and vegetation) through fragmented effort, and this weakened the capacity of both case study regions to influence state and national policy and investment agenda. It also made it more difficult to mobilise and motivate cohesive regional and local efforts with regard to aligning critical natural resource actions. Additionally, a less-focused national framework resulted in a decline in coordinative effort within the states with regard to holistic resource condition and trend monitoring. This had the potential to lead to a reactive regional governance culture. Being reactive versus proactive to major issues once they emerge would also increase the cost of the responses required.

Within both regions, Caring for Our Country focused more effort on fragmented, multiple project–based investments in monitoring and evaluation research. Many of these project-based approaches were poorly integrated, short-term and often did not contribute well to the building of a strong evidence-based case regarding regional natural resource decline. It could have been that more money was being spent on monitoring and evaluation work, with less influence on improving the tractability of critical NRM problems. Progressing towards a more strategic resource condition monitoring framework would have been cheaper and more effective than a focus on multiple, project-oriented approaches at the regional scale.

In recognition of these issues, since 2007, collaborative, pilot-based work on monitoring and reporting regional natural resource condition and trend within a national accounting context has been progressing in partnership between regional NRM bodies and the Wentworth Group of Concerned Scientists. This could form the basis for positive new thinking and development in this area.

Improving MLG: Potential national reforms to enhance outcomes at regional and local scales

The above illustrates that, over the last few decades, there has been dramatic maturation in Australia's multi-level framework for the governance of natural resources. While the health of different parts of the system may have waxed and waned along the chronology of events explored, overall the system now sets a strong foundation for sustainable governance of our resources in the longer term. Our intent here is to inform directions for continuous improvement rather than to simply articulate system weaknesses. Consequently, based on principles articulated in Ryan et al. (2010), through observations from the above case studies, and through the involvement of regional NRM bodies across Australia, we outline below several high-level reforms that are needed for a healthier and more integrated national multi-level NRM governance system to emerge.

A more enduring national NRM infrastructure

We consider that a more enduring infrastructure would build upon the principles of subsidiarity, integration, holism, relationship orientation, innovation, accountability and adaptiveness. To avoid our national system oscillating from one governance approach to another, we consider that it is important for both the federal and state/territory governments to commit to long-term and durable NRM arrangements at national, state, regional and local scales.

First, we recommend better integration of strategic natural resource management issues within ministerial council arrangements under Australia's Council of Australian Governments (COAG) arrangements. At present, there remains the potential for fragmentation in the treatment of integrated NRM issues across the federal, state, territory and local governments. Consequently, the more integrated consideration of continuous improvements in the nation's NRM governance systems has the potential to fall through the cracks.

A new and effective national institution (or perhaps enhanced scope within the Productivity Commission) is also needed to fill an overview and evaluative gap within our national NRM governance system, particularly given the abolition of the National Water Commission in the 2014/15 Commonwealth budget and the demise of Land and Water Australia in 2009. A lean but independent body established with defined links to COAG arrangements could harness cross-sectoral and academic expertise and provide advice to governments and the Australian people on matters of national NRM interest. It could complement NRM commissions that already exist in some states (e.g. the NSW Natural Resources Commission). Such a body, with a wider and more integrated remit and a focus on the health of our NRM governance system, would provide considerable added value and continuity.

The role of such a body could encompass responsibility for coordinating the monitoring, collection and interpretation of national environmental accounts; setting standards and accrediting NRM service providers; developing national NRM knowledge strategies; coordinating national NRM knowledge activities; commissioning strategic research; providing advice to the Australian Government on national plans and strategies; and monitoring of the nation's overarching NRM governance system and its health. The benefits of an independent body carrying out such roles could include an increase in transparency and trust about NRM decision-making, increasing accountability and enhanced retention of the nation's corporate knowledge concerning such issues. Such an organisation could also be responsible for advocating the integration efforts across disparate policy elements (e.g. NRM and regional development), increasing the stability of some of the key ingredients of good NRM governance and giving public recognition to the importance of building stable NRM infrastructure in Australia.

A national NRM framework and strategy and effort alignment across and within governments

While higher-level strategic policy reform at COAG level is important, it is equally important that there is serious effort taken to lead and integrate improved NRM governance systems across the nation's governments and within the Australian Government's administrative arm. We consider that such reform, in part, addresses the principles of permanence, subsidiarity, integration, holism, relationship orientation, innovation, accountability and adaptability. COAG effort could set the scene for a more outcomes-focused approach (e.g. perhaps via a national NRM framework and strategy) to ensure strategic thinking at the national scale. A national NRM strategy could identify the importance of the nation's assets, set national targets and result in a five- to 10-year integrated investment program for cohesive national and state/territory government Cabinet and Treasury consideration. Such a strategy would need to be genuinely strategic and collectively negotiated with the nation's peak sectors and stakeholders with an interest in NRM.

With a strong framework and strategy in place, effort alignment towards implementation could then focus on mobilising resources within and across governments and aligning the effort of a wide range of industry and community sectors across the nation. A genuinely collaborative Australian NRM framework and strategy would also need to be informed by state/ territory objectives and regional NRM plans (and vice versa) in an iterative fashion. Under such a national NRM framework, key opportunities for targeted policy reform across the nation and within individual states and territories could be pursued via more policy *and* investment-oriented agreements that more directly involve local government.

Such reforms could better guide the Australian Government's contemporary NRM policy and investment funding arrangements in the longer term. Longer-term and outcome-focused national NRM targets could better guide mid–short-term program directions (Caring for Our Country, for example, was just one Australian Government program driven by an annual business plan). Some core, longer-term, flexible state-wide and regional investments need to be retained and enhanced to mobilise more adaptive state government, regional NRM, industry, local government and community capacities. Program and investment alignment across Australian Government agencies would increasingly be required (e.g. water, climate change, drought and disaster assistance, employment programs, Indigenous health).

Additionally, administrative governance for major Australian Government investment programs need greater simplicity and more stable, longer-term contractual delivery systems (e.g. comprise less annual grant-based approaches and more strategic and stable devolved delivery systems that uphold the principles of market-based competitiveness). National programmatic components need to remain for significant cross-jurisdictional and cross-regional agendas where they are better delivered nationally to achieve the nation's agreed priorities. Any community-level grant-based systems that are retained nationally can be strengthened by better aligning them with devolved and integrated regional planning and delivery systems. Finally, a stronger mechanism is needed to bring together Australian Government and state investors with regional NRM bodies to ensure effort is coordinated and benefits maximised.

A framework for integrated regional planning and delivery

This reform, in part, addresses the principles of permanence, subsidiarity, integration, holism, system orientation, relationship orientation, resilience, innovation, accountability and adaptability. Regional NRM bodies are a key component in the nation's NRM infrastructure, but they equally need to be focused on continuous improvement and on strengthening the capacity of key NRM delivery agents at regional, sub-regional and local scale (e.g. landcare groups, industry bodies, Indigenous groups, local government). Regional NRM plans, led and facilitated (but not solely owned) by regional NRM groups, are, in effect, a form of regional-scale strategic environmental assessment. Under an enhanced national NRM framework, the federal and state/territory governments could jointly monitor the health of regional NRM planning and its ability to deliver effective natural resource outcomes. Regional NRM bodies would also need to be more explicitly contracted to play these key planning, effort-mobilisation and capacity-building roles.

Formal federal, state and territory government commitment to progressively improving the standard and effect of regional NRM plans would ensure regional NRM bodies could (see Dale et al. 2013):

- ensure and sustain effective community-wide engagement and capacity building
- effectively undertake regional NRM planning and mobilise community support
- ensure effective partnership development, governance and program delivery
- ensure alignment of national, state and regional priorities
- better align regional NRM plans with statutory land-use plans.

The Australian Government could, by agreement, work with the states to continue to actively support continuous improvement in regional NRM planning and governance. The current system of aspirational, resource condition and management action targets has served regions well to this point and could be continued, taking account of Australian Government planning, state NRM plan and regional plan priorities. This needs to be refined, however, towards an increasing focus on building more resilient landscapes. Most importantly, regional NRM plans should remain the foundation for continuous adaptive management based on regional effort alignment to secure agreed targets, ensuring plan currency and a focus on monitoring plan implementation. Annual regional progress reports could be compiled to keep a focus on target achievement. Regional state of the environment (SoE) or a set of regional natural resource accounts could then influence state and national SoE reporting or accounting systems. State and national SoE reporting or accounting would need to better influence policy-setting and resource allocation within their respective governments than is currently the case.

More collaborative frameworks for research and knowledge management

This reform, in part, addresses the principles of integration, system orientation, relationship orientation, resilience, innovation and adaptability. Stronger alliances between research funders (including Commonwealth environment research facility hubs), state agencies, research providers, regional NRM bodies and other sectors could provide better models for linking more coordinated and brokered NRM research within a stronger strategic governance framework. Research users, such as regional NRM bodies, could have stronger 'purchasing power' through better regional collaborative science partnership and brokerage arrangements, creating additional efficiency with shared research, knowledge and information management at appropriate scales. Increased investment in applied NRM research would increase the evidence base for NRM policy and management at a range of scales across the nation (see Campbell 2005). Since the wind up of the research and development corporation Land and Water Australia there is also no clear national framework for NRM knowledge management and brokerage.

A national system of environmental accounts, reporting and adaptive management

This reform, in part, addresses the principles of integration, holism, accountability and adaptability. Currently, SoE reporting does report on resource condition and pressure indicators for our key natural assets, but there is no clear adaptive framework to identify, implement and evaluate the key actions required (see Wentworth Group 2008). There is also no link between SoE reporting and major direction-setting and resource allocation by Australian and state/territory government cabinets and treasuries. This could be changed by linking the reporting process to the proposed national NRM framework and strategy and via development of a standardised set of national natural resource accounts, perhaps resulting in a major five-year program cycle for Cabinet consideration and the potential for alignment of effort across all sectors (including industry, conservation and landcare).

Such an approach could effectively align effort across existing biodiversity, water and sustainable agriculture programs across federal and state/territory governments. Based on evidence from the national accounts, and coordinated through a national independent NRM body or institution (as mentioned above) and revitalised ministerial council arrangements, a process for continuous improvement in the effectiveness of the nation's NRM governance systems is also required. This could incorporate a strong focus on building a culture of continuous improvement within and among regional NRM bodies. Regional bodies across the nation are increasingly adopting standardised approaches to continuous improvement specifically developed for the NRM sector. Examples of strong emerging approaches can be found in New South Wales, Queensland and South Australia (e.g. Vogel and Zammit 2004). These approaches should continue to be enhanced, supported and coordinated, enabling regional NRM bodies to undergo regular performance reviews focused on continuous improvement and perhaps securing specific investment to facilitate strategic approaches to performance enhancement at the regional scale or collectively.

Conclusions

This chapter has outlined some key principles that are needed to underpin the effective operation of our nation's natural resource governance system at multiple scales. These principles, applicable at any level in the system, include permanence, subsidiarity, integration, holism, system orientation, relationship orientation, resilience, innovation, accountability and adaptability. In this context, we have reviewed the evolution of the current multiple layers that exist within Australia's NRM governance system, but we have focused our attention on the interaction between the national and regional scales. We have intentionally explored these issues from the viewpoint of regional NRM bodies and consider that debate on such reforms needs to be genuinely cross-government and cross-sector.

By applying these key principles, we have considered how current MLG arrangements are playing out at the regional scale through the practical experiences of both Wet Tropics and southern Tasmanian regional case studies. Observations from these case studies draw out current system strengths, weaknesses and trajectories. The experiences outlined in our case studies have been frequently echoed by our regional body colleagues and other key natural resource stakeholders across the nation. We have used these principles and case study observations to guide our thoughts and discussion concerning the sort of reforms required in the overall national multi-level NRM governance system that would have particular resonance for Australia's regions. While the principles articulated need to be operative at all scales, we have applied them specifically to identify key national reforms that might improve the operating environment for NRM at the regional scale. Resolving the health of governance arrangements at all scales, however, will ultimately be required.

Our aim has been to spark increased national debate about what constitutes an effective national system of multi-level natural resource governance and to encourage active dialogue on the sort of targeted reforms that might help improve the health of the system. It should be stressed, however, that in international terms, Australia has a world-class national system for the governance of natural resources, with many strong features and characteristics. This chapter explores some of the current opportunities for progressive and continuous reform and improvement.

At the time of writing, both the Australian Government and, in our case study regions, the Queensland and Tasmanian governments, have been actively engaged in discussion with regional NRM bodies and other sectors about directions for further improvement in the nation's multi-level NRM governance system. There continues to be much scope for all of the nation's governments (federal, state, territory and local) to continue to work closely with all parties involved in NRM towards progressive reform opportunities.

Acknowledgements

The authors would like to thank the support of regional NRM bodies, state, territory and federal government staff and a variety of Australian peak bodies for their active participation in, and contributions to, discussions and debates about the need for continuous improvement in our national governance systems for NRM. We would particularly like to thank NRM Regions Australia for their strong interest in these issues across the nation and the Wentworth Group for their critical review of some of the key issues raised. Finally, we also thank the Commonwealth Government's Australian Research Council, the National Environment Research Program Tropical Ecosystem Hub and the Northern Futures Collaborative Research Network for their financial support.

References

ANAO (2008). *Regional Delivery Model for the National Heritage Trust and the National Action Plan for Salinity and Water Quality: Audit Report 21*. Australian National Audit Office, Canberra.

Australian Government (2001). *Intergovernmental Agreement on a National Action Plan for Salinity and Water Quality between the Commonwealth of Australia, New South Wales, Victoria, Queensland, Western Australia, South Australia, Tasmania, the Northern Territory and the Australian Capital Territory*, nrmonline.nrm.gov.au/downloads/mql:2419/content [Accessed: 26/12/2014].

——. (2011a). *The Review of Caring for our Country: Australia's Natural Resource Management Initiative.* Department of Sustainability, Environment, Water, Population and Communities, Canberra.

——. (2011b). *Monitoring, Evaluation, Reporting and Improvement Strategy.* Department of Sustainability, Environment, Water, Population and Communities, Canberra.

Australian Government & Queensland Government (2009). *Reef Water Quality Protection Plan: For the Great Barrier Reef World Heritage Area and Adjacent Catchments.* Reef Water Quality Protection Plan Secretariat, Queensland Department of the Premier and Cabinet, Brisbane.

Campbell, A. (2005). *Knowledge for Managing Australian Landscapes: Analysing the Australian NRM Knowledge System.* Land and Water Australia, Canberra.

Cash, D., Adger, W., Berkes, F., Garden, P., Lebel, L., Olsson, P., Pritchard, L. & Young, O. (2006). Scale and Cross-Scale Dynamics: Governance and information in a multilevel world. *Ecology and Society,* 11(2): 8. doi.org/10.5751/ES-01759-110208

Commonwealth of Australia (1999). *Managing Natural Resources in Rural Australia for a Sustainable Future: A Discussion Paper for Developing a National Policy.* Commonwealth Government Publishers, Canberra.

——. (2004). *Interim Biogeographic Regionalisation of Australia.* Commonwealth of Australia, Canberra.

——. (2009). *Carbon Pollution Reduction Scheme Bill: Commentary.* Department of Climate Change, Canberra.

Dale A., McDonald G. & Weston N. (2008). Integrating Effort for Regional Natural Resource Outcomes: The wet tropics experience. In: Stork, N. & Turton, S. (eds) *Living in a Dynamic Tropical Forest Landscape.* Blackwell Publications, Malden. doi.org/10.1002/9781444300321. ch32

Dale, A., McKee, J., Vella, K. & Potts, R. (2013). Carbon, biodiversity and regional natural resource planning: Towards high impact next generation plans in Australia. *Australian Planner,* 50(4): 328–39. doi.org/10.1080/07293682.2013.764908

Farrelly, M. (2005). Regionalisation of Environmental Management: A case study of the National Heritage Trust, South Australia. *Geographical Research*, 43(4): 393–405. doi.org/10.1111/j.1745-5871. 2005.00342.x

Folke, C., Carpenter, S., Walker, B., Scheffer, M., Chapin, T. & Rockström, J. (2010). Resilience Thinking: Integrating resilience, adaptability and transformability. *Ecology and Society*, 15(4): 20. doi.org/10.5751/es-03610-150420

Gunningham, N. (2009). The New Collaborative Environmental Governance: The localization of regulation. *Journal of Law and Society*, 36: 145–66. doi.org/10.1111/j.1467-6478.2009.00461.x

Keogh, K., Chant, D. & Frazer, B. (2006). *Review of Arrangements for Regional Delivery of Natural Resource Management Programs*. Departments of Environment Water Heritage and the Arts, Agriculture, Forestry and Fisheries, Canberra.

Lane, M., Robinson, C. & Taylor, B. (2009). *Contested Country: Local and regional natural resources management in Australia*. CSIRO Sustainable Ecosystems. CSIRO Publishing, Collingwood, Australia.

Lockie, S. & Vanclay, F. (eds) (1997). *Critical Landcare*. Key Paper Series No. 5. Centre for Rural Social Research, Charles Sturt University, Wagga Wagga, New South Wales.

McDonald, G. & Weston, N. (2004). *Sustaining the Wet Tropics: A Regional Plan for Natural Resource Management*. Rainforest CRC and FNQ NRM Ltd, Cairns, Australia.

MDBA (2010). *Guide to the Proposed Murray–Darling Basin Plan*. Murray–Darling Basin Authority, www.mdba.gov.au/kid/guide/ [Accessed: 24/12/2014].

Ostrom, E. & Cox, M. (2010). Moving beyond Panaceas: A multi-tiered diagnostic approach for social–ecological thinking. *Environmental Conservation*, 37: 451–63. doi.org/10.1017/S0376892910000834

Parker, C. & Braithwaite, J. (2003). Regulation. In: Cane, P. & Tushnet, M. (eds) *The Oxford Handbook of Legal Studies*. Oxford University Press, p. 119.

Petit, C., Ewing, S., Coffey, B., Geraghty, P., Hocking, G., Meyers, N., Butters, S. & Weston, M. (2011). Exploring the Potential of Knowledge Brokering to Enhance Natural Resource Management: Findings from the Catchment Knowledge Exchange project in Victoria. *Australian Journal of Environmental Management*, 18(4): 233–47. doi.org/10.10 80/14486563.2011.623337

Productivity Commission (2003). *Impacts of Native Vegetation and Biodiversity Regulations: Draft Report*. Australian Government, Canberra.

Ryan, S., Broderick, K., Sneddon, Y. & Andrews, K. (2010). *Australia's NRM Governance System: Foundations and Principles for Meeting Future Challenges*. Australian Regional NRM Chairs, Canberra.

van de Koppel, J. & Rietkerk, M. (2000). Herbivore Regulation and Irreversible Vegetation Change in Semi-Arid Grazing Systems. *OIKOS*, 90: 253–60. doi.org/10.1034/j.1600-0706.2000.900205.x

van Oosterzee, P., Preece, N. & Dale, A. (2010). Catching the Baby: Accounting for biodiversity and the ecosystem sector in emissions trading. *Conservation Letters*, 3(2): 1–8. doi.org/10.1111/j.1755-263x.2009.00090.x

——. (2012). An Australian Landscape-Based Approach: AFOLU mitigation for smallholders. In: Wollenberg, E., Nihart, A., Tapio-Biström, M.-L. & Grieg-Gran, M. (eds) *Climate Change, Mitigation and Agriculture*. Earthscan, London.

Vogel, N. & Zammitt, C. (2004). *Performance Excellence for Regional Natural Resource Management Organisations*. AKM Group and University of Southern Queensland, Toowoomba.

Wentworth Group (2008). *Accounting for Nature. A Model for Building the National Environmental Accounts of Australia*. Sydney.

Williams, J., Beeton R. & McDonald, G. (2005). Means to Ends: Success attributes of regional NRM. In: Kungolos, A., Brebbia, C. & Beriatos, E. (eds) *Proceedings of Second International Conference on Sustainable Development and Planning: Sustainable Development and Planning II*. Bologna, Italy, pp. 691–720.

15

Multi-level Integrated Water Governance: Examples from New South Wales and Colorado

Andrew Ross

Introduction

Water governance refers to the range of political, social, economic and administrative systems that are in place to develop and manage water resources, and the delivery of water services, at different levels of society. The functions of water governance include the definition of sustainable limits and priorities for the use of water resources, the establishment of water-use entitlements and plans and organisations to administer them (Rogers and Hall 2003; Svendsen 2005). Decision-making in a water-governance system takes place at many different spatial, temporal and jurisdictional scales (Cash et al. 2006; Young 2002). This decision-making involves trade-offs and compromises that are shaped by different social and political preferences and governance arrangements in different jurisdictions.

Historically, water governance has been centralised and characterised by top-down decision-making. Most water supply and demand problems were addressed by additional infrastructure development, with regulation employed, where necessary, to address point-source water pollution. Now water management is seen as including a much broader range of issues, including water for the environment, diffuse pollution from agriculture and climate change. Given the complexity of water management and related uncertainties, new approaches are required to guarantee sufficient water of satisfactory quality to meet competing demands. Integrated water supply and demand management and multi-level integrated water governance is needed using blends of regulation, market mechanisms and collaborative networks (Pahl-Wostl et al. 2005; Sabatier et al. 2005). Multi-level governance processes can be defined as systems of continuous negotiation at several territorial tiers, including vertical and horizontal coordination between governments, non-government actors, markets and civil society (Marks 1993).

The dispersion of water governance across multiple jurisdictions can lead to a number of benefits. It can capture variations in externalities arising from the use of water resources, ranging from transnational to local impacts. More decentralised jurisdictions can enable greater flexibility and better reflect heterogeneity of preferences among citizens (Hooghe and Marks 2001). Multiple jurisdictions facilitate innovation and experimentation (Gray 1973). Fragmentation or duplication of authority can, however, present problems in the management of large-scale water resources. Effective coordination across functions, scales and levels presents a key governance challenge (Cash et al. 2006).

Two models for coordination can be distinguished (Hooghe and Marks 2003). General purpose jurisdictions, such as state and local governments and their agencies (Type I), cover a wide range of issues and have a limited number of levels whose membership does not intersect. Special purpose jurisdictions, such as natural resource management organisations in New South Wales (NSW) and water districts in Colorado (Type II), cover a more limited number of issues, but the number of levels is not limited and memberships often intersect. The roles and interactions of these bodies are relatively dynamic. Research suggests that multi-level or polycentric governance (a mixture of Type I and Type II governance) is a more successful model for managing water resources than a hierarchical system (Ostrom 2005; Huitema et al. 2009), even though it can sometimes seem relatively chaotic (Blomquist and Schlager 2008).[1]

---

1   The concept of MLG originated in analyses of intergovernmental arrangements in the European Union (Bache and Flinders 2004). The concept of polycentric governance originated in American studies of city government service provision (Ostrom and Ostrom 1977). When MLG is defined to include both vertical and horizontal integration, and both public and private sector organisations – as in this chapter – these concepts overlap substantially.

Integrated water management involves the joint or coordinated use and management of surface water and groundwater in connected or unconnected resources. Integrated water management helps to enable optimal water use and to prevent adverse impacts of surface water and groundwater use on other water users, third parties and the environment (Blomquist et al. 2004; Ross and Martinez-Santos 2010).

Integrated water planning and management provides an interesting case study of multi-level governance (MLG) because it involves some special cross-boundary coordination challenges. Water catchments do not share the boundaries of social–political systems, and surface water and groundwater boundaries are different. The impacts of groundwater use are often much slower than surface water use, leading to intertemporal management issues.[2]

In the remainder of this chapter, MLG arrangements are explored in a comparative case study of integrated water management and planning in the Namoi region in NSW and South Platte basin in Colorado. These regions are selected for comparative study because they have similar biophysical and socio-economic conditions, including relatively dry climate, variable rainfall, water scarcity and a high proportion of water use in irrigated agriculture. The two regions also share a common spatial and jurisdictional scale: sub-basins under state government jurisdiction. These similarities assist a comparison of the impact of different policy settings and MLG approaches on integrated water use and management.

In both the Namoi and South Platte regions, the main integrated water management problem in recent decades has been how to maintain the benefits of groundwater pumping without adverse impacts on surface water supplies, environmental assets or long-term groundwater resources. This problem has been approached in different ways in the two regions, reflecting their different multi-level water governance arrangements.

---

2   The interactions between some alluvial surface water and (shallow) groundwater resources can be relatively fast – within months – but in most cases the impacts of groundwater pumping on connected surface water and water-dependent ecosystems can take many years, or hundreds of years in some cases.

Integrated water governance in New South Wales and Colorado

Both NSW and Colorado are experiencing increasing water scarcities owing to drier climatic conditions, increasing human populations and increasing consumptive demands for water (Blomquist et al. 2004; Pigram 2006). Some surface water and groundwater resources are being depleted or degraded, and there are increasing concerns about the impacts on riverine environments, wetlands and floodplains. Integrated surface water and groundwater management presents many opportunities to mitigate these problems and to insure against water scarcity. Integrated water management has been actively pursued in Colorado and other states in the western United States, but not in NSW (or most jurisdictions in the Murray–Darling Basin, MDB). What explains this phenomenon, and how has MLG affected the outcome?

Core water governance approaches

Ostrom (2005) distinguishes between constitutional, collective choice and operational rules and rule-making. Constitutional decisions involve the establishment of water decision-making bodies and their membership, collective choice includes making water policies or broad allocations of water resources, and operational rules involve more frequent decisions about the implementation of policies and plans. The choices of water users, policymakers and managers in specific water management areas are shaped and constrained by 'core' principles of water governance and by previous decisions about institutions (laws, rules and management organisations) and instruments. The prior-appropriation system in Colorado requires integrated water management in tributary water resources. Separate surface water and groundwater planning and allocation in NSW does nothing to encourage integrated water management.

In Australia's federal system, water governance takes place at a number of levels at the jurisdictional and river basin scale. Essentially, it is a relatively centralised and hierarchical governance system. The Council of Australian Governments (COAG) (Commonwealth, state and territory) has led responsibility for national water policy. In 2004, COAG established an intergovernmental agreement on a national water initiative

(NWI) (COAG 2004). The NWI provides for comprehensive planning and secure, tradeable water-access entitlements for both surface water and groundwater.

The 1992 MDB agreement covers surface water allocation between MDB jurisdictions. The agreement includes a 'cap' on surface water use in the MDB, but does not include any limit on groundwater use. In the MDB, water plans are the main instrument used for allocating water. Markets are also used, especially for reallocating surface water. Groundwater trade is less well developed than surface water trade.[3] Water-use limits and allocations for each water resource are established by state water plans. Tradeable water-use entitlements are allocated according to the histories of use, usually over periods in the relatively recent past.

The NSW *Water Management Act 2000* gives effect to the COAG 1994 reforms[4] and the NWI by establishing a framework of water management based on clearly defined tradeable water-access entitlements/licences. The *Water Management Act* authorises the preparation of surface water– and groundwater-sharing plans to allocate water resources.[5] The rules for allocation of water are set out in water-sharing plans for specified water-management areas (Montoya 2010). Surface water and groundwater plans have generally been made separately. The Australian Government's *Water Act 2007*[6] requires the preparation of a new, integrated surface water and groundwater plan for the MDB and its catchments.

In the US federal system of governance, each state has 'plenary control' over the waters within its boundaries, and is free to develop whatever system of water-rights administration it chooses (Hobbs 1997). In the western United States, state law underpins the doctrine of prior appropriation, which provides the basic system for the allocation of water resources (Kenney 2005). Under this doctrine, the earliest user of a water source has the right to apply it to a beneficial use and to exclude others. If low stream flows prevent 'senior' rights from diverting the water to which they are entitled, the 'seniors' put a 'call' on the river, requiring all

---

3   Groundwater trade and groundwater–surface water trade is constrained by uncertainties about the long-term impacts of moving groundwater use from one location to another.
4   www.austlii.edu.au/au/legis/nsw/consol_act/wma2000166/ [Accessed: 16/02/2011]. Amendments to the Act enable implementation of the National Water Initiative in NSW.
5   A number of water-sharing plans are now in place covering various water resources in the Namoi region. www.water.nsw.gov.au/Water-management/Water-sharing-plans/Plans-commenced/plans_commenced/default.aspx [Accessed: 16/02/2011].
6   www.comlaw.gov.au/Series/C2007A00137 [Accessed: 24/12/2014].

upstream rights 'junior' to the caller to stop diverting water until adequate streamflow is restored (Howe 2008). In addition, many water resources in the United States overlap state boundaries. These resources are regulated by interstate compacts.

In Colorado, the management and use of surface water and groundwater is closely integrated. In practice, the primary purpose of integrated surface water and groundwater management is to maintain stream flows to protect senior surface water rights holders. This also enables Colorado to comply with interstate river compacts, including the South Platte compact between Colorado and Nebraska. There are four types of groundwater rights.[7] In this comparative case study the emphasis is on tributary groundwater, which is hydrologically connected to a surface water stream. Tributary groundwater is subject to the prior-appropriation system (MacDonnell 1998), and surface water and groundwater are managed as a single connected resource. Tributary groundwater wells can be 'shut down' unless they can ensure that senior surface water rights are maintained.

The development of integrated water use and governance

Water users in both regions have a long history of integrated use and management of surface water and groundwater.

In NSW and Colorado, both surface water and groundwater provide an important source of regional water supplies. The primary source fluctuates according to climatic variation. Integrated water use has led to more flexible use of water and helped adaptation to variable water supplies.

Water users in both regions choose between diverse water supplies on the basis of water availability, cost and quality. Interviews with user associations in both regions indicate that, when water users have a choice, they usually prefer surface water, because the cost of delivered surface water is usually

---

7   Tributary, non-tributary, not non-tributary and designated groundwater. Non-tributary groundwater is almost totally disconnected from surface water. Not non-tributary groundwater is connected but only over a long period of time. The definition for non-tributary groundwater is rigorous. A proposed diversion cannot deplete surface streams of more than 0.1 per cent of the proposed diversion volume in any single year for up to 100 years. www.douglas.co.us/water/colorado-state-water-law/ [Accessed: 09/04/2015].

less than groundwater that they have to extract themselves.[8] Some users depend on groundwater because delivered surface water is unavailable. Many users turn to groundwater during dry periods when less surface water is available.

Surface water and groundwater management has gone through similar phases in the two states (Pigram 2006; Heikkila 2000). Initially, surface water and groundwater use was not restricted. Then, as surface water demand exceeded availability, groundwater use increased. Eventually, this led both users and authorities to be concerned about the impact of groundwater pumping on surface water flows and aquifers. Finally, groundwater pumping was restricted and/or groundwater users were required to make good their impacts on surface water users.

The two jurisdictions have taken different approaches to multi-level water governance arrangements, as shown in Table 15.1.

Table 15.1: Water entitlements and management instruments in New South Wales and Colorado

	New South Wales	Colorado
Water rights	Distribution of water rights determined by political choice; rights have different 'security', depending on priority	Distribution of water rights determined by prior appropriation: 'First in time, first in right' (point of diversion, place and time of use, purpose, amount)
Instruments	Access and allocation rules in state water plans; reallocation of water rights through water markets	'Calls' by senior water rights holders; decrees by courts; junior water entitlement holders have to buy senior rights, mitigate impacts or cease to pump

These differences are illustrated by experience in the Namoi region in NSW and the South Platte region in Colorado.

New South Wales

Integrated water management in NSW has been biased towards surface water supplies and storage. In the 'development' stage of water resource management, various NSW state governments built surface water storages and delivery infrastructure to supply irrigation areas (Wilkinson 1997).

---

8   These interviews were carried out by the author during research for his PhD, which examined integrated surface water and groundwater use in the Murray–Darling Basin and western United States. Water-quality issues, such as sedimentation or salt content, also affect water supply preferences.

The NSW Government issued a substantially greater volume of surface water and groundwater entitlements than long-term average availability of the two resources. In the Namoi region, surface water entitlements are supplied from releases from Split Rock and Keepit dams. The majority of the remaining surface water resource flows are provided for environmental flows (Barma Water Resources et al. 2012), although farmers are allowed to opportunistically harvest water during high-flow events.

During major periods of dry weather, groundwater use in the Namoi increased substantially, leading to adverse impacts such as falling groundwater levels, declining stream flows and increasing pumping costs. Water users and managers understood that surface water and groundwater resources were connected. Surface water and groundwater monitoring networks were put in place and substantial research programs were undertaken (Kelly et al. 2007). However, surface water and groundwater plans have generally been prepared separately. In NSW, surface water plans do not generally consider connections with, or impacts on, groundwater.[9] Groundwater plans usually do consider connections with, and impacts on, surface water, but the analysis is limited (NWC 2009).

Restrictions on surface water and groundwater use were introduced incrementally and separately, with the aim of minimising impacts on water-dependent farming industries and communities. Groundwater restrictions were only developed when groundwater use substantially exceeded sustainable limits, or when groundwater pumping threatened surface water availability. The introduction of restrictions involved periodic negotiations between governments and water-user representatives. The NSW Government placed embargoes on new surface water and groundwater licences in 1976 and 1984 respectively. Volumetric limits were introduced for surface water licences in 1984 to restrict the growth of water use (Wilkinson 1997). In the early 1980s, NSW authorities allowed 'controlled depletion' of groundwater resources, anticipating that wet years would recharge them. An embargo on stressed groundwater systems was imposed in 1985 (Williams 1998). In 1994–95, groundwater

---

9   There are some examples of integrated water planning in South Australia, the Australian Capital Territory (where there is one integrated surface and groundwater plan for the territory) and a few areas in Queensland. The complicated Peel Valley water-sharing plan in the Namoi region includes different sets of rules to manage eight different water resources, with varying degrees of connectivity.

use rose to substantially above annual recharge levels. This prompted further embargoes on new groundwater allocations in the Upper Namoi (NGERP 1999).

Colorado

The key policy problem facing Colorado authorities is how to make beneficial use of both surface water and groundwater resources, while upholding the legal rights of senior water users.

In Colorado, prior appropriation has encouraged the integration of surface water and groundwater management. Surface water users hold the most senior rights and, as groundwater use expanded after World War II, senior surface water users became increasingly concerned about the impact of groundwater pumping on surface water supplies. 'Calls' by senior surface water-rights holders on groundwater pumpers prompted initiatives by users and state authorities, and legal and policy innovations to enable groundwater use to continue.

The *Water Rights Determination and Administration Act 1969* in Colorado required tributary groundwater rights to be adjudicated and included in the prior-appropriation system. From that time, management of tributary surface water and groundwater has been integrated. In order to allow continued use and development of groundwater without jeopardising senior surface water rights, groundwater users have been required to bring forward long-term or temporary plans to supply water to mitigate the impact of pumping on senior surface water-rights holders[10] (Blomquist et al. 2004).

In the South Platte region, shallow alluvial groundwater resources are closely connected with rivers, and their use has an almost immediate impact on surface water stream flow. These effects are noticeable to senior surface water-rights holders within a single irrigation season. The relatively early adjudication of groundwater by 1972 has provided a strong driver towards integrated water management. This led to the development of augmentation plans negotiated between water users and approved by the water courts. In March 1974, water appropriators in the South Platte basin agreed on a set of rules for regulating wells. These rules defined

---

10   There are some differences in the terminology and detail relating to these plans in the Arkansas and South Platte basins.

a timetable for phasing out well pumping, but allowed wells covered by an approved augmentation plan to continue to pump during the summer, provided that they did not injure downstream senior appropriators. The augmentation plans also have to take account of the provisions of the South Platte River compact. These limit diversions from the river between 1 April and 15 October in order to guarantee streamflow to downstream states, including Nebraska.

Multi-level water governance processes, levels and actors

Integrated water management requires effective multi-level coordination and broad stakeholder participation. The successful implementation of integrated water management depends on striking an effective balance between broad direction and coordination and local initiative (Ross and Dovers 2008; Turral and Fullagar 2007).

Table 15.2 summarises water governance in NSW and Colorado. Water governance in NSW is relatively hierarchical and centralised, with government agencies controlling water planning and allocation, whereas water governance in Colorado is multi-centred or polycentric, with functions shared between water courts, water users, water districts and government agencies.

Table 15.2: Water governance in New South Wales and Colorado

	New South Wales	Colorado
Management 'style'	Hierarchical	Polycentric
Management organisation	State government and agencies control water planning and allocation, catchment management agencies and water-user groups play a role in implementation	Water courts arbitrate prior appropriation, water users initiate priority calls and mitigation activities, water districts and government agencies play an important role in implementation

New South Wales

The main factors that influence MLG processes in NSW are water resources and their availability, national and state policies and state water plans. The most influential stakeholders are the NSW minister responsible for water and state officials. The water-planning process is the primary arena for negotiation, where water allocation is determined and water-use conflicts are resolved.

The NSW Government has primary responsibility for managing water in the state. The NSW Minister for Primary Industries has the primary responsibility for the management of NSW water resources.[11] The minister's functions and duties include implementing national agreements and policies, developing and implementing water-sharing policies and plans, administering and enforcing access licences and water-use approvals and distributing water. Water-sharing plans set out water allocations between different uses/users and operational rules for water management.[12] Water-sharing plans have effect for 10 years and are reviewed after five years.[13] The development of water-sharing policies and plans involves ongoing negotiation between governments, water users and third parties.

The Office of Water in the Department of Primary Industries[14] carries out many of the minister's functions, including the development of water policy and plans and the administration, monitoring and enforcement of access licences and water-use approvals. Surface water and groundwater policy and planning functions are joined at the highest level of decision-making. Otherwise, they are separate but coordinated. Technical and implementation functions are often carried out separately. Regional staff at Tamworth and Narrabri are responsible for analysis, liaison, monitoring, metering, inspection and compliance.

Water management committees (WMCs) and community advisory committees (CACs) are established by the minister to prepare and/or provide advice about water sharing. These committees include between 12 and 20 members appointed by the minister. They include representatives of environment protection groups, water users (including irrigators), local councils, traditional owners, catchment management boards, the Office of Water and a nominee of the minister. CACs are similarly constituted to WMCs but have a purely advisory role.

---

11   The Minister for Primary Industries took over these responsibilities following a change of government in March 2011.
12   These rules include shares of surface water to be made available to water-entitlement holders, and cease-to-pump rules for rivers and streams subject to too low or intermittent flow.
13   www.austlii.edu.au/au/legis/nsw/consol_act/wma2000166/s43.html [Accessed: 24/12/2014].
14   www.water.nsw.gov.au [Accessed: 24/12/2014].

In practice, consultation often appears more symbolic than real because it takes place after policy changes have been made and/or does not take sufficient account of stakeholder views (Bowmer 2003). Also, the minister may overrule the consultative document and make a separate plan. This can provoke conflicts and legal action, as in the case of the upper and lower Namoi groundwater plan (Gardner et al. 2009). So far, the NSW Court of Appeal has upheld the statutory application of minister's plans and there is no case of a plan being stopped by court action.

Catchment management organisations are special purpose bodies established under the *Catchment Management Act 1989* or the Catchment Management Regulation 1999. They are established to promote healthy and productive catchments by identifying objectives, strategies and actions to manage natural resources. Catchment management organisations represent an interesting innovation to integrate policy at the regional scale. They have responsibilities for land and environmental conservation and water quality, but not for water allocation, and their effectiveness is constrained by limited personnel and budgets (Ross 2008; Robins and Dovers 2007).

A number of special purpose bodies manage water infrastructure and delivery. State Water owns, maintains, manages and operates major infrastructure to deliver bulk water.[15] Irrigation corporations are privately owned organisations that own and operate water supply infrastructure in specific irrigation areas. Private irrigation districts are legal entities constituted by landholders for the construction, maintenance and operation of water supply and drainage infrastructure. Namoi Water is the peak industry group for irrigated agriculture, and covers 60–70 per cent of all water users (Productivity Commission 2003).

Colorado

The main factors that influence multi-level water governance processes in Colorado are water resources and their availability and the prior-appropriation system of water allocation. The most influential stakeholders are the water courts, special purpose water districts and the state and regional engineers.[16] In Colorado, water courts are the primary arena for determining water allocation and resolving conflicts.

---

15 State Water supplies approximately 6,300 licensed water users on the state's regulated rivers along with associated environmental flows: www.water.nsw.gov.au/water-licensing [Accessed: 11/12/2010].
16 The state engineer is the head of the Colorado Department of Water Resources.

The courts define (adjudicate) and enforce appropriation of rights, including the amount, priority, location and beneficial use of water rights, the approval of exchanges and plans for augmentation. The earliest water-rights decrees in Colorado were adjudicated by the district court system – there are 80 water districts in Colorado. Most administration is still done at the level of water districts. A water commissioner serves each water district. The *Water Rights Determination and Administration Act 1969* authorised the establishment of seven water courts and water divisions, based on the seven major river-drainage basins in Colorado. The judge in each water court is designated by the Supreme Court to review water-right applications within the relevant water division. The judge may appoint a water referee to gather evidence and consider applications (Vranesh 1987).

Well owners that pump from alluvial aquifers are required by law to belong to an augmentation plan, such as the Groundwater Appropriators of South Platte, the Central Colorado Water Conservancy District, or an individual augmentation plan. Groundwater users, working with state authorities, develop decreed or temporary augmentation plans to offset their impacts on senior users. The development of these plans involves ongoing negotiation. Formal legally decreed plans take several years to develop and to be agreed among water users. Most groundwater appropriations are covered by temporary plans reviewed, revised if necessary, and approved by the state engineer on an annual basis. Groundwater users collaborate to obtain surface water when it is plentiful, for example during the snow-melt season. They use various techniques to return water to the river, including infiltration from irrigation ditches and ponds, delivery from special purpose surface water storages or simply not using their purchased entitlement (Blomquist et al. 2004)

The state and division engineers provide information and technical resources to appropriators, the courts and the state legislature allowing them to implement the water-rights system. Appropriators, the state engineer, the engineer's seven divisional offices and water commissioners employed by the state engineer participate in monitoring and enforcing water rights (Knox 2008). In Colorado, while the water courts have primary responsibility for administering water rights and determining claims, the Division of Water Resources has played a key role in developing the science that underpins integrated water management plans, and monitoring and enforcement.

The Colorado Water Conservation Board[17] is appointed by the governor. It formulates policy for water development programs, provides funds for water projects, acquires and manages in-stream flow rights and assists in interstate compact administration.

Many federal departments and agencies play a role in state water management. Key departments include the US Fish and Wildlife Service, which administers the *Endangered Species Act 1973* and fisheries management; the US Environmental Protection Agency, which administers national water standards; and the US Army Corps of Engineers, which develops and operates water infrastructure. The federal government also has a strong presence in water issues in relation to American Indian and international treaty obligations, and public land management. Federal and state laws and programs don't always fit together easily. Federal laws and programs that encourage leaving water in streams can conflict with state water laws and programs that encourage maximum diversion and consumptive use (Kenney et al. 2001).

Under the *Water Conservancy Act 1937*, Colorado's legislature authorised the creation of special purpose water-conservancy districts at the sub-basin scale. Fifty of these public entities, some divided into sub-districts, engage in a wide range of water issues, including development and management of water projects, water conservation, distribution, water-quality protection, flood control, legislation and education. The district's taxing ability allows them to borrow money for projects and repay it with tax revenue. Water conservancy districts may acquire and develop water rights, development augmentation plans and/or deliver water directly. These districts play a key role in integrated water management, regional coordination and innovation. Private associations were created across Colorado in the 1800s to develop, maintain and deliver irrigation water. There are over 700 metropolitan districts and more than 100 water and sanitation districts in Colorado. These entities commonly raise money for infrastructure (Jones and Cech 2009).

A 27-member Interbasin Compact Committee has been established by the legislature[18] and separate basin round tables also were established by the Act to coordinate discussions on water issues and encourage locally driven collaborative solutions.

---

17 cwcb.state.co.us/Pages/CWCBHome.aspx [Accessed: 25/05/2011].
18 *Colorado Water for the 21st Century Act.*

Recent developments in integrated water planning and governance

Recent developments in integrated water governance in NSW and Colorado serve to illustrate some of the pros and cons of the two systems – centralised planning and allocation in NSW and prior appropriation in Colorado. Neither system has made the best use of integrated surface water and groundwater management to adjust to water-supply variability and scarcity.

New South Wales: Namoi region

Following the *Water Management Act 2000*, separate surface water– and groundwater-sharing plans were prepared in the Namoi region. The surface water–sharing plan for the upper and lower Namoi regulated rivers[19] established water allocations based on historical average diversion limits. Annual water allocations to municipal and irrigation users vary according to the amount of water available in the major water storages. Irrigators also have access to supplementary water allocations following high rainfall events and on-farm water harvesting allowances. These arrangements have encouraged large, on-farm surface water storages and discouraged aquifer storage and recovery (Ross 2012).

The groundwater management plan was more controversial and contested. In 1994–95, drought-driven groundwater use in the upper and lower Namoi groundwater management area increased to about double the long-term average aquifer recharge. After a protracted negotiation, taking into account economic impacts of reduced groundwater use (Wolfenden & Van der Lee 2002), stakeholders were unable to agree on a water-sharing plan. In 2003, the NSW Minister for Water issued a draft plan that included water-allocation reductions of 51 per cent in the Lower Namoi and 61 per cent in the Upper Namoi.

Water licence holders were strongly critical of the process for developing the Namoi groundwater-sharing plan. The main argument was about whether entitlement reductions should be equalised 'across the board', as proposed

---

19 The water-sharing plan for the Upper Namoi and Lower Namoi Regulated River Water Sources was gazetted in 2003 (DIPNR 2004). The flows in regulated water sources are controlled by dams and weirs.

in the minister's plan, or adjusted in favour of irrigators who had developed their enterprise and were regularly using a large proportion of their entitlement (active users).[20] The plan was not finalised and implemented until governments and groundwater users negotiated a formula for water reductions that took account of historical use (Department of Natural Resources 2006). While the minister's intervention was necessary to break the negotiation deadlock, active participation of water users was needed to come up with an acceptable formula for reducing groundwater entitlements. Acceptance of the plan was also conditional on financial assistance to help irrigators to make a phased transition to sustainable extraction levels over 10 years.

Colorado: South Platte region

Augmentation plans and temporary (non-decreed) substitute supply plans[21] by groundwater users became the main mechanism for integrated water management in Colorado. From 1972 to 2001, the courts allowed the state engineer to play an independent role in facilitating and approving temporary water-supply plans. These plans allowed groundwater users to continue to pump even without completion of the formal legal procedures required to establish an augmentation plan. The temporary plans were coordinated by a group of well owners, the Groundwater Appropriators of the South Platte. In recent years, the authority of the engineer to approve temporary plans has been challenged, and the balance of influence has swung back towards the courts and the legislature.

Temporary supply plans violated the prior-appropriation doctrine because they did not fully replace 'out of priority' stream depletions. In 2001, the Colorado Supreme Court ruled (*Empire Lodge Homeowners Association v Moyer*) that the legislature did not give the state engineer authority to approve temporary water-supply plans. The state engineer filed proposed new rules in May 2002, but more than 30 water-user entities

---

20 Water-entitlement holders who had invested heavily and were using a large proportion of their entitlement considered that they should get a larger allocation than entitlements holders who were not using their allocations. This formula did not, however, give any preference to entitlements holders who had reduced water use by investing in water-saving technology. Also, many farmers had large investments that depended on regular small supplies of water.

21 These plans include a list of members and wells, estimates of the amount of water to be pumped in the coming and previous irrigation season, and an amount of water to replace a priority depletion and offset injuries to senior rights (MacDonnell 1998).

and individuals opposed the revised rules and the Water Court and the Supreme Court ruled that the state engineer lacked authority to approve replacement plans (*Simpson v Bijou Irrigation*).

In 2003, the governor of Colorado signed a bill allowing annual approvals of substitute water-supply plans for three more years. However, negotiation of these plans for 2002–04 was complicated by the severe drought. In 2004, well-owner associations could not obtain replenishment water and the divisional engineer ordered 450 groundwater wells to cease pumping. This was a perverse outcome at a time of severe water shortage and also had the effect of drying up 30,000 acres of cropland, with immediate, severe impacts on the farms and associated rural communities (Howe 2008). The future for many groundwater pumpers remains unclear.

Key lessons from the case studies

The two case studies illustrate the strengths and weaknesses of Type I and Type II governance systems. Predominantly Type I systems, such as water governance in NSW, resolve coordination problems and conflicts by centralisation of decision-making. This enables a comprehensive and relatively low-cost approach taking account of both socio-economic and environmental issues. It also allows governments flexibility in their approach to resolving (or deflecting) conflicts. The risk of this approach is lack of broad community engagement and support. This can lead to protracted opposition and conflict, as in the case of the Namoi groundwater plan. Type I governance also tends to separate innovation by water users and governments, thus reducing the potential for public–private partnerships.

Systems with strong Type II elements, such as water governance in Colorado, resolve coordination problems and conflicts by disaggregating water governance and encouraging the creation of special purpose organisations to deal with particular coordination problems and conflicts. This approach encourages community ownership and participation and manages costs by limiting the scope of problems to be solved. In Colorado, it has encouraged a good deal of technical innovation by groundwater users, which has, in turn, prompted managerial innovation by government agencies. The risk of this approach is a lack of commonality and consistency. The groundwater augmentation plans in Colorado do not take account of environmental water needs or remote impacts, and the informal groundwater pumping agreements are under pressure owing to increasing municipal demand and climate change, as shown in the developments after the 2002–04 drought.

A report prepared for the Western States Water Council concludes that states should not overtake local planning but should establish policies that facilitate the flow of information from water-resource agencies to local planning agencies. This requires local governments to create and adopt comprehensive plans that include water-resource elements. The states should offer technical and financial support for watershed organisations and should work with stakeholders to find innovative ways of allowing transfers of water from agriculture to urban uses while avoiding or mitigating damage to agricultural economies or environmental values (Bell and Taylor 2008).

The two case studies also illustrate some strengths and weaknesses of court- and government-led governance systems. The government-led bureaucratic system in NSW can respond more quickly and more flexibly when water-use conflicts occur. The minister's power to make a minister's plan allows the government to resolve water-sharing conflicts when users cannot agree among themselves. The risk of this system is a lack of transparency or community engagement, as illustrated by the 2003 Namoi groundwater plan. There is also a risk that a water governance system and plans developed over a long period of time at substantial cost may be undermined or abandoned because of short-term political considerations.

In Colorado, the prior-appropriation system creates certainty for users once adjudication of rights has taken place. Court processes require the issues involved in water-use conflicts to be tabled and dealt with by means of clearly defined processes. Intermediaries (water referees, water commissioners) play an important role in developing agreements. The disadvantage of the system is that it can be relatively costly for participants and that parties without adjudicated rights are excluded from negotiations. Informal agreements reduce costs but may not be robust during water scarcities. In addition, the system can be inflexible in the case of severe water shortages, when senior water rights holders insist on their rights regardless of the social and political costs, as occurred in Colorado after the 2002–04 drought.

Integrated water management requires a blend of jurisdiction-wide and local approaches. This could include:

- a jurisdictional-scale approach to sustainable-use limits, projections of surface water and groundwater availability and demand, and integrated water management strategies
- locally developed integrated surface water and groundwater use, storage and transfer rules, and management organisation.

This multi-level approach can avoid the difficulties involved in drafting and communicating a fully detailed management plan at the river basin or jurisdictional scale, but at the same time ensure a coordinated approach to water management at those scales.

Further research is needed on how to improve links and collaboration between higher level and local processes, over long-term water-planning periods. Research on long-term collaborative processes and institutions for integrated water management is particularly important because of the disjuncture between relatively short-term political cycles and the long-term effects of groundwater use on the other users and the environment.

Finally, the case studies illustrate that there is no magic formula for a robust system of water governance. Effective water governance is likely to include a well-developed legal and policy framework, well-defined and flexible water rights and a range of Type I and II water governance organisations with strong coordination arrangements. But the best water governance arrangements may not be robust in the face of severe, unexpected water scarcities. It is difficult to resolve water-sharing conflicts when the parties cannot find common ground. It is especially difficult to reduce water use when people depend on it.

References

Bache, I. & Flinders, M. (eds) (2004). *Multi-level Governance*. Oxford University Press. doi.org/10.1093/0199259259.001.0001

Barma Water Resources, Thurtell, L. & Wettin, P. (2012). *Environmental Water Delivery: Namoi River*. Prepared for Commonwealth Environmental Water, Department of Sustainability, Environment, Water, Population and Communities, Canberra.

Bell, C. & Taylor. J. (2008). *Water Laws and Policies for a Sustainable Future: A Western States Perspective*. Western States Water Council, Murray, Utah.

Blomquist, W. & Schlager, E. (2008). *Embracing Watershed Politics.* University of Colorado Press, Boulder.

Blomquist, W., Schlager, E. & Heikkila, T. (2004). *Common Waters Diverging Streams.* Resources for the Future, Washington.

Bowmer, K. (2003). Reflections on Developing a Water Sharing Plan. In: Wilson, B.P. & Curtis, A. (eds) *Agriculture for the Australian Environment.* Proceedings of the 2002 Fenner Conference, Charles Sturt University, Albury.

Cash, D., Adger, W., Berkes, F., Garden, P., Lebel, L., Olsson, P., Pritchard, L. & Young, O. (2006). Scale and Cross-Scale Dynamics: Governance and information in a multilevel world. *Ecology and Society*, 11(2): 8. doi.org/10.5751/ES-01759-110208

COAG (2004). *Intergovernmental Agreement on a National Water Initiative between the Commonwealth of Australia and the Governments of New South Wales, Victoria, Queensland, South Australia, the Australian Capital Territory and the Northern Territory.* Council of Australian Governments, Canberra.

Department of Natural Resources (2006). *Key Amendments to the Water Sharing Plan for the Upper and Lower Namoi Groundwater Sources 2003.* Sydney.

DIPNR (2004). *A Guide to the Water Sharing Plan for the Upper Namoi and Lower Namoi Regulated Water Sources.* Department of Infrastructure, Planning and Natural Resources, Sydney.

Gardner, A., Bartlett, R.H., Gray, J. & Carney, G. (2009). *Water Resources Law.* LexisNexis Butterworths, Chatswood, New South Wales.

Gray, V. (1973). Confusion in the States: A diffusion study. *American Political Science Review*, 67: 1174–85. doi.org/10.2307/1956539

Heikkila, T. (2000). *Linked Policy Changes and Resource Management Decisions: A Game Theoretic Analysis of Coordinated Water Management in Colorado.* Research Supported by National Science Foundation and US Environmental Protection Agency, Grant Number R824781. School of Public Administration and Policy, University of Arizona, Tucson.

Hobbs, G. (1997). Colorado Water Law: An historical overview. *University of Denver Water Law Review*, 1(1): 1–72.

Hooghe, L. & Marks, G. (2001). *European Integration Online Papers.* 5(11).

——. (2003). Unravelling the Central State, but How? Types of Multi-level Governance. *American Political Science Review*, 97(2): 233–43.

Howe, C. (2008). Water Law and Economics: An assessment of river calls and the South Platte Well shut down. *University of Denver Water Law Review*, 12: 181–96.

Huitema, D., Mostert, E., Egas, W., Moellenkamp, S., Pahl-Wostl, C. & Yalcin, R. (2009). Adaptive Water Governance: Assessing the institutional prescriptions of adaptive (co-)management from the government's perspective and defining the research agenda. *Ecology and Society*, 14(1): 26. doi.org/10.5751/es-02827-140126

Jones, P.A. & Cech, T. (2009). *Colorado Water Law for Non-Lawyers.* University Press of Colorado, Boulder.

Kelly, B., Merrick, N.P., Dent, B., Milne-Home, W. & Yates, D. (2007). *A Scoping Study on Groundwater Knowledge and Gaps in the Namoi Catchment Management Area.* National Center for Groundwater Management Report, NCGM 2007/1. Cotton Catchment Communities CRC, University of Technology, Sydney.

Kenney, D. (ed.) (2005). *In Search of Sustainable Water Management: International Lessons for the American West and Beyond.* Edward Elgar, Cheltenham.

Kenney, D., Nichols, P. & Murphy, M. (2001). *Water and Growth in Colorado: A Review of the Legal and Policy Issues.* Water Resources Centre, University of Colorado School of Law, Boulder.

Knox, K. (2008). Water Administration in Colorado: The daily practice and legal authority. CBA-CLE, Denver, Colorado.

MacDonnell, L. (1998). *Integrating Tributary Groundwater Development into the Prior Appropriation System: The South Platte Experience.* Completion Report No 148. Colorado Water Resources Research Institute, Denver.

Marks, G. (1993). Structural Policy and Multi-level Governance in the EC. In: Cafruny, A. & Rosenthal, G. (eds) *State of European Community.* Vol. 2. Lynne Rienner, Boulder, Colorado, and Longman, London, pp. 391–410.

Montoya, D. (2010). *Water: Regulatory Frameworks in Rural NSW.* NSW Parliamentary Research Service, Sydney.

NGERP (1999). *Report of the Namoi Groundwater Expert Reference Panel on the Ground Water Allocation Adjustment Process in the Namoi Valley, NSW.* Namoi Groundwater Expert Reference Panel, Sydney.

NWC (2009). *Australian Water Reform 2009: Second Biennial Assessment of Progress in Implemention of the National Water Initiative.* National Water Commission, Canberra.

Ostrom, E. (2005). *Understanding Institutional Diversity.* Princeton University Press.

Ostrom, V. & Ostrom, E. (1977). A Theory for Institutional Analysis of Common Pool Problems. In: Hardin, G. & Baden, J. (eds) *Managing the Commons.* Indiana University Press, Indiana, pp. 157–72.

Pahl-Wostl, C., Downing, T., Kabat, P., Magnuszewski, P., Meigh, J., Schlueter, M., Sendzimir, J. & Werners S. (2005). Transition to Adaptive Water Management; the NeWater Project. *NeWater Report*, 1. University of Osnabrück, Germany.

Pigram, J. (2006). *Australia's Water Resources: from Use to Management.* CSIRO, Collingwood, Australia.

Productivity Commission (2003). *Water Rights Arrangements in Australia and Overseas.* Commonwealth of Australia, Canberra.

Robins, L. & Dovers, S. (2007). NRM Regions in Australia: The 'haves' and 'have nots'. *Geographical Research*, 45(3): 273–90. doi. org/10.1111/j.1745-5871.2007.00460.x

Rogers, P. & Hall, A. (2003). *Effective Water Governance.* TEC Background Papers No. 7. Global Water Partnership Technical Committee, Sweden.

Ross, A. (2008). Australia. In: Jordan, A. & Lenschow, A. (eds) *Innovation in Environment Policy: Integrating the Environment for Sustainability*, Edward Elgar, Cheltenham, pp. 289–310. doi.org/10.4337/9781848445062.00027

———. (2012). Easy to Say Hard to Do, Integrated Surface Water and Groundwater Management in the Murray–Darling Basin. *Water Policy*, 14(4): 709–24. doi.org/10.2166/wp.2012.129

Ross, A. & Dovers, S. (2008). Very Hard Yards: Environmental policy integration in Australia. *Australian Journal of Public Administration*, 67(3): 245–60. doi.org/10.1111/j.1467-8500.2008.00585.x

Ross, A. & Martinez-Santos, P. (2010). The Challenge of Groundwater Governance: Case studies from Australia and Spain. *Regional Environmental Change*, 10(3): 299–310. doi.org/10.1007/s10113-009-0086-8

Sabatier, P., Focht, W., Lubell, M., Trachtenberg, Z., Vedlitz, A. & Matlock, M. (2005). *Swimming Upstream: Collaborative Approaches to Watershed Management*. MIT Press, Cambridge, Massachusetts.

Svendsen, M. (2005). *Irrigation and River Basin Management: Options for Governance and Institutions*. CABI Publishing, Wallingford. doi.org/10.1079/9780851996721.0000

Turral, H. & Fullagar, I. (2007). Institutional Directions in Groundwater Management in Australia, In: Giordano, M. & Villholth, K.G. (eds) *The Agricultural Groundwater Revolution: Opportunities and Threats to Development*. CAB International, Colombo, pp. 320–61. doi.org/10.1079/9781845931728.0320

Vranesh, G. (1987). *Colorado Water Law*. Natural Resources Law Centre, Boulder.

Wilkinson, J. (1997). *Water for Rural Production in NSW: Grand Designs and Changing Realities*. NSW Parliamentary Library Research Service, Sydney.

Williams, R.M. (1998). The History of Community Involvement in Groundwater Policy Development – Lower Namoi Valley New South Wales. *Proceedings of the AWWA 16th Federal Convention*, Melbourne.

Wolfenden, J. & Van der Lee, J. (2002). *Social and Economic Assessment of Options/Recommendations for the Upper and Lower Namoi Groundwater and Sharing Plan*. University of New England, Armidale.

Young, O. (2002). *The Institutional Dimensions of Environmental Change: Fit, Interplay and Scale*. MIT Press, Cambridge.

16

Private Actors in Multi-level Governance: GLOBALG.A.P. Standard-setting for Agricultural and Food Products

Anne McNaughton and Stewart Lockie

Introduction

One aspect of governance and regulation that tends to be persistently overlooked is the role of private actors, particularly as standard-setting agencies. Historically, industry bodies have traditionally set standards in specific fields (Schepel 2005: 145). In recent years, however, private standards have taken on significance as regulatory tools. While much has been written about the implications of private standards and standardisation (e.g. Marx et al. 2012; Casey 2009; Henson and Humphrey 2009; Havinga 2006), very little has been written about how standards become such regulatory tools. Unpacking the 'black box' of standardisation to see how it works is a neglected field of inquiry. This chapter makes a contribution to redressing this situation. We do so by applying the work of regulatory scholars, Julia Black, John Braithwaite and Ian Ayres, to a transnational, private standard-setting organisation, GLOBALG.A.P. We use Black's (2001) work on 'decentred regulation' and Ayres and Braithwaite's (1992) work on 'responsive regulation' to account for private actors as regulators in a multi-level governance structure.

In this chapter, we use the term 'multi-level governance' (MLG) in the sense explained in the introductory chapter of this collection. As *Daniell and Kay* note in their chapter, the term 'multi-level governance' refers to a system of 'continuous negotiation among nested governments at several territorial tiers' (Marks 1993: 392). Subsequent refinements of the term 'stress the non-hierarchical, informal and deliberative aspects of the negotiations under scrutiny' (*Kay*). GLOBALG.A.P. may belong to the 'Type II MLG' to which *Kay* refers (Hooghe and Marks 2001). With its highly developed governance structure, however, we suggest that GLOBALG.A.P has a more enduring quality than would be expected of a Type II system.

In the next section, we discuss standards and standardisation, particularly in the context of the agri-food sector. We also explain the way in which these standards acquire legal force (predominantly through the institution of private law contract). The discussion then turns to the governance structure of GLOBALG.A.P. While the level of detail in this section may be daunting, the point is to demonstrate the sophistication and complexity of this private governance regime that is at least equal to corresponding structures in the public sphere. The work concludes with an encouragement to the reader to consider with fresh eyes the way in which we are governed and to seek out opportunities to engage with these governance processes.

Standards and standardisation

> Private standards have become a much more prevalent part of the governance of global agri-food value chains in the last 10 to 15 years. Private firms and standards-setting coalitions, including companies and NGOs [non-government organisations], have created and adopted standards for food safety, as well as food quality and environmental and social aspects of agri-food production. These are increasingly monitored and enforced through third party certification. This has raised profound questions about the role of public and private institutions in establishing and enforcing food safety norms. (Henson and Humphrey 2009: iii).

Thus begins the Executive Summary of a report prepared for the 32nd session of the Codex Alimentarius Commission, held in 2009. The commission is the principal organ of the Joint Food Standards Programme of the Food and Agriculture Organisation and the World Health Organisation, special agencies of the United Nations. The paragraph quoted contains a number of ideas that this chapter will explore in further detail: the nature of standards, private firms and standard-setting coalitions; and the 'public/private' dichotomy as part of an MLG structure in international trade. We also use this quote as a starting point for commenting on the lack of understanding, on the part of many, of the way in which law works and the way in which law 'manages' power and the power balance in relationships. This lack of understanding leads to flawed arguments about the role of private sector entities in international trade and to claims for law reform that are often misplaced.

Standards and contract

Regardless of who develops any given standard, whether it is a state agency or a private sector body, the standard has no inherent legal force. It derives its legal force either from legislation that mandates compliance with it or from the private law of contract that similarly mandates compliance with it.

One concern that has arisen in recent times is the de facto mandatory nature of some standards. This comes about in one of two ways: either commercial reality dictates to particular participants in a market that, if they wish to have access to that market and remain in that market, they will need to comply with the provisions of a particular standard; alternatively, a particular standard will, for example, be referred to in legislation concerning public health and safety. Such legislation will not necessarily, however, mandate compliance with the standard referred to in the legislation.

Rather, the legislation will stipulate that the goods a retailer offers for sale must be 'safe'; that is, must not be harmful to consumers. It may refer to a particular safety standard, stating that compliance with such a standard would be one way of discharging the retailer's obligation. What such legislation does is to put the responsibility for the safety of goods sold to the public on the retailer. Should a consumer be adversely affected by a product purchased from the retailer, the latter is *prima facie* liable for that injury unless they can prove that they met their duty of care to the consumer. This can be difficult to do. One way of discharging this onus, however, is to provide evidence that they complied with a standard.

In order to protect themselves, retailers will either develop their own standards to manage this risk, or they will adopt standards already established.

Private firms and standard-setting coalitions

Standards set by private firms and 'standard-setting coalitions' (Henson and Humphrey 2009) have become increasingly important in international trade in recent times. They are, in fact, a regulatory tool, although as such they have been largely overlooked by most legal scholars because they originate in the private sector and are seldom the subject of judicial consideration or review. In other words, they fall outside the conventional field of inquiry or investigation of legal scholars. Social scientists more generally have also overlooked aspects of this area of inquiry. Schepel (2005: 2–3) explains this situation thus:

> Standardization is a 'much neglected area of social science research, attracting much less attention than it deserves.' One of the reasons for this, I suspect, is that social scientists like to construct a world according to a series of distinctions – state and market, law and society, public and private, national and international – that are inherently incapable of capturing or explaining standardisation. Standards hover between the state and the market; standards largely collapse the distinction between legal and social norms; standards are very rarely either wholly public or wholly private, and can be both intensely local and irreducibly global.

Schepel's explanation holds true for legal scholars as a subset of social scientists. Legal scholars, like other social scientists, tend to look at 'the law' within the spheres to which Schepel refers (state, market, law, society, public, private, national, international), rather than looking at 'the law' cutting across these spheres. This statement requires further clarification, however: traditionally, legal scholars have concerned themselves with studying norms that have been made 'according to the procedures and passed through the institutions prescribed by law' (Schepel 2005: 2).

Standards, generally speaking, have not been made in this way and have not, traditionally, been regarded as 'laws'. The narrowness of this definition has been one of the problems with explaining and accounting for developments that have been occurring in society. It has led, among other things, to the development of new spheres of inquiry and a new application of terminology: regulation and governance, rather than law and government, for example. Another explanation for the apparent neglect of this area of inquiry by legal scholars is 'the peculiar history and culture of the institutionalised study of law as it has developed in England and of its primary base, the law school' (Twining 1994: xix). Twining's comment applies equally to the Australian context; possibly even to all legal systems based on English common law and its study.

An investigation of standards, their creation and application from a legal perspective sits more comfortably in the area of regulation and governance than it does in the more traditional area of legal inquiry. Perhaps not surprisingly, the sphere of regulation and governance is inherently interdisciplinary; among other things, it examines 'rules' and their application across the spheres referred to above, rather than within them. It also redefines 'rules' more broadly than the definition of 'laws' also referred to above.

Why should legal scholars be concerned with studying standards and standardisation? The answer lies partly in a definition of the term, 'regulation', coined by Julia Black (2001: 142) as:

> a process involving the sustained and focused attempt to alter the behaviour of others according to defined standards or purposes with the intention of producing broadly defined outcome or outcomes.

An element of this definition is the attempt to alter behaviour 'according to defined standards'. Standards are brought into existence for a great variety of reasons: product safety, quality control (of services as well as goods), reducing transaction costs, managing expectations and liability. They cannot be classified solely by their provenance either; that is, whether they have been created by a private, non-state actor or a public, state actor. Depending on the context, standards created in the private sector may be incorporated into legislation and thus made mandatory; voluntary standards contained in legislation may be mandated in the private sector by being incorporated into contracts. Henson and Humphrey illustrate this complexity succinctly, making one clear distinction that many non-lawyers overlook: that private standards can become 'de facto mandatory in a commercial sense through adoption by dominant market actors' (Henson and Humphrey 2009: iii).

Unlike other non-lawyers, Henson and Humphrey do not extrapolate from this that such standards are therefore de jure mandatory. This is an important distinction. Non-lawyers frequently equate a de facto mandatory standard with a de jure mandatory standard because they focus on the exercise of power in the voluntary, contractual relationship that is governed in part by the standard in question. A lawyer will or should realise that these are not the same thing: that law deals with this exercise of power in a different way, namely with competition law. This is an important point and it is worth spending some time unpacking the ideas and assumptions underpinning it.

In the first place, if we say that a standard is 'de facto mandatory', what we mean is that a party is mandating compliance with that standard by another party that is not required in law to comply with the standard. The former can compel compliance with the standard because, in the relationship between the two, its bargaining power is stronger; that is, the latter is of the view that it will be more disadvantageous for it not to comply with the standard than it will be to comply with the standard. On the legal landscape, this places the two parties in a contractual relationship in a market in which one party is in a stronger bargaining position than the other.

As a matter of law, a contract is a voluntary institution; that is, the parties to a contract can choose whether or not they enter into a contract with each other and, if so, on what terms. This is referred to as party autonomy and is a fundamental principle of contract law that is recognised and accepted across all jurisdictions, in all legal systems, or at least in those systems in which parties to such contracts are found (even, interestingly, in those of planned economies: Schmitthoff 1961).[1] Irrespective of the legal system, the negotiating power of a party to a contract is largely irrelevant to the formation of a contract. As a matter of contract law, the assumption is that the parties to a contract have concluded it on the terms they have negotiated as acceptable between them.

Clearly, this ignores the commercial reality of 'standard form' contracts[2] and situations in which the party in the stronger bargaining position can prevail in contracting on their terms, rather than those of their counterpart. It is fair to say that most, if not all, developed legal systems limit the extent to which one party can exert power over the other to 'persuade' or 'compel' the latter to conclude a contract. This is certainly true of the legal systems of developed economies and states. Australian law, for example, has the defences of duress at common law and of undue influence and of unconscionable conduct in equity. It also has certain statutory causes of action such as unconscionability under the Australian Consumer Law (Part IVA of what was formerly the *Trade Practices Act 1974* (Cth)), Part 2, Division 2 of the *Australian Securities and Investment*

---

1   China and Cuba, for example, are signatories to the United Nations Convention on Contracts for the International Sale of Goods: United Nations, *Treaty Series*, Volume 1489, p. 3.

2   A 'standard form' contract is one in relation to which one party has set out all the terms to which they are willing to be bound and presented it to the other contracting party on a 'take it or leave it' basis. Most contracts that consumers conclude with institutions such as banks, insurance companies and utility companies are such contracts.

Commission Act 2001 (Cth) and the *Contracts Review Act 1980* (NSW). The Australian Consumer Law (dealt with under Part XI and Schedule 2, *Competition and Consumer Act 2010* (Cth)) provides for 'unfair' terms in a consumer, 'standard form' contract (as defined under the Act) to be declared void.

Common to all these measures is the fact that they apply, in effect, retrospectively. That is, they do not contain any prerequisites for the formation of the contract itself; rather, they enable one of the contracting parties to avoid the contract (or certain terms in the contract, in the case of the Australian Consumer Law provisions, for example) by showing that their circumstances meet the elements of one of these causes of action. Legal systems in which the rule of law, legal institutions and governance structures are fragile or weak are less likely to have effective, functioning competition regimes such as those found in developed systems. Consequently, market participants in such systems may well behave in a manner that, in other legal systems, would be subject to certain constraints on, and sanctions for, the exercise of market power.

Private standards in the agri-food sector: The case of GLOBALG.A.P.

In the 1990s, public confidence in the ability of the state to regulate for food safety dropped dramatically when it was established that a fatal disease found in cattle – bovine spongiform encephalopathy or 'mad cow disease' – had 'jumped' species and was presenting as Creutzfeldt-Jakob Disease in humans. Responses to consumer concerns about the provenance of what they were eating included, on the part of the state, the introduction in the United Kingdom of the *Food Safety Act*. Among other things, this Act made it an offence for a person to sell food that did not meet food safety requirements (s. 8).

GLOBALG.A.P. is the name of a private sector, voluntary standard-setting organisation that first came into existence in 1997 under the name EurepG.A.P. It was established by the Euro-Retailer Produce Working Group (EUREP) for the purpose of setting standards and procedures for the development of 'GAP' (Good Agricultural Practice) (Bayramoglu and Gundogmus 2009: 52). Apart from consumer concerns regarding food safety, EurepG.A.P. was also responding to concerns of citizens as consumers for the environment and for labour standards, especially in developing countries. Through EurepG.A.P., retailers in Europe set about harmonising their differing standards. Producers dealing with these retailers also became involved with EurepG.A.P. in the process of harmonising certification standards. In the decade following, retailers and producers outside Europe also became involved in this process and, in 2007, EurepG.A.P. was renamed GLOBALG.A.P. to reflect this shift.

Much of the writing about GLOBALG.A.P. and what it represents has tended to have a concerned, if not critical, tone (Wouters et al. 2009; Havinga 2006). It is not the purpose of this chapter to engage directly with those works. In exploring the role of the private sector in the context of MLG, however, this chapter will hopefully also allay some of those concerns. Similarly, considering the perceived Eurocentric nature of GLOBALG.A.P. (Campbell 2005) must also wait for another occasion, as too must an evaluation of GLOBALG.A.P. standards and their implementation. As stated, the purpose of this chapter is to examine the role of private, non-state actors as 'regulators' in the context of MLG. To that end, discussion in this chapter is concerned with understanding the GLOBALG.A.P. standards as regulatory tools, not evaluating their implementation or effectiveness.

What levels, actors and sectors are involved?

As already stated, GLOBALG.A.P. is a private sector organisation that develops voluntary standards in the agri-food sector. According to its website,[3] GLOBALG.A.P. currently has 16 standards across three areas (or scopes): crops, livestock and aquaculture. These include: the Integrated Farm Assurance (IFA) Standard; the Compound Feed Manufacturing Standard (CFM); the Livestock Transport Standard (LT); the Product Safety Standard (PSS) and the Plant Propagation Material Standard (PPM). It has also developed the Risk Assessment on Social Practice Standard (GRASP) and a module for Animal Welfare. These last two instruments are the 'Add-on' element of the 'GLOBALG.A.P + Add-on' certification scheme or 'product'.

---

3   www.globalgap.org/uk_en/what-we-do/globalg.a.p.-certification/ [Accessed: 20/07/2017].

For example:

> The GLOBALG.A.P. Integrated Farm Assurance (IFA) Standard covers the certification of the whole agricultural production process of the product from before the plant is in the ground (origin and propagation material control points) or from when the animal enters the production process to non-processed product (no processing, manufacturing or slaughtering is covered, except for the first level in Aquaculture). GLOBALG.A.P provides the standard and framework for independent, recognized 3rd party certification of primary production processes based on ISO/IEC Guide 65. (Certification of the production process – cropping, growing, rearing, or producing – of products ensures that only those that reach a certain level of compliance with established Good Agricultural Practice (G.A.P.) set out in the GLOBALG.A.P normative documents are certified (GLOBALG.A.P. 2017).

The IFA Standard applies to certain crops: fruit and vegetables, combinable crops, tea, green coffee, flowers and ornamental plants (horticulture); and certain livestock: cattle, sheep, pigs, poultry, turkey; and certain acquaculture.

A recent initiative in GLOBALG.A.P. standards development is the GLOBALG.A.P. Risk Assessment on Social Practice (GRASP),[4] which is the result of nearly five years of stakeholder consultation, supported by the GTZ (Deutsche Gesellschaft für Technische Zusammenarbeit GmbH) and Coop Switzerland in the initial development of the module. In the second phase of the project, GLOBALG.A.P. members, Edeka, Lidl, Metro AG and Migros, also assisted in implementing the GRASP module in selected pilot countries. The development of the module was accompanied by intensive stakeholder dialogue in more than 20 countries on five continents. The results of this process were reviewed together with contributions from further public consultation. GRASP is a voluntary assessment that can be undertaken at the same time as a GLOBALG.A.P. audit. The results of such an assessment are not intended to affect GLOBALG.A.P. certification. They do, however, provide additional information to supply chain partners who have been given access to the results.

---

4   www.globalgap.org/uk_en/for-producers/globalg.a.p.-add-on/grasp/index.html   [Accessed: 9/11/2017].

The purpose of providing this brief insight into what are, in fact, complex instruments is twofold: to indicate the comprehensive nature of the IFA Standard and to demonstrate the breadth of issues with which GLOBALG.A.P. engages. This work draws on research focusing on the nature of standards more generally, particularly those set by entities located in the private sector, and how these standards can be explained as part of the network of regulations governing international trade.

It is in this context that the standards of GLOBALG.A.P. operate. The members, board and committee members and office bearers of the organisation responded to a number of drivers, including, it is suggested, a gap: a regulatory failure. They responded to that failure by developing a sophisticated regime and governance structure that, in turn, has developed and administered the foremost private standard-setting body in the world. In the area of food safety certification, GLOBALG.A.P. is, according to its website, the most widely accepted private sector system in the world. Even allowing for bias in this statement, it is beyond question that GLOBALG.A.P. is the single most significant private sector standard-setting institution worldwide.

Governance structure of GLOBALG.A.P.

The GLOBALG.A.P. governance structure consists of a board, secretariat, Technical Committees and National Technical Working Groups. The following information is available at the relevant links on the GLOBALG.A.P. website.[5]

The board

The board comprises an equal number of producer and retailer representatives elected from the membership and is headed by an independent chairperson. Its task is to determine strategy, design the standards-setting procedure, adopt standards and rules and provide the legal framework for regulating the certification bodies.

---

5   See for example www.globalgap.org/uk_en/who-we-are/governance/ [Accessed: 20/07/2017].

The Technical Committees

The five Technical Committees (for livestock, aquaculture, crops, GRASP and Systems and Rules) comprise members of GLOBALG.A.P. who are experts in the particular field for which the committee is responsible. These members are selected from across the supply chain and are elected for a four-year term. Half represent producers and half represent retail members of GLOBALG.A.P. The committees are responsible for 'developing and defining the standard criteria' (referred to as control points and compliance criteria). They are also responsible for defining the general regulations that 'establish clear criteria for the successful implementation and verification of standards'. The terms of reference for the Technical Committees are available from the GLOBALG.A.P. website. They stipulate the obligations of committee members, including voting procedures and the development of four-year activity plans. The latter include detailed milestones that are re-evaluated annually; they are shared with the National Technical Working Groups and benchmarked schemes and are published on the GLOBALG.A.P. website once they have been approved by the board.

Stakeholder Committees

Previously, there were eight Stakeholder Committees: SHC GRASP, SHC Water, SHC Animal Welfare, SHC Microbiological Risk Assessment, SHC Crop Protection, SHC Flowers and Ornamentals, SHC Producer Groups and SHC Chain of Custody. The Stakeholder Committees were working groups. Their membership was drawn from 'a wide range of industry experts including GLOBALG.A.P. members, non-members, non-government organisations, retailers and suppliers' and their responsibilities included:

- developing change proposals
- preparing initial drafts of the required Control Points and Compliance Criteria, add-on modules or guidelines based on background research
- reviewing public input and making revisions to drafts of standards
- advising the GLOBALG.A.P. Board and Technical Committees.

The Stakeholder Committees have now been replaced by Focus Groups, which are established as needed and work on specific topics as required.

Certification Body Committee

The Certification Body Committee (CBC) is responsible for coordinating and supervising the activities of GLOBALG.A.P.-approved certification bodies. There are currently more than 140 such bodies worldwide. The CBC comprises experts employed by certification bodies that are associate members of GLOBALG.A.P. and are also accredited consistently with ISO Guide 65 to at least one GLOBALG.A.P. scope. The CBC discusses issues concerning GLOBALG.A.P. implementation, provides feedback and represents the activities of the certifying bodies within the GLOBALG.A.P. system. Any changes proposed by the CBC are issued to the Technical Committees for consideration and approval. A CBC subgroup was specifically established for South American certification bodies in early 2012 at their request. This regional subgroup, CBC Latin America, represents local sector interests. It communicates regularly with the CBC (referred to as CBC Central).

Integrity Surveillance Committee

The Integrity Surveillance Committee (ISC) has been in place since 2009. It comprises industry experts who have a local legal background. Committee members are appointed by the board but operate independently. The ISC is part of the GLOBALG.A.P. Integrity Program, which was established in 2008. According to the GLOBALG.A.P. website, there are 'over 1800 trained inspectors and auditors working for more than 150 accredited certification bodies certifying over 530 products and more than 170,600 producers, spread across 120 plus countries in 5 continents'. The Integrity Program was developed to foster and maintain the confidence and trust of stakeholders in the GLOBALG.A.P. product and certification process. The way in which the program works is set out on the GLOBALG.A.P. website.

In essence, however, GLOBALG.A.P. auditors assess certification bodies (CB) by way of a document review and by sampling producers directly to check inspection performance of the CBs. The auditors advise the certifying bodies as well as accreditation bodies of any deviation in the compliance requirements. Audit reports are forwarded to the ISC, which makes the final decision on the approval status of a CB. Where a certification body fails to comply with a second warning concerning non-compliance, a so-called Yellow Card is issued to that CB. This is also published on the website and is only removed once the CB has been successfully reassessed. Should the CB be unsuccessful, a so-called Red Card is issued and also published on the GLOBALG.A.P. website.

When a Red Card is issued, the CB is prohibited from issuing new certificates, or reissuing them, for up to six months. Should such a CB fail its reassessment, its license and certification agreement with GLOBALG.A.P. will be cancelled for at least two years. Each of these sanctions is displayed on the GLOBALG.A.P. website. The ISC reviews cases of non-compliance by CBs 'on an anonymous basis, defines corrective measures and proposes sanctions, which the GLOBALG.A.P. Secretariat then enforces'.

National Technical Working Groups

Several countries have established a National Technical Working Group (NTWG). Forty-two countries have a NTWG for a range of scopes and sub-scopes. These countries include Brazil, Japan, Kenya, New Zealand, Chile, Vietnam, Pakistan, India and Thailand. GLOBALG.A.P. does not require the establishment of such groups but does support, encourage and work with those that are established. Information is also set out on the GLOBALG.A.P. website on how to set up and host a NTWG.

NTWGs play an important role in the GLOBALG.A.P. regulatory structure. They provide an 'in-country' forum in which GLOBALG.A.P. members can consider necessary adaptations to respond to local challenges of implementing GLOBALG.A.P. measures. NTWGs can, and do, develop national interpretation guidelines (NIG) in accordance with the procedure established by GLOBALG.A.P. for this purpose. Draft NIGs are submitted to the GLOBALG.A.P. secretariat for approval, following consultation with the Technical Committees.

Once the NIGs are approved, they are binding on producers and certification bodies with respect to that country. Accreditation bodies 'must ensure that all the accredited certification bodies have adopted the NIG in their auditing and certification activities'. The NTWGs and the NIGs complete the feedback loop between national producers and certification bodies and the GLOBALG.A.P. board, Technical Committees and secretariat. The main activities of the NTWGs include translating official GLOBALG.A.P. documents into languages used in the relevant country; supporting the Technical Committees with proposals for revising the protocols; and, at the request of FoodPLUS, participating in the peer-review processes of benchmarking and recognition activities of schemes operating within their country.

GLOBALG.A.P. as regulator

Applying Black's (2001) definition of 'regulation' (above) to GLOBALG.A.P., it is clear that the regime established by the latter is one of regulation and that the organisation itself is a regulator. We suggest, further, that GLOBALG.A.P. is, in fact, a *responsive* regulator. Elsewhere, we have explored the relationship between GLOBALG.A.P. as a private standard-setting organisation and state agencies in relation to the regulation of food safety and quality (Lockie et al. 2013).

We considered there the interaction of state and private regulation in the national context of Australia, Vietnam and the Philippines, using the concept of responsive regulation (Ayres and Braithwaite 1992) as an analytical device to explore such interdependencies in these particular national contexts. In the next section, however, we use responsive regulation as a lens for considering the responsiveness of GLOBALG.A.P. as a regulator.

Although our focus is on GLOBALG.A.P. as a private regulator, we do not suggest that it regulates *to the exclusion* of public or state regulators. Our deliberations here contribute to the conversations concerning hybrid forms of regulation. In focusing on a private actor as regulator, however, we seek to demonstrate that a private actor is as capable of improving the effectiveness, transparency and legitimacy of its regulation as a public regulator.

GLOBALG.A.P. as responsive regulator

We use two examples to illustrate the responsiveness of GLOBALG.A.P. as a regulator:

1. the concerns of small farmers in developing states about being excluded from European markets because of an inability to meet GLOBALG.A.P. standards
2. support and encouragement for the creation of National Technical Working Groups.

GLOBALG.A.P. and small farmers

In 2005, Saint Vincent and the Grenadines raised concerns with the Sanitary and Phytosanitary (SPS) Committee of the World Trade Organization (WTO) about private standards (WTO 2007). These states were representing the interests of small farmers who had little or no capacity to meet the requirements of the GLOBALG.A.P. standards. As a result, they feared they would lose access to the valuable European markets whose retailers required compliance with those standards as part of their risk management strategy concerning food integrity and safety. In response to these concerns and, almost certainly, motivated by a desire to head off more formal intervention from the WTO and its agencies, GLOBALG.A.P. initiated and developed a project to assist farmers of small holdings to comply with the GLOBALG.A.P. standards. With the support of the UK Department for International Development and the German Society for Technical Cooperation (Deutsche Gesellschaft für Technische Zusammenarbeit, GTZ), GLOBALG.A.P. established an 'Africa Observer' project in 2007 (Will 2010; Homer 2010: 16). The objectives of this project were:

> to identify ways in which the GLOBALG.A.P. standard [could] become more inclusive for smallholder farmers in developing countries and to assist GLOBALG.A.P. to develop new and adjust existing technical standards and tools appropriate for smallholder certification (Will 2010: 9).

This initiative developed to become what is now 'localg.a.p.' and 'localg.a.p. program'. 'Localg.a.p.' is described on the GLOBALG.A.P. website as a:

> cost-effective solution for emerging markets [that] helps producers gain gradual recognition by providing an entry level to GLOBAL.G.A.P. Certification. [I]t helps retailers gain access to quality foods, support their local and regional producers and promote Good Agricultural Practice.

The point here is not to evaluate the effectiveness of the initiative, nor to debate the advantages and disadvantages of this particular approach. It is simply to demonstrate that a private actor, as regulator, responded to criticisms of its regulatory processes in a way that sought not only to improve the effectiveness of that regulation, but also to enhance the legitimacy of the regulator and the transparency of the process.

National Technical Working Groups

The second example of GLOBALG.A.P.'s responsiveness is the acceptance, support and engagement of the National Technical Working Groups. As indicated above, GLOBALG.A.P. does not require members to establish such working groups. However, it enables the creation of such groups as an agency within the regulatory structure created by the private actor. Again, the purpose of the discussion here is not to evaluate the particular approach adopted by GLOBALG.A.P. in recognising and managing the establishment of such groups. The purpose here is simply to recognise that the private regulator has adopted this approach, rather than resisting the participation of members and stakeholders at the local level. Rather than either reject such contributions outright or accept them through an opaque, informal and arbitrary process, the organisation has set up a structure dealing with what can be contributed by these groups, and how and in what way such contributions may be given effect.

Conclusion

Notwithstanding the recognition and acceptance of a plurality of actors in the MLG landscape, the role of the state and public actors seems to occupy the attention of most commentators. Private, non-state actors seem to be considered as subordinate or ancillary players, complementing and supplementing the activities of state actors. While formally subordinate to the authority and competence of the nation state, we suggest that, in fact, GLOBALG.A.P. as a regulator is on an equal footing with public regulators and agencies. In the field of agri-food, food safety, integrity and quality and the management of risk along the production and delivery chain the governance structure is a hybrid of private and public actors.

To properly understand the governance of this field, it is essential that the nature and role of private regulators in general, and GLOBALG.A.P. in particular, are examined and understood. In this chapter, we have used a private sector food safety and quality regulator as the focus of our inquiry. Similar 'regulators' can, however, also be found elsewhere in the market; for example, particularly in relation to financial and professional services. By discussing the way in which standards and standard-setting bodies operate, we hope readers will consider anew the way in which we are governed and will seek out opportunities to engage not only with public, but also with the private governance processes.

References

Ayres, I. & Braithwaite, J. (1992). *Responsive Regulation: Transcending the Deregulation Debate*. Oxford University Press.

Bayramoglu, Z. & Gundogmus, E. (2009). The Effect of EurepGAP Standards on Energy Input Use: A comparative analysis between certified and uncertified greenhouse tomato producers in Turkey. *Energy Conversion and Management*, 50: 52–56. doi.org/10.1016/j. enconman.2008.08.023

Black, J. (2001). Decentring Regulation: Understanding the role of regulation and self-regulation in a 'post-regulatory' world. *Current Legal Problems*, 54(1): 103–46. doi.org/10.1093/clp/54.1.103

Campbell, H. (2005). The Rise and Rise of EurepGAP: European (re) invention of colonial food relations? *International Journal of Sociology of Food and Agriculture*, 13(2): 1–19.

Casey, D. (2009). *Three Puzzles of Private Governance: GLOBALG.A.P. and the Regulation of Food Safety and Quality*. UCD Working Papers in Law, Criminology and Socio-Legal Studies, Research Paper No. 22/2009, Dublin.

GLOBALG.A.P. (2013). GLOBALG.A.P. IFA Standard, Version 4.0, Edition 4.0-2Mar2013, valid from 2 March, 2013.

——. (2017). Integrated Farm Assurance: All Farm Base – Crops Base – Fruit and Vegetables. Control Points and Compliance Criteria. English Version 5.1.

Havinga, T. (2006). Private Regulation of Food Safety by Supermarkets. *Law and Policy*, 28(4): 515–33. doi.org/10.1111/j.1467-9930. 2006.00237.x

Henson, S. & Humphrey, J. (2009). *The Impacts of Private Food Safety Standards on the Food Chain and on Public Standard-setting Processes*. Paper prepared for FAO/WHO, ALINORM 09/32/9D-Part II, Rome.

Homer, S. (2010). *Standards and Market Preferences: Opportunities and Constraints*. Seminar paper: 3rd Installment under the AACP-Funded Series of High Value Agriculture Seminars, www.globalhort.org/ media/uploads/File/Video%20Conferences/VC3%20Issue%20Paper. pdf [Accessed: 17/12/2014].

Hooghe, L. & Marks, G. (2001). Types of Multi-level Governance. *European Integration online Papers (EIoP)*, 5(11), eiop.or.at/eiop/pdf/2001-011.pdf [Accessed: 17/12/2014].

Lockie, S., McNaughton, A., Thompson, L.-J. & Tennent, R. (2013). Private Food Standards as Responsive Regulation: The role of national legislation in the implementation and evolution of GLOBALG.A.P. *International Journal of the Sociology of Agriculture and Food*, 20(2): 275–91.

Marks, G. (1993). Structural Policy and Multilevel Governance in the EC. In: Cafruny, A. & Rosenthal, G. (eds) *The State of the European Community Vol. 2: The Maastricht Debates and Beyond*. Longman, Harlow, pp. 391–410.

Marx, A., Martens, M., Swinnen, J. & Wouters, J. (2012). *Private Standards and Global Governance: Economic, Legal and Political Perspectives*. Edward Elgar Publishing Limited, Cheltenham. doi.org/10.4337/9781849808750

Schepel, H. (2005). *The Constitution of Private Governance: Product Standards in the Regulation of Integrating Markets*. Hart Publishing, Oxford.

Schmitthoff, C.M. (1961). International Business: The new law merchant. *Current Law and Social Problems*, 2: 129–53.

Twining, W. (1994). *Blackstone's Tower: The English Law School*. Stevens and Sons/Sweet and Maxwell, London.

Will, M. (2010). *Integrating Smallholders into Global Supply Chains: GLOBALG.A.P. Option 2 Smallholder Group Certification Generic Manual: Lessons learnt in pilot projects in Kenya, Ghana, Thailand and Macedonia*. April, Deutsche Gesellschaft für Internationale Zusammenarbeit (GIZ) GmbH.

Wouters, J., Marks, A. & Hachez, N. (2009). *In Search of a Balanced Relationship: Public and Private Food Safety Standards and International Law*. Working Paper No. 29. Leuven Centre for Global Governance Studies.

WTO (2007). *Private Standards and the SPS Agreement*. G/SPS/GEN/746: 24 January 2007, WTO Secretariat Note, World Trade Organization, Geneva.

17

Breaking Down the 'One-Size-Fits-All' Approach to Rural and Regional Policy: Enhancing Policy Initiatives through Multi-level Governance

Katherine A. Daniell, Anthony Hogan and Jen Cleary

Introduction

Key Australian rural and regional policy challenges: A brief overview

With the prospect of continuing climate change and the emergence of the Asian century, Australia faces a range of likely impacts on, and policy challenges associated with, food production and natural resource management. Such impacts and changes have included the further intensification of agricultural processes owned by international interests, as well as the intensification of ore, coal and gas extraction, coupled with large-scale policy-reform programs targeted at water management, resources, infrastructure development and structural changes to telecommunications. As a consequence, shifting economic outlooks sit at the heart of an agenda for policy change that significantly impacts on rural and regional Australians' livelihoods and wellbeing.

Yet, change is not unusual in rural and regional Australia (Hogan and Young 2015). The agricultural base that has underpinned the viability of many rural communities has been declining over many years as a result of a sustained technological revolution, which has led to an annual productivity improvement rate of 2.7 per cent since the 1960s (Productivity Commission 2005). Such productivity gains are argued to 'be of benefit to some farmers only if others were subsequently forced from their farms' (Barr 2009: 11). Barr (2009), writing on the transformation of Australian farming communities, argues further that, as the number of farmers decreases, the remaining number of farms must increase in size and continue to achieve technological efficiencies, including reducing the need for rural labour.

He points out that the loss of agricultural jobs has a flow-on effect in rural towns, with young people seeking employment in other industries and other towns and cities. The Bureau of Rural Sciences (2008) reported that, for the 10 years ending 2006, jobs in agriculture had fallen proportionately by one-third, moving from 4.4 per cent of total employment in Australia in 1996 to 3.1 per cent in 2006. In particular, a booming Australian mining industry has been increasingly competing for labour in rural and regional agricultural production areas, which, while welcomed in some regions, causes serious challenges for others. The educational needs of children, teenagers and young adults wanting to pursue studies or broader cultural experiences that are not available in their communities is also a driver of outwards migration and a key concern for the future of some rural communities (e.g. Pearson and Dare 2014).

Independent of the process of rural decline and/or structural change, but also exacerbating it, has been the process of climate change and the impacts of dryness. Increasingly, many small-scale farmers find that they cannot compete within the structure of existing globalising markets and an increasingly unstable climate (Hogan et al. 2010), while, at the same time, large-scale multinational interests are investing in farming at a geographic scale not seen before. These businesses have access to such levels of capital as to be able to climate-proof themselves against changes of weather and climatic trends by owning productive resources in a variety of countries and regions within countries, such that they can farm one region but not another, depending on where, when and how often rain falls or water allocations for irrigation are available. Environmental degradation – including loss of biodiversity and soil health through land salinisation, acidification and the loss of topsoil, as well as serious damage to water-dependent ecosystems such as rivers and wetlands through overuse and invasive species – is also a major challenge, as it typically underpins agricultural productivity (in the case of soil) or other industries vital to rural and regional communities, such as tourism.

The state and drivers of Australia's rural and regional governance system

The governance of rural and regional Australia seems as confused as it is complicated. Evans et al. (2013) highlight that, rather than streamlining the complexities of governance in this space, successive Australian governments have introduced new agencies and decision-making processes that are set up to work around entrenched decision-making processes at lower levels. The intensified layering of administrative and institutional arrangements, not to mention the duplication of decision-making processes in rural and regional Australia, is further complicated by a lack of clear vision for policy in this space (Hogan and Young 2013). Community-based governance processes are also almost systematically altered when there is a change in the Australian Government, as was the case for the Julia Gillard's Labor Government (2010–13), which reinvigorated notions of localised decision-making. This was, albeit, a form of (centralised) managerial localism (Evans et al. 2013) where local bodies were given some say in the development of some local initiatives, subject to the wishes of the Commonwealth Minister for Regional Development.

The importance of crises, such as intense floods, droughts or global economic events, can also not be overlooked as drivers for the development of these complex governance arrangements as such events help to mobilise action around governance changes and provide a window of opportunity for legislative reform in conflict-ridden policy spaces (e.g. Sabatier 1988; Dovers 2013; Daniell et al. 2014). The 'Millennium drought' in Australia, which officially ended in 2012 (*Age* 2012), was certainly one such event that mobilised policy change in the governments of John Howard and Kevin Rudd – Gillard governments, such as the *Water Act 2007* and the associated federal takeover of Murray–Darling Basin (MDB) governance.

With the spending of $4.5 billion in exceptional circumstances (EC) assistance payments from 2001–12, there was also increased impetus for drought policy change in the agricultural policy domain. This was especially due to fears that climate step-changes in south-western Australia and south-eastern Australian might be permanent and linked to climate change (e.g. Wentworth Group 2006), which would make the financial undertakings of the current policy system untenable into the future. In response, an intensification of drought policy work was evident, underscored by values that construct the global challenges of farming as risks that are inherently internal to businesses and, as such, a risk to be carried by the individual entity.

In particular, the Gillard Government went to extensive lengths to encourage the nation's farmers to adapt to the challenges of climate change, while the Intergovernmental Panel on Climate Change continued to document the extent, impact and likely future scenarios of global warming and the acidification of oceans on Australia's weather patterns and capacity to pursue agriculture in given parts of Australia. A distinct climate-impact line was identified in the West Australian wheat belt, where a casual observer can stand and observe the point in the wheat paddocks (east of Merredin) where the rain has stopped falling and where it is unlikely wheat will grow again. A new drought policy trial was implemented in this region (DAFF 2010; ABARES 2012) with the possibilities of rolling measures of it out nationally if it was seen to be successful through part of the Intergovernmental Agreement on National Drought Program Reform,[1] signed under the Gillard Government in 2013.

With the subsequent election of the Liberal conservative government under Tony Abbott in late 2013, policy directions changed, with the government bringing to a halt or deprioritising many of the former government's efforts to address either the impacts of climate change or the environmental impacts of increasingly intensified farming. In the 2014 budget, the Abbott Government withdrew approximately $500 million in funding for the care of land in Australia, despite the serious challenges of soil salinity, acidification, erosion, loss of top soil, and pollution and overuse of many of the nation's waterways. It also sought to wind-up the National Water Commission by the end of 2014. By contrast, a further $1 billion has been allocated to the development of critical infrastructure to support the more efficient export of primary resources overseas by road and through seaports.

---

1   www.agriculture.gov.au/SiteCollectionDocuments/agriculture-food/drought/drought-program-reform/iga.pdf.

Amidst these typical swings in national policy, people living in rural and regional areas have to suffer through the lack of coherence and consistency in policy strategies that have important impacts on their day-to-day lives. There are multiple levels of government and a multiplicity of interests at work in the governance of rural and regional Australia, and it appears to be a far from effective form of governance. Yet, many people continue to express the desire to live in rural and regional Australia and to develop their livelihoods there (Gross and Dumaresq 2014). Others just want to see it prosper as it is an important part of the Australian nation, which is said to be have been built 'on the sheep's back' and agricultural development more broadly, and/or have its environmental qualities preserved for the future generations. Here, Australians concerned about the environment look for coherence in environmental policy (Tennent and Lockie 2015), while people who rely on the rural space tend to look at the nation's economic settings and question how such policy design could possibly be in the interests of small-scale family farmers and similarly sized rural communities (Smith and Pritchard 2015).

Proposal for a way forward

In this complex policy context of often competing values, rural and regional Australia desperately needs a well-developed and considered form of 'multi-level governance' (MLG) – a system of governance where mechanisms exist that provide for arenas of 'continuous negotiation among nested governments at several territorial tiers' (Marks 1993), where authority is not only dispersed vertically between levels of administration, but also horizontally across different sectors of interest and spheres of influence, including non-government actors, markets and civil society (see *Daniell and Kay*). Over the past few years, scholars have described how such systems of governance could be developed (see, for example, Botterill 2011; Cockfield 2015; Collits 2015; Hogan et al. 2015). The Commonwealth's approach the development of institutional structures and policy implementation processes, however, appears to continue to diverge significantly, in that they are typically 'one-size-fits-all' approaches where power is devolved to the federal or state government, depending on the issue.

In taking government in September 2010, Julia Gillard announced a new era in governance (discussed below). Yet, since the Abbott-led Coalition's election victory in 2014, governmental departments continue to operate within basically the same processes and structures as usual. Thus, central to progressing governance in rural and regional Australia, is the need to embrace principles and processes of MLG to enhance these current and longer-term policy initiatives. But how could this come about and why might such moves be justified?

First of all, we suggest that MLG can be used as a potential way of moving beyond current forms of policy centred on values of centralised command-and-control (including managerial localism), to open up possibilities of a more flexible and dynamic approach to decision-making – one that requires continuous negotiation, interaction and revised funding models. We consider that the central tenet of 'negotiated policies' as outputs of MLG processes implies that one-size-fits-all policies are unlikely to result because individual communities and other stakeholders will likely have the opportunity to negotiate appropriate place- and need-specific mechanisms or policies with higher levels of governments, businesses and non-government organisations, which will vary from community to community.

By 'appropriate' mechanisms, a range of MLG arrangements could be imagined where policies are developed. For example, in some cases, it could be envisaged that multi-level negotiation systems are developed between federal and local governments, communities and businesses, effectively bypassing the states, if decision-making processes do not require them (Daniell et al. 2014). Efforts to develop such an approach for specific water policy initiatives have already been observed with the federal government negotiating with, and directly funding, local communities for local policy initiatives (e.g. Kelly 2010). Other systems – for example, for natural resource management that is strongly spatially constrained – may require more nested 'polycentric' (Ostrom 1999; Marshall 2008) or 'adaptive' (Pahl-Wostl 2008) governance structures. The challenge here remains to ensure that no important spatial or administrative/institutional levels are neglected and that effective cross-scale linkages and negotiation systems are developed to support them (Berkes 2002; Cash et al. 2006; Daniell and Barreteau 2014).

In the next sections, we expand our argument by reviewing some current issues and approaches in policymaking arising in the context of global changes and the regional policy agenda, and consider them in the context of the principles of MLG. The analysis relies not only on literature and policy reviews, but also on research and interviews carried out as part of the

Cotton Catchment Communities Co-operative Research Centre (CRC); a Rural Industries Research and Development Corporation–funded project, 'Securing the Wealth and Wellbeing of Rural Communities', undertaken between 2012 and 2014 (Hogan et al. 2014); and the 'Building Adaptive and Sustainable Communities in the Murray–Darling Basin' project of the MDB Futures Collaborative Research Network (2012–14). Bringing these materials together, we then propose a way forward for the development of governmental conditions that could allow for more power-sharing, flexible financing and cross-sectoral capacity development in the field of Australian rural and regional policy.

Issues and approaches arising in Australian regional policy practice

Within regional Australia, there is significant diversity in income levels (Lloyd et al. 2001), employment rates (Garnaut et al. 2001) and mixes of both high and low productivity. Regions may have differing histories of settlement patterns and migration (Hugo 2001) and differences in both the pace and nature of development. Some regions have highly diverse local economies, or larger, more demographically diverse populations concentrated in relatively small areas (e.g. regional Victoria), while other regions are dominated by a single industry or a few industries that are agglomerative in nature and contain smaller and less demographically diverse populations spread over vastly greater spatiality (e.g. remote South Australia, Northern Territory and Western Australia).

Smaller and/or remote communities in geographically large regions, in particular, are highly interconnected across sectors, operate systemically and rely heavily on economies of scope rather than scale (Cleary 2014). In these regions, where distance and low-density populations are a feature, resources are often shared across different sectors so as to minimise higher overhead costs associated with productivity and service provision (Carson and Cleary 2010). They also, however, tend to rely on the same people to lead initiatives and community development or maintenance activities, with many community members struggling to manage the load of work required (Drought Policy Review Expert Social Panel 2008; Collaborative Research Netword (CRN) Project interviews 2013–14).

The Regional Development Australia initiative

In the period since 1996, successive Australian governments (regardless of political affiliation) have increasingly withdrawn from regional development, arguing that this falls constitutionally within the bailiwick of state and territory governments (Maude 2004). Following the installation of the Rudd and Gillard governments in 2007 and 2010, however, Australia moved towards new institutional arrangements that purported to link federal, state and local governments in supporting regional development through the Regional Development Australia (RDA) initiative (Albanese 2008). Federal involvement in regional Australia policy further intensified through the Gillard Government and its signing of an agreement with a group of independent members of federal parliament that provided a basis for specifically addressing the needs of rural and regional Australia. The agreement provided for the establishment of a Department of Regional Australia, and funds for infrastructure development for rural and regional Australia. In announcing this agreement, Gillard, echoing her predecessor's views (APSC 2009), said that Australia was entering a new era of governance, where one-size-fits-all policies would no longer work. We can immediately see here the presence of contrasting perspectives on the governance of regional Australia, with positions shifting considerably from one with more clearly demarcated lines of responsibility and limited accountability to one with far more enmeshed forms of interaction that lack an articulation of either policy strategy or lines of accountability through local and state governments (see also *Mulgan* for discussion of accountability in MLG systems).

Despite its apparent intentions in putting its new RDA structure in place, however, the Gillard Government ended up pursuing a one-size-fits-all policy. In Victoria, Queensland, Western Australia and the Northern Territory, the RDA structure directly replaced existing area consultative committees and sat alongside existing regional development structures. In South Australia, Tasmania and New South Wales, the structure was superimposed over existing arrangements; that is, both area consultative committees and regional economic development boards were replaced by RDA committees. In South Australia and New South Wales, for example, regional economic development was vigorously pursued by regional economic development boards through a range of projects, programs and service delivery, while area consultative committees acted in an advisory role to the Australian government but without direct involvement in 'on-ground' projects or service delivery.

This RDA policy implementation process did not take into account pre-existing governmental arrangements or differences in regional decision-making. It also ignored the existing internal process that the various local bodies had developed to meet the diversity of contextual challenges that exist among regions. It also ignored the different foci that have historically determined the activities undertaken by the various regional bodies and it ignored existing reporting processes, imposing a new set of reporting requirements that were mirrored across all states and territories, despite the differing operational arrangements that existed prior to the creation of the new structure. In the case of the RDA initiative, economies of scale related to funding requirements and reporting employed to achieve efficiencies within government departments increased the burden on these RDA bodies and thus created inefficiencies at the local scale.

The development and implementation of this RDA policy certainly did not appear to stem from negotiations between existing community, regional and government bodies, as a more connected MLG system approach would suggest but, rather, were imposed from above with little consultation.[2] In the face of climate change and other global changes, however, the fundamental imperative will be for regional, rural and remote communities to adapt to the changing environmental conditions that will affect their sustainability and capacity for development. At the local and regional level, this will undoubtedly require the flexibility to respond appropriately to the contextual factors that continue to shape these communities.

A flexible policy and regulatory environment in which suitably tailored adaptation approaches can be enacted is, therefore, critical. Such arrangements need to support appropriate institutional social infrastructure that is responsive to regional difference and, most importantly, nimble and flexible enough to enable local responses to local conditions. This analysis would imply a potential need to change the current RDA policy to increase its flexibility and break down the one-size-fits-all implementation process.

Under the Abbott Government, RDAs were retained, albeit with a stronger focus on local economic development rather than the broader realm of social inclusion that was the case under the previous government.

---

2   CRN interview respondents also note that, in implementation, the RDAs are structured in a way that supports a stronger government directive approach, rather than the more collaborative nature of previous regional area consultative committees, but that individual RDAs are attempting to make the best of the new arrangements for their communities.

Deputy prime minister Warren Truss, in his address to the 2014 SEGRA (Sustainable Economic Growth for Regional Australia) conference delegates in Alice Springs (Truss 2014) announced changes to RDA governance whereby chairs and deputy chairs would be appointed by the Australian Government, and committee members would be appointed by chairs. He also highlighted the current situation in which some states have tripartite arrangements, as outlined above, and said that this would continue to be supported in those states and territories. His address signalled that, while the federal government 'still had an important role to play in supporting economic development in all regions' and would continue to work closely with all RDA committees, it would take a more 'hands off' approach and seek to streamline administrative and reporting requirements:

> I have taken time to consider the structure based on the views of all stakeholders. I have spoken with state and territory ministers responsible for regional development, my parliamentary colleagues, many RDA committee members, as well as representatives of the community in the hope that it might be possible to develop a model where all three tiers of government worked together to sponsor a well resourced national network of regional development organisations working to grow stronger regions across the nation … but the prospects of all states agreeing to participate in a common RDA network anytime soon seems remote. I hope the goal will be achieved one day (Truss 2014).

In other words, Truss considered that developing formal coordination (or 'meta-governance') of multi-level RDA governance systems across the country was at the time too challenging. This could leave room for more freedom to 'fit' RDA work to local needs, but only a fuller evaluation of the system would allow this to be investigated.

One other linked area of policy flexibility that requires particular attention is the current existence of funding silos between RDAs and rural industry-focused research and development corporations (RDCs). Price (2015: 226) points out that Australia invests a significant amount (approximately $3 billion per annum) in research and development associated with such industries. We note, however, that there often appears to be little interface between research that is focused on rural industries and the communities in which those industries operate. The question needs to be asked as to how the notion of 'regional development' can be effectively enacted when the research and development process operates largely independent of regional planning. Ideally, the gap between these processes needs to be bridged to enhance future rural and regional development. Embedding research and researchers in regional Australia may be one means of working towards that goal.

In October 2017, the Turnbull Government completed a review of the RDA Committees' structures and functions. The review proposed a new that focus 'on growing strong and confident regional economies ... in order harness innovation and drive economic growth'. Such growth, the charter suggests, would result from 'creating local jobs, attracting investment and driving innovation' (RDA 2017). Comments from the 2016 Regional Development Australia National Forum showed that, despite a number of challenges reflecting those already discussed, RDAs are increasingly seen as creating significant value in the regions as 'honest brokers' between local, state and federal governments, and they are indeed becoming increasingly 'agile, flexible and independent' in their ways of functioning.[3] Despite a top-down beginning, significant bottom-up and collaborative working arrangements and contextualisation of the RDAs over their lifespan have emerged in many instances, demonstrating the transient nature of MLG systems. Such transitions and common patterns in MLG system changes will be explored in more depth in the conclusion (*Daniell and Mercer*).

Drought policy adjustments and the guide to the draft Murray–Darling Basin Plan

The command-and-control approach to federal policy development and implementation is not unique to the RDA process. Other significant regional government policies have been developed, or at least started out, with minimal or one-sided consultative processes. An expert social group convened extensive and independent consultations to establish a drought policy. This group reported its findings to government (Drought Policy Review Expert Social Panel 2008). The government, in turn, developed its policy and proceeded to pilot it, without open consultation, in a specific part of Western Australia. Policy advocates and farmers across the eastern seaboard were concerned by this process, as the findings of the pilot were likely to have widespread ramifications for farming across Australia,

---

3   Based on comments contained in the notes from participants in the forum: rda.gov.au/national-forum/files/20161116-Regional-Development-Australia-National-Forum.pdf [Accessed: 12/04/2017].

although they also acknowledge the issues concerning the existing EC policy.[4] The proposed guide to the Murray–Darling Basin Plan (MDBA 2010) was launched in a similar way.

Consultants were hired to prepare specific pieces of scientific work, and a small community advisory committee was consulted to inform the governmental policy development process run by the new, independent Murray–Darling Basin Authority (MDBA). An outcome was then announced to the Australian community, which was followed by a highly mediatised barrage of critique and anger. Independent federal politician Tony Windsor, responding to the intense level of community backlash against the plan, observed that a way forward that addressed the water needs of the river system and the viability of rural communities would need to be worked out on a 'valley by valley or even town by town basis'. The diversity of rural and regional communities across the basin would require a flexible approach that could drill down to the community level, rather than the current one-size-fits-all top-down approach, if even 'better–better' (rather than 'win–win') solutions were to be hoped for (ABC 2010).

Similarly, in the research undertaken in rural communities across Australia within the 'Securing the Wealth and Wellbeing of Rural Communities' project (Hogan et al. 2014), we found that policies and the command-and-control approaches to their implementation across both federal and state jurisdictions were often cited by project participants as impacting on the viable futures of those communities. For example, in Tasmania, the federal policy decision to connect 'spoke' communities to the new National Broadband Network (NBN) before larger 'hub' communities (in an attempt to benefit those rural communities seen to be most in need of broadband services to progress economic growth through digital business opportunities) 'failed dismally' in the words of one interviewee.

Without the required economies of scale achievable in connecting multiple users in larger communities (e.g. Launceston), participants reported that one major telecommunications company was reluctant to change their service provision model in the smaller communities because initial implementation costs were too high. This resulted in subscribers

---

4   For example, community tensions about appropriate farm management and equity were observed around the policy in CRN interviews, as exemplified by the comment: 'The people who had been tight and saved money when it came to Exceptional Circumstances couldn't access money, yet those who splashed money around and had nothing in reserve received Exceptional Circumstances.'

to that company in those communities often having to stay with this service provider until broadband services were available through that provider, or maintain mobile telephony service with that provider (due to contractual requirements of post-paid service plans) and subscribe to a different service provider (who was providing NBN connections) for the new broadband internet services. In this instance, project participants cited a lack of engagement and consultation along with knowledge gaps about how on-ground services work as the primary unintended consequences of the policy decision. Indeed, we found that engagement, consultation and a knowledge of the differing social and economic situations of rural communities were fundamental factors in assisting rural communities to plan for their futures (Cleary and Carson 2014).

Potential for moving beyond one-size-fits-all

Before moving to consider how more flexible mechanisms of policy development may be realised, it is first necessary to step back for a moment and consider current methods of development and implementation of policy strategy. Hogan (2010) reports on several key ways in which policy is developed in Australia. Just some of these include: policy that is politician-driven (e.g. the current agreement for regional Australia); reactive policy, often politician-driven in response to media reports and public outcry (e.g. a parliamentary inquiry to quell anger on the guide to the basin plan); policy that comes up through government department internal policy development processes (e.g. the current draft drought policy and asylum seeker detention centre site choice); and policy driven through the Council of Australian Governments (COAG).

The problem with these processes, as Hogan (2010) observes, is that they do not generally provide mechanisms for systematic and well-organised public participation and broader stakeholder engagement in decision-making. Rather, policies are developed within the closed processes of government departments or in the shadows of Parliament House. Such governmental policy development processes often follow the adage of *decide, promote, defend* (and amend if you have to). Consultations, when they occur (e.g. for drought policy process and the guide to the basin plan), are typically one-sided, allowing the hearing of only limited views from the public and without the identification of further opportunities for the public to participate in discussions. Such processes in contentious policy areas are well known to incite widespread backlash and run the risk of developing locally inappropriate and unimplementable policies (Daniell 2012), as well as disempowering communities (Arnstein 1969).

Other internalised governmental policy development processes do provide for a level of consultation and negotiation between the Commonwealth and the jurisdictions, for example in the two-tiered decision-making processes of ministers and departmental heads that feeds into COAG (e.g. the Primary Industries Ministerial Council and its Primary Industries Standing Committee, as well as the Natural Resource Management Ministerial Council and its Natural Resource Management Standing Committee). Typically within such processes, the bureaucracy tables its policy issues and concerns through heads of department. Once a consensus position or series of options is agreed upon, recommendations go to the ministerial committee for endorsement and, where appropriate, a request is made for action or endorsement through COAG.

While the agendas that such committees address can be seen on public websites, the processes do not provide for open public and stakeholder participation in the policy development process. What it does allow for is the opportunity for well-organised and resourced interest groups to lobby policymakers, with a view to influencing decision-making. The workings of such processes are readily open to participant observation in the ever-popular coffee shops conveniently situated on the ground floor of most Commonwealth government departments in Canberra. More independent bodies, such as statutory authorities (e.g. Safe Work Australia), sometimes provide for more broadly based public and stakeholder participation in decision-making where representatives of industry and unions have a seat at the decision-making table and an opportunity to negotiate with the authority. But again, the process is far from transparent and open in engaging stakeholders from different jurisdictional levels.

The funding mechanism underpinning federal policy development in Australia can be as critical to the success of federal initiatives as the concepts within the policy itself. Commonly within the federal budget, funds may be allocated to a policy strategy wherein such funds must be expended within the existing financial year. With budgets typically announced in May, it is not uncommon for such projects to be initiated late in the calendar year, with the requirement that projects be completed by 30 June the following year. Such funding strategies provide little opportunity for projects to develop the necessary synergies and momentum to address entrenched policy problems. To address substantive policy problems, funds need to be allocated to policy strategies with much longer time frames in place, and be provided for projects that can run over many years.

An increasingly global issue is the expectation from citizens that they have the right to participate in all aspects of decision-making that impact upon them if they feel the desire to do so, as well as that decision-making processes are underpinned by a policy of transparency. Commentators note that it is not only democratic legitimacy issues that are driving open and inclusive approaches to policy development, but also the need to develop implementable policies that have the best chance of being successful while minimising unintended consequences. This is as the knowledge, resources and authority to make and implement decisions are increasingly dispersed between a large range of stakeholders, including different levels of government, management bodies, research organisations, private companies, non-government organisations and the general public (Rhodes 1988; Fischer 2000; Daniell et al. 2010a, 2010b). Mike Oliver's (1990; 1996) work on disability policy, following the adage of *nothing about us without us*,[5] serves as an excellent example of this work from the perspective of an international movement.

More locally, however, Australia has witnessed a range of alternative policy development processes that have begun to embrace more open MLG approaches to decision-making.[6] Such processes were also evident in a social-planning approach developed at the state government level and involving close collaboration by the state government with local government and community organisations. For example, the process known as area assistance schemes[7] was concerned with the allocation of limited resources that were available to address the priority community infrastructure needs of disadvantaged and developing communities. Local priorities were established through an annual community consultative rating process that was informed by needs analysis (e.g. local community profiles) developed by local government. Community development

---

5   'Nothing About Us Without Us', Wikipedia contributors, *Wikipedia, The Free Encyclopedia*, en.wikipedia.org/w/index.php?title=Nothing_About_Us_Without_Us&oldid=780235527 [Accessed: 29/05/17].
6   'Multi-level Governance Symposium' 12–13 June 2010, Crawford School of Economics and Government, The Australian National University, crawford.anu.edu.au/events/content/video/?year=2010&id=31.
7   See, for example, Bamforth et al. (2016).

officers worked closely with local communities to help them articulate their service needs, to understand the competing needs in the community and to facilitate a community-supported decision-making process.

These concepts of shared levels of systemic disadvantage, competing social needs, the need to be sensitised as to how one is affected, the need for engagement and facilitated social change are common aspects of the social demands placed on rural communities by climate change, amongst other factors. Set before our community is the challenge of how governance processes for rural and regional Australia may be established that facilitate recognition of being affected, of shared social impacts, of the uneven and unavoidable distribution of disadvantage, and the development of socially responsible means of mitigating such effects with a view to securing just and peaceful outcomes across our society. Understanding and developing the potential of appropriate types of MLG processes to open up opportunities for the necessary adaptations to, and mitigations of, the social effects of climate change, therefore, seems a promising way forward to break down the common one-size-fits-all approach to rural and regional Australian policy.

Mapping a way forward for the development of MLG approaches to policy challenges in rural and regional Australia

As we see it, there is ample evidence of MLG systems having been effectively developed between communities, appropriate levels of government, business and other stakeholder groups that have led to widely acceptable and effectively implemented policies, even if this is often just at a regional rather than national level (see, for, example the following chapters in this volume: *Jarvie and Stewart* on indigenous policy in the Murdi Paaki region of New South Wales; *Mercer and Jarvie* on early childhood education reform through COAG; *Andrews* on the governance arrangements of the Lake Eyre Basin) or international level (see, again in this volume, *McNaughton and Lockie* on GLOBALG.A.P. standard-setting for agricultural and food products), and improvements could be made (see, for example, in this volume, *Dale et al.* on Australian natural resource management (NRM) governance systems; *Iwanicki et al.* on strengthening NRM and urban planning governance system interactions; *Hogan* on the governance of differences in hearing; and *Norman and Gurran* on governance arrangements for coastal and climate change planning).

In fact, following the catastrophic reaction to the release of the guide to the draft of the Murray–Darling Basin Plan, the new CEO of the MDBA sought to change the authority's approach from a top-down one that excluded stakeholders to a 'localism' approach (Knowles 2011; Dare and Daniell 2017) that would engage and value different communities' views and inputs in the negotiations over the construction of the plan. The approach proved successful in that the Murray–Darling Basin Plan was passed by the parliament in 2012 with minimal negative reaction from rural and regional communities.

Our way forward involves distilling the lessons of these effective negotiation systems and adapting their application to policy challenges in rural and regional Australia. This will be an important and ongoing task for researchers, policymakers and stakeholders alike. From the examples briefly outlined in this chapter, we conclude with four priorities that would significantly propel us into the more widespread uptake of MLG approaches to policy challenges in rural and regional Australia.

The first key priority for the endeavour of developing effective MLG systems is the need to develop the enabling conditions at all levels of government that will allow them to move towards power-sharing and continuous negotiation systems that fit the policy challenges of rural and regional Australia. The Australian Public Service Commission has also noted the significance of this challenge (APSC 2009). Therefore, if the federal government is serious about effecting positive change in rural and regional Australia, strong political and bureaucratic leadership is required to reform the way government develops and implements policy, which will enable improved governance systems that function along the principles espoused by the United Nations of being 'participatory, consensus oriented, accountable, transparent, responsive, effective and efficient, equitable and inclusive, and follows the rule of law' (e.g. UNESCAP 2010).

The development of trust between stakeholders, including in governments, is also important, as highlighted by *Dugdale*, and *Jarvie and Stewart*. Considering these principles for good governance, an important first step in governance reform is to understand that 'town hall meetings' do not meet half the governance criteria that they are perhaps expected to, namely being participatory, consensus-orientated, effective, efficient, equitable and inclusive (Daniell 2011). This means understanding the mechanisms for engagement of the public that allow active involvement and exchange and the implementation of a range of participatory methods to foster dialogue and negotiation to match the needs of the policy issue (see Rosenhead and Mingers 2001; Slocum 2003; and Creighton 2005 for some examples). This expertise in participatory engagement methods already exists in Australia and effort is only required to muster and support its use for the development and delivery of more collectively negotiated, widely accepted and effective rural and regional Australian policy.

The second priority is to attempt to develop improved articulation between centralised rural and regional policy and planning processes and those occurring at more local levels, so that different regions can play a stronger role in envisaging and working towards their preferred futures in a coordinated manner. The European Union (EU) has, for example, introduced the 'Smart Specialisation' platform, supported by a number of coherence policies and structural funds, that is aimed to support regions to develop strategies for growth and to reduce inter-regional inequities. Specifically, the smart specialisation initiative includes:

> a focus on identifying niche areas of competitive strength, solving major societal challenges – bringing in a demand-driven dimension, innovation partnerships emphasizing greater co-ordination between different societal stakeholders and aligning resources and strategies between private and public actors of different governance levels.[8]

In the Australian situation, such a focus might involve determining what niche areas of strength different communities have and how these could be better enhanced in the future – for example, through targeted funded linkages with regional university groups and businesses/government services on specific topics (e.g. health care, tourism, cotton, grape production, irrigation efficiency, cultural pursuits) – to build further capacity and economic and community growth in these areas.

Third, broader consideration needs to be given to creating an interface between decision-making in RDCs with RDAs. Collaboration within and across industries, as well as the communities in which rural industries operate, has long been a priority of the Rural Industries Research and Development Corporation.[9] The reality is, however, that the research plans of RDCs give little regard to collaborations with rural communities, with the possible exception of employment-related research. It seems

---

8   'Smart Specialisation', *EU Science Hub*, ec.europa.eu/jrc/en/research-topic/smart-specialisation [Accessed: 29/05/17].

9   See www.rirdc.gov.au/ for more information.

fundamental, therefore, that an interface needs to be developed between RDCs and RDAs so that more industry research considers the communities within which it operates and that provides community members with the opportunity for real input into the development of publicly funded research and development within their communities. The same could be said for other government-based and academic research on Australian rural and regional policy challenges, including water, environmental, Indigenous and health policy.

Finally, there is the need to draw attention to the important task of 'meta-governance' that focuses on setting up the conditions and rules that can foster MLG systems with 'good governance' characteristics (described in the first priority, above) to develop and thrive. As Jessop (2004) suggests, this meta-governance role, which could be taken on by people inside and outside government, should foster a requisite variety in the types of MLG systems set up, be reflexive and forward thinking, and supervise the combination and implementation of this variety of appropriate systems that meet the needs of the policy issues for which they are developed. Effectively performing this meta-governance role could, therefore, lead to the welcome end of one-size-fits-all policies for remote, rural and regional Australia and give our diverse communities the opportunity to participate actively in developing the policies that are so important for their futures. This is not likely to be a simple task, considering the historical and ongoing tendency to centralise decisions affecting regions and apply them in a standardised manner with little input from communities. For example, in response to a proposal by the NSW Government to appoint regional 'advisory committees', Bland (1944) noted:

> and there is no reason to assume that projects for soil erosion, for afforestation, and for electric power will not be handled by the respective central departments now concerned with these things. The effect of this method for promoting regional development is obvious. Whether or not the regions have local representatives on the committees appointed by the Reconstruction Division is immaterial. The committees are purely advisory. Effective control remains at the centre, and the central departments will implement the schemes. In other words, the development of the regional resources will be removed from the control of the people of the regions, and the traditional centralised administration will be more securely established than ever. The effect will be to retard the emergence of any regional consciousness.

We remain hopeful, however, that a multiplicity of regional and rural 'consciousnesses' will be able to play an integral role in shaping future Australian rural and regional policy reforms, if sufficient energy and resources can be put into the development of more effective and diversified, but still coordinated, MLG systems across the country.

References

ABARES (2012). *Drought in Australia: Context, Policy and Management.* Australian Bureau of Agricultural and Resource Economics and Sciences, Australian Government, www.droughtmanagement.info/literature/GovAustr_drought_in_australia_2012.pdf [Accessed: 26/07/2017].

ABC (2010). Windsor on the Murray Darling. *The 7.30 Report*, www.abc.net.au/7.30/content/2010/s3038776.htm [Accessed: 28/10/2010].

Age (2012). Minister Declares End of Drought, news.theage.com.au/breaking-news-national/minister-declares-end-of-drought-20120427-1xpgi.html [Accessed: 11/12/14].

Albanese, A. (2008). Regional Development Australia. Statement by the Minister for Infrastructure, Transport, Regional Development and Local Government, the Hon Anthony Albanese MP, 20 March 2008.

APSC (2009). *Delivering Performance and Accountability.* Australian Government, Canberra, www.apsc.gov.au/publications-and-media/archive/publications-archive/delivering-performance [Accessed: 26/07/2017].

Arnstein, S.R. (1969). A Ladder of Citizen Participation. *Journal of the American Institute of Planners*, 35(4): 216–24. doi.org/10.1080/01944366908977225

Bamforth, J., Gapps, B., Gurr, R., Howard, A., Onyx, J. & Rawthorne, M. (2016). *Planning, Funding, and Community Action The Area Assistance Story.* Diversity in Organizations, Communities & Nations, a book imprint by Common Ground Publishing, Champaign, IL.

Barr, N. (2009). *The House on the Hill: The Transformation of Australia's Farming Communities.* Land and Water Australia in association with Halstead Press, Canberra.

Berkes, F. (2002). Cross-Scale Institutional Linkages: perspectives from the bottom up. In: Ostrom, E., Dietz, T., Dolsak, N., Stern, P., Stonich, S. & Weber, E.U. (eds) *The Drama of the Commons*. National Academy Press, Washington, D.C.

Bland, F.A. (1944). *A Note on Regionalism*. The Institute of Public Administration, Australia, pp. 176–82. doi.org/10.1111/j.1467-8500.1944.tb02045.x

Botterill, L.C. (2011). Fair Share: Correspondence. *Quarterly Essay*, 43: 129–31.

Bureau of Rural Sciences (2008). *Country matters – 2008 Social Atlas of Rural & Regional Australia – Employment*. Department of Agriculture, Fisheries and Forestry, Canberra.

Carson D. & Cleary J. (2010). Virtual Realities: How remote dwelling populations become more remote over time despite technological improvements. *Sustainability*, 2(5): 1282–96. doi.org/10.3390/su 2051282

Cash, D.W., Adger, W., Berkes, F., Garden, P., Lebel, L., Olsson, P., Pritchard, L. & Young, O. (2006). Scale and Cross-Scale Dynamics: Governance and information in a multilevel world. *Ecology and Society*, 11(2): 8. doi.org/10.5751/ES-01759-110208

Cleary, J. (2014). *Recycling Dependency: The Grant Economy Propping up Rural, Regional and Remote Australia*. Proceedings of the SEGRA Conference, 7–10 October, Alice Springs.

Cleary, J. & Carson, D. (2014). Project Engagement. In: Hogan, A., Carson, D., Cleary, J., Donnelly, D., Houghton, K., Phillips, R. & Tanton, R. (eds) *Community Adaptability Tool: Securing the Wealth and Wellbeing of Rural Communities*. RIRDC Publication No. 14/041, Canberra, pp. 17–27, rirdc.infoservices.com.au/items/14-041 [Accessed: 12/12/14].

Cockfield, G. (2015). From State Direction to Community Self-Efficacy: the devolution of responsibility for regional development in Australia. In: Hogan, A. & Young, M. (eds) *Rural and Regional Futures*. Routledge, London, pp. 38–57.

Collits, P. (2015). Regional Policy in Post-War Australia: much ado about nothing? In: Hogan, A. & Young, M. (eds) *Rural and Regional Futures*. Routledge, London, pp. 19–37.

Creighton, J.L. (2005). *The Public Participation Handbook: Making Better Decisions through Citizen Involvement*. Jossey-Bass, San Francisco, California.

DAFF (2010). *Stronger Rural Communities: Program Guidelines*. Australian Government Department of Agriculture, Fisheries and Forestry, Canberra.

Daniell, K.A. (2011). Enhancing Collaborative Management in the Basin. In: Connell, D. & Grafton, R.Q. (eds) *Basin Futures: Water Reform in the Murray–Darling Basin*. ANU E Press, Canberra, pp. 413–38.

——. (2012). *Co-engineering and Participatory Water Management: Organisational Challenges for Water Governance*. UNESCO International Hydrology Series. Cambridge University Press. doi.org/10.1017/CBO9780511998072

Daniell, K.A. & Barreteau, O. (2014). Water Governance across Competing Scales: Coupling land and water management. *Journal of Hydrology*, 519(Part C): 2367–80. doi.org/10.1016/j.jhydrol.2014.10.055

Daniell, K.A., Coombes, J. & White, I. (2014). Politics of Innovation in Multi-level Water Governance Systems. *Journal of Hydrology*, 519(Part C): 2415–35. doi.org/10.1016/j.jhydrol.2014.08.058

Daniell, K.A., Máñez Costa, M.A., Ferrand, N., Kingsborough, A.B., Coad, P. & Ribarova, I.S. (2010a). Aiding Multi-level Decision-Making Processes for Climate Change Mitigation and Adaptation. *Regional Environmental Change* 11(2): 243–258.

Daniell, K.A., Mazri, C. & Tsoukiàs, A. (2010b). Real World Decision-Aiding: a case of participatory water management. In: Rios Insua, D. & French, S. (eds) *e-Democracy: A Group Decision and Negotiation Perspective*. Advances in Group Decision and Negotiation Series, Vol. 5, Part 2. Springer, pp. 125–50. doi.org/10.1007/978-90-481-9045-4_8

Dare, M. & Daniell, K.A. (2017). Australian water governance in the global context: Understanding the benefits of localism. *Policy Studies*, 38(5): 462–481. dx.doi.org/10.1080/01442872.2016.1188908

Dovers, S. (2013). The Australian Environmental Policy Agenda. *Australian Journal of Public Administration*, 72(2): 114–128. doi.org/10.1111/1467-8500.12013

Drought Policy Review Expert Social Panel (2008). *It's About People: Changing Perspective. A Report to Government by an Expert Social Panel on Dryness*. Report to the Minister for Agriculture, Fisheries and Forestry, Canberra, September, www.agriculture.gov.au/SiteCollection Documents/ag-food/drought/publications/dryness_report.pdf [Accessed: 18/07/2017].

Evans, M., Marsh, D. & Stoker, G. (2013). Understanding Localism. *Policy Studies*, 34(4): 401–07. doi.org/10.1080/01442872.2013.822699

Fischer, F. (2000). *Citizens, Experts, and the Environment*. Duke University Press, Durham. doi.org/10.1215/9780822380283

Garnaut, J., Connell, P., Lindsay, R., & Rodriguez, V. (2001). *Country Australia: Influences on Employment and Population Growth*. ABARE Research Report 2001:1. Canberra.

Gross, C. & Dumaresq, D. (2014). Taking the Longer View: Timescales, Fairness and a Forgotten Story of Irrigation in Australia. *Journal of Hydrology*, 519(Part C): 2483–92. doi.org/10.1016/j.jhydrol.2014.08.056

Hogan, A. (2010). Beyond Merciless Critique – Reflections on the Contribution of Sociology in the Policy Space. *Working Notes*, Issue 1, 29 June, sociologyatwork.org/beyond-merciless-critique/ [Accessed: 13/12/14].

Hogan, A., Berry, H., Ng, S.P. & Bode, A. (2010). *Decisions Made by Farmers that Relate to Climate Change*. Rural Industries Research and Development Corporation, Canberra.

Hogan, A., Carson, D., Cleary, J., Donnelly, D., Houghton, K., Phillips, R. & Tanton, R. (eds) (2014). *Community Adaptability Tool: Securing the Wealth and Wellbeing of Rural Communities*. RIRDC Publication No. 14/041, Canberra, rirdc.infoservices.com.au/items/14-041 [Accessed: 12/12/14].

Hogan, A., Cleary, J., Lockie, S., Young, M. & Daniell, K.A. (2015). Localism and the Policy Goal of Securing the Socio-Economic Viability of Rural and Regional Australia. In: Hogan, A. & Young, M. (eds) *Rural and Regional Futures*. Routledge, London, pp. 260–81.

Hogan, A. & Young, M. (2013). Visioning a Future for Rural and Regional Australia. *Cambridge Journal of Regions, Economy and Society*, 6: 319–30. doi.org/10.1093/cjres/rst005

Hogan, A. & Young, M. (eds) (2015). *Rural and Regional Futures*. Routledge, London.

Hugo, G. (2001). What is Really Happening in Rural and Regional Populations? In: Rogers, M.F. & Collins, Y.M.J. (eds) *The Future of Australia's Country Towns*. Centre for Regional Communities, La Trobe University, Bendigo.

Jessop, B. (2004). Multi-level Governance and Multi-level Metagovernance. In: Bache, I. & Flinders, M. (eds) *Multi-level Governance*. Oxford University Press, pp. 49–74. doi.org/10.1093/0199259259.003.0004

Kelly, M. (2010). Peregian Springs Urban Recycled Water Project. Statement by The Honourable Dr Mike Kelly AM MP, Tuesday 9 March 2010.

Knowles, C. (2011). Opening Address. Sustaining Rural Communities Conference, www.mdba.gov.au/media/mr/mdba-chair-mr-craig-knowles-speech-sustaining-rural-communities-conference-narrabri [Accessed: 18/07/2017].

Lloyd, R., Harding, A. & Hellwig, O. (2001). Regional Divide? A Study of Income Inequality in Australia. *Sustaining Regions*, 1(1): 17–30.

Marks, G. (1993). Structural Policy and Multilevel Governance in the EC. In: Cafruny, A.W. & Rosenthal, G.G. (eds) *The State of the European Community, Vol 2: The Maastricht Debates and Beyond.* Harlow Longman, Boulder, CO, pp. 391–410.

Marshall, G.R. (2008). Nesting, Subsidiarity, and Community-Based Environmental Governance beyond the Local Level. *International Journal of the Commons*, 2(1): 75–97. doi.org/10.18352/ijc.50

Maude, A. (2004). Regional Development Processes and Policies in Australia: a review of research 1990–2002. *European Planning Studies*, 12(1): 3–26. doi.org/10.1080/0965431031000163567O

MDBA (2010). Guide to the proposed Basin Plan. Murray–Darling Basin Authority, Australian Government, Canberra.

Oliver, M. (1990). *The Politics of Disablement.* Macmillan, London. doi.org/10.1007/978-1-349-20895-1

——. (1996). *Understanding Disability – From Theory to Practice.* Macmillan, London. doi.org/10.1007/978-1-349-24269-6

Ostrom, E. (1999). Coping with Tragedies of the Commons. *Annual Review of Political Science*, 2: 493–535. doi.org/10.1146/annurev.polisci.2.1.493

Pahl-Wostl, C. (2008). *Climate Change – A Global Challenge for Water Governance.* ExpoZaragoza 2008, www.zaragoza.es/contenidos/medioambiente/cajaAzul/18S6-P3-Pahl%20WostlACC.pdf

Pearson, L. & Dare, M. (2014). Alternate Futures for Murray–Darling Basin Communities. MDBFutures Workshop presentation, 20 May 2014, Collaborative Research Network, University of Canberra.

Price, R. (2015). Rural Research and Regional Innovation – Are Past and Present Research Funding Policies Building Future Resilience in the Bush? In: Hogan, A. & Young, M. (eds) *Rural and Regional Futures.* Routledge, London, pp. 226–46.

Productivity Commission (2005). *Trends in Australian Agriculture.* Canberra.

RDA (2017). RDA Reform. Regional Development Australia, rda.gov.au/review/

Rhodes, R.A.W. (1998). *Beyond Westminster and Whitehall.* Urwin-Hyman, London.

Rosenhead, J. & Mingers, J. (eds) (2001). *Rational Analysis for a Problematic World Revisited.* John Wiley and Sons, Chichester.

Sabatier, A. (1988). An Advocacy Coalition Framework of Policy Change and the Role of Policy-Oriented Learning Therein. *Policy Sciences,* 21: 129–68. doi.org/10.1007/BF00136406

Slocum, N. (2003). *Participatory Methods Toolkit: A Practitioner's Manual.* King Baudouin Foundation and the Flemish Institute for Science and Technology Assessment (viWTA) in collaboration with the United Nations University – Comparative Regional Integration Studies (UNU/CRIS), unu.edu/hq/library/Collection/PDF_files/CRIS/PMT. pdf [Accessed: 10/12/10].

Smith, E. & Pritchard, B. (2015). Australian Agricultural and Rural Policy Since World War II: the pursuit of agricultural efficiency. In: Hogan, A. & Young, M. (eds) *Rural and Regional Futures.* Routledge, London, pp. 58–70.

Tennent, R. & Lockie, S. (2015). Natural Resource Management in Australia: a historical summary. In: Hogan, A. & Young, M. (eds) *Rural and Regional Futures.* Routledge, London, pp. 71–83.

Truss, W. (2014). Keynote Address. SEGRA 2014 Connecting Matters Conference, 8 October 2014, Alice Springs, minister.infrastructure. gov.au/wt/speeches/2014/wts024_2014.aspx [Accessed: 26/07/17].

UNESCAP (2010). *What is Good Governance?* United Nations Economic and Social Commissions for Asia and the Pacific, www.unescap.org/ sites/default/files/good-governance.pdf [Accessed: 26/07/2017].

Wentworth Group (2006). *Australia's Climate is Changing Australia: The State of Australia's Water.* Wentworth Group of Concerned Scientists, www.myoung.net.au/water/publications/Australias_Climate_ is_Changing_Australia.pdf [Accessed: 18/07/17].

18

What Remains Unwritten? Developing a Critical Evaluation of Multi-level Governance and its Futures in Australian Public Policy and Politics

Katherine A. Daniell and Trish Mercer

Paying attention to the unwritten

This book has a vocation to raise awareness on forms of multi-level governance (MLG) in Australian public policy and associated politics. As an overview of key observations from the conceptual and case study chapters has already been provided in large part in the introduction, this conclusion instead focuses on issues that are yet to be raised.

Among the potentially long list of untreated issues, we have elected to focus on three key themes. First, we investigate the counter-evidence to the development of MLG approaches and how, where and when 'non-negotiable' inflexible approaches to governance across levels are most likely to flourish, using examples from national policy initiatives. Second, we investigate the issue of research practice and methodologies employed in studying MLG processes presented in and beyond this volume, which have yet to be systematically elicited. These two investigations allow us to postulate why certain case studies have appeared in this volume and not others, as well as why there is a relatively large gap between the theoretically focused and case study example chapters. It then leads us into a final section of new theorisation to state the conditions – or rather cultures and political value systems – under which different types of MLG systems may appear and be reorganised. We can hence postulate where such systems will likely have the brightest and darkest futures across Australia's public policy and political system, and to what extent future research and focus on specific MLG practice may or may not prove fruitful.

Investigating a relative absence of MLG

To understand where there is an absence of MLG in Australia, we return to the definitions of MLG processes provided in Chapter 1 (*Daniell and Kay*), which we took as being systems of 'continuous negotiation among nested governments at several territorial tiers' (Marks 1993: 392) where there is not only a vertical dispersion of authority between levels of administration, but also a horizontal dispersion across different sectors of interest and spheres of influence, including non-government actors, markets and civil society (Bache and Flinders 2004; *Daniell and Kay*). We are thus theoretically looking for governance systems that are controlled by specific actors where there is little to no (obvious) ongoing negotiation about how policy development and implementation does, or will, function. We consider that the most likely places to find such systems are where: (a) negotiations have broken down, reached a stalemate, trust has evaporated or led to a lack of progress that results in a crisis and need for an actor to take urgent unilateral action; (b) the policy issue is so minor that it is of little interest to any more than one main actor; or (c) where one particular actor is so powerful that they do not need to negotiate but can effectively direct or coerce other actors to perform the governance activities they desire.

From an analysis of policy sectors in Australia, we have struggled to identify clear examples of minor policy issues (b), since the large majority of policy decisions will affect someone or some group's interests. We still theorise that such 'routine' policy areas likely do exist where bureaucrats can propose small policy changes that will pass through government approval processes with little interest or criticism from anyone inside or outside government. Areas such as municipal rubbish collection in regional areas could be an example, although there will always be some stakeholders who hold views on how it could or should be done differently. In federal governance systems, we propose that such situations are more likely in policy areas where 'coordinate' federalism can exist; that is, where there is little to no jurisdictional overlap and tiers of government can operate largely separately (*Mulgan*). In the other two categories, however, especially on largely non-negotiated policy responses to crises (a), sometimes with an element of powerful and directive leadership (c), examples are more plentiful.

For example, in the controversial area of gun control, we can see the pivotal influence of a specific actor on an area of policy stalemate. Proposals for uniform gun laws were discussed intermittently at the Commonwealth–state level from 1969, but had failed to progress given state government reluctance and opposition from pro-gun interest groups (Prasser 2006). In April 1996, the murder of 35 people at Port Arthur by a lone gunman with a high-powered semiautomatic gun was the catalyst for a major Commonwealth policy initiative. John Howard, the newly elected prime minister, acted decisively and with great speed to secure agreement from both the Commonwealth parliament and state and territory governments to the standardisation of firearms legislation and an accompanying gun buyback of newly illegal weapons from their owners. While Howard was not in the end required to act unilaterally, he was nonetheless prepared to employ media reports of a possible referendum in order to win agreement from the second tier of government to act together, given the overlapping federal and state jurisdictional responsibilities in this area. A policy impasse had thus been broken by the actions of a strong player who has been credited with managing both the politics and the policy effectively to achieve significant reform, although the actual impact of the National Firearms Agreement on firearm deaths continues to be debated (Prasser 2006; Leigh and Neill 2010).

In a similar way, the global financial crisis (GFC) of late 2008 provided Labor Prime Minister Kevin Rudd with the impetus for the federal government to drive through the national Home Insulation Program (HIP) as part of the GFC economic stimulus package. In the lead-up to the GFC, there had been joint Commonwealth–state work on energy efficiency initiatives but, with flagging economic confidence and the prospect of a sharp increase in unemployment, the Rudd Government decided to act unilaterally and took a deliberate decision not to involve state governments in order to roll out HIP within extremely tight time frames. The HIP was closed in February 2010, following the tragic deaths of four young insulation installers and more than 200 house fires related to the program. In their analysis of the HIP's limited achievements and massive failures, Hamdhan and Lewis (2013) underline the truncated nature of the consultation process, including minimal input from state and territory officials and key industry stakeholders.

The Royal Commission, appointed by the following Coalition Government under Tony Abbott to inquire into HIP, forensically analysed the program's failures and also drew attention to the Commonwealth's failure to engage directly with the states and territories, which held the regulatory powers for occupational health and safety (Hanger 2014). In 2015, the report *Learning from Policy Failure* into three major government policy initiatives (all conveniently under the Labor leadership of Rudd and Julia Gillard) by Peter Shergold (formerly head of the Department of Prime Minister and Cabinet), concluded that a major factor underpinning the poor decisions made in the program was failure in the operation of the Cabinet, with decisions being taken by a Cabinet committee that did not include the line minister (Shergold 2015). Whereas Howard reaped the political benefits of strong leadership in a crisis on a contested policy issue, Rudd's similarly decisive actions in a rather less contested policy area (but one seen to be owned by the state governments) had disastrous political and human implications.

Before discussing what we can take away from these insights in terms of the role of MLG, or lack thereof, in Australia, it is also worth mentioning two other examples that arise from chapters in this book. The first is the case of the Murray–Darling Basin takeover by the federal government (*Daniell et al.*). This followed a similar path to the previous two examples where the 'Millennium drought' and catastrophic state of the basin's environment and communities provided the state of crisis, motivation and window of opportunity for Water Minister Malcolm Turnbull to push through the national *Water Act 2007*, which would establish the federal Murray–Darling Basin Authority (MDBA) to manage the basin's water resources, doing away with the previous state-, territory- and Commonwealth-negotiated arrangement of the Murray–Darling Basin Commission. After a shaky start and retreat by the MDBA from negotiating with the basin's stakeholders while working on an 'evidence-base' for water planning – which resulted in the parliamentary inquiry into the guide to the draft of the Murray–Darling Basin Plan (see Daniell 2011; Crase 2011) – MLG and more collaboratively negotiated operating mechanisms returned in order to ensure the passage of the initially heavily contested basin plan.

The other policy area to consider is that of Indigenous affairs and to what extent the heavily negotiated and flexible ways of working described in *Jarvie and Stewart* can be taken into account considering that, soon after the collaborative Council of Australian Governments (COAG) Policy Trials (2002–07), came the unilateral Northern Territory (NT) National Emergency Response or 'The Intervention' (see Hunter 2007; Sanders 2008). This time the crisis point and call to action was taken up by Minister Mal Brough, a former army officer (Stewart and Jarvie 2015), with the strong endorsement of Prime Minister Howard, following the release of a report into widespread child abuse in NT Aboriginal communities (Wild and Anderson 2007). Discussion, relationship-building and the approach of working in partnership with Indigenous communities and their leaders dramatically halted when, following the passing of federal legislation with bipartisan political support, the Australian Defence Force (ADF) and an army of public servants (for approximate numbers, see FaHCSIA 2011) were sent into the Northern Territory to improve security, health and living conditions in Indigenous Australian communities there.

The Intervention was headed by Major General Dave Chalmers as a 'non-force' operation, but soon became so controversial that the ADF wanted the role handed over to a civil servant (James 2007). Stewart and Jarvie (2015), through policy evaluation of these programs, outline that many of the public servants involved were just happy to get back to their traditional roles of doing things and seeing tangible outputs of their work, rather than building relationships and having to rely on different skills to ensure some progress was being made, as was the case under the COAG Murdi Paaki trial (*Jarvie and Stewart*). They also highlight how policy lessons from the trial's evaluations were unlikely to be taken up by government in subsequent phases of policy reform, which was due in large part to bureaucratic forms and cultures that do not lend themselves easily to 'working across boundaries' or reflecting on and amending practices when they may no longer suit the prevailing political winds.

What we see instead in these examples is a government – with sufficient strength of political leadership – taking the opportunity, often when policy progress is perceived to stall and/or negotiations break down, to revert to a command-and-control hierarchical approach to management that is inherent in its bureaucratic design, with the negotiation arena restricted to government bodies and their close allies. These examples also help to illustrate policy-framing contests in MLG systems, and how different framings of policy at different levels can be detrimental to building high trust and continuous negotiation.

In terms of intergovernmental relations, in 2006–07, the Coalition Government was facing a phalanx of Labor-led state and territory governments and this final term in office was marked by strong central government initiatives by Howard (Walter 2010). In the NT Intervention, there was typically some negotiation between levels and sectors (e.g. a range of federal government departments, ADF, the NT Government and some service providers) and some MLG occurring, but this was strongly skewed to the powerful federal government interests (rather than community or private stakeholders), and to where the money and resources that could be quickly thrown at the policy issue lay. In the case of the Rudd Government's HIP, the Commonwealth's drive for pushing the program through was to contribute to a macro-economic policy strategy in a time of crisis. The effort was, in its entirety, arguably successful in its main objective of helping the Australian economy to avoid recession. It was deeply flawed, however, at the state and local level due to its rushed and unilateral implementation, without adequate negotiation, which proved to be the program's downfall.

It is here that the study of governance systems with a relative absence of negotiation across a broad range of policy stakeholders connects clearly to the observations of Australia's federalism literature. In particular, we can see linkages around issues of power and resources that can set in train systems of coercive federalism, rather than the more pragmatic, collaborative or cooperative forms that exist at times within COAG and other flexible and negotiated systems (Mathews 1977; Hollander and Patapan 2007; Fenna 2012; Smullen 2014; *Kay*; see also *Mercer and Jarvie* for another collaborative COAG working example). We also see how blurred responsibilities in many areas can lead to tension (see also Painter 2001; *Fawcett and Marsh*; and *Mulgan* on accountability), slow progress and a political willingness to 'cut through' with unilateral action to solve the impasse and attempt to 'get the job done' by controlling and directing its implementation. This appears to be particularly prevalent when the political complexion is polarised between the Commonwealth and the next tier of government – intuitively because of the greater likelihood of negotiations breaking down due to differing core values.

There thus remains a dream of being able to centralise power in Australia, as in other countries, with a unified system of government, which is most often lived out here through periods of crisis and is increasingly being enacted little by little (see Fenna 2012 or Smullen 2014 for a more nuanced interpretation). It is also the moment when a governing mentality of 'welfare statism' and the need for strong government intervention to support social development and security, more common in the 1950s, again becomes more acceptable to the voting public (see *Dugdale* for more discussion on this 'governmentality'). In a real crisis, like a natural disaster, there is a general hope that the government and army will pitch in to protect and help people to recover with dignity; they are our risk managers of last resort (see Matthews 2009).

Thus, in terms of what was largely unwritten in this volume, we can see here that MLG systems in Australia can break down and away from collaborative flexible forms (Type II), be replaced by more traditional bureaucratic forms of MLG (Type I) or, on occasion, be a governance system outside this classification. We have presented some initial thoughts on why such moves might be made due to political impetuses linked to crises (which can be real or concocted) and perceived complications of negotiating with diverse policy stakeholders. This, however, raises a deeper underlying question about the evolution of MLG types and systems: specifically, what general configurations of MLG are found where (i.e. policy domains and countries/regions), and how and why do they reconfigure between types over time?

We cannot hope to respond to this question fully in this chapter and, in fact, it could form the basis for many future volumes. Posing it, however, does lead us into discussing another element of the work in this volume that remains largely unwritten – the issue of research methodologies used to develop the work and case studies on MLG processes. We will first reflect on this, before providing some preliminary thoughts and analyses on the aforementioned question.

MLG systems research practice: Emerging methodological possibilities

As explained earlier in this book, we consider MLG to be processes of ongoing negotiation across boundaries. These processes are influenced by institutional and administrative structures at a range of levels and across sectors. Some of these structures, especially the cross-jurisdictional ones like COAG or regional management groups (e.g. for natural resource management or regional development), and how they support or constrain effective cross-boundary working, are studied in the case study chapters. The researchers of these chapters focus on the 'practice' of policymaking and how different forms of working can lead to changes in policy support structures and a range of both internal (i.e. for the negotiating actors involved) and external outcomes (i.e. the impacts of the policy). In a number of cases, authors also look at the quality of the coordination between actors from different jurisdictions and groups, and how they work (or fail to effectively work) together across a range of typical boundaries, including departmental, sectorial, government level and administrative area, public–private and official–community member. Coupled to this analysis is a focus on the factors that supported and enabled this coordination, or led to its demise, such as legislative or political changes and leadership or the support of champions (see *Daniell and Kay* for a more in-depth analysis on the book's contributions).

Here we maintain a critical stance and ask: *how did the authors* carry out this analysis of practices, structures, negotiations and interpreting the different stages of policy development through MLG practice? And, how might researchers interested in MLG processes go about analysing them in the future?

For the most part, our authors are silent on the research methods they used, except to note in a number of cases their involvement as policy actors who were themselves taking part in many of these negotiations (see, for example, *Dugdale*; *Mercer and Jarvie*; *Hogan*; *Jarvie and Stewart*; *Iwanicki et al.*; *Andrews*). Some of the methods or data collection tools can, however, be implicitly determined from the text, such as the use of archival analyses that has been focused by some level of involvement in the policy area over many years (e.g. *Troy*; *Hogan*); literature-based reviews, with or without case examples from experience and/or the literature (e.g. *Kay*; *Fawcett and Marsh*; *Mulgan*; *Kerr*; *Dugdale*; *Daniell et al.*); comparative policy or institutional analyses (e.g. *Ross*; *Norman and Gurran*; *Andrews*; *Dale et al.*); and personal recollections of process and structure design and negotiations, coupled to meeting notes and other records (e.g. *Mercer and Jarvie*; *Jarvie and Stewart*; *Andrews*).

We see in Andrews, for example, comments such as 'it was necessary for the group to first design an appropriate framework', implying that Andrews was part of 'the group' involved in designing and negotiating the MLG processes for management of the Lake Eyre Basin. She then clarifies the role she played personally in different phases of the process, helping to establish the viewpoint of her analyses, and draws on archival records (reports and papers) from the process that provide the data for her comparative analyses of two instances of multi-level working, using definitional components of MLG from a number of authors (e.g. Peters and Pierre 2004) to draw her conclusions. Participant observation during negotiations, plus informal discussions with others involved in these processes, were thus also likely to contribute to the data relied upon to construct the 'rich' case descriptions that border on ethnographic methods in this chapter and others.

Since 'behind-the-scenes' negotiations of the types common in MLG, or any other policy change process, are notoriously difficult to research (Daniell et al. 2014), this book contributes some useful and original contributions to the literature because many of the authors have been embedded themselves in the processes they have studied and have thus had valuable insight into these processes that outside researchers may find hard to gain. For others to emulate such studies, however, it is important to discuss the kinds of research methods that were used with varying degrees of rigour in these studies, which could be applied to the study of similar MLG processes in the future. Although MLG has been conceptualised largely through the political science literature, its emphasis on actors and the processes of interaction and collective construction of policy between them across scales and levels means that it is well placed to profit from the use of actor- and process-focused research methods from not only the political sciences, but also disciplines such as sociology, anthropology, linguistics, psychology and the management sciences (see also *Fawcett and Marsh*).

In particular, and as with the study of policy translation (Mukhtarov and Daniell 2017), MLG analysis could benefit from greater use of 'engaged' research approaches and associated methods. Specifically, methods where researchers are embedded close to, or participating in, the negotiating action will be vital to understanding MLG processes better. These include ethnographic and 'follow-the-policy' methods (e.g. Mosse 2004, 2011; Peck and Theodore 2012), as well as alternative appellations such as 'mobile methods' (McCann and Ward 2012) and the need to 'study through' policy and governance systems to understand 'tracing ways in which power creates webs and relations between actors, institutions and discourses across time and space' (Wedel et al. 2005: 40). Indeed, many 'interpretative policy methods' more generally fit this mould and would be most applicable to uncovering the tensions and reflecting the values in discourses that occur through the negotiation processes of MLG (e.g. Yanow 2000; Wagenaar 2006; Hendriks 2007).

Other research approaches from an alternative body of literature – the management and decision sciences – could also prove useful for uncovering and understanding negotiation processes. Specifically, the use of 'intervention research' is another engaged research approach that could be pursued by researchers interested in the inner workings of MLG systems. Intervention research is defined as 'purposive action to create change' (Midgley 2000). Unlike some of the interpretive methods, it purposely emphasises the need for an abductive approach (cycles of deductive and inductive work) via the use of models or 'rational myths' that shape and can be tested in interventions to create 'actionable knowledge' (Hatchuel and Molet 1986; David 2000; Daniell 2012). As outlined and used in Daniell et al. (2014) for investigating the politics of innovation in MLG systems by actors taking part in or organising policy negotiations, such an approach can allow access to behind-the-scenes struggles, as well as provide insight into why MLG system negotiations may break down and, ultimately, exclude some actors and preference others.

Both of these groups of approaches rely on similar data collection techniques such as field notes, reports, participant observation, records of communications (emails, letters, media, meeting and workshop notes, photos, videos and audio recordings), interviews, oral histories and questionnaires, but have slightly different underlying philosophical positions. We can see elements of these reflected in some of the case studies previously outlined. Specifically, an approach closer to intervention research is evident in *Jarvie and Stewart*, *Andrews*, *Mercer and Jarvie* and *Iwaniki et al.* – due to the use of policy and 'ways of working' model creation and testing – where the researchers were policy practitioners who set out to create change, but also developed and reflected on their knowledge creation to inform future action.

What is valuable in these approaches is the reflexivity that it promotes for policy actors and researchers around their own practices and impacts. The ethical issues associated with such research can, however, be complicated, especially when such policy and governance projects are not framed as traditional research projects at the beginning of their life and are thus not subject to ethics approval. Rather, the lead researchers were at the time subject to other codes of conduct, such as that of the Australian public service, and they subsequently needed to consider how to avoid breaching those codes (e.g. through breaking of confidence), as other public figures do when they research and write their memoirs and analyse certain events in which they have played a role.

We consider, as has been discussed at greater length in Daniell et al. (2009, 2014), that there is no easy way to deal with some of these ethical complexities, but being upfront about them and reasoning them through (including what aspects of processes should be revealed and how people are identified) will allow such research approaches to take their place alongside the more established policy and governance research methods. Indeed, encouraging this kind of research and reflexivity about policy practice in the future could help not just the research community but also be of benefit to policy actors in government and other spheres of influence to enhance a culture of policy learning, evaluation and experimentation. It is also a productive avenue for the development of academic–practitioner partnerships around public policy, which could help both groups reflect on and learn from policy interventions leading to future improvement.

New perspectives on MLG and transitions between systems

Drawing on various illustrations of MLG from the authors of this book – and on a number that are obviously missing – and what their synthesis can tell us, we wish to reflect in this section on the question posed earlier on the evolution of MLG types and systems, as well as where they are most commonly found in the Australian context.

First of all, we postulate that Type I MLG systems are more likely to be found and thrive in the older and potentially more entrenched policy areas such as health, education, industrial relations, defence and traditional or long-lived public services (e.g. urban and rural infrastructure, such as roads, sewerage, water and electricity supply). In part this is due to the long-term responsibility for these areas that has been enshrined as part of constitutions and the sovereign realm of certain jurisdictions. This sets up a particular dynamic of state- and/or federally led negotiations that can often become institutionalised. It is not that simple, however, as there are many examples of pockets of more flexible Type II processes that operate during periods of reorganisation or when there is a need to integrate an innovation (e.g. integrating early childhood education into the policy domain of Australian education; see *Mercer and Jarvie*). In a similar vein, we observe that newer issues without obvious constitutional recognition are more likely to find themselves in a Type II MLG configuration, which is similar to why MLG Type II processes evolved in the European Union (EU). These include issues and policy areas such as telecommunications and internet regulation (including cyber security), extreme events and pandemics and climate change. Such areas often require negotiations across a broad range of actors in a non-hierarchical and fluid manner, as actors with the up-to-date knowledge, capacity and authority to act are split across the public, private and community sectors.

In other long-term 'wicked' policy issues, such as sustainable development (e.g. managing the health and functionality of the environment in the face of pressures for human and economic development), overcoming Indigenous disadvantage and security and migration issues, we are more likely to see significant flip-flopping between Types I and II of MLG as progress in either form advances, but not as desired by different interests.

Specifically, and as already alluded to (*Daniell and Kay*), MLG Type II arrangements are flexible but can also be fragile in response to changes in support from participating parties, leading to changes in structures and practices of negotiation. Change and learning to work differently with a variety of actors continuously over time can be tiring, and require a special set of unique skills (Stewart and Jarvie 2015; *Jarvie and Stewart*; *Mercer and Jarvie*; *Daniell et al.*). This means that events such as the loss of leaders and champions in different jurisdictions can lead to breakdown of the MLG negotiation system and installation of an alternative, as described earlier. Breakdowns in trust (i.e. to negotiating in good faith) can also lead to the need for a modified MLG system (see *Dugdale* on the need for 'high-trust' governance environments).

Institutionalisation of cross-boundary structures can help to support MLG system maintenance for slightly longer periods (see, for example, *Norman and Gurran* on regional groups for urban and coastal planning; or *McNaughton and Lockie* on GLOBALG.A.P.). The form of negotiations may still vary over time, however, depending on the complexity and flexibility of these structures and what subsidiary working structures they create (e.g. the COAG examples in *Mercer* and *Jarvie and Stewart*). In a national context, we observe that it can prove difficult for a federal (or state) government to manage multiple MLG Type II negotiation processes around a particular policy with different stakeholders across a specific region, especially when there are varying levels of conflict and capacity for effective governance.

Once either MLG negotiation systems begin to fail or frustration (real or manufactured) by federal level policymakers and politicians sets in (e.g. in Indigenous policy or the managing of the Murray–Darling Basin) it appears that, rather than re-resourcing these systems to improve their functionality, the desire for one centrally enforced (or 'one-size-fits-all') policy becomes stronger. The switch to a less flexible MLG Type I system (or even to an absence of MLG systems (MLG Type 0)) with clearer lines of authority and accountability can then be enacted when an appropriate window of opportunity opens.

This fluctuation of MLG types in certain policy areas also appears to underline the challenge of Australian society's competing cultural values over how we ought to be organised, who ought to be responsible for decision-making and what kind of justice regime we ought to enact through these decisions and specifically for where.[1] Indeed, different forms of competing MLG types can be mapped onto the hierarchist, individualist, egalitarian and fatalist cultural types (also known as Grid-Group Cultural Theory; see, for example, Douglas 1978; Wildavsky 1987; Thompson et al. 1990; Tukker and Butter 2007; Daniell 2014), as presented in Figure 18.1.

Grid: subject to rules +

Fatalist - Type 0 MLG No one in control; breakdown of negotiations; waiting for events creating windows of opportunity that make unilateral action possible	Hierarchist – Type I MLG Government control; top-down centralised management; primary negotiations are between levels of government
Individualist – Type II MLG Business and individual actor control; primary negotiations are between economic managers (business, individuals, government and other groups)	Egalitarian – Type II MLG Control is shared; participatory multi-actor processes of negotiation (community groups, governments, businesses and others) and learning by doing

Group: ties – … *Group: ties +*

Grid: subject to rules –

Figure 18.1: MLG cultural typology (based on Grid-Group Cultural Theory)

Source: Katherine A. Daniell and Trish Mercer

---

1   This reflects the politics of who wins and loses and, specifically, Lasswell's (1936) question of who gets what, when and how. Due to the importance of claims of territorial justice in many MLG cases, this needs to be supplemented, however, by the question of 'where'.

In any society or political system there is the potential for all of these types – related to the strength of relationships between people (Group ties) and the strength of rules governing individual behaviour (Grid: subject to rules) – to be represented and in tension at the same time, with politics helping to establish which ones take preference in different policy areas and at different times. As shown in Figure 18.1, the type of negotiations set up in a hierarchist system are likely to be those in and between functioning bureaucracies at different administrative levels.

These could be most easily likened to a Type I MLG system, although it does not represent all Type I configurations that may not be hierarchical or centralised as such (see Hooghe and Marks 2003). In an egalitarian system, MLG negotiations are more likely to be inclusive of participants with an interest in the policy area, regardless of which sector or group they represent. The focus would be on working together (for the 'common good') and establishing horizontal rather than vertical accountability (see *Mulgan*). This is representative of a Type II MLG system. In an (ideal) individualist system – another Type II MLG system – negotiations in the governance system would be between individuals, businesses and other groups seeking to maintain and enhance their own interests and freedoms (rather than focusing on the common good).

Finally, the fatalist category represents the discussion earlier in this chapter of the breakdown of effective MLG systems – what we will name Type 0 MLG, even if some spontaneous negotiations may occur opportunistically and to shore up power and passage of policies.

We believe that such a conceptualisation could be useful to both MLG and federalism scholars as it can help to understand the actual and preferred negotiation systems that are seen over time in particular policy sectors. For example, applying this rather crudely to *Troy's* example, we can observe a movement in housing policy from a hierarchist (with an egalitarian ideal) to an individualist-focused negotiation model (with a bit of fatalism thrown in). In natural resource management there has been oscillation between all four categories, even though a number of our authors focus on the development of more egalitarian MLG approaches (e.g. *Andrews*; *Norman and Gurran*; *Iwanicki et al.*). Indigenous policy MLG systems, while also highly variable, can be productive when they lean towards egalitarian approaches, as in the COAG Murdi Paaki Trial (*Jarvie and Stewart*), but appear to be plagued with significant levels of fatalism (see above discussion regarding the NT Intervention approach) that, in the long term, creates one of the most detrimental (non)governance types.

Taking this analysis further and looking more closely at the reform record of COAG, established in December 1992, we can also observe some underlying cultural value systems of various leaders in their approaches to negotiating specific policy issues through COAG. This history also illustrates the vulnerability of both Type I (more hierarchical, or at least focused on clear separation of powers) and Type II (both more egalitarian or individualist) multi-level policy processes to any shift in the supporting political environment. The ascension of Malcolm Turnbull to the prime ministership in September 2015, for example, was hailed as 'a potential game-changer', given the singular role of the prime minister in COAG agenda-setting and Turnbull's apparent willingness to have all reform options on the table (Tiernan 2015: 400–01).

The atmosphere at his first COAG meeting on 11 December, and at the leaders' retreat the previous day, reflected this new openness and optimism – a change in cultural and symbolic positioning – with the communiqué emphasising that a 'new' economic and federation reform agenda would be progressed through 'collaboration', 'shared responsibility' and employing 'a flexible approach' (COAG Communiqué, December 2015), that signalled a change from Type I (or 0) preferences to Type II MLG configurations. By the next COAG meeting in April, however, which was held in the context of increased fiscal pressures and pre-election political positioning, this positive environment for collaborative governance had evaporated: state and territory leaders showed little appetite for pursuing Turnbull's proposal (announced publicly) to levy income tax on their own behalf, and the development of a new competition- and productivity-enhancing reform agreement was relegated to treasurers to produce (COAG Communiqué, April 2016) – a return to Type I configurations.

Yet, even in this inauspicious environment, it was notable that for two of COAG's wicked policy issues – Indigenous economic development and reducing violence against women and their children – there was recognition of the importance of community involvement in policy development. For example, leaders agreed to work in partnership with Indigenous leaders and communities to progress an Indigenous economic development framework. This shows, as discussed previously, that the MLG system type is policy-issue dependent and it is difficult to paint particular governments and their COAG working structures as just of one cultural complexion. Rather, requisite variety or varying percentages across the policy portfolio of issues exists and will remain in ongoing tension due to vying political interests.

In summary, each one of these MLG systems authorises and legitimates the action of different groups of people (see *Kerr*) and holds its own coherent set of values and boundary-crossing (or sector-bridging) logics, which warrant further investigation in future research and policy practice. We hope that this conceptualisation will allow both researchers and policy practitioners to understand the MLG systems within which they work or have an interest, and how ongoing negotiations around Australian public policy for different issues might be strengthened and adapted into the future.

Acknowledgements

Adrian Kay and John Wanna are thanked for their review comments, which have helped to extend the quality of the discussion presented in this chapter.

References

Bache, I. & Flinders, M. (eds) (2004). *Multi-level Governance*. Oxford University Press. doi.org/10.1093/0199259259.001.0001

COAG Communiqués (2015 & 2016). www.coag.gov.au/meeting-outcomes [Accessed: 18/07/17].

Crase, L. (2011). The Fallout to the Guide to the Proposed Basin Plan. *The Australian Journal of Public Administration*, 70(1): 84–93. doi.org/10.1111/j.1467-8500.2011.00714.x

Daniell, K.A. (2011). Enhancing Collaborative Management in the Basin. In: Connell, D. & Grafton, R.Q. (eds) *Basin Futures: Water Reform in the Murray–Darling Basin*. ANU E Press, Canberra, pp. 413–38, press.anu.edu.au/publications/basin-futures [Accessed: 31/05/2017].

——. (2012). *Co-engineering and Participatory Water Management: Organisational Challenges for Water Governance*. UNESCO International Hydrology Series, Cambridge University Press. doi.org/10.1017/CBO9780511998072

———. (2014). *The Role of National Culture in Shaping Public Policy: A Review of the Literature*. HC Coombs Forum Discussion Paper, June 2014, The Australian National University, Canberra, tinyurl.com/national-culture-public-policy [Accessed: 29/12/2014].

Daniell, K.A., Coombes P.J. & White, I. (2014). Politics of Innovation in Multi-level Water Governance Systems. *Journal of Hydrology*, 519(Part C): 2415–35. doi.org/10.1016/j.jhydrol.2014.08.058

Daniell, K.A., White, I. & Rollin, D. (2009). Ethics and Participatory Water Planning. Proceedings of the 32nd Hydrology and Water Resources Symposium: 'H2009', 30 November – 3 December. Newcastle, pp. 1476–87.

David, A. (2000). La recherche-intervention, cadre général pour la recherche en sciences de gestion? In: David, A., Hatchuel, A. & Laufer, R. (eds) *Les nouvelles fondations des sciences en gestion*. Vuibert, collection FNEGE, Paris, pp. 193–213.

Douglas, M. (1978). Cultural Bias. Occasional Paper No. 35. Royal Anthropological Institute of Great Britain and Ireland, London.

FaHCSIA (2011). Northern Territory Emergency Response Evaluation Report. Australian Government Department of Families, Housing, Community Services and Indigenous Affairs (FaHCSIA), Commonwealth of Australia, Canberra.

Fenna, A. (2012). Centralising Dynamics in Australian Federalism. *Australian Journal of Politics and History*, 58: 580–90. doi.org/10.1111/j.1467-8497.2012.01654.x

Hamdhan, A. & Lewis, C. (2013). The Home Insulation Program: a classic case of policy failure? www.academia.edu/11538221/The_Home_Insulation_Program_A_Classic_Case_of_Policy_Failure [Accessed: 20/05/16].

Hanger, R.I. (2014). *Report of the Royal Commission into the Home Insulation Program*. Commonwealth of Australia, Canberra.

Hatchuel, A. & Molet, H. (1986). Rational Modelling in Understanding and Aiding Human Decision-Making: About two case studies. *European Journal of Operational Research*, 24(1): 178–86.

Hendriks, C.M. (2007). Praxis Stories: Experiencing interpretive policy research. *Critical Policy Studies*, 1(3): 278–300. doi.org/10.1080/194 60171.2007.9518523

Hollander, R. & Patapan, H. (2007). Pragmatic Federalism: Australian federalism from Hawke to Howard. *Australian Journal of Public Administration*, 66(3): 280–97. doi.org/10.1111/j.1467-8500.2007.00542.x

Hooghe, L. & Marks, G. (2003). *Unraveling the Central State, but How? Types of Multi-level Governance*. Political Science Series. Institute for Advanced Studies, Vienna.

Hunter, B. (2007). Conspicuous Compassion and Wicked Problems: the Howard government's national emergency in Indigenous affairs. *Agenda*, 14(3): 35–54.

James, N. (2007). Keeping it Civil in Cases of Controversy, *The Drum*, 2 October, Australian Broadcasting Corporation, www.abc.net.au/news/stories/2007/10/02/2048395.htm

Lasswell, H.D. (1936). *Who Gets What, When and How*. Whittlesey House, New York.

Leigh, A. & Neill, C. (2010). Do Gun Buybacks Save Lives: Evidence from panel data. *American Law and Economics Review*, 12(2): 509–57. doi.org/10.1093/aler/ahq013

Marks, G. (1993). Structural Policy and Multilevel Governance in the EC. In: Cafruny, A. & Rosenthal, G. (eds) *The State of the European Community Vol. 2: The Maastricht Debates and Beyond*. Longman, Harlow, pp. 391–410.

Mathews, R. (1977). Innovations and Developments in Australian Federalism. *Publius*, 7: 9–19. doi.org/10.2307/3329459

Matthews, M. (2009). Fostering Creativity and Innovation in Cooperative Federalism – the uncertainty and risk dimensions. In: Wanna, J. (ed.) *Critical Reflections on Australian Public Policy*. ANU E Press, Canberra, pp. 59–70, epress.anu.edu.au/anzsog/critical/pdf/ch06.pdf [Accessed: 29/12/14].

McCann, E. & Ward, K. (2012). Assembling Urbanism: following policies and 'studying through' the sites and situations of policy making. *Environment and Planning A*, 44: 42–51. doi.org/10.1068/a44178

Midgley, G. (2000). *Systemic Intervention: Philosophy, methodology, and practice*. Kluwer Academic/Plenum Publishers, New York. doi.org/10.1007/978-1-4615-4201-8

Mosse, D. (2004). Is Good Policy Unimplementable? Reflections on the Ethnography of Aid Policy and Practice. *Development and Change*, 35: 639–71. doi.org/10.1111/j.0012-155X.2004.00374.x

——. (2011). Politics and Ethics: ethnography of expert knowledge and professional identities. In: Shore, C., Wright, S. & Pero, D. (eds) *Policy Worlds: Anthropology and the Analysis of Contemporary Power*, Berghahn Books, New York and Oxford, pp. 50–67.

Mukhtarov, F. & Daniell, K.A. (2017). Diffusion, Adaptation and Translation of Water Policy Models. In: Conca, K. & Weinthal, E. (eds) *The Oxford Handbook of Water Politics and Policy*. Oxford University Press.

Painter, M. (2001). Multi-level Governance and the Emergence of Collaborative Federal Institutions in Australia. *Policy and Politics*, 29: 137–50. doi.org/10.1332/0305573012501260

Peck, J. & Theodore, N. (2012). Follow the Policy: a distended case approach. *Environment and Planning A*, 44: 21–30. doi.org/10.1068/a44179

Peters, B.G. & Pierre, J. (2004). Multi-level Governance and Democracy: a 'Faustian bargain'? In: Bache, I. & Flinders, M. (eds) *Multi-level Governance*. Oxford University Press, pp. 75–89. doi.org/10.1093/0199259259.003.0005

Prasser, S. (2006). Aligning 'Good Policy' with 'Good Politics'. In Colebatch, H.K. (ed.) *Beyond the Policy Cycle: The Policy Process in Australia*. Allen and Unwin, Sydney.

Sanders, W. (2008). In the Name of Failure: a generational revolution in Indigenous affairs. In: Aulich, C. & Wettenhall, R. (eds) *Howard's Fourth Government: Australian Commonwealth Administration 2004–2007*. UNSW Press, Sydney, pp. 187–205.

Shergold, P. (2015). *Learning from Policy Failure. Why Large Government Policy Initiatives Have Gone So Badly Wrong in the Past and How the Chances of Success in the Future Can Be Improved.* Commonwealth of Australia, Canberra.

Smullen, A. (2014). Conceptualising Australia's Tradition of Pragmatic Federalism. *Australian Journal of Political Science*, 49(4): 677–93. doi.org/10.1080/10361146.2014.964660

Stewart, J. & Jarvie, W. (2015). Haven't We Been This Way Before? Evaluation and the Impediments to Policy Learning. *Australian Journal of Public Administration*, 74(2): 114–127. doi.org/10.1111/1467-8500.12140

Thompson, M., Ellis, R. & Wildavsky, A. (1990). *Cultural theory.* Westview Press, Boulder, Colorado.

Tiernan. A. (2015). Reforming Australia's Federal Framework: priorities and prospects. *Australian Journal of Public Administration*, 74(4): 398–405. doi.org/10.1111/1467-8500.12180

Tukker, A. & Butter, M. (2007). Governance of Sustainable Transitions: About the 4(0) ways to change the world. *Journal of Cleaner Production*, 15(1): 94–103. doi.org/10.1016/j.jclepro.2005.08.016

Wagenaar, H. (2006). Interpretive Policy Analysis. In: Fischer, F., Miller, G. & Sidney, M. (eds) *The Handbook of Public Policy Analysis: Theory, Politics and Methods.* Boca Raton, CRC Press, pp. 429–41. doi.org/10.1201/9781420017007.ch29

Walter, J. (2010). *What Were They Thinking? The Politics of Ideas in Australia.* UNSW Press, Sydney.

Wedel, J., Shore, C., Feldman, G. & Lathrop, S. (2005). Towards an Anthropology of Public Policy. *Annals of the American Academy of Political and Social Science*, 600: 30–51. doi.org/10.1177/0002716205276734

Wettenhall, R. (2011). Global Financial Crisis: the Australian experience in international perspective. *Public Organization Review*, 11(1): 77–91. doi.org/10.1007/s11115-010-0149-9

Wild, R. & Anderson, P. (2007). *Ampe Akelyernemane Meke Mekarle: 'Little Children are Sacred'*, Report of the Northern Territory Board of Inquiry into the Protection of Aboriginal Children from Sexual Abuse 2007. Department of the Chief Minister, Northern Territory.

Wildavsky, A. (1987). Choosing Preferences by Constructing Institutions: a cultural theory of preference formation. *American Political Science Review*, 81(1): 3–21. doi.org/10.2307/1960776

Yanow, D. (2000). *Conducting Interpretive Policy Analysis*. Sage, Thousand Oaks. doi.org/10.4135/9781412983747

List of Contributors

Dr Kate Andrews worked with people across the Lake Eyre Basin (LEB) designing and establishing the Lake Eyre Basin Coordinating Group – Australia's only community-designed and managed cross-border natural resource management organisation (developed alongside the LEB Intergovernmental Agreement). She became its first CEO. Since then, Kate has worked with Land & Water Australia as their first Knowledge and Adoption Manager, and then across northern Australia as a consultant, chairing Territory Natural Resource Management for six years and participating in numerous national committees such as the Australian Landcare Council. Kate is currently the Executive Officer for NRM Regions Australia, a collaboration of the 56 regional NRM organisations across Australia.

Kathryn Bellette has a background in environmental science and has worked in environment and development portfolios of the South Australian Government in both executive and board roles. She works across interfaces, bringing together different levels of governance, disciplines and sectors on matters relating to the achievement of ecologically sustainable development. As an academic at Flinders University, she taught across three schools and two faculties. Roles include General Manager of the Onkaparinga Catchment Water Management Board, Director of Strategic Planning at Planning SA and Director Strategy and Assessment of the South Austrailan Environment Protection Authority.

Dr Kathleen Broderick has over 30 years' professional experience in natural resource management. She has combined management with research contributions to Water Quality Improvement in the Great Barrier Reef Catchments, irrigation development in the Tasmanian Midlands and salinity management in the Collie Catchment.

Kathleen has written several key papers examining governance of natural resources and community participation in resource management. She has contributed to many national initiatives, including the expert reference panel of the National Rural Industries Research and Development Council's 'Consolidating Targeted and Practical Extension Services for Australian Farmers and Fishers' project. She currently works with the seven natural resource management regions in Western Australia, with governments, and with communities undertaking changes.

Dr Jen Cleary is a rural geographer with research interests in rural social and economic policy and community decision-making processes. She is CEO of Centacare Catholic Country South Australia, and Adjunct Associate Professor with the Centre for Global Food and Resources at the University of Adelaide.

Allan Dale is a Professor of Tropical Regional Development at The Cairns Institute, James Cook University. He has a strong interest in integrated governance, with a particular focus across the tropical world, northern Australia and the Great Barrier Reef. Allan has extensive research and policy expertise in building strong governance systems, but particularly in regional development and natural resource management. Allan was the CEO of Terrain NRM and, before that, was responsible for natural resource policy in Queensland. He has a long research background in analysing complex and multi-level governance systems (including with CSIRO and Griffith University) and is an Honorary Professorial Research Fellow with Charles Darwin University's Northern Institute.

Dr Katherine A. Daniell is a Senior Lecturer in the Fenner School of Environment and Society at The Australian National University. Katherine's work focuses on collaborative approaches to policy and action for sustainable development. Her works include the monograph *Co-engineering and Participatory Water Management: Organisational Challenges for Water Governance* (2012). She is also editor of the *Australasian Journal of Water Resources*. Katherine has held research roles in the ANU Centre for European Studies, the HC Coombs Policy Forum, the ANU Centre for Policy Innovation and IRSTEA in France.

Paul Dugdale is the Director of the ANU Centre for Health Stewardship and Chair of the Australian Healthcare and Hospitals Association. He has pursued a dual career in academia and health service provision, with policy roles in health financing and tertiary service planning, and operational roles in public health and hospital management. Paul's publications include the books *Doing Health Policy in Australia* (2008) and *Patient Safety First: Responsive Regulation In Health Care* (2009, with Judith Healy).

Paul Fawcett is Associate Professor of Governance at the Institute for Governance and Policy Analysis, University of Canberra. His new book, *Anti-Politics, Depoliticization, and Governance*, was published by Oxford University Press in September 2017 (co-edited with Matthew Flinders, Colin Hay and Matthew Wood).

Nicole Gurran is Professor of Urban and Regional Planning at the University of Sydney, where she leads Urban Housing Lab@Sydney and directs the university's Australian Housing and Urban Research Institute (AHURI) research centre. She has led and collaborated on a series of studies on aspects of urban policy, housing, sustainability, climate change and planning, funded by AHURI, the Australian Research Council (ARC), as well as state and local government. She has authored and co-authored numerous publications and books including *Australian Urban Land Use Planning: Principles, Systems and Practice* (2011), and *Urban Planning and the Housing Market* (2017, with Glen Bramley).

Anthony Hogan is Honorary Professor in the Faculty of Health Sciences, University of Sydney, and Adjunct Research Professor at the Australian Centre for Christianity and Culture, Charles Sturt University, Canberra. He is a qualified welfare worker and rehabilitation counsellor with over 25 years' experience working with people with disability. He has published several textbooks and many research articles on social aspects of living with hearing difference, including *Hearing Impairment and Hearing Disability: Towards Paradigm Change in Hearing Services* (2015, co-edited with Rebecca Phillips).

Dr Iris Iwanicki is a planning consultant experienced in development assessment, policy and research, and is a historian. As Manager of Environmental Services with the District Council of Willunga, she managed the Willunga Basin strategic planning process that applied sustainability and water management as part of future planning. She subsequently assisted the Onkaparinga Catchment Water Management Board to apply consistent planning policies within the catchment area. Previously a member of the Pastoral Board of South Australia and the Heritage Authority, she has participated in tertiary teaching, development assessment panels and was formerly the Deputy Presiding Member of the SA State Development Assessment Commission.

Dr Wendy Jarvie is an Adjunct Professor at the School of Business, University of New South Wales, Canberra, where she undertakes research in the role of evidence, innovation and learning in public policy and works for the World Bank in early childhood development in the Pacific. Prior to that she was a Deputy Secretary in the Employment and Education departments of the Australian Public Service and managed evaluations and strategy development at the World Bank in Washington.

Adrian Kay is Senior Professor in the Institute of Policy Studies at Universiti Brunei Darussalam. Previously he was Professor of Government in the Crawford School of Public Policy at The Australian National University. Prior to an academic career, Adrian was a graduate trainee at Lehman Brothers and then spent several years on the UK Government's European Fast Stream, including an extended period on secondment at the European Commission in Brussels. His research areas lie at the intersection of comparative and international public policy, with a particular focus on health. Adrian's research has received funding from the Australian Research Council, National Health and Medical Research Council, Economic and Social Research Council in the United Kingdom as well as the Leverhulme Trust.

Russell Kerr currently administers research students in the College of Arts & Social Sciences at The Australian National University. He is co-editor (with R.B.J. Walker) of a forthcoming collection of Barry Hindess's work, titled 'Elephants in the Room: Tracks and Dispatches; Selected Writings on Liberalism, States and Empire'. Among his current projects is a book titled 'Disappearing Islands: Liberty and Colony in Western Political Thought'; he has presented chapters in New Orleans, Atlanta, Ljubljana, Baltimore and Havana. In addition to the research project 'Becoming and Politics' with Sakari Hänninen, Russ is editing a volume on international relations with Mark Franke called 'The Cost of Kant'.

Stewart Lockie is Distinguished Professor of Sociology and Director of the Cairns Institute at James Cook University. He is a Fellow of the Academy of the Social Sciences in Australia and foundation editor of the journal *Environmental Sociology*. Professor Lockie's research addresses natural resource and environmental governance, social impact assessment and risk management.

the theory and practice of changing modes of governance, new forms of democratic participation and the practice of public policy and service reform. She has published widely in academic and practitioner media and has acted as advisor to governments and governing institutions at all levels. She is co-author of a number of books including *Working Across Boundaries* (2002), *Power, Participation and Political Renewal* (2007) and *Hybrid Governance in European Cities: Neighbourhood, Migration and Democracy* (2013).

Patrick Troy is an Emeritus Professor at the Fenner School of Environment and Society, The Australian National University. He has worked as an engineer in the private sector and in state and local government, as a planner in New South Wales and as senior administrator in the Commonwealth. He is a Fellow of the Planning Institute of Australia and Academy of the Social Sciences in Australia. He is currently an Adjunct Professor for the Urban Research Program at Griffith University and a Visiting Professor for the City Futures Research Centre, Faculty of Built Environment, at the University of New South Wales.